The Ethics of War and Peace

The Ethics of War and Peace

An Introduction to Legal and Moral Issues

Third Edition

Paul Christopher

PEARSON
Prentice
Hall

Upper Saddle River, New Jersey 07458

Library of Congress Cataloging-in-Publication Data

Christopher, Paul
  The ethics of war and peace : an introduction to legal and moral
issues / Paul Christopher. — 3d ed.
    p.   cm.
  Includes bibliographical references and index.
  ISBN 0-13-092383-4
  1. War—Moral and ethical aspects.   2. Just war doctrine.   3. War
(International law)   I. Title.
  U22.C528   1999
  172'.42—dc21   98-52775
                                                            CIP

Editorial Director: Charlyce Jones Owen
Senior Acquisitions Editor: Ross Miller
Assistant Editor: Wendy B. Yurash
Editorial Assistant: Carla Worner
Director of Marketing: Beth Mejia
Marketing Assistant: Kimberly Daum
Managing Editor (Production): Joanne Riker
Production Liaison: Marianne Peters Riordan
Manufacturing Buyer: Christina Helder
Cover Design: Suzanne Behnke
Cover Illustration: Dorling Kindersley Media Library
Copy Editor: Melissa Messina
Composition/Full-Service Project Management: Brittney Corrigan-McElroy,
  Interactive Composition Corporation
Printer/Binder: Courier Companies, Inc.

Credits and acknowledgments borrowed from other sources and reproduced, with permission, in this textbook appear on appropriate page within text.

Pearson Education LTD.   Pearson Education North Asia Ltd
Pearson Education Singapore, Pte. Ltd   Pearson Educación de Mexico, S.A. de C.V.
Pearson Education, Canada, Ltd   Pearson Education Malaysia, Pte. Ltd
Pearson Education–Japan   Pearson Education, Upper Saddle River,
Pearson Education Australia PTY, Limited   New Jersey

10   9   8   7   6   5   4

ISBN 0-13-092383-4

CONTENTS

PREFACE

The most important decision that nations make is whether to use force for political objectives. In a democracy, all responsible citizens feel the weight of such decisions. The most important decision that military leaders have to make is how to fight the wars that their governments have authorized. I believe both that (1) human beings should not intentionally harm other human beings and (2) human beings may sometimes employ violence to protect themselves or others from harm. I call these two claims *moral truths* and, if one accepts both of them, it is obvious that they will occasionally conflict with one another. A central theme of this book is how conflicts between these two truths are best resolved. Specifically, I discuss those conditions that justify the use of force, and what the limits should be on the amount and types of force that may be used.

Because reasoning about moral and ethical issues does not lend itself to the same precision as mathematics, we must learn how to make responsible judgments based on relevant principles instead of learning how to plug facts into a formula for decision making. Rather than being a book about right answers, this is a book about right reasoning. My goal is for my readers to know not just what I believe but to understand why I believe as I do. I wish to thank my colleagues and students at the United States Military Academy, who steadfastly refused to accept any of my claims uncritically and whose incessant, detailed, always thoughtful, and sometimes brutal criticisms constantly forced me to reevaluate and refine my thinking on Just War. I especially benefited from discussions with Al Bishop, Tim Challans, Gary Coleman, Randy Dipert, Merritt Drucker, Peter Fromm, Cathy Haight, Anthony Hartle, Bryan Keifer, Van Martin, Wallace Matson, Mark Mattox, David Newell, John Petrik, Louis Pojman, Rainer Spencer, Steve Tryon, Sandra Visser, Scott Weaver, Ted Westhusing, Robert Williams, and Dan Zupan. Others who read the entire manuscript and made numerous worthwhile suggestions include Lin Bredenfoerder, Gareth Matthews, Fariborz Mokhtari, and Alan Schactman.

The author also thanks the following reviewers for their constructive criticism: Louis R. Beres, Purdue University; Major Kristine V. Nakutis, U.S.

Military Academy; Fariborz L. Mokhtari, Norwich University; and Wayne S. Osborn, Iowa State University.

Even as I send this manuscript to press, I am aware that some of my beliefs are probably false. Unfortunately, I don't know which ones they are. I trust that readers of this third edition will continue the tradition of accepting nothing I say uncritically, and that by engaging in a rigorous, open-minded dialectic we can all learn to think more clearly and competently about issues relevant to war and peace.

Paul Christopher
Lunenburg, Massachusetts

INTRODUCTION

Hugo Grotius, writing in the seventeenth century, observed that, concerning war, we must not believe either that nothing is allowable or that everything is. Today we might refer to the views Grotius was rejecting as **pacifism** and *realism*. The pacifist, abhorring the suffering caused by violence, concludes that war is the consummate evil and rejects it under all circumstances. The realist, beginning from a similar assessment regarding the evil nature of war, concludes that the resort to force constitutes a rejection of the rule of law and that there are no limits on what might be done to those who start wars in order to restore law and order.

These views reflect a tension between the negative duty not to intentionally harm innocent people, on the one hand, and the positive obligation that innocent persons be protected, on the other hand. These two moral inclinations or precepts seem to be at the center of debate concerning when to wage war and how to wage it. The pacifist views the prohibition against harming others as the more fundamental of the two; the realist takes the positive duty to protect others as the more basic. I call these divergent viewpoints *moral truths*. Moral Truth 1 is that it is wrong to intentionally harm innocent people; Moral Truth 2 is that we are sometimes justified in using force to protect innocent people from harm. Historically, the *Just War Tradition* has provided one means of resolution when these obligations conflict with one another. Today, many tenets of this tradition are reflected in both the national laws of individual nations and the international laws of war, as formalized at the Geneva and Hague Conventions and in the United Nations Charter.

In an earlier edition of this book, I observed that recent events in the conduct of war seem to call into question the relevance of certain aspects of the Just War Tradition for modern wars. Examples from Vietnam, Cambodia, Afghanistan, the former Yugoslavia, Pakistan, India, the Middle East, and the World Trade Center and Pentagon attacks of September 11, 2001, might lead one to conclude that the Just War Tradition and the international laws that reflect it are often ineffective in protecting innocents and ameliorating suffering in the international arena. Additionally, members of civilized nations are in constant debate on issues such as the use of land mines; chemical, biological, and nuclear weapons; the bombing and blockading of cities; the responsibility for war crimes; and the status of terrorists as combatants or criminals. Rather than an increased moral clarity on these issues, some argue, there seems to be an increased uncertainty, compounded perhaps by new technology, the proliferation of weapons of mass destruction, and religious or political fanaticism.

Nevertheless, despite the numerous infractions and ongoing debates, I remain convinced of the importance and defensibility of the Just War Tradition. The care taken to protect noncombatants and national monuments by the United States, Great Britain, and their allies in the 2003 war with Iraq was a conscious, dedicated effort to adhere to the Just War Tradition in the conduct of hostilities. While some can certainly point to examples of violations of either the laws of war or the tenets of the Just War Tradition, these do not constitute a persuasive argument against their appropriateness or defensibility, any more than do the occasional violations of civil laws show them to be ineffectual. In a sometimes murky international legal arena characterized by unratified conventions, bilateral treaties, and customary laws it is the Just War Tradition that holds moral nihilism at bay and provides some guidelines for when nations may resort to arms and how. Attempts to develop a system of international law to regulate the use of force have largely been an effort to codify the tenets of the Just War Tradition. Although the Just War Tradition is not without certain problems, problems that become increasingly obvious when the Just War principles are reduced to positive laws, it remains the primary moral force behind international agreements on the conduct of hostilities.

In this work I critically examine the Just War Tradition in terms of both *jus ad bellum* (justice of war) and *jus in bello* (justice in war) as each is reflected in international law. *Jus ad bellum* concerns the conditions that make the use of force permissible and is primarily a political responsibility. *Jus in bello* concerns the rules governing how war should be conducted and is largely the responsibility of members of the military profession.

Although I have tried to be objective throughout, there are certain prejudices apparent in the way I have structured the text, and I want to be up front with my readers concerning the biases that I bring to this project before we begin.

I have decided not to include a chapter discussing the view that morality has no place in international relations (often called **political realism,** or realpolitik), even though there are still some who adhere to this position. Political realism is criticized by Hugo Grotius, the author of *The Law of War and Peace,* and I summarize his arguments on this topic in Chapters 5 and 6.

I also omit any detailed discussion of the view that war is hell, and the best thing one can do in hell is to get out of there by the fastest possible means: *Inter arma silent leges* (in war the laws are silent). This view is referred to as **military realism,** and those who hold it argue that the side that initiates war commits a criminal act and, in so doing, the members of that side thereby forfeit any right they might have had to protection under the law. Put another way, one cannot reasonably expect to violate the rule of law in pursuit of selfish interests and later seek protection under the law when those who were violated strike back. As General Sherman, a senior military leader during the American Civil War put it, "War is cruelty, and you cannot refine it; and those who brought cruelty on our country deserve all the curses and maledictions a people can pour out."[1] Although I have not dedicated a chapter to this topic, I have included criticisms of military realism, where appropriate, in various discussions throughout the text.

On the other end of the spectrum, I have not dedicated a chapter to addressing various versions of pacifism, although I discuss early Christian pacifism in the historical context of Just War theory in chapter 2. It seems to me that for pacifism to qualify as a moral doctrine, it must be formulated so that nonviolence is always the only acceptable alternative. I have never met anyone who did not believe that nonviolent methods are *almost always* preferable to violent ones. For pacifism to qualify as a moral doctrine, however, it must be formulated so that there is never a justification for the use of violence. This does not seem plausible to me from either a theoretical standpoint or as a practical guide. For example, from the fact that all of the nations of the world have formally rejected the first use of military force, it follows that there should be no more wars. But of course, conflicts are ongoing at various places around the world, and it is highly unlikely that this will change anytime soon.

Using violence to defend oneself or one's community against unjust predation, genocide, terrorism, or the imminent threat of hostilities seems at least permissible and is perhaps even obligatory on some occasions. In any event, we will proceed under the assumption that the use of violence is at least sometimes permissible and then attempt to determine what the conditions are that permit it, as well as what the limits are on how it might be employed.

These two topics—when to employ force and how—form the broad margins that will guide us in our investigation. We will begin our study by examining the history of the Just War Tradition in terms of these two dimensions. It is important that we begin with some historical background, I believe, because the key to understanding modern Just War doctrine (and the laws of war that reflect it) is to study its past. If we can understand the moral or prudential principles that inspired the development of the Just War Tradition, we will be better able to evaluate its relevance in light of modern technology and tactics. Thus, when we examine Hugo Grotius's contention that war should be declared only by a lawful authority, we will be just as interested in understanding the reasons why he believes this is so as we are in learning the implications of this rule for the use of force in today's world.

In those chapters that are concerned with the historical development of the Just War Tradition, the reader will notice that I focus the discussions primarily on the works of one or two representative historical figures. The historical sections of this work are not meant to be a comprehensive study of the history of Just War but an overview of how the Just War Tradition has evolved and why. In each case, I have attempted to select authors whose work articulates key developments and who make important contributions to the topic, although I expect that some will disagree with my choices.

Section I outlines the modern concept of Just War as it evolved from a fusion of early Roman law and Judeo-Christian teachings. Focusing on the work of Marcus Tullius Cicero, Saint Ambrose, Saint Augustine, Saint Thomas Aquinas, and Francisco de Vitoria, I trace the development of the Just War Tradition from its beginnings in Ancient Rome and show how it was gradually transformed into a corpus of international law following the Thirty Years' War.

In Section II I address more specifically the relationship between the Just War Tradition and the international laws of war. After examining the historical development of the major tenets of *bellum justum* in Section I, we will be ready to understand their relationship to positive international law. We also will examine various motives for obeying laws—especially international laws—including the role of sanctions. Those whose work we will examine include Hugo Grotius and H. L. A. Hart.

One of our goals in Section II will be to explore why the laws of war are so often ignored on modern battlefields. We will want to determine whether this is a product of the formulation of the laws themselves or whether it is inherent in the very notion of having laws without a common authority to legislate them and enforce compliance, as is the case with international law.

Section III explores some of the tensions in certain aspects of the laws of war. We will examine issues related to obedience to orders, responsibility for war crimes, military necessity, reprisals, weapons of mass destruction, and terrorism, and we will discuss how these issues contribute to problems with the enforcement of international law. My intention here is to demonstrate that if the Just War Tradition is going to be a viable factor today and in the future, certain ambiguities in its formulation, especially as it is currently reflected in international legal documents, must be resolved.

Finally, Section IV addresses a number of contemporary problems related to service in the officer corps as a profession, such as whether an officer is morally obligated to serve in wars he or she believes to be unjust and issues related to multilateral and unilateral peacekeeping and peacemaking missions under the aegis of the United Nations.

While I have written each section so that it may be read independently of the others, I have used a building-block design where subsequent arguments are grounded in previous ones. Thus when we examine the military principle of obedience to superior orders, we will be able to appreciate the competing viewpoints as being representative of Augustine's and Aquinas's perspectives on an individual's duties to authority. Certainly, however, one will be able to understand fully the difficulties posed by the principle of obedience, as well as my analysis of these difficulties, without having read the chapters discussing Augustine's or Aquinas's views on war.

Note

1. William T. Sherman, quoted in John M. Gibson, *Those 163 Days* (New York: Coward, McCann & Geoghegan, 1961), p. 21.

SECTION

I

THE JUST WAR TRADITION

The modern concept of **bellum justum** was first compiled, refined, and formalized by Christian theologians and philosophers beginning with Saints Ambrose and Augustine in the fourth and fifth centuries. The tradition of recognizing constraints on the conduct of war is, however, much older. In this section we will outline the development of the Just War Tradition from Ancient Rome to the beginnings of modern international law.

Chapter 1 sketches the early foundations of the Just War Tradition from which the Christian philosophers derived their ideas. Chapter 2 contains a discussion of early Christian pacifism and how it succumbed to Just War arguments. Chapter 3 examines St. Augustine's doctrine of Just War. And finally, we will explore in chapter 4 the secularization of the Just War Tradition by the Scholastics, based on reason and natural law. In later sections we shall see how these early Just War concepts became embodied in positive international law.

Chapter

1

JUST WAR IN ANTIQUITY

The policy of recognizing prescriptions concerning the just conduct of war is not a product of "Christian charity" or even of Western civilization, but is found in some form across all cultures for which we have detailed historical records. Fifth century B.C. China recognized rules that stipulated that no war should begin without just cause; that the enemy be notified of pending attacks; that no injury be done to the wounded; and that the persons and property of innocents be respected.[1] Different territorial groups of the Aztec Empire fought battles with fixed numbers of warriors at set times on predetermined battlefields, which they called "wars of flowers."[2] Laotse, a Chinese philosopher from the sixth century B.C. and founder of the Tao religion, wrote

> *A good general effects his purpose and stops. . . .*
> *Effects his purpose and does not take pride in it.*
> *Effects his purpose as a regrettable necessity.*
> *Effects his purpose but does not love violence.*[3]

Sun Tzu, a fifth century B.C. Chinese soldier and philosopher who has been highly influential in the development of Chinese military doctrine and who has had (and continues to have) tremendous influence on U.S. military doctrine, advised

Treat the captives well, and care for them.

This is called "winning the battle and becoming stronger."

Hence what is essential in war is victory, not prolonged operations. And therefore the general who understands war is the Minister of the people's fate and arbiter of the nation's destiny.[4]

The ancient Egyptians thought humanitarian actions in war were important enough to be included among their records of glorious actions, including, in one instance, the rescue of enemy sailors whose ship had been sunk in battle.[5] And in the *Book of Manu*, produced by the Hindu civilization in India around the fourth century B.C., we find humanitarian rules for regulating land warfare that are strikingly similar to many aspects of present-day international law regarding the conduct of war.

> When the king fights with his foes in battle, let him not strike with weapons concealed in wood, nor with such as are barbed, poisoned, or the points of which are blazing with fire. Let him not strike one who in flight has climbed on an eminence, nor a eunuch, nor one who joins the palms of his hands in supplication, nor one who flees with flying hair, nor one who sits down, nor one who says "I am thine"; nor one who sleeps, nor one who has lost his coat of mail, nor one who is naked, nor one who is disarmed, nor one who looks on without taking part in the fight, nor one who is fighting with another foe; nor one whose weapons are broken, nor one afflicted with sorrow, nor one who has been grievously wounded, nor one who is in fear, nor one who has turned to flight; but in all cases let him remember the duty of honorable warriors.[6]

The Babylonian leader Sennacherib treated the Jews according to principles of justice and even distinguished those responsible for initiating the war from those soldiers who fought it. Concerning his directives after the battle against Jerusalem in 690 B.C., we are provided with the following account:

> I assaulted Ekron and killed the officials and patricians who had committed the crime and hung their bodies on poles surrounding the city. The [common] citizens who were guilty of minor crimes, I considered prisoners of war. The rest of them, those who were not accused of crimes and misbehavior, I released.[7]

In Western culture, the Just War Tradition is no less pronounced. In the *Laws*, Plato argues that wars are necessary evils, fought to gain peace; because wars are often unavoidable, he outlines restrictions pertaining not only to *jus in bello* but also to *jus ad bellum*. In the *Republic*, Socrates provides the following guidance for soldier guardians of an ideal state:

> They will not, being Greeks, ravage Greek territory nor burn habitations, and they will not admit that in any city all the population are enemies, men, women, and children, but will say that only a few at any time are their foes, those, namely, who are to blame for the quarrel. And on all these considerations they will not be willing to lay waste the soil, since the majority are their friends, nor to destroy the houses, but will carry the conflict only to the

point of compelling the guilty to do justice by the pressure of the suffering of the innocent.[8]

And later, in the *Laws,*

> Any person making peace or war with any parties independently of the Commonwealth shall likewise incur the pain of death. If a section of the state makes peace or war with any on its own account, the generals shall bring the authors of the measure before a court, and the penalty for conviction shall be death.[9]

In these passages Plato grants special status to noncombatants and innocents and reserves decisions regarding the initiation and cessation of hostilities to "proper authority."

Aristotle, like Plato, regards war (or the threat of war) as being inevitable and expresses concerns about sufficient justifications for going to war. "No one chooses to be at war or provokes war for the sake of war.... [We] make war that we may live at peace."[10] He is the first to use the phrase "just war,"[11] and in *Rhetorica ad Alexandrum* he provides guidance concerning justifications for going to war and for when to seek peace.

> The pretexts for making war on another state are as follows: when we have been the victims of aggression, we must take vengeance on those who have wronged us, now that a suitable opportunity has presented itself; or else, when we are actually being wronged, we must go to war on our own behalf or on behalf of our kindred or benefactors; or else we must help our allies when they are wronged; or else we must go to war to gain some advantage for the city, in respect either of glory, or of resources, or of strength, or of something similar.... [And] we must realize that it is the universal custom of mankind to abandon mutual warfare, either when they think that the demands of the enemy are just, or when they are at variance with their allies, or weary of war, or afraid of their enemy, or suffering from internal strife.[12]

Xenophon's historical narratives point to Greek concern for considerations of justice in both when and how to wage war;[13] and the popular playwright Euripides dramatizes the prohibition against harming prisoners of war.[14] Another example from around the same period may be found in the policies of Aristotle's student Alexander the Great. Concerning one of his battles against the Persians for control of Greek cities (Battle of Halicarnassus, 334 B.C.), we are provided with the following account:

> Although the defenders used cross-fire to good effect and delivered another partly successful sally, it became apparent that Alexander's siege engines would break a way into the city.... At the end of the day a company of Macedonian veterans drove the Greeks and Persians back in disorder and

might have broken into the city if Alexander had not sounded retreat in order to spare the civilian population. Shaken by their heavy losses, the garrison-commanders decided to withdraw into the two citadels by the harbor. . . .

Alexander broke into the city, . . . and forbade any reprisals against the civilians.

***

This was characteristic of him throughout his life; after his victory at the Hydaspes River he "ordered the burial of the dead, his and the bravest of the enemy." Except for the Greek mercenaries he let the defeated go free. He did not demand indemnities or impose conscription, and when hillsmen came down to surrender he sent them back to cultivate their own properties in peace.[15]

Polybius records examples of injustice in the conduct of war and contrasts such action with the concerns for justice on the battlefield shown by both Phillip and Alexander.[16] And Julius Caesar chronicles his beneficence toward defeated foes in his *Civil Wars*, and in a letter to Cicero he writes

You are right to infer of me . . . that there is nothing further from my nature than cruelty. Whilst I take great pleasure from that fact, I am proud indeed that my action wins your approval. I am not moved because it is said that those, whom I let go, have departed to wage war on me again, for there is nothing I like better that I should be true to myself and they to themselves.[17]

Other cultures also developed constraints on how war should be conducted. The ancient Hebrews had certain rules governing warfare, as the following passage from Deuteronomy shows:

When you draw near to a city to fight against it, offer terms of peace to it. And if its answer to you is peace and it opens to you, then all the people who are found in it shall do forced labor for you and shall serve you. But if it makes no peace with you, but makes war against you, then you shall besiege it; and when the Lord your God gives it into your hand you shall put all its males to the sword, but the women and the little ones, the cattle, and everything else in the city, all its spoil, you shall take as booty for yourselves; . . . When you besiege a city for a long time, making war against it in order to take it, you shall not destroy its trees by wielding an axe against them; for you may eat of them, but you shall not cut them down. . . . Only the trees in the field which you know are not trees for food you may destroy and cut down that you may build siegeworks against the city that makes war with you, until it falls.[18]

Finally, there are even historical cases of limiting the brutality of war through arms control. For example, during the Japanese invasion of Korea in 1590, the principal weapon carried by Japanese soldiers was the musket, reputed to be the best in the world at the time. In less than a century, however, firearms had virtually disappeared from Japan because they were inconsistent with the ethos of Japanese warriors.[19]

Although this sampling of unrelated examples provides guidelines that differ from what we would consider appropriate, they nevertheless identify explicit restraints on both *jus ad bellum* and *jus in bello* that reach back to the beginning of recorded history. Later we will attempt to understand why commonly held notions of justice so often break down in warfare. For now, however, let us examine in more detail the work of a Roman philosopher whose ideas directly influenced the development of our present tradition of Just War, Marcus Tullius Cicero.

THE JUST WAR TRADITION IN ANCIENT ROME

In *De Re Republica* 3, XXIII, written in the first century B.C., Cicero provides the precursor of our modern concept of *jus ad bellum*.

> A war is never undertaken by the ideal state, except in defense of its honor or safety. . . .
>
> Those wars which are unjust are undertaken without provocation. For only a war waged for revenge or defense can actually be just. . . .
>
> No war is considered just unless it has been proclaimed and declared, and unless reparation has first been demanded.[20]

Wars fought for revenge for wrongs done (we might say retribution) are included in wars fought in defense of honor. Cicero has in mind wars fought in response to unprovoked acts of aggression either against Rome or Rome's allies. Elsewhere in the same section from which the previous quotation was taken we find the following: "Our people, by defending their allies, have gained domination over the whole world."

Cicero also notes that war should be a last resort, turned to only when discussion is unsuccessful.[21]

Other necessary conditions for *jus ad bellum* are the following:

1. War must be declared by proper authority.
2. The antagonist must be notified of the declaration of war.
3. The antagonist must be afforded the opportunity to make a peaceful settlement prior to the initiation of hostilities.

Concerning these last conditions, Rome had a detailed procedure whereby whenever she had a grievance against another city, ambassadors under the direction of a distinguished statesman would go to the offending city and demand reparations. The ambassadors then returned to Rome and waited thirty-three days for a response. If they received none, the same representative and his party would again travel to the other nation and threaten war. If the offending nation still refused, the designated statesman would inform the Roman Senate of the failure to achieve reparations, and the Senate could decide to resort to force to carry out its claims. Once the Senate voted for war, the ambassadors were again sent to the hostile nation to announce the declaration of war and symbolically throw a javelin on enemy soil. The only time these elaborate procedures were not followed was when the enemy was not organized as a state, when Rome was already under attack, or in the case of civil war.[22]

According to Roman law, a war was just if it conformed to these procedures. Thus Roman law provided a means whereby Rome could "objectively" assess justice in the international arena; war waged in accordance with these conditions was *formally* just.

Moreover, under Roman law, only those who were formally recognized as members of the military profession had the authority to act on behalf of the state by engaging in state-sanctioned warfare. Officers who fought in battles after they had been discharged or their units deactivated could be guilty of murder. Cicero writes

> When Popilius decided to disband one of his legions, he discharged also young Cato, who was serving in the same legion. But when the young man out of love for the service stayed on in the field, his father wrote to Popilius to say that if he let him stay in the Army, he should swear him into service with a new oath of allegiance, for in view of the voidance of his former oath he could not legally fight the foe. So extremely scrupulous was the observance of the laws in regard to the conduct of war.[23]

In a second example concerning a youth who was discharged while serving in Macedonia, Cicero relates that the young man was warned "to be careful not to go into battle; for the man who is not legally a soldier has no right to be fighting the foe." The Roman Empire was such a dominant force— morally and militarily—that in formulating her laws, she assumed the role of an objective observer operating from behind a "veil of ignorance," regarding which side of the law she might be on. In other words, the Roman Senate adopted "just" laws based on principles so obvious and reasonable that they must be universally recognized, and imposed them on herself and those nations with whom she interacted. In this sense, Rome is the "lawgiver" and these laws are *jus gentium*, or world law. Nevertheless, even though the Roman term *jus gentium* is usually rendered as "international law" or "law of nations," it is worthwhile to note that historically the term referred to laws declared by the Roman Senate, not by any international organization. The Roman Senate assumed the same "ideal observer" role that is assumed by the representatives to modern international conventions at Geneva, The Hague, and the United Nations. Thus Roman *jus gentium* seems to meet the objections of those who criticize modern international law, because there is no recognized common authority with the power of sanctions. We will return to this topic in more detail in later discussions of contemporary international law.

Roman rules governing how war should be fought also were delineated. In *De Officiis,* Cicero notes that "there are certain duties that we owe even to those who have wronged us . . . [and] there is a limit to retribution and punishment."[24] Cicero emphasizes that only soldiers sworn to duty with active military units may legally wage war, and he adds

> Not only must we show consideration for those whom we have conquered by force of arms, but we must also ensure protection to those who lay down their arms and throw themselves upon the mercy of our generals, even though the battering ram has hammered at their walls.[25]

It is possible, of course, to produce numerous examples where such rules were ignored. This does not, however, show that these rules were without effect, anymore than a particular breach of private law by a citizen proves that a particular domestic law is inoperable. Some would argue that wars and war crimes are a mark of the human condition, an unfortunate but inevitable dimension of human behavior. Perhaps this is true. But the mere statement that a particular act constitutes a war *crime* is sufficient to show that one recognizes normative constraints on the conduct of Just War.

What this myriad of examples from different cultures and historic periods suggests is that concern for justice in war is a human, rather than simply a Christian, characteristic.

Let us now turn our attention to the Christian theologians who compiled, codified, and modified the pagan Just War Tradition to make it compatible with Christian doctrine.

Topics for Further Discussion

1. Plato's *Republic* and the Book of Deuteronomy both contain some limits on what may be done to the environment in warfare. Is it reasonable to place restraints on environmental damage during warfare? Develop a set of guidelines showing how the environment should be treated in wartime.

2. Statesmen in Ancient Rome established formal criteria for ascertaining whether force was justified in a particular situation. Why did they establish these *jus ad bellum* criteria rather than just decide whether to resort to force on a case-by-case basis? What are the advantages and disadvan-

tages of committing to a set of formal criteria for future decisions concerning the use of force?

3. Cicero noted that soldiers who continued to fight in campaigns after they had been discharged from military service might be charged with murder. Do you agree with such a policy? Why do you suppose that Cicero believed this topic worthy of discussion?

4. In Ancient Rome, wars waged according to Roman law were formally just. Explain the difference between *formal justice* and *objective justice*.

Notes

1.   W. A. P. Martin, "Traces of International Law in Ancient China," in *International Review* XIV (1883), pp. 63–77.

2.   Geoffrey Parrinder, ed., *World Religions: From Ancient History to the Present* (New York: Facts on File, 1971), p. 78.

3.   *The Book of Tao*, reprinted in *War and Peace*, vol. 5 of *Classical Selections on Great Issues* (Washington D.C.: University Press of America, 1982), p. 526.

4.   *The Art of War*, Sun Tzu, trans., with an introduction by Samuel B. Griffith (New York: Oxford University Press, 1963), p. 76.

5.   Samuel Birch, *The Manners and Customs of the Ancient Egyptians*, vol. III (New York: Scribner and Welford, 1878), p. 264. There also is a record of a peace treaty between Ramses II and the Hittites that specifies, among other things, mutual exchange of political fugitives and emigrants with assurances of humane treatment to the same by both sides. See James Henry Breasted, *Ancient Records of Egypt: Historical Documents*, vol. 3 (New York: Russell & Russell, Inc., 1962), pp. 163–72.

6.   *The Law of War: A Documentary History*, vol. I, edited by Leon Friedman with a foreword by Telford Taylor (New York: Random House, 1972), p. 3.

7.   Ibid., p. 3.

8.   Plato, *The Republic*, Bk. V 471a5–b5 in *The Collected Dialogues of Plato*, edited by Edith Hamilton and Huntington Cairns (Princeton, N.J.: Princeton University Press, 1961).

9.   Plato, *Laws*, Bk. XII 955b9–c6, in *The Collected Dialogues of Plato*; see also *Laws*, 1 (629c8–d9).

10. Aristotle, *Nichomachean Ethics* (1177b6), in *The Complete Works of Aristotle*, vol. 2 (Princeton, N.J.: Princeton University Press, 1985), p. 1861.

11. Ibid., *Politics* 1256b25, p. 199.

12. Ibid., 1425a10–18, 1425b11–16, pp. 2277–78. Some scholars attribute this work to Anaximenes of Lampsacus, a contemporary of Aristotle, but T. Case argues that it is a genuine work written earlier than Aristotle's *Rhetoric* and that therefore it cannot be by Anaximenes. See W. D. Ross, *Aristotle: A Complete Exposition of His Works and Thought* (New York: Meridian Books, 1959), pp. 22, 293 (note 51).

13. Xenophon, *Cyropaedia* vii, 1, 41, translated by J. S. Watson and Henry Dale (London: George Bell & Sons, 1891), p. 208; and *Anabasis* vii, 1, 29, in the same collection, p. 213.

14. Euripides, *The Heracleidae* (960–67), translated by Ralph Gladstone in *The Complete Greek Tragedies*, edited by David Grene and Richard Lattimore (Chicago: University of Chicago Press, 1955), p. 152.

15. N. G. L. Hammond, *Alexander the Great: King, Commander, and Statesman* (Park Ridge, N.J.: Noyes Press, 1980), pp. 78, 81.

16. Polybius, *The Histories of Polybius,* vol. 1, Bk. V, 9–11, translated from the text of Hultsch by Evelyn S. Shuckburgh (Westport, Conn.: Greenwood Press, 1974), pp. 367–69.

17. Caesar, quoted by Cicero in a letter to Atticus dated March 26, 49 B.C. in *Cicero: Letters to Atticus,* vol. II, translated by E. O. Winstedt (New York: Macmillan, 1912), pp. 261–63.

18. Deut. 20: 10–20.

19. Gwynne Dyer, *War* (New York: Crown Publishers, 1985), pp. 56–57.

20. Marcus Tullius Cicero, *De Re Publica,* Bk. 3, XXIII, translated by Clinton Walker Keyes (New York: G. P. Putnam's Sons, 1928), pp. 211–13.

21. Cicero, *De Officiis,* Bk. I, XI, translated by Walter Miller (Cambridge, Mass.: Harvard University Press, 1961), p. 35.

22. Arthur Nussbaum, *A Concise History of the Law of Nations* (New York: Macmillan, 1954), pp. 21–23.

23. Cicero, *De Officiis,* Bk. I, XI, p. 39. U.S. officers and soldiers also take oaths of allegiance, as we shall see in later discussions.

24. *De Officiis,* Bk. I, XI, p. 35.

25. Ibid., p. 37.

Chapter

2

CHRISTIANITY AND THE JUST WAR TRADITION

In the first few centuries following Christ's Crucifixion, up until the time of Constantine's conversion to Christianity, many Christians refused military service. Some scholars have speculated that they did so primarily because of the requirement for idolatry rather than on pacifist grounds.[1] The Roman military traditionally required that all higher ranks, Centurion upward, sacrifice to the emperor; and even though lower ranks did not have to participate actively, they had to be present at the ceremony, swear allegiance to the emperor, and wear a badge bearing the emperor's effigy. At the beginning of the fourth century, however, the requirement for idolatry was extended to all ranks in order to identify the Christians who were at the time being subjected to severe persecution. Those who refused to perform the required idolatry were tortured and executed. In the well-known case of the Forty Martyrs (A.D. 316), Licinius, in attempting to rid his forces of Christians, forced forty of them to either renounce Christianity or lie naked on a frozen lake all night.[2]

Records of Christians in the military are frequently cited as evidence that it was not pacifism but the expansion of the requirement for idolatry and increased persecution that caused many Christians to avoid military service. While much of the historical evidence most often cited is undoubtedly accurate, there is another interpretation of the evidence that is more consistent with the available information and convinces some that many early Christians also were pacifists. Tertullian, writing in A.D. 199, prays "for security to the empire; for protection to the imperial house; for brave armies," but explicitly prohibits Christians from wearing a sword irrespective of the requirement for idolatry.

But now inquiry is made about this point, whether the military may be admitted unto the faith, even the rank and file, or each inferior grade, to whom

17

there is no necessity for taking part in sacrifices or capital punishments. . . . One soul cannot serve two *masters*—God and Caesar. . . . But how will a *Christian man* war, nay, how will he serve even in peace, without a sword, which the Lord has taken away? . . . [The Lord] in disarming Peter, unbelted every soldier. No dress is lawful among us, if assigned to any unlawful action.[3]

Another record from that period that expressly prohibits violence (and warfare) but does not address military service is found in the following passage from Lactantius, tutor to Constantine, written about A.D. 313:

It is not therefore befitting that those who strive to keep to the path of justice should be companions and sharers in the public homicide. For when God forbids us to kill, He not only prohibits us from open violence, which is not even allowed by the public laws, but he warns us against the commission of those things which are esteemed lawful among men. Thus it will be neither lawful for a just man to engage in warfare, since his warfare is justice itself, nor to accuse anyone of a capital charge, because it makes no difference whether you put a man to death by word, or rather by sword, since it is the act of putting to death itself which is prohibited. Therefore with regard to this precept of God, there ought to be no exception at all; but that it is always unlawful to put to death a man, whom God willed to be a sacred animal.[4]

One way to reconcile the issues of pacifism and idolatry is to recognize that Christians could serve in the army (perhaps on occupation duty, as part of a police force, or simply as deterrents), without necessarily committing violent acts. This seems to be implied by Origen (A.D. 245) who, in responding to charges by Celsus that Christians were guilty of *contemptissima inertia,* or most contemptible apathy, because they refused to join in the defense of the state that maintained the communal order, argues that "none fight better for the king than we do . . . we fight on his behalf, forming a special army—an army of piety—by offering our prayers to God."[5]

And Marcus Aurelius, in crediting prayer by the great numbers of Christian members of his Thundering Legion with saving the entire unit from perishing from thirst in A.D. 173, observed

I called out of the ranks those whom we call Christians, and, having questioned them, I perceived what a great multitude of them there were and raged against them: which indeed I should not have done, because I afterward perceived their power. For they did not begin by the contemplation of spears or arms or trumpets (which is hateful to them because of the God which they keep in their conscience . . .), but by prostrating themselves on the ground.[6]

Presumably Aurelius "raged against them" because of their unwillingness to fight.

Bainton argues for a similar explanation and concludes that "ecclesiastical authors before Constantine condemned Christian participation in warfare, though not necessarily military service in time of peace."[7]

We can conclude that, while the expansion of the requirement for idolatry to all ranks in the fourth century did keep Christians from military duty, their service prior to this time was not inconsistent with their pacifist beliefs. Let us now turn to an examination of the basis for this early pacifism.

EARLY CHRISTIANITY AND PACIFISM

The prohibition against Christians engaging in warfare was derived from certain passages from the New Testament that seemed to expressly prohibit doing violence to others. The most poignant of these passages are quoted next.

How blest are the peacemakers; God shall call them his sons. (Matt. 5:9)

You have learned that our forefathers were told, "Do not commit murder, and anyone who commits murder shall be brought to judgment." But what I tell you is this: Anyone who nurses anger against his brother must be brought to judgment. If he abuses his brother he must answer for it to the court; if he sneers at him he will have to answer for it in the fires of hell. (Matt. 5:21–22)

You have learned that they were told, "An eye for an eye, and a tooth for a tooth." But what I tell you is this: Do not set yourself against the man who wrongs you. If someone slaps you on the right cheek, turn and offer him your left. If a man wants to sue you for your shirt, let him have your coat as well. If a man in authority makes you go one mile, go with him two. . . .

You have learned that they were told, "Love your neighbor and hate your enemy." But what I tell you is this: Love your enemies and pray for your persecutors . . . ; And if you greet only your brothers, what is there extraordinary about that? Even the heathen do as much. You must therefore be all goodness, just as your heavenly Father is all good. (Matt. 5:43–48)

They then came forward, seized Jesus, and held him fast.

At that moment one of those with Jesus reached for his sword, drew it, and he struck at the High Priest's servant and cut off his ear. But Jesus said to him, "Put up your sword. All who take the sword die by the sword." (Matt. 26:50–53)

Never pay back evil for evil. Let your aims be such as all men count honorable. If possible, so far as it lies with you, live at peace with all men. My dear friends, do not seek revenge, but leave a place for divine retribution; for there is a text which reads, "Justice is mine, says the Lord, I will repay." But there is another text: "If your enemy is hungry, feed him; if he is thirsty, give him a drink; by doing this you will heap live coals on his head." Do not let evil conquer you, but use good to defeat evil. (Rom. 12:17–21)[8]

Of course, these passages cannot be interpreted simply as prohibitions against *Christians* doing violence to others or to one another. If Christians have this duty because what Christ said is true, then everyone must have the same duty.[9]

Part of the problem with using these passages as the basis for pacifism is that in order to interpret them as espousing pacifism, one must distill certain values from them—for example, submissiveness or nonresistance—and argue that such values imply passivity. But if we adopt this interpretation, then no one should ever serve as a police officer, guard, or in any other position that might require force; and such an extreme reading runs contrary to other passages in the New Testament that recognize the legitimate authority of the state as a keeper of the peace and enforcer of the laws.

In fact, many of the same or similar passages in the New Testament can be interpreted in ways that seem to justify violence in certain circumstances. For example, one might argue that while the New Testament preaches love and warns against hate, it nowhere prohibits violence as a means of distributing justice; it is only violence done in anger or with vengeance that we are warned against. In fact, if we continue the previous quotation from Romans, we get a discussion of the legitimate use of force in the name of justice.

> Every person must submit to the supreme authorities. There is no authority but by act of God, and the existing authorities are instituted by him; consequently anyone who rebels against authority is resisting a divine institution, and those who so resist have themselves to thank for the punishment they will receive. For government, a terror to crime, has no terrors for good behavior. You wish to have no fear of the authorities? Then continue to do right and you will have their approval, for they are God's agents working for your good. But if you do wrong, then you will have cause to fear them; it is not for nothing that they hold the power of the sword, for they are God's agents of punishment, for retribution on the offender. (Rom. 13:1–4)

This passage undoubtedly permits violence as a means of distributing justice and maintaining communal order.

A second problem for a pacifist interpretation is that it requires that one accept both the Old Testament and New Testament as presenting different moral standards. Without this discontinuity it is impossible to reconcile pacifism with *lex talionis* (Exod. 21–24). If, however, the violence of the Old Testament is understood as a legitimate means of retributive justice rather than as a form of revenge, the two texts are not incommensurate. In the following paragraph, Elizabeth Anscombe notes that the "an eye for an eye" passage is often misunderstood in this way:

> It is characteristic of pacifism to denigrate the Old Testament and exalt the New: something quite contrary to the teaching of the New Testament itself, which always looks back to and leans upon the Old. How typical it is that

the words of Christ "You have heard it said, an eye for an eye and a tooth for a tooth, but I say to you . . ." are taken as a repudiation of the ethic of the Old Testament! People seldom look up the occurrence of this phrase in the juridical code of the Old Testament where it belongs, and is the admirable principle of law for the punishment of certain crimes, such as procuring the wrongful punishment of another by perjury. People often enough *now* cite the phrase to justify private revenge; no doubt this was often "heard said" when Christ spoke of it. But no justification for this exists in the personal ethic taught by the Old Testament. On the contrary. What do we find? "Seek no revenge," (Leviticus xix, 18). . . . And "If your enemy is hungry, give him food, if thirsty, give him drink," (Proverbs xxv, 21).[10]

According to Anscombe's interpretation, the "an eye for an eye" passage should be understood not as a mandate for punishment but as a limit on what one can do in the name of retributive justice—that is, do no more in retribution than has been wrongly done to you. Anscombe goes on to add that the passages from the New Testament often cited as dictating pacifism are instead admonitions against wrongdoing and hatred, and they do not at all preclude the use of force as a legitimate means for administering justice.

Another difficulty for grounding pacifism in Christianity arises because of what is not said in the New Testament. Despite the presence of Roman soldiers throughout Palestine and numerous references to them in the New Testament (they are baptized by John the Baptist and provide Paul safe escort from Jerusalem to Caesarea), nowhere do we find soldiering prohibited or even frowned upon as a profession.

Ironically, the same text in which many have found the tenets of pacifism has provided for others the basis for the reprehensible, unconstrained violence of the Crusades. The pronouncement in Matthew, "You must not think that I have come to bring peace on earth; I have not come to bring peace, but a sword" (10:34); and Luke, "Whoever has a purse had better take it with him, and his pack too; and if he has no sword, let him sell his cloak to buy one" (22:35–38); and also Christ's treatment of the peddlers in the temple—all have been used as passages justifying the Crusades.

Because of the ambiguity of the New Testament on the issues of warfare, military service, and using violence in the name of justice, many early Christians concluded that Christ's nonresistance to the law meant a nonresistance to lawlessness. As adherents to Christianity grew, these beliefs regarding the laws of the state threatened the very fabric of communal order. The requirement to respond to this early pacifism forced the Church to build upon the Roman notion of just use of force and to develop the tradition of *jus ad bellum* that we recognize today. By expressly permitting Christian participation in *Just War*, Church leaders such as Saints Ambrose and Augustine hoped to keep the new *Holy* Roman Empire under Constantine safe from invading barbarians, as we shall see in our subsequent discussions on the development of *bellum justum*.

Nevertheless, the Just War doctrine that the early Christian theologians codified and developed continues to be a cause for consternation by those who argue that Christ's message implies pacifism. Modern defenders of Christian pacifism explain the development of early Just War doctrine as a compromise between the practical or worldly notion of duty to society that was embodied in Roman traditions, with the ideal or utopian notion of purity of the soul that they found in the New Testament. They believe that pacifism is precisely what was compromised when Christianity became the official religion of the state.[11]

James Turner Johnson argues convincingly that the development of the Christian Just War Tradition does not represent a compromise between Christian and Roman values but should more accurately be described as a synthesis of these values.[12] Analysis of the writings of the early Christian scholars shows that all of them opposed war and violence per se and that the debate really centered on whether Christians might seek the temporal goods represented by the state. Those who defended pacifism argued the position that Christians must hold themselves aloof from the affairs of this world in preparation for the next one. Those who advocated the notion of Just War, on the other hand, held that in some cases the quest for temporal goods (such as justice or communal order) might be a duty grounded in Christian ideals.[13]

One example that illustrates this is Ambrose's dictum that wrong behavior is not limited to just doing harm, but that it also is wrong to fail to prevent another from inflicting harm when one has the ability. As Ambrose puts it, "He who does not keep harm off a friend, if he can, is as much in fault as he who causes it."[14] Even though this statement is taken verbatim from Cicero (*De Officiis*, Bk. I, VII, 23), it would hardly do to call this a compromise of the values of the New Testament, especially since Ambrose rejects self-defense. Instead, it should be understood as a principle that permits one to resolve conflicts in values: in this case, the prohibition against the use of violence on the one hand and the responsibility to protect the innocent based on the principle of brotherly love on the other hand. Johnson sums up the thrust of this development in the following way:

> The achievement of just war theory was . . . to combine the general opposition to violence and bloodshed with a limited justification of the use of violence by Christians. This limited justification required that the use of force be to protect a value that could not otherwise be protected, and it justified military service as an instrument for such protection of value. The presumption against violence nonetheless remained, so that the justification could never become absolute: permission was always accompanied by limitation.[15]

The central notion here is that the use of force requires justification—the presumption is always against violence—but violence may be permitted to protect other values. Hence the New Testament passages that advocate non-violence might be taken to express a **prima facie duty,** rather than an absolute one (as the pacifists would have it).

One important consequence of such thinking is that the Roman legal notion of Just War is gradually replaced with a moral or religious notion where the forces of good combat the forces of evil. Saint Augustine, especially, expands the just causes for war by including those wars ordained by God. Couple this with Pauline teaching that earthly political authority is divinely sanctioned and it is a short step to the Holy War, or Crusade. Likewise, the belief that God directly intervenes in or even orchestrates battles—a belief inspired by numerous biblical passages—permits one to view warfare as a kind of trial by combat between states, with God tipping the scales in favor of the righteous.

Another consequence of these developments was the establishment of the Church as a unifying, political authority. This helped undermine the notion that the will of the monarch was the sole source of law and justice in the temporal world. If the sovereign could be called to the bar to answer for his actions, then there must exist higher criteria by which he might be judged—namely, God's. Such criteria would, of course, apply to all monarchs: hence, ecclesiastical authority in political affairs.

In a later section we will see how Christian Just War theory evolves into a secular set of legal dicta similar to those of ancient Rome whence they originated but with considerably more detail. As we turn to the writing of Saint Ambrose (and Saint Augustine in the next chapter), we will attempt to distinguish the secular principles of *bellum justum,* generally originating in Greek and Roman works, from those that have theological origins.

SAINT AMBROSE

Prior to becoming the Bishop of Milan, Ambrose occupied the position of Roman governor of northern Italy, essentially a military post. He viewed the Roman Empire as the warder of peace, the *pax romana,* and preached that the ongoing assaults on the empire by Germanic tribes were divinely inspired as retribution for Roman paganism. His primary importance for our study lies in his admonition to Christians that they not keep themselves aloof from the affairs of the state in anticipation of an imminent fulfillment of the **eschatological promise**—an argument that Augustine develops further in *The City of God.*

Borrowing heavily from Cicero, Ambrose outlines the duties that Christian citizens owe to their community. These duties are derived from the **Four Cardinal Virtues:** prudence (wisdom), justice, fortitude (courage), and temperance.[16] One must manifest these virtues in his temporal life in order to attain eternal life.

It is certain that virtue is the only and the highest good; that it alone richly abounds in the fruit of a blessed life; that a blessed life, by means of which eternal life is won, does not depend on eternal or corporal benefits, but on virtue only. A blessed life is the fruit of the present, and eternal life is the hope of the future.[17]

Ambrose adds that "what is useful is the same as what is virtuous" and that this may be "divided into what is useful for the body, and what is useful unto godliness."[18] Christians have a duty to do that which is useful or virtuous, both in terms of serving God and in their daily activities. This emphasis on the duties that Christians have in their temporal lives is at once a rebuttal to those Romans who accused Christians of *inertia* or apathy, and an admonition to those Christians who held themselves aloof from temporal affairs in anticipation of the eschatological Armageddon.

The dominant virtue is justice, and the examples that Ambrose uses to illustrate his message are especially revealing concerning his thinking on Just War theory. In a discussion on how these virtues are integrated and manifested in one's daily life, Ambrose uses virtue in making battlefield decisions as his example, and in so doing provides us with his views on *justum bellum*. In a passage that reads like a modern treatise for military commanders on certain tactical and moral principles of warfare, he writes

It is clear, then, that these [cardinal] and the remaining virtues are related to one another. For courage, which in war preserves one's country from the barbarians, or at home defends the weak or comrades from robbers, is full of justice; and to know on what plan to defend and to give help, how to make use of opportunities of time and place, is the part of prudence and moderation, and temperance itself cannot observe due measure without prudence. To know a fit opportunity, and to make return according to what is right, belongs to justice.[19]

By making justice most fundamental or the highest virtue, Ambrose lays the ground rules for how conflicts between competing duties should be arbitrated.

Likewise, his discussion of right conduct in war is developed in a discussion of the duties that are part of our temporal lives—such as the military duty for selfless service to the state. Concerning this duty to one's country, he writes

We read, not only in the case of private individuals but even on kings. . . . If anyone gains the people's favor by advice or service, by fulfilling the duties of his ministry or office, or if he encounters danger for the sake of the whole nation, there is no doubt but that such love will be shown him by the people that they all will put his safety and welfare before their own.[20]

In an example found in the same chapter from which the previous quotation is taken, Ambrose discusses David (among others), who accepts the role of king against his wishes because it is his duty to do so. And in a remarkable passage, Ambrose holds up David's actions in war as a model of *jus in bello*.

> He had bound the people to himself freely in doing his duty . . . when he showed that he loved valor even in an enemy. He had also thought that justice should be shown to those who had borne arms against himself the same as to his own men . . . [and] he admired Abner, the bravest champion of the opposing side whilst he was their leader and was yet waging war. Nor did he despise him when suing for peace, but honored him by a banquet. When killed by treachery, he mourned and wept for him. He followed him and honored his obsequies, and evinced his good faith in desiring vengeance for the murder; for he handed on that duty to his son in the charge that he gave him, being anxious rather that the death of an innocent man should not be left avenged, than that any one should mourn for his own.[21]

This passage is especially significant because it implies two principles that are key tenets in our modern notion of *jus in bello*. The first is that soldiers have a duty to the innocent, even when it means the risk of their own lives. In this case, that duty is manifested by David's willingness to risk his son's life in order to bring justice to the wrongdoer. In Ambrose's philosophy, brotherly love demands the use of force.

Second, Ambrose clearly notes that the guilt for initiating the war does not necessarily extend to those who are fighting it. This is the notion of *moral equality among soldiers*. David accepts Abner as a moral equal because of the way he fights in the war—independent of the rightness or wrongness of the war itself. The message is that soldiers are to be respected (or punished) based on their conduct as soldiers, even when they are members of the enemy's forces. Because soldiers are judged by their actions on the battlefield rather than in terms of the political considerations of the war itself, they are protected rather than punished when their status as combatants (that is, soldiers) is terminated, whether by capture, surrender, or injury.

In addition to the aforementioned principles that Ambrose introduces, he also borrows freely from Cicero's ideas regarding *jus in bello*. Citing an example used by Cicero, he notes that virtue does not lie in victory and that it is a shameful victory unless it is gained with honor. "In truth," he adds, "it is a noble thing for a man to refuse to gain the victory by foul acts."[22] He also argues against excessive cruelty and admonishes Emperor Theodosius for needless bloodshed at the siege of Thessalonica.

> I urge, I beg, I exhort, I warn . . . that you who were an example of unusual piety . . . should not mourn that so many have perish. . . . I dare not offer the sacrifice if you intend to be present. Is that which is not allowed after

shedding the blood of one innocent person, allowed after shedding the blood of so many?[23]

Ambrose, like Cicero, champions the notion of justice for the vanquished and distinguishes the innocent from the guilty among the enemy. Although these *jus in bello* principles do not appear in Augustine's writing on Just War, they will be adopted by subsequent exponents of Just War theory and will thereby find their way into canon law.

As we read Ambrose we should remember that nowhere is his intention to provide a theory of when and how one should wage war—this he considers an obvious by-product of living a virtuous life. His point is to convince Christians that those who would attain the kingdom of heaven must live a virtuous life in the temporal world, and included in such a life is the duty to promote and, when necessary, enforce justice. He believed unequivocally that Christians had a duty to support and defend the great empire that had brought peace and imposed order on the sin-ridden combative world. By remaining aloof from civil affairs, one fails "to render unto Caesar" those things which are due him; and one of these duties is the requirement to contribute to the peace and justice of one's community—even by the use of arms, if necessary. Of course, it was crucial that soldiers conduct themselves virtuously in the manner in which they fought.

One additional aspect of Ambrose's work that warrants our attention, if only for its subsequent importance in Augustine's Just War thinking, is God's role in deciding the outcome of wars. Old Testament passages where God orders his chosen people to wage war and then grants them victory were not lost on either Ambrose or Augustine. In a treatise written at the request of Gratian, Emperor of the West, who was preparing to repel a Gothic invasion, Ambrose writes

> Go forth, sheltered, indeed, under the shield of faith, and gird with the sword of the spirit; go forth to the victory, promised of old time, and foretold in oracles given by God. . . .
>
> No military eagles, no flights of birds, here lead the van of our army, but Thy Name, Lord Jesus, and Thy worship. This is no land of unbelievers, but the land whose custom it is to send forth confessors—Italy.[24]

In the same work, Ambrose blames earlier successes by the Goths against the empire on Roman paganism. Thus he argued that if Rome would reject paganism, God would protect Rome from the ravages of the barbarians. He quotes the prophecy found in Ezekiel 39 that the people of Israel will repulse an attack by the Gog, and concludes, "That Gog is the Goth, whose coming forth we have already seen, and over whom victory in days to come is promised, according to the word of the Lord."[25] This notion of divinely inspired wars constitutes a break with Cicero's theory of Just War and will comprise a key element of Augustine's idea of *jus ad bellum.*

Topics for Further Discussion

1. For some early Christian scholars, Christianity entailed positive duties as well as negative ones. How can such an interpretation of Christianity be used as an argument against pacifism? How might the same position be stretched in order to justify crusades?

2. Provide two recent examples where political or military leaders have invoked their deity as a justification for the use of force.

3. Various forms of pacifism derive from the principle that it is always wrong to do harm to others. Elizabeth Anscombe objects to this principle because "it makes no distinction between the blood of the guilty and the blood of the innocent." Develop an argument either attacking or defending Anscombe's position.

4. Why does the view that political leaders are divinely appointed (or sanctioned) present a problem for Just War theory?

5. Ambrose tells us that good soldiers not only respect their enemies but that in some cases they also mourn enemy dead. Explain why you agree or disagree with this view.

6. Ambrose argues that one's virtues are the "only and highest good," and he stipulates that justice is the highest virtue. How does Ambrose reconcile his view that justice is the highest virtue with Christ's command that all persons be meek?

Notes

1. Elizabeth Anscombe defends this position in "War and Murder" in *War and Morality,* edited by Richard A. Wasserstrom (Belmont, Calif.: Wadsworth Publishing Co., 1970), pp. 48–49. See also Arthur F. Holmes, "The Just War," in *War: Four Christian Views,* edited by Robert G. Clouse (Downers Grove, Ill.: Inter Varsity Press, 1981), pp. 117–35.

2. John Eppstein, *The Catholic Tradition of the Law of Nations* (Washington, D.C.: Catholic Association for International Peace, 1935), pp. 45–46.

3. Tertullian, *On Idolatry* 19, translated by S. Thelwall, in *The Ante-Nicene Fathers* 3, reprinted in *War and Christian Ethics,* edited by Arthur F. Holmes (Grand Rapids, Mich.: Baker Book House, 1975), pp. 43–44. The previous quotation from Tertullian is taken from *Apology,* found in the same source, p. 40. Tertullian's work is not always consistent on this topic. In one instance, he argues that no Christian can engage in warfare (*On Idolatry* 19), while elsewhere he seems to hold that a soldier who converts to Christianity may still be a faithful Christian: "With Him [God] the faithful citizen is a soldier, just as the faithful soldier is a citizen." ("The Chaplet," aforementioned source, p. 46). Presumably he means that soldiers who convert to Christianity may assist the emperor by prayer, but not with the use of arms. Christians who are not already soldiers are prohibited from military service.

4. Lactantius, *De Divinis Institutionibus* VI, 20, found in Eppstein, *The Catholic Tradition,* pp. 38–39.

5. Origen, *Contra Celsum.* 8:73, reprinted in Holmes, *War and Christian Ethics,* p. 49.

6.   Eppstein, *The Catholic Tradition*, p. 34.

7.   Roland H. Bainton, *Christian Attitudes Toward War and Peace* (New York: Abingdon Press, 1960), p. 81.

8.   All biblical quotations are taken from *The New English Bible: New Testament* (London: Oxford University Press & Cambridge University Press, 1961).

9.   See Jan Narveson "Pacifism: A Philosophical Analysis," *Ethics*, vol. 75, pp. 259–71. Reprinted in Wasserstrom, *War and Morality*, p. 66. For an interesting discussion of Narveson's argument, see Yehuda Melzer, *Concepts of Just War* (Leyden: A. W. Sijthoff, 1975), p. 122.

10.   Elizabeth Anscombe, "War and Murder," in Wasserstrom, *War and Morality*, p. 48.

11.   For example, see Stanley Windass, *Christianity Versus Violence* (London: Sheed and Ward, 1964), who claims that early Christians "prostituted" themselves to secular authority.

12.   James Turner Johnson, *The Quest for Peace* (Princeton, N.J.: Princeton University Press, 1987), p. 45.

13.   Ibid., pp. 52–53.

14.   St. Ambrose, *Duties of the Clergy*, Bk. I, XXIV, 115, in *Nicene and Post-Nicene Fathers*, vol. X, edited by Philip Schaff (Grand Rapids, Mich.: Eerdmans Publishing Co., 1969), p. 30.

15.   Johnson, *Quest for Peace*, pp. 51–52.

16.   St. Ambrose, *Duties of the Clergy*, Bk. I, XXXVI, 179, p. 20. These are the same virtues Cicero discusses in *De Officiis*, Bk. I, XV–XVII, which have their origins in Plato, *Laws* 631 and *The Republic* 427e. Ambrose, like Plato, gives prudence (wisdom) and justice special billing.

17.   St. Ambrose, *Duties of the Clergy*, Bk. II, V, 18, p. 46.

18.   Ibid., Bk. II, VI, VII, pp. 47–48.

19.   Ibid., Bk. I, XXVII, 129, p. 22. This example is an interesting choice by Ambrose because the Greek word for virtue, *arete*, was used by Homer to refer specifically to military virtue, that is, courage. Plato and others use the term more broadly of course.

20.   Ibid., Bk. II, VII, 30, p. 48.

21.   Ibid., Bk. II, VII, 33, p. 49.

22.   Ibid., Bk. III, XV, 91, p. 82. The case of Caius Fabricius is discussed by Cicero in *De Officiis*, III, XXII.

23.   St. Ambrose, Letter LI, "To Theodosius after the Massacre at Thessalonica," in *Nicene and Post-Nicene Fathers*, vol. X, pp. 450–53. Theodosius was excommunicated until he had done public pennance.

24.   St. Ambrose, *On the Christian Faith*, Bk. II, XVI, 136, 142, in *A Select Library of the Nicene and Post-Nicene Fathers*, vol. X, pp. 241–42. The Roman army was defeated before Gratian arrived and this moderated Ambrose's predication for predicting military outcomes.

25.   Ibid., 138, p. 241.

Chapter

3

Saint Augustine and the Tradition of Just War

Saint Augustine is widely recognized as being the father of modern Just War theory. In this chapter we will summarize his principles of *bellum justum* and also the arguments he offers to support these principles.

Augustine was a student of philosophy before his conversion, and many of the ideas he espoused were taken directly from Plato and Cicero, while others were derived from his interpretation of the Gospel. In either case, he invariably attempts to support his views—including those that have their origins in Greek and Roman philosophy—with evidence from the Old and New Testaments. One problem with defending Greek and Roman Just War principles with Christian premises is that if the premises can be called into question, then the conclusions themselves become suspect, even though they may originally have been derived from secular premises. The later jurists and philosophers of the Middle Ages will use Augustine as their starting point, but will strive to formulate their Just War arguments to be less dependent on revealed premises, as we shall see in later chapters.

A second consideration to keep in mind when studying Augustine's writing is that in defending Catholic orthodoxy against both the pagans and the many divisions within the Church itself, he develops his own philosophy of history, political philosophy, and conception of humans as moral agents (his psychology), and an understanding of Augustine's innovations in these topics is often crucial in understanding how he arrives at certain aspects of his theory of Just War. While our purpose is to understand Augustine's thinking on *bellum justum*, it will be necessary to discuss, at least to some extent, both his philosophy of history and his psychology in order to accomplish this.

We will divide our exposition into three broad sections: Augustine's philosophy of history, his political philosophy, and his views of human beings as moral agents. Let us begin, however, with a brief background.

Augustine was born in A.D. 354 and converted to Christianity in 386. During his lifetime (in A.D. 383), Christianity was adopted as the official state religion of the Roman Empire (although all but one of the emperors had been Christians since Constantine became a convert and issued the Edict of Milan proclaiming toleration of Christians in A.D. 312).[1] Augustine also lived during a period of decline for the Roman Empire, which included the sack of Rome by Alaric the Visigoth in 411—an event that shocked the Roman world. His own city, Hippo, in northern Africa, felt the pressure of barbarian expansion, and during the last two years of Augustine's life the only thing that separated his community from being overrun was the Roman army. In fact, Hippo fell to the Vandals under Genseric in 431, the year following Augustine's death.[2]

In addition to these external secular threats to Augustine's world, his life also was a period of great divisiveness within the Church, with multiple sects claiming orthodoxy and vying for leadership and followers. Augustine himself was once a follower of the Manichaeans (a dualistic religion whose founder, Mani, claimed to be a prophet sent by Christ), although after his conversion he worked hard to expose the heretical nature of their beliefs; his *De Libero Arbitrio* is largely directed toward this end.[3]

One difficulty in extracting a single coherent theory of *bellum justum* from Augustine stems from the fact that much of his work, especially that relevant to our topic, was written either (1) in response to inquiries by Christians concerning their religion, (2) in an effort to stem the growing divisiveness in the Church, or (3) to respond to attacks against the Church by either the pagans or other religious sects. His thoughts on *bellum justum* are nested in such works, and there is no single source where we can find even a majority of his views on our topic.

For example, his writing against the British monk Pelagius is primarily a defense of God's grace as a necessary condition of salvation. The Pelagians denied the doctrine that mankind was inescapably cursed through Adam's **Original Sin** and asserted instead a doctrine whereby salvation was wholly dependent on a virtuous life attainable by everyone through the judicious exercise of their free will.[4] Inherent in this position was the contention that men should maintain their purity by remaining aloof from all political affairs. In responding to this heresy, Augustine explains, among other things, that the soul has the franchise on the normative worth of human actions. Thus it is what one holds in one's heart—that is, one's intentions—rather than one's actions that are weighed by God. This idea is crucial to Augustine's principle of **benevolent severity,** which he often invokes as a justification for violence.

In addition to defining Manichaeanism and Pelagianism as heresies, Augustine excludes Donatism from Christian orthodoxy. In his writing against the Donatists he is largely concerned with condemning their practice of granting a second baptism; but he also seeks to refute their contention that all political institutions are diabolical. In defending political institutions (such as the Roman Empire), Augustine defends the institutional use of force as a means of maintaining peace and order.

Augustine's *The City of God* is a response to accusations by the pagans that the decline of Rome at the hands of the barbarians was the divine retribution of Jove. It is also meant to provide Christians with an explanation for the barbarian successes against the (by then) Christian Empire—an explanation especially needed because of Ambrose's admonishment that earlier barbarian successes were due to the pagan nature of the empire.

Considering the motivation for these works, along with the fact that Augustine's thoughts on various topics were developed over the last forty years of his life, one can easily understand why they do not lend themselves to scrutiny as a tight, consistent philosophy on *bellum justum*. With this in mind, let us turn to his work.

PHILOSOPHY OF HISTORY

We begin with the charge, levied by Rome's pagans, that the sack of Rome by Alaric was divine retribution by Jove for the Empire's adoption of Christianity. This charge was not easily dismissed, even by the faithful, for it was plausible to think that an event of such catastrophic proportions must be the work of God. To accept the idea that God would permit the earthly bastion of Christianity to be raped by pagans was not consistent with commonly held beliefs about the omniscient, omnipotent, and omnibeneficent nature of the Christian God. Many of the faithful, faced with explaining God's actions, concluded that the demise of the Empire signaled the onset of the **eschatological** promise. And indeed, the eternal empire, the *pax romana*, that had endured for centuries seemed to be coming to an end.

Augustine responded to these issues with a philosophy of history that he develops in *The City of God*.[5] He begins by addressing the pagan charge that Christianity was the cause of the Empire's demise. After researching and chronicling all of the calamities, spiritual and physical, that he could say had ever befallen Greece or Rome under paganism, Augustine concludes

> Yet which of these disasters, suppose they happened now, would not be attributed to the Christian religion by those who thus thoughtlessly accuse us, and who we are compelled to answer? And to their own gods they attribute none of these things, though they worship them for the sake of escaping lesser calamities of the same kind, and do not reflect that they

who formerly worshiped them were not preserved from these serious disasters.[6]

Augustine goes on to explain that humanity's suffering is both a punishment and a remedy for sin. World history is a process, culminating in the Last Judgment, whereby men and women suffer as redemption for Original Sin. Specific events in the epic of time, such as wars, battles, or the fall of empires, are the means whereby God at once punishes and absolves humanity for its sins. Political turmoil and, indeed, all events in the temporal world must be understood as being part of the divine plan.

Augustine argues that there are two cities on earth that coexist and whose inhabitants commingle. The **civitas Dei** came into being with the beginning of time, when God created the universe[7]; the **civitas terrena** came into being with the Fall of Man and will cease to exist when humanity's redemption is complete, as signified by the Last Judgment. The latter is limited to the temporal world, and its citizens are those who are without **efficacious grace:** a society of the reprobate. The former consists of heaven plus those very few elect persons on earth who have been granted efficacious grace. Both earthly groups are infected with the curse of Original Sin and are "slaves to sin," but the members of *civitas terrena* are motivated *solely* by self-love (**cupiditas**) which manifests itself as a lust for wealth, glory, and power and is at the root of the pain, suffering, and corruption of the human condition.

The former group (the elect) have been granted efficacious grace and are motivated by an unselfish love of God (**caritas**) which gives them the strength to exercise their will in always choosing the lesser over the greater evil.[8]

Because both the elect and the reprobate coinhabit the same *terra firma* and are equally infected with the curse of Original Sin, each experiences the wars of the flesh against the spirit and of man against man, although each is affected differently by the experience.

> For even in the likeness of the sufferings, there remains an unlikeness in the sufferers; and though exposed to the same anguish, virtue and vice are not the same thing . . . the same violence of affliction proves, purges, clarifies the good, but damns, ruins, exterminates the wicked. For, stirred up with the same movement, mud exhales a horrible stench, and ointment emits a fragrant odor.[9]

A crucial aspect of Augustine's theory is that neither the *civitas terrena* nor the *civitas Dei* is equated with the Roman Empire (or the Church): Both societies—the elect and the reprobate—transcend political boundaries. His point here is not to discredit the Roman state, but simply to diminish the relevance of its rise and fall, its successes and failures, as they relate to Christianity and God's divine plan. In fact, it is only through earthly suffering that mankind will attain redemption. Wars are one means by which humans receive both retribution and absolution for their sins, thus even victories by the wicked have a purpose in the divine plan.

> For even when we wage a just war, our adversaries must be sinning; and every victory, even though gained by wicked men, is a result of the first judgment of God, who humbles the vanquished either for the sake of removing or of punishing their sins.[10]

We see that this account of history at once responds to the pagan charge that the sack of Rome was inspired by Jove, as well as the Christian heresy that it was the beginning of Armageddon. Augustine manages to mitigate considerably the significance of all discrete earthly catastrophes by explaining them as mileposts along the road to mankind's redemption.

Another key aspect of Augustine's philosophy of history is its emphasis on a world society wherein the citizens of *civitas Dei* and *civitas terrena* share a common bond in that they all are descended from Adam and all share the curse of his sin.[11] Even the elect have no cause for self-exaltation, because their selection is invariably arbitrary. The significance of Augustine's notion of a *world society* of mankind that transcends political and national boundaries cannot be overstated. While the idea is not new (having its origins in the Book of Genesis), Augustine is the first to state it definitively, and to state it to an audience that itself transcends national and political boundaries: Christians.[12] The significance of a world society lies in the implication that judgments concerning *bellum justum* do not apply simply to Christians (or Romans) but to all of mankind. Of course, this premise concerning the unity of mankind can be supported just as well by secular arguments, as we shall see later.

POLITICAL COMMUNITIES

How do states fit into Augustine's philosophy? The classical Greek–Roman view was that the state is the highest form of human society; it made possible the attainment of knowledge, justice, and happiness. The most perfect state that the world had ever known was the Roman Republic. The Christian view, on the other hand, was that true (or perfect) knowledge, justice, or happiness could be attained only through God. The disparity between these two views gave rise to different positions concerning the relationship that Christians should recognize with their state. The belief that Ambrose had sought to rebut—namely, that Christians ought to hold themselves aloof from all political concerns—was still very much alive and may have been rejuvenated by Alaric's sack of Rome.

Augustine derives his views on the state directly from his beliefs concerning the way good and evil are realized in the temporal world. Plato's Theory of Forms greatly influenced Augustine's belief that evil is a corruption of the perfection of something good: "For who can doubt that the whole of that which is called evil is nothing else than corruption?"[13]

Everything that God creates is good (and perfect). This is true of both man and, because it is an essential aspect of man's nature, human society. But one aspect of man's perfection is that he is not *necessarily* good—he has free will. It is this free will that caused man to turn from God (in an effort to aggrandize himself) and that thereby introduced evil into the world.

Evil, in Augustine's view, has no **ontological status.** It does not itself exist independently but is the corruption of that which is perfect—it is the privation of good. Mortality, suffering, and vice had no place in human nature as it was created; it was man's injudicious exercise of his free will that caused his fall from grace and introduced imperfection (which we perceive as evil) into the temporal world. The result is that all mankind, and all that mankind creates, is contaminated with the malady of Original Sin and bears the attribute of this imperfection. Political entities, of course, fall into this category. The ideal state (e.g., Plato's *Republic*), where perfect peace, justice, and knowledge obtain, is possible only in the City of God; when compared to the eternal city, earthly kingdoms are no better than "robber bands."[14]

But we must not assume that Augustine's pessimistic assessment of political entities implies that they are *entirely* evil. On the contrary, Augustine believes that people must live in communities, and he, following Plato and Aristotle, builds his notion of a state on that of a family. He argues that people are social creatures *by nature*, and that one who dwells outside of a *polis* (state) must be either a beast or a god. For Augustine, the family is primitive and an association of families is natural. And just as a family is organized hierarchically, a state must be so organized for the sake of order. As Augustine puts it, "Obedience to princes is a compact of all human society."[15] In response to a charge by Petilianus the Donatist that states are invidious, Augustine responds that men have some duties that they share in virtue of their humanness and others commensurate with their natural abilities and social roles. Each person must fill the social role for which he or she is destined and must strive to serve God in terms of that role. Rulers especially have a duty to serve God through their rule, and their performance of this duty affects all of those under their rule.

> Accordingly, when we take into consideration the social condition of the human race, we find that kings, in the very fact that they are kings, have a service which they can render to the Lord in a manner which is impossible for any who have not the power of kings.[16]

One form that this "benefit to others" can take is to ensure peace. And indeed, the primary purpose for which man organizes his small family groups and communities into states is to ensure peace. In the *civitas Dei,* there is no need for laws or a government because there is no need for restraint or coercion. On earth, however, beginning with the **first fratricide,** man, unable to govern himself, has needed civil government and authority to maintain peace and thereby seek whatever happiness can be attained in this world.

> The earthly city, which does not live by faith, seeks an earthly peace, and the end it proposes, in the well-ordered concord of civic obedience and rule, is the combination of men's wills to attain the things which are helpful to this life.[17]

Included in the "things helpful to this life" are temporal goods that are only attainable when there is order and peace. Enjoyment of the pleasures that such goods provide is not contrary to a Christian life.

> This whole class of human arrangements, which are of convenience for the necessary intercourse of life, the Christian is not by any means to neglect, but on the contrary, should pay a sufficient degree of attention to them, and keep them in memory.[18]

This "class of arrangements" by which states contribute to the "necessary intercourse of life" includes the availability of such temporal goods as leisure, art, and material possessions, and while Augustine advises his readers not to shun such temporal goods and the pleasure they provide, he warns that he is referring simply to the enjoyment of discrete instances of pleasure rather than avarice or lust for pleasure: It is one's lust for possessions (and fame, glory, etc.) that is the real evil, not the attainment of them. For example, a general, king, or bishop could become famous and wealthy as a coincidental result of magnanimous actions done entirely for the welfare of others. In spite of this, he might remain humble in his actions and generous in his love. According to Augustine, it is what one holds in one's heart (one's intentions) that determines moral worth rather than consequences. It follows that temporal acquisitions themselves are not to be shunned.

> Money will be thy means of pilgrimage, not the stimulant of lust; something to use for necessity, not to joy over as a means of delight. . . . Thou art passing on a journey and this life is but a wayside inn. Use money as the traveller at an inn uses table, cup, pitcher, and couch, with the purpose not of remaining, but of leaving them behind.[19]

The outward peace achieved in the *civitas terrena*, which not only permits people to live a commodious life but also enables them to aspire to righteousness, is at best a fleeting, inconstant peace, whereas that peace attained in the *civitas Dei* is a perfect, eternal peace. Mankind, as a whole, moves through time toward redemption and eternal peace.

Thus Augustine at once argues that the *ideals* of justice and peace are reserved for the *civitas Dei*, but that justice and peace are still the proper goods of the temporal world, and these can only be attained by humanity organizing into states—that is, people need a political Leviathan to motivate and to effect social harmony and commodious living. "For peace is a good so great, that even in this earthly and mortal life there is no word we hear with such pleasure, nothing we desire with such zest, or find to be more thoroughly satisfying."[20] Borrowing from Plato, Augustine assures us that "even robbers take care to maintain peace with their comrades, that they may with greater effect and greater safety invade the peace of other men."[21]

Nevertheless, while all people desire peace,

> Whoever hopes for this so great good in this world, and in this earth, his wisdom is but folly . . . for in the very great mutability of human affairs such great security is never given to any people, that it should not dread invasions hostile to this life.[22]

Human society, like the individuals who comprise it, is perfect by nature, but corrupt by convention. If society were perfect, as it is in the *civitas Dei*, there would be peace for all inhabitants for "there will be perfect righteousness where there will be perfect peace."[23] Earthly society is, however, corrupt; consequently, humans must continually struggle, often violently, to achieve peace that, when attained, is at best imperfect and ephemeral. As a social being, a person's desire for peace is natural (and therefore good); as a fallen being, a person's *cupiditas* makes the achievement of peace impossible. Nevertheless, all mankind desires peace.

> Whoever gives even moderate attention to human affairs and to our common nature, will recognize that there is no man . . . who does not wish to have peace. For even they who make war desire nothing but victory—desire, that is to say, to attain to peace with glory. . . . It is therefore with the desire for peace that wars are waged. . . . For even those who intentionally interrupt the peace in which they are living have no hatred of peace, but only wish it changed into a peace that suits them better. They do not, therefore, wish to have no peace, but only one more to their mind.[24]

The *idea* of human society, as conceived by God, is one where there is perfect peace and harmony among all members; the instantiation of it on earth, however, is plagued with conflict and violence. Still, people seek peace to the extent possible, and thereto organize themselves into states and pass laws, and maintain vigilance, *and even fight wars*, all in an effort to deter or restrain the inevitable effects of human *cupiditas*. Without states, there would be Hobbesian chaos, hence Christ's admonition to his followers to "render onto Caesar those things which are Caesar's" and John the Baptist's charge to the

Roman soldiers to "be content with your wages and do harm to no man." Augustine concludes

> The natural order which seeks the peace of mankind ordains that the monarch should have the power of undertaking war if he thinks it advisable, and that the soldiers should perform their military duties in behalf of the peace and safety of the community.[25]

Up to this point, Augustine deviates little from the classical views on state authority he inherits from Cicero, although his explanations for them are entirely his own because they are framed in the context of Christianity. In his discussion of the just causes for war, however, he modifies Cicero's definition of a Just War (one fought for safety or honor) to reflect his religious beliefs concerning good and evil in the world, and he adds to those wars that are to be considered just those which are ordained by God.

> Just wars are usually defined as those which avenge injuries, when the nation or city against which warlike action is to be directed has neglected either to punish wrongs committed by its own citizens or to restore what has been unjustly taken by it. *Further, that kind of war is undoubtedly just which God Himself ordains.* [italics added][26]

We noted previously that Augustine viewed war as a means whereby God could both punish man for his sins and grant him absolution. The consequences of this reasoning become apparent in the following passage:

> War begun at God's command is certainly waged justly in order to frighten or break down or subjugate human pride: it is not waged for human cupidity, it cannot be contrary to the incorruptible God or His saints: who are also pleased by the exercise of patience, the humbling of the proud, the bearing of paternal discipline. Nor has anyone power over soldiers except from the command or permission of God.[27]

This account of war as an instrument of God is a key area where Augustine breaks dramatically with his Greek and Roman predecessors. Whereas the Roman tradition held that "no war is just unless it is entered upon after an official demand for satisfaction has been submitted or warning has been given and a formal declaration made,"[28] this could no longer be operative in Augustine's notion of righteous wars fought at the behest of God. And because one of the duties of rulers is to carry out God's will, the wars they initiate become *ipso facto*, God's wars. Wars, then, are not formally or objectively just, as they were under the Roman system, but become just based on the command of the ruler. Examples of this reasoning can be found in recent Middle East and Eastern European wars fought at the command of rulers alleging to be intermediaries for divine will. Frederick Russell provides an illuminating analysis of the further consequences of this innovation.

> [Augustine's] just war was thus total and unlimited in its licit use of violence, for it not only avenged the violation of existing legal rights but also avenged the moral order injured by the sins of the guilty party regardless of injuries done to the just party acting as a defender of that order. As sins as well as crimes, seen in the context of a broadened concept of justice whereby not only illegal but immoral or sacrilegious acts were punishable, the transgressions were both a crime against the law and a sin against righteousness.[29]

Beginning with Augustine, war (as well as the violence of the magistrate) became more than just a legal remedy for injustice; it became a moral imperative—and even more significant, it could be fought for the benefit of the vanquished.

> For the person from whom is taken away the freedom which he abuses in doing wrong is vanquished with benefit to himself; since nothing is more truly a misfortune than that good fortune of offenders, by which pernicious impunity is maintained, and the evil disposition, like an enemy within the man, is strengthened. . . . And in mercy, if such a thing is possible, even wars might be waged by the good, in order that, by bringing under the yoke the unbridled lusts of men, those vices might be abolished which ought, under a just government, to be either extirpated or suppressed.[30]

Later writers will attempt to replace this view of righteous war with an objective legal notion of *bellum justum*, founded on the Roman tradition, but only after many *jihads* are fought by Christians in the name of righteousness.

HUMAN BEINGS AS MORAL AGENTS

We have explained humanity's **concupiscence** as a consequence of Original Sin. If man (humanity) is destined to sin and suffer until his redemption is complete (as signified by the Last Judgment), can he still be held accountable (either to God or to his fellows) for his sinning, given this inevitable predisposition to sin? Moreover, given that God has foreknowledge of every thought and act that man will ever consider or perform, how can it be said that man has any free will at all? And if man has no free will, how can he be culpable for his misdeeds?[31]

Augustine responds to these questions by distinguishing what is foreseen from what is necessary, and concludes, "It is manifest that our wills by which we live uprightly or wickedly are not under a necessity; for we do many things which, if we were not willing, we should certainly not do."[32] It is our will, he argues, that God foresees,

> [And] it is not the case that because God foreknew what would be in the power of our wills, there is for that reason nothing in the power of our wills. . . . For a man does not sin because God foreknew that he would sin. Nay, it cannot be doubted but that it is the man himself who sins when he does sin, because God, whose foreknowledge is infallible, foreknew not that fate, or fortune, or something else would sin, but that the man himself would sin, whom if he will not, sins not.[33]

And because people do not know whether or not they are saved, or that they will persist in salvation until death,[34] they have no choice but to judiciously exercise their free will in order to minimize their sinning.[35]

The crucial point here is not that people can altogether avoid sinning, but that they can *endeavor to avoid* (or minimize) sinning—and herein are individuals judged by God. Thus it is what one wills or intends, rather than one's actions themselves, which have normative worth. And in fact, we find that Augustine's psychology completely subordinates actions to intentions. This focus on inward dispositions is Augustine's way of reconciling the requirement for man to strive to maintain his purity for divine judgment with the pragmatic need to live in the sin-ridden, temporal world. In response to a letter from Marcellinus, which maintained that certain Christian principles were incompatible with the rights and duties of citizens—namely, "Recompense to no man evil for evil," and "Whosoever shall smite thee on one cheek, turn to him the other also; and if any man take away thy coat, let him have thy cloak also; and whosoever will compel thee to go a mile with him, go with him twain"—Augustine responds

> These precepts pertain rather to the inward disposition of the heart than to the actions which are done in the sight of men, requiring us, in the inmost heart, to cherish patience along with benevolence, but in the outward action to do that which seems most likely to benefit those whose good we ought to seek . . . and the benevolence which prevents the recompensing of evil for evil must be always fully cherished in the disposition. At the same time, many things must be done in correcting with a certain benevolent severity.[36]

Consider, for example, the parable of the Good Samaritan (Luke 10): Imagine that the Samaritan had happened on the victim while the robbery and the beating were in progress. Would not the principles of charity and brotherly love mandate that one stop the evil deed, even if it meant harming the perpetrators of the injustice? Augustine would surely answer in the affirmative because such action would be motivated by *caritas*. For Augustine, Christ's statement, "Blessed are the peacemakers," does not refer to a passive inactivity but to an active process.[37]

Moreover, for Augustine, the need for social order is so great that its requirements often override individual rights. He believes that when the values one cherishes come into conflict, a good citizen has no choice but to act virtuously and attempt to effect justice in accordance with one's abilities and duties. Often this entails committing acts that might otherwise be deemed evil, but which, in certain circumstances and depending on the disposition of one's heart, might be morally obligatory. This is nicely illustrated in the following passage, where he discusses a judge who must torture an accused man in order to ascertain his guilt or innocence:

> What shall I say of these judgments which men pronounce on men, and which are necessary in communities, whatever outward peace they enjoy? Melancholy and lamentable judgments they are, since the judges are men who cannot discern the consciousness of those at their bar, and are therefore frequently compelled to put innocent witnesses to the torture to ascertain the truth. . . . And what is still more unendurable—a thing, indeed, to be bewailed, and, if that were possible, watered with fountains of tears—is this, that when the judge puts the accused to the question, that he may not unwittingly put an innocent man to death, the result of this lamentable ignorance is that this very person, whom he tortured that he might not condemn him if innocent, is condemned to death both tortured and innocent. . . . for [he might] declare that he has committed the crime which in fact he has not. . . . And consequently, he [the judge] has both tortured an innocent man to discover his innocence, and has put him to death without discovering it. If such darkness shrouds social life, will a wise judge take his seat on the bench or no? Beyond question he will. For human society, which he thinks it a wickedness to abandon, constrains him and compels him to this duty. . . . These numerous and important evils he does not consider sins; for the wise judge does these things, not with any intention of doing harm, but because human society claims him as a judge.[38]

This is not an application of some type of utilitarianism where certain lesser evils are obligatory in order to maximize aggregate utility. In Augustine's formulation, the obligatory action (or rule) might result in less utility than alternatives, as it does in the aforementioned example of torturing an innocent person; but "it is impossible for a man's acts to be evil, when his thoughts are good."[39]

Thus, does Augustine recognize that there are exceptions "made by the divine authority to its own law," including the prohibition against the taking of human life, and that exceptions may either be derived from a special commission granted for a limited time, or based on a just law that applies generally.[40] Concerning those exceptions that apply generally, Augustine cites the magistrate who, like a father toward his son, must behave with benevolent severity.[41] "Whoever lives according to God . . . ought to cherish toward evil men a perfect hatred . . . [so that he] hates the vice and loves the man."[42]

Concerning those exceptions to divine law that are based on a special commission, Augustine cites the example of a soldier who is himself "but a sword in the hand of him [the ruler] who uses it, [and] is not himself responsible for the death he deals."[43] And not only does the soldier carry out his orders with impunity, he is obligated to obey those orders. "The soldier who has slain a man in obedience to the authority under which he is lawfully commissioned is not accused of murder by any law of his state; nay, if he has not slain him, then he is accused of treason." And in fact, instances of men inflicting harm on others in the line of duty may even be considered a form of charity because man as a social animal is not disposed to harm his fellow human beings.[44] Of course, soldiers who kill out of hatred for the enemy or a lust for violence are answerable to God for these "inner dispositions."

Augustine also makes it clear that a soldier is not guilty of wrongdoing when acting under orders and is still bound to obey, even in those cases where the war itself is an unjust one.

> Julian was an infidel Emperor, an apostate, a wicked man, an idolater; Christian soldiers served an infidel Emperor. . . . If he called upon them at any time to worship idols, to offer incense, they preferred God to him: but whenever he commanded them to deploy into line, to march against this or that nation, they at once obeyed. They distinguished their everlasting from their temporal master; yet they were, for the sake of their everlasting Master, submissive to their temporal master.[45]

Here Augustine restricts the responsibility for *jus ad bellum* to the political arena, thereby setting the stage for the modern tradition of limiting the soldier's moral culpability to the battlefield itself.

While Augustine recognizes exceptions to the divine law against taking another's life, he accepts Cicero's arguments against private killing, and also Ambrose's prohibition against killing in self-defense.

> As to killing others in order to defend one's own life, I do not approve of this, unless one happens to be a soldier . . . acting in defense of others according to the commission lawfully given him.[46]

Augustine can make this distinction between the defense of others and self-defense, because he, like Ambrose, believes that the defense of others is a charitable or altruistic act, whereas self-defense is a selfish one. The former could be done with "love in one's heart," while the latter would be motivated either by hatred or self-love. This prohibition against self-defense will be reversed in the thirteenth century by St. Thomas Aquinas, who otherwise adopts Augustine's view on *justum bellum* with little change.

CONCLUSION

Most of Augustine's precepts on man's political duties can be found either in Plato's *Republic* and *Laws*, Aristotle's *Politics*, or Cicero's *De Officiis* and *De Re Publica*.[47] The significance of his work lies in the synthesis achieved between this classical philosophy and the Christian religion. Nevertheless, Augustine can rightly be called the father of the modern Just War Tradition, because it is his synthesis that is picked up and developed by later writers such as Gratian and Aquinas.

While Augustine supposes that there may be divinely ordained wars, he retains the Roman Just War principles: (1) There must be a just cause; (2) Wars must be declared and carried out by proper authority; and (3) The final objective must always be peace. Moreover, Augustine insists that soldiers should never fight for fame or glory, or with a spirit of vengeance. He admonishes soldiers and leaders to always keep faith with the enemy and show mercy to the vanquished. And, finally, he establishes war as a purposeful, public act, with prescribed moral limits, which, though itself abominable, occasionally becomes necessary for the sake of peace and justice.

The premises that are central to Augustine's argument can just as easily be stated *sans* theism: (1) Man is *by his very nature* a social being; (2) Social groups must have some means of ensuring order and keeping the peace; and (3) Social groups require a hierarchical structure, and so on. Where the Greek and Roman tradition advocated equality for citizens, Augustine sought to extend it to mankind. Clearly Augustine, like Plato, Aristotle, and Cicero, places squarely on the shoulders of civil government the responsibility to maintain order, effect justice, and seek peace.

What is different—and a dramatic difference it is—is the tint of good and evil with which Augustine imbues all justice and injustice in the world. His understanding of political institutions as being instruments of mankind's redemption in God's divine design colors political actions with a kind of indeterminate hallowness. His blurring of the distinction between good and evil on one hand and the legal and the unlawful on the other hand leads him to accept war and violence as legitimate means of attacking subjective assessments of evil. His subordination of actions to intentions opens the door to even the most heinous acts done for a "good purpose." The moral law as determined by the Church became the law of the land. What had been restrained by objective criteria under pagan rule now became subject to ideological zealotry and Crusade.

Topics for Further Discussion

1.   All historical events, according to Augustine, including wars, are part of God's divine plan, whereby mankind moves through time toward

redemption. If true, this seems to make *jus ad bellum* considerations moot. Consider: If God has already determined which wars will be fought (and which side will prevail), what is the point of any nation conducting *jus ad bellum* deliberations to determine whether to resort to arms? How might Augustine respond to this objection? Do you find this response persuasive?

2. Augustine argues that certain social roles require persons filling them to act with "benevolent severity" toward others. Such behavior is permissible (and sometimes obligatory), he argues, because one's intentions determine the moral worth of actions rather than the consequences of said actions.

   a. Certain philosophers (notably John Stuart Mill) have objected that Augustine's position confuses the rightness of actions with the character of the agent performing the actions. The moral worth of actions, they argue, is determined by their consequences; the moral character of agents is determined by their intentions. How might Augustine respond to this objection? Do you find this response persuasive?

   b. Augustine discusses "benevolent severity" in terms of social roles. Do you believe that a person's professional competence in a particular role can be relevant to the moral worth of his or her actions? In other words, can persons be morally blameworthy for a lack of competence? Are professionals—such as doctors, lawyers, military officers—different in this regard compared to tradespersons? Why or why not?

3. One consequence of Augustine's influence is that wars are often viewed as battles of good against evil. How might such a perception affect one side's adherence to *jus in bello* rules? Should the relative rightness of one's cause affect whether the *jus in bello* rules are followed?

4. Augustine argues that soldiers (and all mankind) must carry out the commands of their lawfully appointed leaders, and that subordinates are not responsible for any wrongs they commit at the command of their superiors. Do you agree with this view? Why or why not?

5. Augustine argues that while it is permissible (or obligatory) to defend other innocent persons against unjust predation, self-defense is morally wrong. What is Augustine's justification for this counterintuitive position? Develop at least one objection to it.

Notes

1. The single non-Christian emperor after Constantine was his youngest son, Julian the Apostate, who reigned from 351 to 363.
2. For a brief summary of key biographical information, see "Augustine, St.," by R. A. Markus in *The Encyclopedia of Philosophy*, vols. 1, 2 (New York: Macmillian, 1967), pp. 198–206. Markus includes an annotated bibliography at the end of his essay.

3. The Manichaean heresy was an effort to account for sin in the world by positing eternal forces of good (light) and evil (darkness). The problem posed for Christians was how to account for evil in a monotheistic religion; that is, if we credit God with all the good in the world, must we not also blame God for all the evil? See *Nicene and Post-Nicene Fathers*, vol. IV, "The Anti-Manichaean Writings" (Grand Rapids, Mich.: Eerdmans Publishing Co., 1956), pp. 3–365. The most important of these works for our study is Augustine's "Reply to Faustus the Manichaean," pp. 155–345.

4. The Pelagians cited Augustine's *De Libero Arbitrio* as evidence for their position. Augustine's *Retractations*, where he elaborates on the relationship between grace and free will, was a response to the Pelagian position. For a more detailed discussion, see B. B. Warfield, "Introductory Essay on Augustine and the Pelagian Controversy," in *A Select Library of the Nicene and Post-Nicene Fathers*, vol. V, pp. xiii–lxxi.

5. For a cogent commentary on this work, see John Neville Figgis, *The Political Aspects of Augustine's "The City of God"* (Gloucester, Mass.: Peter Smith, 1963).

6. *Nicene and Post-Nicene Fathers*, vol. II, Bk. III, 31, p. 63.

7. Ibid., Bk. XI, chap. IX, p. 210. Augustine argues that the *civitas Dei* came into being when God created the angels, which occurred simultaneously with the creation of light.

8. Ibid., Bk. XIV, 28, pp. 282–83.

9. Ibid., Bk. I, 13, p. 6.

10. Ibid., Bk. XIX, 15, p. 411.

11. "God created only one single man, not, certainly, that he might be a solitary, bereft of all society, but that by this means the unity of society and the bond of concord might be more effectively commended to him, men being bound together not only by similarity of nature, but by family affection. And indeed, He did not even create the woman that was to be given him as his wife, as He created the man, but created her out of the man, that the whole human race might derive from one man." Ibid., Bk. XII, 21, p. 241. Augustine also argues that Christians have an additional bond in that they all refer to God as "Father."

12. Earlier religions most often construed God in terms of a spatial or spatio-temporal existence. Thus when one traveled to another country or locality, one worshipped the gods of that land. The Jewish religion marked a significant break from this tradition, because here God watched over the Tribe of Israel, independent of where they lived geographically—hence the wrath of the pharaoh because of Jewish refusal to worship Egyptian deities. Christianity (and later Islam) differs again in that God transcends national as well as spatio-temporal bounds—that is, there is only one God for all of mankind.

13. *Nicene and Post-Nicene Fathers*, vol. IV, "Against the Epistle of Manichaeus," 35, p. 147.

14. *Nicene and Post-Nicene Fathers*, vol. II, *The City of God*, Bk. IV, chap. IV, p. 66.

15. *Nicene and Post-Nicene Fathers*, vol. I, *Confessions*, Bk. III, VIII, 15, p. 65.

16. *Nicene and Post-Nicene Fathers*, vol. IV, "The Letters of Petilian, The Donatist" Bk. II, XCII, 202, 210, pp. 577, 583.

17. Augustine, *The City of God*, Bk. XIX, 17, p. 412.

18. *Nicene and Post-Nicene Fathers*, vol. II, "On Christian Doctrine," Bk. II, 25, 40, p. 548.

19. *Nicene and Post-Nicene Fathers*, vol. VII, "On the Gospel of St. John," Tractate XL, 10, p. 229.

20. Augustine, *The City of God*, Bk. XIX, chap. 11, p. 407.

21. Ibid., Bk. XIX, 12, p. 407. (See also Plato's *Republic* 351c.)

22. Ibid., Bk. XVII, 13, p. 352.

23. *Nicene and Post-Nicene Fathers*, vol. VIII, "Expositions on the Book of Psalms," CXL VII, 22, p. 670.

24. Ibid., Bk. XIX, 12, p. 407.

25. *Nicene and Post-Nicene Fathers*, vol. IV, "Reply to Faustus the Manichaean," Bk. XXII, 75, p. 301.

26. Augustine, *Questiones in Heptateuchum*, Bk. VI, 10a, quoted in John Eppstein, *The Catholic Tradition of the Law of Nations* (Washington, D.C.: Catholic Association for International Peace, 1935), p. 74.

27. Ibid., p. 301. I have used Eppstein's translation from *The Catholic Tradition of the Law of Nations*, p. 70, for this passage, as it is much clearer than the Stothert translation in the *Nicene Fathers* edition.

28. Cicero, *De Officiis*, Bk. I, 36, p. 39.

29. Frederick H. Russell, *The Just War in the Middle Ages* (London: Cambridge University Press, 1975), p. 19.

30. *Nicene and Post-Nicene Fathers*, vol. I, "Letters of St. Augustine," CXXXVIII, 14, pp. 485–86.

31. For a short summary of the key arguments and Augustine's response to them, see "A Treatise on Grace and Free Will," in *Nicene and Post-Nicene Fathers*, vol. V, pp. 433–65.

32. *The City of God*, Bk. V, 10, p. 92. I omit the more difficult question of how man receives his "just desert" for the prudent exercise of his free will, except to add that although the great majority (all those without efficacious grace) are inescapably damned, the severity of their punishment is linked to the severity of their sins. The Catholic Church will later soften this position through the Doctrine of Purgatory. For the inception of the Doctrine of Purgatory (later developed by Pope Gregory I) and a discussion of the biblical passages on which it is founded, see *The City of God*, Bk. XXI, 13, 24, pp. 463–64, 470.

33. Ibid., p. 93. For clarity, I have made a minor change in the wording of the second sentence. Augustine provides a parallel argument for happiness: "Though God knows what we shall will in the future, this does not imply that we do not make use of our will. . . . I say because God foreknows your future happiness, and because nothing can happen otherwise than as He has foreknowledge, it does not follow that we must suppose you will not be happy through your own will." *The Problem of Free Choice*, translated by Dom Mark Pontifex, Bk. III, 3.8 (Westminster, Md.: The Newman Press, 1955), p. 147.

34. *The City of God*, Bk. XI, 12, p. 212.

35. They must also pray daily not to be led into temptation and for forgiveness of trespasses. *Nicene and Post-Nicene Fathers*, vol. V, "On Nature and Grace," chap. 80, p. 149.

36. *Nicene and Post-Nicene Fathers*, vol. I, "Letters of St. Augustine," CXXXVIII, II, 9, 13–14, pp. 483, 485. The New Testament passages cited are from Rom. 12 and Matt. 5, respectively.

37. See Eppstein, *The Catholic Tradition of the Law of Nations*, p. 91.

38. *The City of God*, Bk. XIX, 6, pp. 404–05.

39. *Nicene and Post-Nicene Fathers*, vol. I, "Expositions on the Book of Psalms," XCLVIII, 2, p. 673.

40. *The City of God*, Bk. I, 21, p. 15.

41. *Nicene and Post-Nicene Fathers*, vol. I, "Letters of St. Augustine," CXXXVIII, II, 14, p. 485.

42. *The City of God*, Bk. XIV, 6, p. 266.

43. *The City of God*, Bk. I, 21, p. 15.

44. See Richard Shelly Hartigan, "Saint Augustine on War and Killing: The Problem of the Innocent," in *Journal of the History of Ideas* 27 (1966), p. 203; Louis Swift, "Augustine on War and Killing: Another View," in *Harvard Theological Review* 66 (1973), pp. 376–77; and Paul Ramsey, *The Just War: Force and Personal Responsibility* (New York: Charles Scribner's Sons, 1968), pp. 159–60. Hartigan argues that Augustine's analogy between soldier and executioner fails because soldiers kill those who are not guilty. Swift responds (citing Ramsey) that it is not an assumption about the "individual, subjective, moral guilt of the opponent . . . [but] his objective or functional guilt . . . which results from his objective participation in actions disruptive to peace and public order."

45.   *Nicene and Post-Nicene Fathers,* "Expositions on the Book of Psalms," CXXV, 7, pp. 602–03. For an excellent and more detailed discussion of this point, see Herbert A. Deane, *The Political and Social Ideas of St. Augustine* (New York: Columbia University Press, 1963), pp. 143–50. Elsewhere, Augustine argues that "good laws can be issued by a man who is not good." (*The Problem of Free Choice,* translated by Dom Mark Pontifex (Westminster, MD: The Newman Press, 1955), Bk. I, 5.11, p. 45)

46.   *Nicene and Post-Nicene Fathers,* vol. I, "Letters of St. Augustine," XLVII, 5, p. 293. This is a modification to what he had written years earlier in *De Libero Arbitrio: Evodius:* "It is a much lesser evil for the assassin than for the man who defends his own life, to be killed. It is far more dreadful that an innocent person should suffer violence than that the assailant should be killed by the intended victim." (Bk. I, 5.12, pp. 44–45). Augustine's final position in this section is unclear. He responds to Evodius by distinguishing between earthly punishment through temporal law and "secret" punishment by Divine Providence. I believe that his conclusion here is that this is an example where man must choose the lesser of two sins. See p. 91 of *The Problem of Free Choice.*

47.   We also find in Augustine an implication that there are "natural rights" common to all peoples that cannot be "legislated away," for example, the right to common passage, which the Amorites refused the Israelites and which was justification for war. This point will be crucial to later philosophers writing on Just War, especially Hugo Grotius.

Chapter

4

SECULARIZATION OF THE JUST WAR TRADITION

The process whereby Roman and Christian ideas concerning Just War evolved into international law is complex and spans many centuries. Theologians, canonists, and jurists, many of them now obscure, all contributed to the transition. In this chapter we will highlight some of the key mileposts in this process by focusing on two representative and influential writers whose original contributions significantly affected the development of the laws of war: Thomas Aquinas and Francisco de Vitoria.

The period between the work of Augustine and that of Aquinas saw a transition from the stability of the magnificent Roman Empire to the continuous feudal conflicts of the Dark Ages. The emergence of numerous, autonomous political communities with a shared unifying dimension—the Catholic Church—motivated the development of more formal rules governing warfare and gave birth to the Code of Chivalry.[1] Ironically, the breakup of the Catholic Church during the Reformation led to savage ideological wars that were void of rules (e.g., the Thirty Years' War) and gave birth to Grotius's famous work on international law.

Likewise, the Spanish treatment of Native Americans in the New World inspired a number of significant contributions to the law of nations by writers such as Vitoria, Valdez, and Suarez. In each case, it seems as though moral judgments concerning the conduct of war were formulated in response to actions that outraged the public conscience. Perhaps the public recognition of wrongs most often motivates the development of formal rules to outlaw acts that people's private sense of justice already recognizes as being manifestly improper.[2] Certainly the changes in conduct of war and the technological innovations that occurred during this period necessitated parallel developments in the Just War Tradition.

As secular, central authority diminished with the demise of the Roman Empire, localized conflicts increased. An increasingly powerful Catholic Church sought to fill the void created by the decentralization of secular power. Around the year A.D. 600, St. Isidore, the Archbishop of Seville, produced an encyclopedic compilation of past writings on Just War that became a source document for later scholars.[3]

In the year 989, the Church attempted to restrict the conduct of the constant warfare through an edict known as the Peace of God.[4] This edict sought to regulate the participants in war by prohibiting actions against certain classes of people such as clerics, monks, peasants, women, pilgrims, merchants, and shepherds; the edict also prohibited attacks on churches, cemeteries, farm animals, and fruit trees. While this had little immediate effect (probably because it was not supported by feudal law), the ideas contained in the edict concerning innocents would be picked up by later writers, most notably Grotius, and would thereby find their way into the *jus in bello* rules of international law.

In 1027, the Peace of God was supplemented with the Truce of God, which restricted warfare to certain days of the week and certain seasons of the year.[5] A third attempt at controlling the conduct of war was made by the Second Lateran Council in 1139 when it prohibited crossbows, bows and arrows, and siege weapons. Through these efforts the Christian Church became an early proponent of *jus in bello* restrictions—with the limitation that these restraints only restricted what Christians could do to other Christians; non-Christians were not afforded protection until many centuries later. Ironically, the event that contributed most to reducing the countless private wars that cursed the period was the Church's successful redirection of the violence within Christendom against an external foe through the Crusades.

From a historical perspective, the first really pivotal event in the development of the Just War Tradition following Augustine occurred in 1148 when a Benedictine monk, Gratian of Bologna, published an exhaustive compilation of canon law, the *Concordia discordantium canonum*. Gratian's *Decretum*, as the work was known, became the focal point for the Just War debate.

The *Decretum* is important, not because of its original content, but because of its topical organization and detailed treatment of the central issues. Gratian sought to reconcile the many divergent, even contrary, works on canon law, and in his discussions he included selections from historical documents, various civil laws, and extensive ecclesiastical sources, hence the title *Concordia discordantium canonum*.

Gratian, like Augustine, argues that "with the true servants of God even wars are pacific as they are entered upon not through cruelty or greed and have as their object peace, the repression of the wicked and the deliverance of the good."[6] He devotes a separate chapter (*Pars Secunda, Causa* XXIII) to war; and while the content of this chapter does little more than reproduce most of the texts of Augustine (the Roman influence also is apparent through the texts of Isidore), it is presented in a manner that encourages study and invites commentary. Up until the publication of the *Decretum*, canon law was considered a branch of theology; but after the circulation of Gratian's work, canon law became an independent discipline. In fact, the influence of this work was so great that it inspired a new school of canon lawyers called the Decretists, which in turn gave birth to the Decretalists.[7] As one scholar of the period notes, "To Master Gratian we owe the introduction of the concept of the just war into modern international jurisprudence."[8]

While many of the commentators on Gratian's work made important contributions to the Just War Tradition, the next pivotal breakthrough occurred during the intellectual renaissance of the thirteenth century, following the new availability of the Aristotelian corpus in Europe. Aristotle's emphasis on grounding arguments in principles derived from induction (coupled with the sheer brilliance of his analyses) influenced many to believe that revealed moral and scientific truths, at least those concerning the temporal world, could be deduced independently of the Gospel. This is not to imply a questioning of the veracity of that which is revealed through the Old and New Testaments; it simply means that because the truths written in the mind of the immutable God must necessarily be manifested in God's instantiation of the world, induction from the state of the world can therefore reflect glimpses of these truths.

Foremost among the Aristotelians of the period was Thomas Aquinas, whose work we will now examine.

SAINT THOMAS AQUINAS

Just as Augustine turned to Cicero and Plato for inspiration, Thomas Aquinas turned primarily to Aristotle and Augustine. His work on *bellum justum* is significant for a number of reasons. First, Aquinas summarizes the key elements of Augustine's work on Just War (available to Aquinas through Gratian) and reduces them to abstract rules grounded in clearly stated principles. Aquinas believed that human reason was the sole arbiter between right and wrong moral choices (and by extension, just and unjust human laws).[9]

The first principles that give the impetus to rational (hence moral) choice are accessible to all humans through perception of natural inclinations. This is crucial because it recognizes that all humans share identical natural inclinations (we might call these "fundamental social values"), even though these universal inclinations often provide the basis for different human laws for different peoples at different times.[10] That is, all mankind has access to the *eternal law* (written in the mind of God) by discerning the fundamental tendencies of nature (*natural laws*); and by reflecting on these tendencies, rational agents can develop knowledge of the principles that underlie moral judgments. These principles serve as the grounding for different *human laws*. Aquinas himself explains the significance of this.

It follows therefore that natural law in its first common principles is the same among all men, both as to validity and recognition (i.e., something is right for all and is so by all recognized).[11]

One of mankind's natural inclinations is to live in society. This necessitates some form of government as well as laws to ensure justice and order. "The common good of the state cannot flourish unless its citizens be virtuous"; therefore, "the proper effect of law is to lead its subjects to their proper virtue."[12] In fact, the state is a natural condition and the end (*telos*) of all states is the same: to bring about justice and order.

Because justice and order are the end for which all states exist, a ruler's authority cannot legitimately extend to decisions concerning this end, but only to the means whereby this end might be realized. This is significant because it implies that laws or commands by rulers (governments) that interfere with justice and order are invalid and need not be obeyed.

Human laws are the rational ordinances enacted and promulgated by the states (and their rulers) for the common good, understood by Aquinas to mean the preservation of order and maintenance of justice. These laws might necessitate the destruction of life, limb, and property and the deprivation of liberty, whenever such action is necessary to uphold justice or maintain order. That which is murder or theft for a private person may become a praiseworthy act when performed by someone vested with public power. Public officials also may act to address injustices that arise from causes outside of the state. Because the raison d'etre of political rulers is to promote the common welfare, they have a duty to ensure the safety of their community from external enemies.[13]

This brings us to Aquinas's second major contribution to the Just War Tradition: his comprehensive statement concerning *jus ad bellum*. Before addressing this, however, we should note that the position we have been attributing to Aquinas rests entirely on secular premises. As Russell observes, "Aquinas' use of Aristotle prevented him from attempts to transform the church's spiritual superiority into the legal supremacy advocated by [certain] canonists."[14] And in Aquinas's own words, "the theologian considers a sin principally as an offense against God, whereas the moral philosopher considers it as being contrary to reason."[15]

None of Aquinas's three conditions for a Just War are new, but he is the first to place all three of them together as independently necessary and jointly sufficient. Moreover, he elaborates on them and supports them with sound, and often original, argumentation. In the section of his *Summa Theologica* where he specifically addresses war, Aquinas stipulates that for a war to be just it must be declared by the authority of a head of a state (proper authority), for a proportionally good reason (just cause), and with a morally good aim (right intention).[16]

The requirement that wars be declared has its origins in Roman law. Although Aquinas does not mention a specific time between the declaration and commencement of hostilities (recall that Roman law stipulated thirty-three days), the very act of declaration invites the second party to the pending hostilities the opportunity to offer redress in lieu of war. This is crucial because it establishes the principle that for a war to be just, the aggrieving nation must have refused to render satisfaction. While he does not specifically state that war must only be used as a last resort in this section, Aquinas does specify elsewhere that a cause cannot be considered just unless the aggrieved party has first tendered the opportunity for a peaceful settlement and been refused.[17] Thus war becomes a means of sanction for some injury received in those cases where there is no alternative means of seeking redress. This point is developed in greater detail by subsequent writers such as Francisco Suarez, and it will evolve into the modern principle that war must always be a "last resort."[18]

Concerning the requirement that wars be declared *only* by proper authority, Aquinas argues that if one can seek redress from some higher authority, then one is not justified in resorting to violence. States, however, have no common authority to which they may appeal for arbitration, and "just as it is lawful for them to have recourse to the sword in defending the common weal against internal disturbances, . . . so too it is their business to have recourse to the sword of war in defending the common weal against external enemies." Quoting Augustine (*Contra Faustum,* 22.75), Aquinas adds, "The natural order conducive to peace among mortals demands that the power to declare and counsel war should be in the hands of those who hold the supreme authority."

Concerning the requirement for just cause, Aquinas provides three examples taken directly from Augustine (*Questiones in Heptatuechum,* 10). "A just war is wont to be described as one that avenges wrongs, when a nation or state has to be punished for refusing to make amends for wrongs inflicted by its subjects, or to restore what it has seized unjustly."

Although Aquinas does not directly address defensive wars (presumably he considers their justification obvious), he does discuss personal self-defense in the chapter following his discussion of war. Here he makes it clear that a defensive act can become aggression if one uses more violence than is necessary in repelling an attack.[19] We will return to the issue of self-defense momentarily in our discussion of double effect.

Finally, Aquinas again follows Augustine in his stipulation that wars may not be undertaken without rightful intentions, such as the advancement of good, the securing of peace, the punishment of evildoers, or the avoidance of evil. The examples he gives of wrongful intentions also are taken directly from Augustine (*Contra Faustum,* 22.74). "The passion for inflicting harm, the cruel thirst for vengeance, an unpacific and relentless spirit, the fever of revolt, the lust of power, and such like things." He adds that even if a war is declared by legitimate authority for a just cause, it can be rendered unjust through a wicked intention.

Aquinas concludes his discussion of offensive wars by again invoking the words of Augustine (*Epistle ad Boniface* 189). "We do not seek peace in order to be at war, but we go to war that we may have peace. Be peaceful, therefore, in warring, so that you may vanquish those whom you war against, and bring them to the prosperity of peace."

Aquinas also addresses the right of subjects to rebel against an unjust sovereign. While he adopts the Augustinian doctrine that sedition is wrong because it is opposed to a special kind of good, namely "the unity and peace of the people," he also breaks sharply with Augustine with the following important caveat:

> A tyrannical government is not just, because it is directed, not to the common good, but to the private good of the ruler, as the Philosopher states. Consequently there is no sedition in disturbing a government of this kind, unless the tyrant's rule be disturbed so inordinately, that his subjects suffer greater harm from the consequent disturbance than from the tyrant's government.[20]

Notice that Aquinas is careful to stipulate that the harm done by the means employed in effecting justice must not exceed the harm that is being done by the injustice one seeks to correct. This introduction of *proportionality* as being a necessary condition for the resort to revolution will be picked up by later writers and will become a necessary condition for any resort to force.

The final dimension of Aquinas's philosophy that we will explore is his doctrine of **double effect.** Recall that both Ambrose and Augustine had prohibited self-defense because it is motivated by *cupiditas,* while defense of others is motivated by brotherly love (a form of *caritas*). Aquinas's predisposition to natural law and his Aristotelian background would not let him accept this position, and his doctrine of double effect is his retort to the prohibition against self-defense. This doctrine states that acts that have both a good and bad effect are permissible, provided that the bad effect is an unintended side effect, that it is proportional to the objectively good effect, and that there is no alternative way of achieving the good effect. Thus one can kill an attacker in self-defense if he or she does not intend (will) the attacker's death (either as an end or a means), but simply endeavors to defend one's own life, and the death of the attacker is "outside the intention" or *per accidens.*

While Aquinas's doctrine of double effect is developed to justify self-defense, and even though he himself does not extend it to acts of war, it has had such a profound effect on Just War thinking and international law that it is worthwhile to reproduce Aquinas's own words here.

> Nothing hinders one act from having two effects, only one of which is intended, while the other is beside the intention. Now moral acts take their

species according to what is intended, and not according to what is beside the intention, since this is accidental. . . . Accordingly, the act of self-defense may have two effects, one is the saving of one's life, the other is the slaying of the aggressor. Therefore, this act, since one's intention is to save one's own life, is not unlawful, seeing that it is natural to everything to keep itself in "being," as far as possible. And yet, though proceeding from a good intention, an act may be rendered unlawful, if it be out of proportion to the end.[21]

Notice that the innate disposition to remain "in being" (i.e., alive) is not itself a sufficient justification for the secondary or "bad effect," because one could conceivably save one's own life by acquiescing or fleeing; Aquinas also must condone the *foreseen harm* that will occur to another as a direct result of one's defense of self. His solution (ironically) is to use Augustine's own distinction between intended consequences (which have normative worth) and incidental consequences (which are morally neutral) to provide this justification. The crucial step that permits Aquinas to make this innovation is an acceptance that unintended (bad) consequences can be foreseen without undermining the permissibility of intended (good) consequences, as long as the bad consequences are proportional to the intended ones.

The application of double effect to the conduct of war has been the topic of much debate and consternation, and we shall return to it. For now, however, let us focus on the writer who first extended Aquinas's double effect to include collateral damage on the battlefield: Francisco de Vitoria.

FRANCISCO DE VITORIA

Vitoria studied philosophy at the College Saint-Jacques in Paris, where he edited a commentary on the *Secunda Secundae* of Aquinas's *Summa Theologica*, written by one of his teachers. After receiving his doctorate, Vitoria returned to his native Spain and won the "Chair of Prime," the most important chair of theology, at the University of Salamanca, a position he held until his death in 1546. His most famous works, and the ones with which we are concerned, *De Indis* and *De Jure Belli*, were published for the first time from the lecture notes of two of his students ten years after his death.[22] Although together they total fewer than sixty pages, these works contain innovative insights concerning both *jus ad bellum* and *jus in bello*.

The catalyst for his lectures on international law was the treatment of the Native Americans by the Spanish Conquistadors. Vitoria, like many of his contemporaries, was profoundly disturbed by the treatment of the indigenous peoples, and his *De Indis* is an attempt to ascertain whether the many massacres and plunderings by the Spanish in the New World were right or wrong. Law provided no answers: Indians were subject neither to Spanish civil law nor, as heretics, to Christian law.

Vitoria examines no fewer than six arguments that purport to justify seizing possession of Native Americans' land and property (e.g., the Indians were heretical, guilty of mortal sin, unsound of mind, not rightful owners to begin with) and shows each of them to be groundless.[23] Concerning the subjugation of the native people, he is equally thorough in his analysis and refutes such arguments as they should be subjugated either for their own good (i.e., Aristotle's contention that war could justly be waged against those whose nature dictates that they should be governed, *Politics* 1256b22–25), or in order to "compel them to come in" to the Christian faith, or by authority of "a special grant from God."[24]

Vitoria concludes that "the aborigines undoubtedly had true dominion over public and private matters, just like Christians."[25] Moreover, he insists that Spain had no right to wage war against the Indians and that neither the emperor nor the Pope could authorize such a war. He adds that, even if the Indians themselves attacked the Spanish out of fear, the Spanish might defend themselves, but only "so far as possible with the least damage to the natives, the war being a purely defensive one."[26]

Vitoria concludes that an obligation to observe certain minimum standards of conduct prevails between all peoples at all times and that even in a defensive war, nations have a duty to hold their own soldiers accountable for these minimum standards of behavior (even against aliens). These standards include, for example, that no looting or burning shall be permitted without express orders from the prince or general in command—irrespective of the absence of any positive laws to the same.

Vitoria's position is pivotal because it recognizes an international society of independent states, each with reciprocal obligations and prohibitions on their conduct vis-à-vis one another. His refutation of various Spanish justifications for seizing the territory and property of the native peoples establishes what is now recognized as a state's right to territorial integrity. His rebuttal to Spanish arguments justifying domination of Native Americans establishes what we now call a nation's right to political sovereignty. These rights, articulated in response to the Spanish abuse of Native Americans, are central to our modern international law.

In his *De Jure Belli*, Vitoria addresses the problem of war more directly and specifies restrictions on both *jus ad bellum* and *jus in bello*. He is the first to insist on an objective analysis of the justifications for going to war and, in so doing, revokes the monarch's monopoly on decisions regarding the resort to arms. It is not enough, he argues, for a prince to believe he has a just cause; the decision must also, as Aristotle asserts, come up to the standard of a wise man's judgment.

> It is essential for a just war that an exceedingly careful examination be made of the justice and causes of the war and that the reasons of those who on

grounds of equity oppose it be listened to. . . . For truth and justice in moral questions are hard of attainment and so any careless treatment of them easily leads to error, an error which will be inexcusable. . . . [All] who are admitted on summons or voluntarily to the public council or the prince's council ought, and are bound, to examine into the cause of an unjust war. . . . [For they] can avert the war, if they lend their wisdom and their weight to an examination into its causes. Therefore they are bound so to do. . . . Again, a king is not by himself capable of examining into the causes of a war and the possibility of a mistake on his part is not unlikely and such a mistake would bring great evil and ruin to multitudes. Therefore war ought not to be made on the sole judgment of the king, nor, indeed on the judgment of a few, but on that of many, and they wise and upright men.[27]

Of course, what is missing is a list of objective criteria for what constitutes just cause; but this is not Vitoria's concern here: He has previously repeated Augustine's (and Aquinas's and Cicero's) examples of just causes and also enumerated many examples of unjust causes. Here he is concerned that extreme care be taken to ensure that cases under consideration do indeed warrant a resort to arms—that the legitimate authority is not guilty of "vincible and deliberate error" in declaring a cause just—and also that "greater evils do not arise out of the war than the war would avert."[28] In this sense, justice is "objectively" satisfied by method (as it was in the Roman tradition), rather than by a subjective judgment. If the formal method is followed correctly, Vitoria reasons, then the cause is *as just as we can attain to as imperfect beings.*[29]

Vitoria's contribution to the tradition of *jus in bello* is likewise significant because of his commitment that "the deliberate slaughter of innocents is never lawful in itself," for it is "forbidden by natural law."[30] By "innocent," Vitoria means all who do not directly take part in the fighting. This is a distinct break with Augustine, who saw war in terms of a moral struggle between the forces of good and evil, where the enemy represents the embodiment of evil. Vitoria begins his arguments regarding the inviolability of innocents with a quotation from Exodus 23: "The innocent and the righteous slay them not"; he continues:

> The basis of a war is a wrong done. But a wrong is not done by an innocent person. Therefore war may not be employed against him. . . . [Moreover] it is not lawful within a State to punish the innocent for the wrongdoing of the guilty. Therefore this is not lawful among enemies. . . . [W]ere this not so, a war would be just on both sides . . . a thing which, as has been shown, is impossible. And the consequence is manifest, because it is certain that innocent folk may defend themselves against any who try to kill them.[31]

Vitoria goes on to enumerate specifically those who are to be included in the class of innocents, and names women, children, farmers, foreign travelers, clerics and religious persons, and *the rest of the peaceable population.* He also stipulates that even among the Saracens and other nonbelievers the innocent shall not be harmed because, "A prince has no greater authority over foreigners than his own subjects. But he may not draw his sword against his own subjects unless they have done some wrong. Therefore, not against foreign citizens."[32] But Vitoria realizes that absolute injunction against harming civilians is unattainable; he must temper the ideal of not harming any innocents with the reality of combat if he is to be credible. This leads him to develop another crucial innovation: the application of Aquinas's doctrine of double effect to collateral damage in war. Vitoria notes:

> Sometimes it is right, in virtue of collateral circumstances, to slay the innocent, even knowingly, as when a fortress or city is stormed in a just war, although it is known that there are a number of innocent people in it and although cannons and other engines of war cannot be discharged . . . without destroying innocent together with the guilty. The proof is that war could not otherwise be waged against even the guilty and the justice of belligerents would be balked.[33]

In the paragraph following the aforementioned quotation, Vitoria cautions—most prophetically—against possible abuses of the principle he has just espoused.

> Great attention must be paid . . . to see that greater evils do not arise out of the war than the war would avert. . . . In sum, *it is never right to slay the guiltless, even as an indirect and unintended result, except when there is no other means of carrying on the operations of a just war.* [italics added]

Vitoria concludes with a quotation from Matthew 13, to "let the tares grow, lest while ye gather up the tares ye root up also the wheat with them."

Thus Vitoria at once develops the most powerful case to date for granting special status to innocents, and he also provides the first statement of military necessity as a justification for overriding this protection.[34]

Notice that each of the criterion Vitoria gives us under the doctrine of double effect is a necessary condition, and that only all three of them together constitute **sufficient justification** for invoking this doctrine in order to excuse the foreseeable deaths of innocents.

This leads us to another dimension of Vitoria's exposition of *justum bellum,* which, like his application of double effect as a justification for collateral damage, continues to be a source of consternation even today: the question of whether a war can be just on both sides. Recall that in a previously quoted passage (page 55, note 31), Vitoria uses the premise that a war cannot be just on both sides as manifest in order to prove (by a ***reductio ad absurdum***) that even among the enemy, innocents must not be slain. Elsewhere, however, he makes a further distinction concerning justice and injustice in war, which clouds the issue somewhat.

> Assuming a demonstrable ignorance either of fact or of law, it may be that on the side where true justice is the war is just of itself, while on the other side the war is just in the sense of being excused from sin by reason of good faith, because **invincible ignorance** is a complete excuse. [emphasis added][35]

Vitoria's objective here is to distinguish between guilt and culpability. The innuendo that a war may be considered just by both sides is, however, picked up by subsequent writers and has been a magnet for criticism of Just War theory ever since. Arthur Nussbaum, for example, observes

> The traditional doctrine of just war is essentially religious; where its religious spirit evaporates, only a shallow and stale residue remains. Certainly, the issue of just war deserves discussion in any course or textbook on international law, but only as a matter of analysis and historical information. . . . The just-war-on-both-sides problem is illustrative. It is there that insoluble troubles befell the writers who tried to elaborate the just war concept in a legal or semi-legal way.[36]

In his specific discussion of Vitoria's treatment of this topic, Nussbaum notes, "His objective was laudable, indeed, but one can hardly agree with the obliteration of the difference between the objective criterion of justice and the subjective criterion of good faith."[37]

But Nussbaum's criticism is, it seems to me, unfair and out of context. Surely we understand Vitoria's intention in grouping together guiltless and blameless—he is concerned with reparations and punishments after the war— even if we do not agree with his method. Vitoria's objective here is not to develop a system of international law, but to provide guidance to his monarch (and his monarch's subjects) on the proper moral choices concerning war. This is even more apparent when we consider that the topic is broached in conjunction with a discussion on whether a subject's beliefs concerning the justice or injustice of a war affect one's obligation to serve in it. Vitoria concludes that "if a subject is convinced of the injustice of a war, he ought not to serve in it, even on the command of his prince."[38]

The common thread in Vitoria's reasoning is that, ultimately, each person, sovereign or citizen, can do no more than what that individual believes to be right. (He adds that each must vigorously seek the truth to the best of one's ability.) One who does, with good intentions, what he or she sincerely but mistakenly believes to be right is guilty of wrongdoing without necessarily deserving punishment.

Moreover, Vitoria also employs the distinction between objective justice and culpability when he notes that "a war may be just and lawful in itself and yet owing to some collateral circumstance may be unlawful."[39] This is because wars are political acts waged for the common good. Therefore, when the costs of waging the war are excessive, even though there exists a just cause, "it is indubitable that the prince is bound rather to give up his own rights and abstain from war."[40] It follows that a prince could begin a war believing it to be just (i.e., with good intentions), and subsequently discover it to be unjust because of, for example, new information or costs to his nation. In such cases, the war would be objectively unjust, but the monarch who initiated the war would be "excused," as Vitoria puts it, because he acted in good faith.

In all cases, Vitoria is concerned with providing practical instructions to his readers, whether they are citizens or heads of state, on how they should act in particular situations, and he necessarily bases his alternatives on subjective beliefs rather than objective facts. Of course, he, along with the rest of us, would like these to be the same. In cases where the ideal is not realized, however, Vitoria addresses the subsequent question of moral and legal culpability after the fact. Thus he addresses his remarks to those contemplating war, those engaged in war, and those who are victorious in war. We can see this clearly in his summary, which he organizes into three canons corresponding to three time periods.

> First Canon: Assuming that a prince has authority to make war, he should first of all not go seeking occasions and causes of war, but should, if possible, live in peace with all men, . . . [and] only under compulsion and reluctantly should he come to the necessity of war.

> Second Canon: When war for a just cause has broken out, it must not be waged so as to ruin the people against whom it is directed, but only so as to obtain one's rights and the defense of one's country and in order that from that war peace and security may in time result.

> Third Canon: When victory has been won and the war is over, the victory should be utilized with moderation and Christian humility, and . . . so far as possible should involve the offending state in the least degree of calamity and misfortune, the offending individuals being chastised within lawful limits; . . . [for] it is thoroughly unjust that *"Quidquid delirant reges, plectantur Achivi."* (For every folly their kings commit the punishment should fall upon the Greeks.)[41]

Here Vitoria makes explicit the practical nature of his enterprise. This comes into even sharper relief when contrasted with the way a subsequent Spanish writer and student of Vitoria's work, Francisco Suarez, accomplishes the same results by specifying that

> Three periods must be distinguished with respect to every war: its inception; its prosecution, before victory is gained; and the period after victory. The three classes of persons already mentioned must also be distinguished,

namely: the sovereign prince, the intermediate group of leaders [military officers], and the soldiers of the rank and file.[42]

By specifying different rules for each group and each time period, Suarez alleviates the difficulty caused by linking postwar justice to prewar decision making. Of course, the link is still there, but the mechanism for dealing with it is in distinguishing discrete time periods rather than by blurring the objective notion of *jus ad bellum*, which jurists demand.[43]

Finally, we must keep in mind that when Vitoria discusses national prerogative, his purpose, like that of Ambrose, Augustine, and Aquinas before him, is to determine the normative status of alternatives. A sovereign could not be called before the bar except by God, and then only after the sovereign's death. There could be no legal judgment on a sovereign's actions. Vitoria's enterprise was to provide guidance that would assist a ruler in choosing the moral alternative. Vitoria's work had legal connotations only insofar as it motivated rulers to decree laws restricting the behavior of their own citizens vis-à-vis foreigners. We cannot criticize Vitoria for the inefficacy of his theory of international law.

Nussbaum's criticism stems from the jurist's insatiable quest for objectivity; and, indeed, the purpose of law (at least a sufficient purpose) is to make objective commonly recognized morality, hence the idea that legislators *declare* rather than "make" laws. But laws always require interpretation, both in terms of application to particular situations and degree of culpability, because principles of justice, like moral principles, cannot be stated in terms of a general rule that can be applied mechanically to empirical data.[44] In the next chapter we will return to the topic of international law in more detail.

Vitoria specifies reprisals as a type of case where the use of force may intentionally be directed against innocents. He argues that a nation's leaders have a duty "to vindicate the right against the wrongdoing of their subjects," and that "the neglect and breach of this duty grants the prince of the injured party the right to recoup himself even from innocent folk."[45]

Vitoria believes that leaders have an obligation to hold their own subjects accountable for their wrongdoings, even when these wrongdoings are directed against members of another nation. When a leader neglects this duty, the leaders of those wronged have a right to seek justice through reprisals, even if the perpetrators of the initial wrong are outside of the victim's civil jurisdiction. In practice, this means that if certain members of Group A commit a wrong against the members of Group B, and the leaders of Group A fail to take appropriate actions to redress those wrongs, the members of Group B may attempt to recoup themselves against any of the members of Group A in reprisal. And even if they are unable to right the wrongs committed, they may still conduct reprisals to prevent the commission of further wrongs.

This attempt at justifying "evil for evil" between states makes a mockery out of the very notion of justice that underlies the resort to force in the first place; justice returns against the guilty, not the innocent. Even if we only consider reprisals for their deterrent effect, it seems morally repugnant to use threats against the innocent as a means of deterring crime.

Vitoria's work inspired subsequent Spanish writers such as Suarez, who transcribes Vitoria's ideas into the language of jurists and elaborates on the distinction between combatants and innocents, and Vasquez, who envisions a society of free states with reciprocal rights, regulated by a law of nations and independent of either imperial or ecclesiastical authority. We shall pass over their work, however, to examine in detail the views of a Dutchman, widely regarded as the father of international law, Hugo Grotius.

Topics for Further Discussion

1. Aquinas believed that individuals could often ascertain God's will concerning right conduct, independent of revealed truths. Why did he believe this?

2. Vitoria argued that there are laws governing the treatment of all humans, even non-Christian "aborigines." Where did he believe these laws came from? Provide a secular defense for the view that there are at least some universal moral truths relevant to human behavior.

3. Vitoria accepts that monarchs are fallible. Why is this important to his work?

4. Vitoria extends Aquinas's doctrine of double effect to collateral damage in war. What might be some problems with this in practice?

5. On June 26, 1993, U.S. naval ships attacked the Iraqi intelligence headquarters in reprisal for an assassination attempt against former U.S. President George Bush. The evidence implicating the Iraqi government was conclusive. Of the twenty-three Tomahawk missiles fired in the attack, however, three missed the target and landed in a residential section of Baghdad, thereby killing numerous civilians.

    a. Was the U.S. response in this case a justified reprisal using Vitoria's criteria?

    b. Article 51 of the United Nations Charter states the following: "Nothing in the present charter shall impair the inherent right of individual or collective self-defense if an armed attack occurs against a member of the United Nations." Does this article justify acts of reprisal (in lieu of war) against states sponsoring terrorism?

6. In March 2003, after numerous warnings, a United States-led coalition of forces invaded Iraq on the grounds that the Iraqi government had failed

to cooperate with United Nations inspectors as agreed at the conclusion of hostilities in 1991, and had failed to comply with several United Nations mandates that they eliminate all weapons of mass destruction. Explain why (or why not) this military action met the conditions of just cause and last resort.

7. How is it possible—or why is it not possible—for a war to be just on both sides? Why is the distinction between objective justice and what citizens believe relevant to this discussion?

Notes

1. A similar development occured in Ancient China from about the fifth century B.C. to the death of Alexander (referred to by the Chinese as the Age of *Chan-kuo*, or warring states). The unifying dimension recognized by the Chinese was the emperor (among other things). See W. A. P. Martin, "Traces of International Law in Ancient China," in *International Review* XIV (1883), pp. 63–77.

2. Every modern war seems to have stimulated innovation and refinement of the laws of war. Henri Dunant's founding of the International Red Cross in 1863, an event inspired by his memories of the Battle of Solferino, is another interesting example, as is the League of Nations' initiative after World War I and the United Nations' initiative after World War II. Perhaps it is the improvement in mass communication techniques that has brought the public conscience into play and served as the catalyst for these recent accelerated refinements in the Just War Tradition.

3. Isidore's most significant work was the *Etymologies*. The fifth book concerns the laws of war and the eighteenth addresses the various kinds of war. For a brief summary of Isidore's contribution, see William Ballis, *The Legal Position of War: Changes in Its Practice and Theory from Plate to Vattey* (New York: Garland Publishing, 1973), pp. 43–45; Richard Shelly Hartigan, *The Forgotten Victim: A History of the Civilian* (Chicago: Precedent Publishing, 1982), pp. 37–38.

4. Hartigan, *The Forgotten Victim*, pp. 651–76.

5. Ibid., p. 68. Hartigan notes that the Peace of God and the Truce of God represent two separate movements that often are referred to in their later combined form as the Truce of God. The year 1027 represents the date that both movements were formally combined at the Council of Elne.

6. Gratian, *Decretum*, *Pars*. II, *causa* xxii, Q.1, in John Eppstein, *The Catholic Tradition of the Law of Nations* (Washington, D.C.: Catholic Association for International Peace, 1935), p. 89.

7. Frederick Russell, *The Just War in the Middle Ages* (London: Cambridge University Press, 1975), especially chaps. 4 and 5, "The Just War According to the Decretists" and "The Just War According to the Decretalists," pp. 86–212. Russell uses 1190 as the date dividing the two groups, but he notes that "the distinction between Decretists and Decretalists is not easy to draw, since after 1190 many canonists commented on both . . . " (p. 86).

8. Ibid., p. 85. According to one source, the period between 1471 and 1500 produced at least thirty-nine different editions of the *Decretum*.

9. St. Thomas Aquinas, *Summa Theologica* I–II, Question 91, First Article (henceforth Q.91, A.1) "On the Various Types of Law," in *The Political Ideas of St. Thomas Aquinas*, edited by Dino Bigongiari (New York: Hafner Publishing Co., 1957), p. 11.

10.   Ibid., Q.95, A.2, pp. 57–59: Human law is derived from the precepts of natural law, though human laws are different for different peoples at different times; Q.97, A.1, p. 79: The process of perfecting temporal laws is an ongoing one, based on reason.

11.   Ibid., Q.94, A.4, p. 50. Aquinas's classification of laws into eternal, natural, and human is strikingly similar to the view of the Romans expressed in this passage from Cicero: ". . . [supreme] Law is not a product of human thought, nor is it any enactment of peoples, but something eternal which rules the whole universe. . . . Law is the primal and ultimate mind of God, whose reason directs all things either by compulsion or restraint. . . . Therefore, just as the divine mind is the supreme law, so, when reason is perfected in man, that also is law; and this perfected reason exists in the mind of the wise man; but those rules which, in varying forms and for the need of the moment, have been formulated for the guidance of nations, bear the title of laws rather by favor. . . ."[22] Cicero goes on to argue that these "laws of perfect reason" (such as a prohibition against rape and a disposition to jeopardize one's own safety for the community) are binding, regardless of any temporal laws which may or may not exist. See *Laws*, II. iv, and v, 8–13, in Cicero, *De Re Publica and De Legibus* (New York: G. P. Putnam's Sons, 1928), pp. 381–85.

12.   Ibid., Q.92, A.1, A.2, pp. 25–26.

13.   "Aquinas wrote to the Duchess of Brabant that since princes were instituted by God to further the common good, they therefore had the duty to defend it," quoting Russell, *The Just War in the Middle Ages*, pp. 261–62. Aquinas also stipulates that because wars are fought on behalf of the common good, rulers may not resort to war when the cost of fighting exceeds the good for which it is being fought.

14.   Russell, *The Just War in the Middle Ages*, p. 289.

15.   *Summa Theologica* I–II, Q.97, A.6, quoted in Frederick Copleston, *Thomas Aquinas* (London: Search Press, 1976), p. 199.

16.   *Summa Theologica* II–II, Q.40, A.1, pp. 106–09. All of the quotations concerning justification for war that follow are from the First Article of Question 40, except as noted.

17.   Ibid., I–II, Q.105, A.1, p. 104.

18.   Suarez writes, "I hold that a war may also be justified on the ground that he who has inflicted an injury should be justly punished, if he refuses to give just satisfaction for that injury, without resort to war. This conclusion is commonly accepted . . . [provided] we assume that the opposing party is not ready to make restitution, or to give satisfaction; for if he were so disposed, the warlike aggression would become unjust. . . ." See *The Three Theological Virtues: On Charity*, Disputation XIII, Sections 4, 5, in *Selections from Three Works of Francisco Suarez, S. J.*, vol. 2, translated G. L. Williams, A. Brown, and J. Waldron, in *Classics of International Law*, vol. 2, edited by James Brown Scott (Oxford, England: Clarendon Press, 1944), pp. 817–18.

19.   Ibid., Q.41, A.1, pp. 113–14.

20.   Ibid., Q.42, A.2, p. 117. The passage from Aristotle to which Aquinas refers in this quotation states that "governments which have a regard to the common interest are constituted in accordance with strict principles of justice, and are therefore true forms; but those which regard only the interest of the rulers are all defective and perverted forms. . . ." *Politics*, Bk. 3, chap. 6, 1279a16–17. From *The Complete Works of Aristotle*, vol. 2, edited by Jonathan Barnes (Princeton, N.J.: Princeton University Press, 1984), p. 2030. The seed in Augustine that permits Aquinas to make this break is, I believe, Augustine's statement that, "A law which is not just does not seem to me to be a law." *De Libero Arbitrio*, Bk. I, 5.11, in *The Problem of Free Choice*, translated by Dom Mark Pontifex (Westminster, Md.: The Newman Press, 1955), p. 44.

21.   Ibid., Q.64, A.7. I believe that the doctrine of double effect was inspired by the following passage from Bk. 5, chap. 10, of Aristotle's *Nicomachean Ethics*. "Thus there are three types of injury that occur in communities and associations: (1) injuries committed in igno-

rance are mistakes, when the person affected, the act, the instrument, or result were not what the agent supposed they were. He thought he was not hitting anyone, or not with that particular missile, or not that particular person, or not for this purpose, but a result was obtained which he had not intended. . . . ; (2) When the injury inflicted happens contrary to reasonable expectation, it is a mishap; (3) when it happens not contrary to reasonable expectation, but without malice, it is a mistake. . . ." (1135b). Aristotle does not release from culpability those who make "mistakes," however.

22.   For more detail on Vitoria's life, see the Introductory Essay by Ernest Nys in *De Indis Et De Ivre Belli Reflectiones,* in *Classics of International Law,* edited by James Brown Scott (Washington, D.C.: Carnegie Institute of Washington, 1917), pp. 9–100. All quotations from Vitoria are taken from this edition. The information in my introductory paragraph is taken from Nys's essay. For a summary of his views on *jus ad bellum,* see Ballis, *The Legal Position of War,* pp. 77–90; for a summary of his contributions to *jus in bello,* see Hartigan, *The Forgotten Victim,* pp. 81–91.

23.   *De Indis,* Section I, para. 4–23, pp. 120–27.

24.   Ibid., II, pp. 130–48.

25.   Ibid., II, 16, p. 149.

26.   Ibid., concerning the emperor: II, 1, 2, pp. 131–35; concerning the Pope: II, 6, p. 137; concerning the right to self-defense: III, 6, p. 155. Note that Charles V was both the emperor and the king of Spain when this was written.

27.   Ibid., III, 21, 24, pp. 173–74.

28.   Ibid., III, 20, p. 173, and III, 37, p. 179.

29.   Of course, there are bound to be mistakes just as there are in the enforcement of municipal law. Consider a well-publicized criminal trial: Attorneys on both sides carefully scrutinize prospective jurors, experts are brought in to testify for and against various "factual" data, fervent arguments are articulated on both sides, national "experts" speculate on the evening news as to the outcome, and the jury decides. But what have they decided? They make a reasonable decision based on the information they have, and we call this formal justice. We hope, of course, that our system of formal justice gives us objective or ideal justice in most cases, just as Vitoria did for his "system" in the international arena.

30.   Ibid., III, 13, p. 171, and III, 35, p. 178.

31.   Ibid., III, 35, p. 178.

32.   Ibid., III, 13, pp. 170–71.

33.   Ibid., III, 37, p. 179.

34.   Vitoria adds military necessity as a necessary condition for his application of the doctrine of double effect to war. At certain times in history, military necessity will be considered a sufficient condition for setting aside considerations of *jus in bello.* We return to this issue and examine it in considerable detail in chapter 9.

35.   Ibid., 32, p. 177. See also *De Indis,* III, p. 155, where he states that "there is no inconsistency, indeed, in holding the war to be a just war on both sides, seeing that on one side there is right and on the other there is invincible ignorance."

36.   Arthur Nussbaum, "Just War—A Legal Concept?" in *Michigan Law Review* 42 (1943), p. 478. The argument that international law is not genuine law is not new. In the early seventeenth century, Grotius introduces the reason for his writing *The Law of War and Peace* thus, "Such a work is all the more necessary because in our day, as in former times, there is no lack of men who view this branch of law [international law] with contempt as having no reality outside of an empty name" (*Prolegomena* 3, p. 9).

37.   Ibid., p. 460.

38.   Ibid., 22, p. 173.

39.   Ibid., 33, p. 178.

40.   Ibid.

41.   Ibid., 60, p. 187.

42.   Francisco Suarez, *The Three Theological Virtues,* Disputation XIII, Section VII, in *Selections from Three Works,* edited by G. L. Williams, A. Brown, and J. Waldon, in *Classics of International Law,* vol. 2, edited by James Brown Scott (Oxford, England: Clarendon Press, 1944, reprint of 1917 edition), p. 836. Suarez also notes that the possibility of a war being just on both sides is absurd.

43.   Suarez also addresses the practical issue of deciding when to resort to arms, and he concludes that rulers must follow the "more probable" truth. Ibid., p. 836.

44.   This may be the point Aristotle is making in his introduction to the *Nicomachean Ethics* I, 2, when he notes that one should "look for precision in each class of things just so far as the subject matter admits . . . [in moral philosophy] the end aimed at is not knowledge but action" (1094b12–1095a10). *The Complete Works of Aristotle* vol. 2, edited by Jonathan Barnes (Princeton, N.J.: Princeton University Press, 1984), p. 1730.

45.   Ibid., 41, p. 181. I am limiting this discussion to reprisals conducted in lieu of war, rather than reprisals conducted as retribution for war crimes, as this is Vitoria's context.

SECTION

II

THE LEGAL POSITION OF WAR

The writers we have examined so far have all advocated certain Just War principles as moral imperatives. The next contributor we will examine, Hugo Grotius, attempts to transform the tradition of Just War from a set of moral principles into positive international law. In chapter 5 we will survey Grotius's theory of jurisprudence and international law and identify the principles that Grotius uses to ground the laws of war. In chapter 6 we will examine Grotius's laws of war themselves and discuss their relevancy in light of new political and technological realities. While much of what Grotius advocates may seem outdated (such as a prohibition against using poison spears), irrelevant to our enterprise (such as his rules governing ambassadors), or simply contentious (such as his careful division of prohibitions into natural and customary), the principles on which he bases his arguments are still cogent and worthy of our attention, and these will be our focus.

Grotius's ideas provoke controversy. Many jurists, like Nussbaum in the last chapter, for example, argue that international law could more appropriately be called international morality; where there is no common authority, they argue, and hence no power to enforce violations, there is no positive law. In chapter 7 we will examine the difficulties that criticisms such as Nussbaum's raise for Grotius's argument and explore ways in which he might have responded to them. We will save our critical assessment of the content of the laws of war for Section III.

Chapter

5

HUGO GROTIUS: FATHER OF INTERNATIONAL LAW

Huig de Groot was born in Holland in 1583. He graduated from the University of Leiden at fourteen years of age and received the degree of Doctor of Law from the University of Orleans two years later. In 1609, he published his first work on international law, a treatise in defense of freedom of the seas (*Mare Liberum*), which was actually a chapter in a larger unpublished work titled *Commentary on the Law of Prize*. He conceived his most important work, *The Law of War and Peace*, while he was in prison on political charges, and he wrote it between 1623 and 1625, following his escape to France.[1]

Rightly regarded as the father of international law, Grotius's extensive influence and many contributions to the science of jurisprudence defy summarization here. We can, however, examine the rules for the conduct of war that he formulated, articulated, and systematized, and we can explain why those rules were so suited to the needs of his world and how they are relevant to our world today. To prepare the way for that examination and analysis, we will profit from putting Grotius's work in the context of his time, noting the relationship between morality and law in his theory of jurisprudence and understanding his theory of international law.

During the Middle Ages, the international order of Europe rested primarily on the ecclesiastical authority of the Catholic Church. With the Church being the dominant central authority—for matters political as well as spiritual—international legal questions were seen as subjective moral determinations in the Augustinian tradition, rather than objective empirical issues as they had been in the Roman tradition. But Grotius confronted a society marked by (1) the replacement of feudal systems with national states, (2) the increase in world trade and colonialism, and (3) the fragmentation of the Christian

Church. Without a powerful ecclesiastical authority to mediate and arbitrate interests between increasingly powerful states, many of them with worldwide expansionist and trade interests, force became a common medium of political intercourse. National animosities that had been held in check for centuries by a unity of religion found expression on the battlefield.

A particularly abominable outcome of the new societal conditions, namely the Thirty Years' War, dominated much of Grotius's life. This was a "righteous," religious war wherein the only outcome acceptable to the opponents was either the conversion or the annihilation of the opposing side. Even when the Roman Church might have exercised its influence in urging moderation of violence, it did not. On the contrary, Church leaders often seemed determined to destroy forever the heresy of the Reformation through the annihilation of its adherents. This was a war fought on behalf of God and, like the Israelites in the wars of the Old Testament, its soldiers were not constrained by any rules whatsoever.[2] In Grotius's own words, it was the conduct of this war that motivated him to write *The Law of War and Peace*.

> I have had many and weighty reasons for undertaking to write upon this subject. Throughout the Christian world I observed a lack of restraint in relation to war, such as even barbarous races should be ashamed of; I observed that men rush to arms for slight causes, or no cause at all, and that when arms have once been taken up there is no longer any respect for law, divine or human; it is as if, in accordance with a general decree, frenzy had openly let loose for the committing of all crimes.[3]

Grotius's objective was to supplant the impotent and corrupt ecclesiastical authority with an external, objective, secular authority that the competing political interests (i.e., nation–states) would accept—a corpus of international laws. In the following famous passage he establishes with finality that the domain for his enterprise is all of humankind, regardless of race, religion, or national affiliation: "What we have been saying [that natural laws are binding on all mankind] would have a degree of validity even . . . if there is no God, or [if] the affairs of men are of no concern to Him."[4] Let us now turn to Grotius's work.

LAW AND MORAL PRINCIPLES

The central theme of *The Law of War and Peace* is that the relations between states should always be governed by laws and moral principles just as relations are between individuals. This assertion is pivotal because, if true, it restricts both the authority of the Church and that of sovereign states (and their rulers). Such limitations on secular and Church authority are necessary if international laws are to have any force. But in order for his argument to persuade, Grotius must first show that just as there are moral principles operative in interpersonal relations there are analogous moral principles that are at the foundation of municipal (civil) laws. Only then can he stand any chance of convincing us that analogous rules apply (or should apply) in the society of states.

Grotius tackles the first issue by grounding municipal law in a law of nature that is, as he puts it, "unchangeable—even in the sense that it cannot be changed by God."[5] Our discussion of international law must build, therefore, on the foundations that Grotius lays in his theory of natural law. Let us start by identifying the different types of law that Grotius recognizes and examining how they are related to one another in his system of jurisprudence.

Grotius divides all laws into two broad types: natural law and volitional law. Of the former, he says,

> The law of nature is a dictate of right reason which points out that an act, according as it is or is not in conformity with rational nature, has in it a quality of moral baseness or moral necessity.

and later,

> In discussing the law of nature, the question is this, whether an act can be performed without injustice; and injustice is understood to be that which is utterly repugnant to a rational and social nature.[6]

When Grotius uses the term **natural law,** he is referring to phenomena in the realm of interpersonal relationships, the same way a scientist explains phenomena concerning inanimate bodies in terms of the laws of physics.[7] He argues that there is something in the nature of humans as rational, social beings that is manifested in human interaction as behavioral patterns. When humans objectively apprehend the patterns, they can express them as abstract universal or natural laws. Such laws are as universal and timeless for human beings as are the laws of nature that explain and predict the interaction of inanimate substances. These universal laws are the first principles from which human reason deduces *moral truths.*

Volitional laws, on the other hand, may be set aside under certain circumstances, such as in wartime; or they may be changed to reflect the particular needs of a people or the times in which they live. Volitional laws may be either human or divine.[8] In either case, they should never be contrary to the laws of nature; and, in fact, volitional laws that decree anything contrary to the laws of nature are invalid.[9] Human volitional laws can be modified by consent and reflect the times, customs, and necessities of those who consent to them. Volitional laws are best understood as an ever-changing, evolving expedient to commodious living. Natural laws, which often provide the principles or foundation upon which volitional laws are conceived, cannot be set aside with the "tide of men's fortunes." For example, laws in times of war differ from those in peacetime, even though the same fundamental principles provide the foundations for them all.

Volitional human laws are of three types. One type concerns domestic relationships, such as those between a father and his children or a master and his employees. The remaining types Grotius calls "municipal laws" and "laws of nations." Both of these are based on consent, either explicit or implicit, and can be either written or simply customary. We will return to each type of law in more detail in the course of this exegesis.

The fundamental tenet of Grotius's conception of natural law is that human beings are social creatures—civil society must have existed in the state of nature (even if states did not) because it proceeds from "essential traits implanted in man."[10] These traits include the disposition to sympathize with others, a disposition to fulfill promises, the ability to know and act in accordance with general principles, the ability to use language, and a proclivity to inflict penalties on individuals in accordance with their just deserts.

Thus not self-preservation but life in society forms the fundamental basis for natural law.[11] While self-preservation is an instinctive disposition, it is not the most fundamental value as evidenced by man's (and other social creatures') willingness to encounter great personal risk to protect families and communities.

This concept is crucial because from it Grotius concludes that *neither persons nor states have an absolute right to self-defense.* Even if a person was being attacked by a ferocious wild beast, for example, the right of self-defense would not justify his seizing another's child and tossing it to the attacking animal in order to divert the danger away from himself. Thus the right of self-defense is limited at least to the extent that one cannot impose unreasonable dangers on other innocent persons to save oneself.

The type of society that is natural to humans is not one of loose anarchic associations but is a society that consists of ordered communities where individuals may live in concord with their fellows. Furthermore, society is not simply an expedient (as Thomas Hobbes claims), for man's very nature as a social being would "lead him into the mutual relations of society [even] if he had no lack of anything."[12]

Because it is in man's nature that he live in society, "it is a rule of the law of nature to abide by pacts" so that members may oblige themselves to one another.[13] The disposition to live in society and abide by pacts is the source of municipal law that is thereby grounded in the consent of those whom it affects. Grotius summarizes part of the relationship between natural law and municipal law, thus

> For the very nature of man, which even if we had no lack of anything would lead us into the mutual relations of society, is the mother of the law of nature. But the mother of municipal law is that obligation which arises from mutual consent; and since this obligation derives its force from the law of

nature, [human] nature may be considered, so to say, the great-grandmother of municipal law.[14]

Grotius adds that, while expediency is not the motive behind municipal laws, they are reinforced by it in that expediency provides the "opportunity" for civil government and municipal laws that help cultivate the social life. Thus man's rational nature compels him to adopt municipal laws that are an expedient to increased welfare.

Natural laws either obligate, prohibit, or, by forfeit, permit. Most volitional laws concern affairs that are neither obligatory nor prohibited under natural law; that is, they are permitted. Such laws are, however, binding, because individuals have given their consent to them, either explicitly or implicitly, and this constitutes having entered a pact with others who are subject to these laws and, of course, "abiding by pacts is a rule of nature."[15] This formulation successfully grounds obedience to volitional law in moral principles without claiming that the content of particular municipal laws (such as those concerning swimming or fishing above the milldam) have inherent moral significance. An example will be helpful here.

Grotius notes that all persons have a natural right to those goods necessary for survival. Natural law does not prohibit ownership of additional goods, and volitional law extends the right of ownership to these. "Thus ownership, such as now obtains, was introduced by the will of man; but, once introduced, the law of nature points out that it is wrong for me, against your will, to take away that which is subject to your ownership."[16] The law of nature that grants everyone the right to that which is necessary for survival can never be superseded by volitional law, and any law that deprives people of their basic survival needs is invalid because it is contrary to natural law. Ownership of necessities is, therefore, guaranteed by natural law, whereas ownership of additional goods is permitted by natural law (in that it is not forbidden) and legislated by volitional law; and volitional law is itself grounded in natural law through the innate human disposition to abide by pacts.

The significance of this to our enterprise is that it means that no one—not even heads of state such as Muammar Khadaffi, Manuel Noriega, Richard Nixon, or Saddam Hussein—is outside of either natural or volitional laws. Moreover, treaties entered into by leaders on behalf of their nations constitute instances of volitional laws and cannot be abrogated without the consent of all parties. As Grotius puts it,

> Speaking of the observance of the law of nature and of divine law, or of the law of nations; observance of these is binding upon all kings, even though they have made no promise. . . . Nevertheless, it must be admitted that when such a promise is made, the sovereign power is in a way limited . . . [because] a true promise confers a legal right upon the promisee.[17]

This leads us to an apparent difficulty for Grotius: Are citizens obligated to obey unjust laws—specifically, to serve in an unjust war? Grotius must work with two traditional perspectives. The first is the Augustinian view emphasizing domestic peace and order. Augustine derives his position from Paul's letter to the Romans: "Let every person be subject to the governing authorities. . . . [He] who resists the authorities resists what God has appointed, and those who resist will incur judgment" (Rom. 13:1–2). Augustine interprets this to mean that humans must obey even unjust laws for the sake of order.

> The people of Christ, whatever be their condition—whether they be kings, princes, judges, soldiers, or provincials, rich or poor, bond or free, male or female—are enjoined to endure this earthly republic, wicked and dissolute as it is.[18]

Aquinas defends the second perspective. He argues that one's individual conscience must always be the final arbiter of moral choices. He grounds his position in an understanding of human nature quite different from Augustine's. Augustine believes that humans are *naturally* disposed to sin; hence, the very purpose of political authority is to *impose* an imperfect peace on stained beings. Aquinas, on the other hand, sees in people's rational and social nature a disposition to beneficence: "The first precept of [natural] law [is] that *good is to be done and ensued, and evil is to be avoided.*"[19] The purpose of civil authority is to foster "the unity and peace of the people," and when a duly constituted authority fails to accomplish this, it may be deposed. "Man is bound to obey secular princes insofar as this is required by the order of justice. Wherefore if the prince's authority is not just but usurped, or if he commands what is unjust, his subjects are not bound to obey him."[20]

Aquinas is not questioning the divine authority of civil government, but he locates it in the office rather than the individual who fills the office; and because all human beings are fallible, a ruler's commands can never be absolutely binding on his subjects.

The premises of the two thinkers contradict each other: Augustine holds that revelation is always the foundational source of moral truth; Aquinas contends that humans can discover moral truths through reason.[21] In the former case, the last word concerning right and wrong conduct comes "from the top"—from God through either papal authority or the state—while in the latter view, the last word comes from humans using their reason. Augustine generally equates morality with legality; Aquinas sees moral truths as the foundation of positive laws.[22] Grotius's position on this topic initially seems to favor the Augustinian perspective, but further analysis shows that it fuses together the two views.

Grotius certainly denies to citizens the right to resist a tyrannical ruler and includes among his list of unjust wars those waged by an oppressed people to gain freedom.[23] This seems paradoxical when contrasted with the progressive character of his work as a whole—enough so that one classic writer on international law attributes this apparent inconsistency to the needs of the times in which Grotius wrote.

> What is the explanation of these views, so foreign to the spirit of his teaching and his personal condition? . . . his frowning upon rebellion and the favoring of authority were in accordance with what were considered to be the essential needs of the times. . . . At a time of general uncertainty and of loosening of traditional ties of society, national and international, order was looked upon as the paramount dictate of reason. . . . Considerations of this order must have weighed heavily with one in whose work the desire for peace was the dominant motive and ever-recurring theme.[24]

This commentator goes on to note that "behind the facade of general disapproval of the right of resistance there lay qualifications so comprehensive as to render the major proposition almost theoretical."[25] And indeed, Grotius adds that there is a right of resistance in those cases either where a ruler transgresses against the laws of the state, abandons his responsibility or authority, undertakes to place the state in subjugation, oversteps the authority granted him by the people, or shows himself the enemy of the people, or when the right to resist has been reserved by the people in the constitutional document.[26] Certainly these reservations seem to render impotent the earlier prohibition against rebellion. Why then does Grotius take such pains to emphasize that even unjust laws must be obeyed, and that bad rule is better than no rule at all?

There is, I believe, a better explanation for Grotius's position than simply, "It was required by the times." Understanding his rationale on this topic provides us with a worthwhile insight into his enterprise as a whole. Recall that although Grotius takes his notion of natural law from Aquinas, he applies it in a manner that gives it relevance between nations as well as between individuals. While Aquinas argues that all just human laws are derived from natural law, his first precept of natural law—do good and avoid evil—has little usefulness in terms of formulating specific rules of behavior and simply does not make any sense at all when applied to abstract political entities.

Remember that Grotius argues that people's natural disposition to abide by pacts is at the root of volitional laws, a form of consensual agreement between individuals. The same reasoning applies to international obligations that, although they obtain between states, *are made by individuals*. Because he has grounded positive law in the natural law precept that rational beings have a *prima facie* obligation to abide by pacts, Grotius must be very careful concerning the conditions whereby he justifies overriding this obligation. He cannot permit disobedience to municipal law based on subjective assessments by individuals, because exceptions that are operative between individuals in domestic society will have parallel applications in the international society of states. In fact, Aquinas's advocacy of individual conscience as the final arbiter of right and wrong action would make international obligations a farce. If Grotius is going to be successful in establishing legal constraints on sovereign nations based on their implicit consent as evidenced by customary practices, he cannot allow "the camel to get its nose under the tent" by permitting states the wherewithal to revoke their consent at will. The only justifications for reneging on promises must be conflicts with other natural law obligations. By insisting that individuals are always bound by municipal laws based on their consent and the universal obligation to keep pacts (except when such laws conflict with natural law), he has prepared the way to stipulate a like requirement for states.[27]

This is a marvelous "compromise" by Grotius, because he successfully grounds positive law in morality, as Aquinas advocates, without completely subordinating it to individual conscience. Still, he is able to leave the door open for civil disobedience based on the incompatibility of municipal laws with the principles of natural law—an outcome that legal systems based entirely on consent are unable to achieve.[28]

The last point we need to address in our present discussion of law and morality concerns sanctions. Grotius argues that the law of nature is a real law that has its sanction in force, because according to natural law, "Every man has the right to punish wrongdoers."[29] Notice that he does not assert that others have a duty to punish wrongdoers, only that it is permissible. In municipalities, the offices of preventing and punishing wrongdoers are specialized, and each individual's right to undertake such action is restricted by volitional laws.[30] In other words, only civil authorities may undertake to punish wrongdoers, and *they have an obligation to do so.* We can readily see why this is so when we consider that the members of society at large have agreed to give up their individual right to punish wrongdoers with the stipulation that the state will do it for them. Agents of the state, therefore, hired for this purpose, have a duty to the members of their community to act in their behalf in apprehending and punishing wrongdoers.

In places where there is no constituted authority, "the old natural liberty remains, especially in places where there are no courts, as, for example, on the sea."[31] In the international society of states, then, nations have a right to punish wrongdoers, but they do not have a duty to do so except in cases where they are so compelled because of treaty obligations.

Grotius grounds his conception of international law by drawing a domestic analogy to civil (municipal) law. The analogy fails to satisfy, however, because it is highly questionable that states have moral obligations to one another that are analogous to those that individuals have to one another in domestic society. We must wait until our discussion of international law to see how Grotius responds to this objection.

THE LAW OF NATIONS

Besides the problem of sanctions, two additional difficulties confronted Grotius in developing a system of international law. First, he had to identify a core body of laws upon which to build a *corpus juris*. Grotius claims that nations do in fact observe implicit laws, just as individuals in domestic society observe implicit laws as a matter of custom. He describes the laws between nations, *jus inter gentes,* as follows:

> The law which is broader in scope than municipal law is the law of nations; that is the law which has received its obligatory force from the will of all nations, or of many nations. . . .

> The proof for the law of nations is similar to that for unwritten municipal law, it is found in unbroken custom and the testimony of those who are skilled in it.[32]

Grotius argues that familiar precedents reflect the moral dispositions that are natural to humans as rational social beings, and that one can determine the operative laws of nations through the analysis of past and present customs.

> When many at different times, and in different places, affirm the same thing as certain, that ought to be referred to a universal cause; and this cause, in the lines of inquiry which we are following, must be either a correct conclusion drawn from the principles of nature, or common consent. The former points to the law of nature; the latter, to the law of nations.[33]

Only a prodigy such as Grotius could be familiar with the incredible volume of records from past civilizations that he filters for moral practices and refines into principles. Because he found the wellsprings for his research in the civilizations of Ancient Greece and Rome, he appealed to national leaders who themselves were steeped in classical traditions. The laws of war that he devised rested on familiar precedents.

The second problem that confronted Grotius is the difficulty of anchoring laws between nations in a law of nature that concerns moral agents. Grotius recognizes that the proper domain for natural law is individual relationships within a society, but he also recognizes a society of nations wherein each member nation consents to laws for the benefit of all. So the law of nations, as he conceives it, is based *almost* entirely on consent (*pacta sunt servanda*), rather than on natural law. Just as reason dictates that individuals must follow certain principles if they are to maintain domestic society, so reason dictates that certain principles must regulate a society of independent states. In this way, the laws of nations are similar to municipal laws in that they come into being through consent.

Just as the laws of each state have in view the advantage of that state, so by mutual consent it has become possible that certain laws should originate as between all states, or in a great many states; and it is apparent that the laws thus originating had in view the advantage, not of particular states, but of the great society of states. And this is what is called the law of nations.[34]

Thus, Grotius is able to legitimize his enterprise by using a timeless, international consensuality as his precedence. Consensus, however, can mean agreeing on the rule to be adopted, without necessarily agreeing on the reason for that rule—and in moral philosophy, the reason is everything. Rules grounded entirely in expediency will be followed only as long as following is expedient. Grotius must account for a lack of moral foundation in a legal system seemingly based on expediency.

Recall that Grotius's account of domestic society stipulated that not only were some municipal laws derived from the law of nature but all municipal laws were affected by it because of man's natural obligation to keep promises and abide by pacts. Grotius risks misunderstanding when he uses the moral obligations inherent in interpersonal relationships as the basis for assuming that such obligations obtain in international relationships because of the fundamental dissimilarities between the subjects of law involved in each case: that is, moral agents on one hand and abstract entities on the other.

The proposition that abstract entities can incur moral as well as legal obligations vis-à-vis human beings or other abstract entities is highly controversial, even today. It was simply a nonstarter in Grotius's precorporate world.[35] But if we reject natural law's application to the international community, we deprive international law of moral force. A system of laws grounded only in consent (sans moral force) and recognizing no common constituting authority or force of sanction is likely to have little effect.[36] Under such a formulation, the only reason a sovereign state would conform to a law would be that to conform would be in its best interests. And then, of course, there would be no need for law in the first place. Moreover, if international law is based solely on consent, then nations can withhold their consent or repudiate it whenever conditions change, because there is no common authority to mandate compliance. To give international law normative force, one must link it to moral principles the same way Grotius links municipal law to human nature.

Grotius achieves this link by arguing that the same natural laws governing man's relationships with his fellows also apply to relationships between states. This is not a domestic analogy argument where the state is considered an individual "writ large." Grotius regards the state as an expedient formed so that group functions may be delegated to individuals who act on the group's behalf.[37] The moral principles that govern the individuals conducting national affairs apply to the relations that they establish between their states. And because it is always moral agents who make decisions and initiate actions on behalf of the constituents of a state (who are themselves moral agents), such actions must be governed by the natural laws inherent in man's nature as a rational, social being. People do not cease to be responsible moral agents because they act in an official capacity as agents of a state. Nor do the principles of natural law cease to apply when one "interacts" with an abstract entity representing an association of persons. Even though abstract entities are the subjects of international law, the responsibility for compliance, as well as the culpability for infractions, always rests with individuals.[38] This understanding harkens back to Grotius's earlier insistence that the laws of nature are binding on all people—monarch or Pope included.

A final point: This application of the principles of natural law to international law does not imply that municipal and international laws are similar in content. We should keep in mind that in most cases volitional laws—municipal and international—are expedients; their moral force is derived from the obligation to keep promises, not something inherently normative in the laws themselves.

In chapter 7 we will return to the issue of sanctions and other difficulties for international law; for now, however, let us turn to chapter 6 and examine the Just War principles that Grotius proposes.

Topics for Further Discussion

1. Grotius compares scientific laws that dictate (or explain) the "behavior" of inanimate objects in the natural world with his *natural laws,* and he believes that the latter have the same efficacy in governing human choices in the political and social world of interpersonal relationships as physical laws have in the world of innaminate objects. Develop an analogy between a scientific law or theory and human relationships. Example: Boyle's law of gasses predicts how gas molecules will perform according to certain variables. Think of human beings as the individual molecules and their individual character as a variable (e.g., the temperature or environment). Develop an argument either defending or attacking such an analogy.

2. Grotius argues that people do not have an absolute right to self-defense. Develop three examples that illustrate your position on this issue.

3. Grotius uses a family metaphor to explain the relationship among human nature, promise keeping, municipal law, and the law of nature. Develop a "family tree" that visually depicts this relationship.

4. Grotius is careful to ground his theory of international law in morality. Why does he consider this crucial?

5. Is it reasonable to expect abstract entities such as nations to have moral obligations to one another as Grotius maintains? Might we extend Grotius's arguments regarding international society to corporations in the business community? Explain.
6. Why does Grotius assert that natural laws are binding "even on God"? How might the effects of the Thirty Years' War have influenced his thinking on this topic?
7. Grotius, following Aristotle and Aquinas, argues that there are natural laws that govern human interaction, and that these are derived, at least in part, from the rational and social characteristics of human nature. Explain why you agree or disagree with this view.

Notes

1. Hugo Grotius, *The Law of War and Peace*, translated by Francis W. Kelsey (Indianapolis and New York: Bobbs-Merrill Co., 1962). The biographical information is from the Introduction by James Brown Scott, pp. ix–xliii. All quotations from Grotius are taken from this source.
2. One commentator describes the period in the following way: "War to extermination thus became the only means of obtaining peace. This was the strictly logical basis of the decree of the Holy Inquisition, which Philip II solemnly approved, condemning to death the entire population of the Netherlands. . . . Plunder and pillage were supported by reference to the divinely approved 'spoiling of the Egyptians' by the Israelites. The right to massacre unresisting enemies was based upon the command of the Almighty to the Jews in the twentieth chapter of Deuteronomy. The indiscriminate slaughter of whole populations was justified by a reference to the divine command to slaughter nations round about Israel Torture and mutilation of enemies was sanctioned by the conduct of Samuel against Agag, of King David against the Philistines, of the men of Judah against Adoni-bezek. Even the slaughter of babes in arms was supported by a passage from the Psalms—'Happy shall he be, that taketh and dasheth thy little ones against the stones.'" Andrew Dickson White, *Seven Great Statesmen* (New York: The Century Co., 1912), pp. 84, 85.
3. *The Law of War and Peace*, *Prolegomena* 28, p. 20.
4. Ibid., *Prolegomena* 10, p. 13. Grotius is careful to add that he is only referring to the minimum standards for acceptable behavior; he notes that there are additional revealed constraints on Christians. This is a brilliant tactic, because it effectively limits ecclesiastical criticism to content rather than process (i.e., the parameters of the theory rather than the theory itself).
5. Ibid., Bk. I, chap. 1, X, p. 40. Grotius's law of nature is derived from that of Aquinas.
6. Ibid., Bk. I, chap. 1, X, p. 38, and chap. 2, I, p. 52.
7. Grotius also compares natural law to mathematics, "Just as God cannot cause two times two should not make four, so He cannot cause that which is intrinsically evil be not evil." Ibid., Bk. I, chap. 1, X, p. 40; and elsewhere, "The fundamental principles of the law of nature are as manifest and clear as those things we perceive through the senses," *Prolegomena*, 39, p. 23.
8. Grotius further divides divine law into "universal divine law and divine law peculiar to a single people." Ibid., Bk. I, chap. 1, XV, pp. 45–50. In this sense, divine laws are those given by God to either all mankind or one people.

9. Ibid., Bk. II, chap. 16, XXVI, p. 425.

10. Ibid., *Prolegomena* 12, p. 14. Much of Grotius's position on natural law is taken from Aquinas and Aristotle. "[5] Yet it is natural for man, more than for any other animal, to be a social and political animal, to live in a group. [6] This is clearly a necessity of man's nature. . . . [8] If, then, it is natural for man to live in the society of many, it is necessary that there exist among men some means by which the group may be governed. . . ." Thomas Aquinas, *On Kingship*, Bk. I, chap. I, in *The Political Ideas of St. Thomas Aquinas*, edited by Dino Bigongiari (New York: Hafner Publishing Co., 1957), pp. 175–76.

11. Ibid., *Prolegomena* 6–8, pp. 11–13. "Man is, to be sure, an animal, but an animal of a superior kind, . . . among the traits characteristic of man is an impelling desire for society, that is, for the social life—not of any and every sort, but peaceful, and organized according to the measure of his intelligence, with those who are of his own kind; . . . Stated as a universal truth, therefore, the assertion that every animal is impelled by nature to seek only its own good cannot be conceded."

    In this passage, we see Grotius's political idealism, framed in the tradition established by Aristotle, Cicero, and Aquinas. Cicero, for example, argues that divine laws are laws of perfect reason and gives as examples the prohibition against rape and the duty to sacrifice one's self for one's community. Contrast this view with that of Thomas Hobbes, who argues that people are naturally disposed to selfish actions and therefore it is self-interest and self-preservation that are the fundamental values that motivate people to form social groups.

12. Ibid., *Prolegomena* 16, p. 15.

13. Ibid., *Prolegomena* 15, p. 14.

14. Ibid., *Prolegomena* 16, p. 15.

15. Much of what Grotius states is best understood in the context of the Thirty Years' War. For example, the Papacy assumed the authority to void any promises or treaties at will. Grotius responds by arguing that volitional laws, both human and divine, are a variety of promises that are binding even on God. As Grotius puts it, "According to civil law also a person can be said to be bound by his own act, either in this sense, that an obligation results not from the law of nature also but from the municipal law, or from both together, or in the sense that the obligation gives a right to action in a court of law. Therefore we say that a true and proper obligation arises from a promise and contract of a king, which he has entered into with his subjects, and that this obligation confers a right upon his subjects; . . . and *this holds even between God and man*." [italics added] Bk. II, chap. 14, VI, p. 384.

16. Ibid., Bk. I, chap. 1, X, p. 39.

17. Ibid., Bk. I, chap. 3, XVI, p. 121. For Grotius, with his strong background in business and contract law, the terms *promise* and *pact* presume the same obligation.

18. Augustine, *The City of God*, Bk. II, chap. XIX, p. 34. Augustine includes a citizen's obligation to serve in unjust wars in his position. The only time a citizen can disobey civil authority is when what one is enjoined to do contradicts a command of God; that is, the only unjust laws are those that are contrary to God's will. Thus, his oft-quoted statement, "Unjust laws are not laws at all." See the previous discussion of this issue in chapter 3.

19. Aquinas, *Summa Theologica* I–II, Q.94, A.2, in *The Political Ideas*, p. 45.

20. Aquinas, *Summa Theologica* II–II, Q.104, A.6, p. 172.

21. Aquinas holds that there are two types of reason, speculative and practical, and, as he puts it, "The precepts of natural law are to practical reason what the first principles of demonstrations are to speculative reason." Practical reason, then, deduces moral truths from the principles of natural law. Ibid., I–II, Q.94, A.2, p. 44.

22. Again, Aristotle's influence is noticeable. In the *Nicomachean Ethics* V, 9, 10, Aristotle notes that municipal laws are only just incidentally (1137a12), and that when justice and

law conflict (due to law's inevitable lack of total universality), it must give way to justice (1137b20–32).

23. Grotius writes, "Liberty, whether of individuals or of states. . . . cannot give the right to war." What Grotius means here is that the lack of liberty *by itself* cannot justify war, because it may have been entered into by lawful means. This is because although "by nature no one is a slave," individuals must have the right to enter slavery if they choose, otherwise they are not truly free. *The Law of War and Peace*, Bk. II, chap. 22, XI, p. 551.

24. H. Lauterpacht, "The Grotian Movement," in *International Law: A Contemporary Perspective*, edited by Richard Falk, Friedrich Kratochwil, and Saul L. Mendlovitz (Boulder, Colo.: Westview Press, 1985), p. 26. Lauterpacht undoubtedly has in mind the terrible violence of the Reformation. In 1570, after excommunicating Queen Elizabeth, Pope Pius V announced that all of her subjects were released from any obligation of obedience to her. And although both Martin Luther and John Calvin, two of the central Protestant figures of the Reformation, were reluctant to endorse rebellion, even against tyrants, both eventually did give their approval to some form of resistance. Calvin argues that while private individuals should never rebel against their rulers, neither should they obey them when "they lead us away from obedience [to God]." He specifies that other political leaders, such as magistrates, have a duty to resist the "fierce licentiousness of kings," and that those who do not "betray the freedom of the people." Luther accepts that "a Christian may offer resistance, not as a Christian but as a citizen or member of the body politic." Thus we see approval of violence as a means of political resistance, but not as a remedy for individual grievances. See *Christianity and Revolution: Radical Christian Testimonies 1520–1650*, edited by Lowell H. Zuck (Philadelphia: Temple University Press, 1975). The quotations from Luther and Calvin are taken from pp. 140 and 134, respectively, and the discussion of Pope Pius V's advocacy of rebellion is found on p. 187.

25. Ibid., p. 27.

26. *The Law of War and Peace*, Bk. I, chap. 4, VIII–XI, XIV, pp. 156–59.

27. "Whatever the king does in acts belonging to his kingly office should be considered the same way as if the state did them. . . . After an oath has been taken he [the king] cannot render it void, because here also separate persons are required. . . . To swear so that you would be bound only if you should yourself be willing is altogether ridiculous, and contrary to the nature of an oath." Ibid., Bk. II, chap. 14, I, III, pp. 381–82.

28. Consider: If positive law is completely unrelated to morality, then one might argue that the only motives for obeying the law are either self-interest or the fear of sanctions. Under this account, a state would need a large percentage of the population involved in law enforcement! If, on the other hand, positive law is an imperfect formalization of moral principles, then one should always obey one's conscience when it conflicts with the law.

29. *The Law of War and Peace*, Bk. II, chap. 20, IX, p. 476.

30. "Since in our private affairs and those of our kinsmen we are liable to partiality, as soon as numerous families were united at a common point judges were appointed, and to them alone was given the power to avenge the injured, while others are deprived of the freedom of action wherewith nature endowed them." Ibid., Bk. II, chap. 20, VIII, p. 473. Compare Grotius's conception of the origins of municipal law to the following extracts from John Locke, written a century later: "The execution on the law of nature is [in the state of nature] put into every man's hands, whereby every one has a right to punish the transgressors of that law. . . . Every offense that can be committed in the state of nature may in the state of nature be also punished equally, as it may in a commonwealth: for though it would be beside my present purpose to enter here into the particulars of the law of nature, or its measure of punishment, yet it is certain there is such a law, and that too as intelligible and plain to a rational creature . . . as the positive laws of commonwealths; . . . for so truly are a great part of the municipal laws of countries, which are only

so far right, as they are founded on the law of nature, by which they are to be regulated and interpreted. . . . The inconveniences [caused] by the irregular and uncertain exercise of the power every man has of punishing the transgressions of other make them . . . willing to give up every one his single power of punishing to be exercised by such alone as shall be appointed to it amongst them; and by such rules as the community, or those authorized by them to that purpose, shall agree on. And in this we have the original right of both the legislative and executive power, as well as of the governments and societies themselves." John Locke, *Two Treatises of Government* (New York: New American Library, 1963), Bk. II, Sections 7, 12, 127, pp. 312, 315, 397.

31.   *The Law of War and Peace*, p. 474.

32.   Ibid., Bk. I, chap., 1, XIV, p. 44.

33.   Ibid., *Prolegomena* 40, pp. 23–24.

34.   Ibid., *Prolegomena* 17, p. 15.

35.   It is interesting that Grotius's early legal experience was gained representing Dutch shipping interests in foreign courts. His first work on international law was written to address issues in international shipping and commerce.

36.   It is doubtful that the informal sanctions that we often employ in international society today—isolation from the world community, economic boycott, and various forms of ill will—would have been effective in Grotius's highly nationalistic, postwar world.

37.   Grotius's enterprise may be understood as a denial of the Machiavellian view, popular in his day, that in international politics nothing is unjust that is expedient. See *Prolegomena* 3, p. 9.

38.   Grotius's formulation was virtually ignored until after World War II, but it has since become more acceptable. As one expert on international law writes, "When I take up the Nuremberg cases in my class in International Law, I find it quite difficult to convey to the students how radical those proceedings appeared to be in 1947. At that time, the contention that there should be individual accountability under international law seemed to constitute an unfounded and dangerous precedent." Anthony D'Amato, *International Law: Process and Prospect* (Dobbs Ferry, N.Y.: Transnational Publishers, 1987), p. 149. The following quotation from Justice Jackson's opening remarks at the Nuremberg trials makes this point with finality: "The principle of personal liability is a necessary as well as logical one if international law is to render real help to the maintenance of peace. An international law which operates only on states can be enforced only by war because the most practicable method of coercing a state is warfare. . . . Of course, the idea that a state any more than a corporation commits crimes, is a fiction. Crimes always are committed only by persons. While it is quite proper to employ the fiction of responsibility of a state or corporation for the purpose of imposing a collective liability, it is quite intolerable to let such a legalism become the basis of personal immunity. The [Nuremberg] Charter recognizes that one who has committed criminal acts may not take refuge in superior order nor in the doctrine that his crimes were acts of states." *Trial of the Major War Criminals Before the International Military Tribunal*, vol. 2, "Transcript of 21 Nov. 1945" (Nuremberg, Germany, 1947), p. 150. See also "The International Tribunal at Nuremberg" in *War and Morality*, edited by Richard A. Wasserstrom (Belmont, Calif.: Wadsworth Publishing Co., 1970), pp. 107–8.

Chapter

6

HUGO GROTIUS
AND THE JUST WAR

Grotius's effort to establish a concise corpus of international law for the conduct of war represents the culmination of a thousand years of gradually reducing moral principles to objective criteria. Grotius realized, however, the impossibility of a completely objective standard of justice; for the conduct of human affairs, even the most objective criteria must be subjectively applied. Hence his work includes not only a system of specific laws but also a discussion of the principles behind them (their purpose or "intention") and guidance concerning their application. Because no legislative body existed to formally "declare" his system of international jurisprudence as positive law, Grotius had to depend on reason and custom as the authority behind his laws and on private conscience and public condemnation as his sanctions. We will return to the efficacy of these foundations in more detail in our discussion of modern international law (chapter 7).

Grotius's laws of war deserve examination from two distinct and independent perspectives: *jus ad bellum* and *jus in bello*. His primary objective is to prevent war; failing to prevent it, he seeks to minimize its brutality. The specific proscriptions of these two dimensions of the theory of Just War are disproportionately represented in modern international legal documents, although the principles upon which they are based are evident, as we shall see. Let us begin with his conditions for *jus ad bellum*.

Grotius's abhorrence of war is a recurring theme in his work. In the dedication of *The Law of War and Peace* to Louis XIII of France, Grotius writes,

> It is worthy of your devotion to duty, worthy of your exalted estate, not to attempt to despoil anyone of his rights by force of arms, not to disturb ancient boundaries; but in war to continue the work of peace, and not to commence war save with the desire to end it at the earliest possible moment. . . . This will be a very great achievement. Yet the peoples of Christian lands are so

bold as to ask of you something further, that, with *the extinction of warfare everywhere*, through your initiative peace may come again. [italics added][1]

While Grotius's objective is to avoid war, he is not a pacifist. "For both extremes [pacifism and realism] a remedy must be found, that men may not believe either that nothing is allowable, or that everything is."[2]

Recognizing that national perspectives can never be truly objective, he lays out a detailed set of criteria for nations to use in evaluating situations that might warrant the use of force. These criteria constitute his concept of *jus ad bellum* and must be met in order for a war to be formally just.

Jus ad Bellum

Modern Just War theory recognizes as many as eight conditions that are necessary to justify a nation's resorting to arms. Grotius discusses seven of these, but accepts only six. Since the seven he does address have their origins in works that we have discussed in previous chapters, our summary of them here will be brief. We will examine the one modern addition to the list last.

The first necessary *jus ad bellum* condition that must be satisfied prior to the resort to arms is that there be a *just cause*. For Grotius, this means that the nation contemplating the resort to arms must identify an injury received. He often frames his examples of just causes in terms of violations of rights.[3] In addition to defense of self or property, other just causes arise when a ruler, even a ruler in another state, "inflicts upon his subjects such treatment as no one is warranted in inflicting," and to punish or prevent humanitarian abuses "for the good of mankind in general."[4] Grotius considers punishment just only when it aims at some good, because "reason forbids a man to do anything whereby another may be harmed, unless this action has some good end in view."[5] Clearly, then, Grotius classifies as just only those wars that are waged either in self-defense or to inflict punishment *after* an injury has been received. This effectively forbids wars of anticipation or security.

> Fear with respect to a neighboring power is not a sufficient cause. For in order that self-defense may be lawful it must be necessary; and it is not necessary unless we are certain, not only regarding the power of our neighbor, but also regarding his intention; the degree of certainty required is that which is accepted in morals.[6]

And elsewhere he states "that the possibility of being attacked confers the right to attack is abhorrent to every principle of equity."[7] War, then, is a legal remedy—albeit an extraordinary one—that is undertaken only in response to a serious injustice and only after ordinary procedures of resolution have failed.

Grotius's discussion of unjust and doubtful causes is as telling as is his list of just ones. In his treatment of "advantage" as an example of an unjust cause (the shortest subchapter in the text, reproduced here in its entirety), he exclaims,

VI. Advantage does not confer the same right as necessity.[8]

He later adds that if there is any doubt about whether a cause is just, one must refrain from war, because "in consequence of war a great many sufferings usually fall upon even innocent persons. Therefore in the midst of divergent opinions we must lean toward peace."[9]

The expression "just cause" is misleading because the term seems to imply a *sufficient justification*. We should keep in mind that a just cause is a *necessary condition* for the resort to arms, it is not itself a sufficient reason: Even if a nation has received an injury constituting a just cause for war, it cannot go to war justly unless the remaining *jus ad bellum* conditions are met.

The second *jus ad bellum* criterion is *proportionality*. By this notion, Grotius intends to ensure that the good toward which the war aims is proportional to the evil that the war will cause.

The king who undertakes a war for trivial reasons, or to exact unnecessary penalties, is responsible to his subjects for making good the losses which arise therefrom. For he perpetrates a crime, if not against the foe, yet against his own people, by involving them in so serious an evil on such grounds.[10]

The requirement that wars be proportional to the costs entailed in prosecuting them serves two purposes. First, it demands a utilitarian calculation of the consequences that will result from resorting to arms. In this regard, Grotius makes the enlightened statement (two centuries before Bentham and Mill) that "kings who measure up to the rule of wisdom take account not only of the nation which has been committed to them, but of the whole human race."[11] Note that rulers cannot meet the condition of proportionality by considering only the war's consequences for the citizens of their own nation; rulers must also consider how their actions might affect others in the world community. And, elsewhere, Grotius notes that if the rulers harbor any doubts concerning the balance of good over evil that will result from the use of force, then war must not be undertaken.[12]

The condition of proportionality also requires a specific political end toward which the war is directed, an end determined in advance of the use of force. It is, after all, impossible to determine whether the political objective stimulating armed conflict is proportional to the expected costs without first clearly articulating the political objective. Once a nation sets its political objectives, fighting aimed specifically at other objectives may well generate costs that violate the condition of proportionality and thereby render the war unjust.

A war justly begun might therefore become unjust during its execution because of violations of the condition of proportionality.

For example, the United Nations authorized the use of force against Iraq in response to Iraq's unprovoked 1990 invasion of Kuwait. After defeat of the Iraqi armed forces in Kuwait, the Commander of the United Nations forces, General Norman Schwartzkopf, advocated pursuing the Iraqi army into Baghdad in order to destroy the Iraqi army and to topple Saddam Hussein's government. Such an action would have exceeded the U.N. resolution authorizing force, however, and may have violated the condition of proportionality by generating costs aimed at a new political end rather than the one established at the outset. Nevertheless, given his role as tactical advisor, General Schwartzkopf's recommendation was appropriate from a military perspective. General Schwartzkopf apparently did not keep in mind that the franchise on *jus ad bellum* decisions belongs solely to the political establishment. As a result, at a news conference he publicly lamented that his recommendation for invading Iraq was not approved, later had to retract his public statements, and was "corrected" by his superiors for his indiscretion.[13]

This example is startlingly similar in principle to General Douglas MacArthur's public insistence that U.S. forces expand their military operations into Manchuria in pursuit of the North Korean army, thereby exceeding the stated political objective of the Korean War—a decision for which General MacArthur was relieved of his command by President Truman.

These examples make the crucial point that the political objective of the war should always be determined by public officials representing their nation's citizens. This objective must be articulated before the start of hostilities, and any change to the war's political objective must also be a political decision, subject to the same *jus ad bellum* criteria as the resort to force in the first place. In any case, the political objectives of Just War are always limited in that wars of annihilation, "even against the wicked," are always unjust, and that wars should be fought "only so far that crimes may be remedied and corrected."[14]

In retrospect, many believe that both Douglas MacArthur and Norman Schwartzkopf were exactly correct in their respective assessments of the best political course of action—after all, North and South Korea have remained at odds for decades and a U.S.- and British-led coalition had to invade Iraq in 2003 in order to enforce compliance with previous U.N. mandates. But that is beside the point. We are concerned with the process by which decisions are made rather than whether a particular decision was the best one. Elected officials make political decisions; military leaders act on them.

Some people have argued that the First Gulf War between Iraq and the United Nations was unjust because the number of Iraqi casualties (an estimated 40,000 Iraqi soldiers killed in combat and thousands of civilians dead from hardship and disease as a result of extensive damage to the Iraqi infrastructure) was out of proportion to the political objectives of the war. This "backward looking" criticism seems to me to be sophistry for two reasons. First, the responsibility for the deaths of Iraqi soldiers must rest with the Iraqi government. Iraq could have prevented or ended the war at any time by complying with the mandate of the United Nations Security Council. Second, the criticism confuses *how the war should have been fought* (*jus in bello*) with the question of *whether it should have been fought* (*jus ad bellum*). Perhaps the destruction to Iraq's infrastructure was excessive—especially the alleged bombing of sewage and water treatment facilities. If so, this is a criticism of how the United Nations coalition fought the war; it is logically independent of the *jus ad bellum* criterion that the political objectives of the war be proportional to the terrible costs reasonably associated with the resort to force. We will return to the *jus in bello* issues in later discussions.

The next *jus ad bellum* condition requires that there be a *reasonable chance of success*. Grotius rejects the "give me liberty or give me death" aphorism on the grounds that "life is of greater value than liberty."[15] This view constitutes not a rejection of fighting for freedom but a rejection of futile or suicidal resistance. This condition also has important implications for timing a nation's surrender.[16]

The fourth condition demands that nations *publicly declare* their wars. The purpose here is twofold. Declaration of war provides the offending party the opportunity to offer redress in lieu of violence.[17] Second, nations must conduct war in a manner that establishes "with certainty that war is not being waged by private initiative but by the will of each of the two peoples or their [lawful] heads."[18] In other words, public declaration opens to public debate the judgment of whether the injury received warrants a resort to arms. As an example, Grotius cites the Roman Senate's practice of debating whether to undertake war *after* they had first ruled that the war could be justly undertaken.

Some modern critics argue that the requirement for public declaration is no longer reasonable, because the time it takes to initiate an attack today is but an instant compared to the time it took to raise an army and march to enemy territory in Grotius's age. In practice, they claim, it would be foolish for a nation to declare its intention to go to war in a manner that affords the opposing nation the opportunity for a preemptive attack.

This "why should I obey the law or do what I recognize to be morally right when others do not?" objection is not very convincing. As Grotius notes in responding to a similar objection,

> This consideration does enter into deliberations regarding war, I admit, but only on grounds of expediency, not of justice. . . . But that the possibility of being attacked confers the right to attack is abhorrent to every principle of equity. Human life exists under such conditions that complete security is never guaranteed to us.[19]

Moreover, it is not at all clear that a declaration of war provides a significant advantage to the offending nation. Even when we consider strategic bombs or missiles, which are the most instantaneous and decisive means for initiating war, the present state of the world is such that those nations that would be most affected by a preemptive attack (instead of a retaliatory one), maintain a constant vigilance against the same.[20] It is not at all clear that a nation would gain a significant strategic advantage by initiating an attack without warning instead of declaring an intention to attack unless demands are met. Declarations appear strategically nonsensical only if a nation's political goals include the complete subjugation of another nation. One need only recall Saddam Hussein's continued public assurances that he had no hostile intentions toward Kuwait right up to the time of the invasion, or Adolf Hitler's similar prevarications regarding his European neighbors prior to World War II. A thief does not care whether the bank is open or not, and he certainly is not going to announce his intention.

Finally, a public declaration of war conveys to the population of the offending nation a unity of purpose in the population of the declaring nation. It announces to their counterparts that "an injustice has been committed and we are prepared to resort to arms to correct it." This must certainly provide a great incentive to "settle out of court." The fact that it is a public declaration distinguishes it from a kind of political blackmail, which is by its very nature secretive.

A fifth *jus ad bellum* criterion is that only a *legitimate authority* may declare war. Grotius is careful to specify that this does not include "public officials not having sovereign power," but only the duly constituted ruler who speaks with the authority of the populace and who does not have recourse to a higher authority for arbitration.

This condition is more complex than it first appears, especially for democratic governments. In the United States, for example, the Constitution specifies that the authority to declare war rests with the Congress. Nevertheless, ever since 1945, the United States has been involved in full-scale wars in Korea, Vietnam, and the Middle East, as well as significant military actions in Grenada, Lebanon, Libya, and Panama, without a single declaration of war by Congress. The War Powers Resolution, passed in 1973 over President Nixon's veto, was an attempt by Congress to regain the authority for waging war. It stipulates (among other things) that while the president may commit troops to combat without congressional approval (although he must notify and consult with Congress within forty-eight hours), combat must end within sixty days unless Congress extends the deadline. The resolution allows the president the authority as the commander in chief to respond rapidly to fast-changing events while Congress debates the continued use of armed intervention.

Although Presidents Richard Nixon, George Bush, and Bill Clinton all claimed the War Powers Resolution to be an unconstitutional limitation on the president's power as commander in chief, the U.S. Supreme Court has not adjudicated the debate. One need only recall the confusion concerning the commitment of American forces against Iraq in 1990–91 to realize the difficulty this ambiguity poses for the condition of legitimate authority.

Recall that after the United Nations passed a resolution authorizing the use of force, President George Bush announced his intention to mass U.S. combat forces in the Middle East and to use these forces to effect Iraq's withdrawal from Kuwait. While the U.S. Congress became embroiled in a debate on whether U.S. troops should be committed to combat, President Bush made it perfectly clear that while he would welcome congressional support, he did not require it and that he would employ U.S. forces with or without congressional approval. His "threat" became moot on January 12, 1991, when the U.S. Senate voted 52 to 47 in favor of the use of force.

Suppose, however, that just three senators had voted the other way; suppose the vote had been 50 to 49 *against* supporting President Bush's plan?

On other occasions, American presidents have used force without congressional approval, but there has never been a case of a president using force *despite congressional disapproval*. The U.S. Constitution seems clearly to grant only Congress the authority to declare war. Would the military establishment have carried out the orders of the president, who is, as the commander in chief of the armed forces, its superior officer? Or would it have obeyed the congressional mandate and refused to enter Kuwait? The oath of allegiance that all U.S. military officers take upon receiving their commission is "to support and defend the Constitution of the United States against all enemies, foreign and domestic." This differs from the oath of enlisted personnel, who swear to "obey the lawful orders of my officers and those appointed over me." The difference in the wording of the two oaths seems to imply that the officer corps would have a duty to support a congressional mandate in accordance with the Constitution, even if this meant disobeying their commander in chief.[21]

Despite the way that issues internal to the United States might be resolved in such cases, the *jus ad bellum* requirement that only a legitimate authority declare war—one that speaks on behalf of the people of the nation— would be met in principle either way, as far as the international community is concerned.

Finally, Grotius specifies that war must always be a *last resort*, undertaken only when all of the other five conditions have been met and when no other means achieves satisfactory resolution. He proposes that attempts be made to obviate war by conference, by arbitration, by lot, or by single combat. He considers war so heinous an evil that in order to avoid it "an innocent citizen may be delivered into the hands of the enemy, in order to prevent the ruin otherwise threatening the state."[22] He concludes that "a cause for engaging in war which either may not be passed over, or ought not to be, is exceptional."[23]

During the First Gulf War between Iraq and the United Nations, there was much debate over whether the U.N. coalition forces had given economic sanctions and the blockade of Iraqi ports a fair chance to work prior to initiating an outright attack. One argument held that the U.N. coalition had violated the criterion of last resort by using force when it did. This criticism completely misunderstands that the "last resort" condition is meant to restrain nations that are considering initiating hostilities—it is not relevant to nations that have already been attacked! The first purpose of maintaining a standing army is to deter aggression; but another purpose is to be able to respond immediately when deterrence fails. The condition of last resort was met as soon as Iraqi soldiers invaded Kuwait. During the Second Gulf War the issue of last resort was even more controversial and divisive, with Russia, France, and Germany adamantly opposing military action.

The traditional *jus ad bellum* condition that Grotius omits is the Augustinian stipulation that war only be undertaken with *right intention* (sometimes referred to as "right aim"). Grotius argues that while all of his conditions must be subjectively assessed, they are objective in the sense that they apply to relationships between states. Intentions, on the other hand, refer to the internal states of individual agents. Thus they cannot change the justice or injustice of the war itself. In Grotius's words,

> With these words [on intentions] you may rightly associate the passage of Augustine: "The eager desire to injure, the cruelty of vengeance, the unappeased and unappeasable mind, the savagery of rebellion, the lust of ruling, and whatever else there is akin, these are the things which are justly censured in warfare."
>
> However, when a justifiable cause is not wanting, while these things do indeed convict of wrong the party that makes war, yet they do not render the war itself, properly speaking, unlawful. Hence no restitution is due as a result of a war undertaken under such conditions.[24]

We can see that if a war is formally and materially just, the intentions of the ruler(s) cannot invalidate this judgment. Nevertheless, we should keep in mind that the political objective toward which the war aims cannot be the annihilation or subjugation of a people. Even in defeat, political communities do not completely lose their right to territorial integrity or political sovereignty.

Another widely accepted Just War condition not added by Grotius requires that a war, to be just, must be *fought justly*.[25] Earlier I mentioned that the two components of Just War theory, *jus ad bellum* and *jus in bello*, are separate and distinct. I believe this interpretation is appropriate for two reasons. First, *jus ad bellum* concerns relationships between states; just and unjust conduct on the battlefield concerns the actions of individuals. As Grotius notes, war describes a condition that can exist between nations (or other political collectives); it is not a description of action.

Second, soldiers can never be responsible for the crime *of* war, *qua* soldiers. Resort to war is always a political decision, not a military one. As Grotius observes,

> It does not fall within the province of the general to conduct negotiations with regard to the causes or the consequences of a war; . . . Even though the general has been placed in command with absolute power, that must be understood to apply only to the conduct of the war.[26]

Michael Walzer captures this distinction nicely when he notes that it does not matter whether soldiers fight because of a legal obligation (conscription) or a patriotic duty; theirs is never the crime of aggression because they always believe that their cause is just.[27] In Francisco Vitoria's language, soldiers are always infected with "invincible ignorance"—and who could wish it otherwise? Standing armies are recruited, trained, and maintained to defend the community in times of danger. And although defending one's community or family may be the right of every citizen in primitive society, in civilized society that right has been taken away from the population at large and isolated in the office of soldier. It is, therefore, a duty for the soldiers to defend those constituents who have entered a pact with them to this end. It would be a traitorous abrogation of public trust to swear an oath of preparedness to perform certain duties on demand in return for "meals and support by the state," and then, after accepting the benefits of the agreement, to refuse to fulfill the duties stipulated when called upon to do so. No citizen logically could wish it so. (We will return to this topic in greater detail in a later chapter.)

Political leaders, on the other hand, are responsible for engaging in political intercourse with other nations on behalf of their respective citizens. The most extreme form this intercourse can take is the resort to arms. Of course, the earlier discussed requirement that the political objective of the war be proportional to the cause for which the war is fought remains applicable. If the political objective of such violent intercourse is not proportional to the wrong received a war might be fought unjustly. In this case, the *jus ad bellum* condition that would be violated is proportionality.

That political leaders can create circumstances that lead to unjust fighting does not, however, imply that soldiers *qua* soldiers have no responsibility under the Just War Tradition. They bear heavy responsibilities, though not of a *jus ad bellum* nature. The responsibility for the conduct of the war is, as Grotius notes, always a military one. In fact, all soldiers are always morally and legally responsible for their actions on the battlefield, regardless of whether the actions are based on superior orders.[28] In other words, soldiers must disobey unlawful orders regarding the conduct of war, even if they are given by an elected official. A good example of this in practice is Field Marshal Erwin Rommel's decision to burn Hitler's written order that all Allied soldiers found behind German lines be killed.[29] (We will return to the issue of superior orders in considerable detail in chapter 9.)

The conceptual difference between political leaders and soldiers seems clear enough, even if, at certain high levels (e.g., the commander in chief of the United States or the secretary of defense) one person may bear both political and military responsibilities. Likewise, U.S. military personnel are considered "citizen–soldiers" because although they do give up some of the rights of private citizens (such as the right to hold public office or be "politically active") they are allowed to vote. Still we have no trouble distinguishing between the two roles, even when a single individual fills both of them. Because political leaders are responsible for the crime *of* war (*jus ad bellum*) and military persons are responsible for crimes *in* war (*jus in bello*), it does not seem useful to make actions in war a condition for determining the justification of the war itself.

Certainly we can imagine a nation's soldiers fighting an unjust war they believe to be just; and we can imagine them conducting themselves either justly or unjustly in such a war. Moreover, we can imagine a Just War in which some soldiers fight in accordance with the *jus in bello* rules and others do not. That some soldiers violate the rules of war does not invalidate the justification for the resort to arms in the first place, anymore than an elected official's misuse of his or her office would invalidate the democratic processes whereby the official was elected. For example, a finding that the Allied bombing of Germany during World War II violated the laws of war because it resulted in the intentional and unnecessary deaths of innocent civilians would not by itself negate Great Britain's and France's right to defend themselves against German aggression.

The two moral truths between which this *bellum justum* dualism attempts to adjudicate are (1) the prohibition against intentionally harming innocents, and (2) the positive duty to protect oneself and other innocents from harm. In response to the argument that the attempt to protect innocents through war always directly results in the death of other innocents and, hence, is immoral, Grotius responds that in cases where all alternatives violate either the same natural law, or natural laws of equal import, one must choose the alternative that minimizes the amount of evil that will occur. In such cases, as he puts it, "the lesser evil assumes the character of the good."

It is especially important to keep in mind that Grotius saw *The Law of War and Peace* as a handbook for individual rulers to use in conducting their international affairs. In that sense, his work constitutes a proposed system of national laws prescribing the conduct of international relations.

The United Nations Charter limits its references on war to *jus ad bellum*. Article 2 of the Charter states that "(3) All Members shall settle their disputes by peaceful means in such a manner that international peace, security, and justice are not endangered. (4) All members shall refrain in their international relations from the threat or use of force against the territorial integrity or political independence of any state."[30] Article 51 states that nothing "shall impair the inherent right of self-defense if an armed attack occurs against a Member of the United Nations."[31] Articles 33 through 40 all deal with means for settling disputes, short of the resort to arms. Taken together, these articles reflect those aspects of the Just War Tradition that should appropriately be articulated in international law—namely, just cause and last resort.

Grotius makes it clear that wars must be carried on "with not less scrupulousness than judicial processes are wont to be."[32] He insists that even in war, when normal municipal laws are set aside, certain other laws "which are of perpetual validity and suited to all times" must be obeyed.[33] These laws constitute his theory of *jus in bello*.

Grotius is careful to point out that questions of *jus ad bellum* are not relevant to *jus in bello* proscriptions or, put another way, one may not set aside the rules of war on behalf of a just cause.[34] Let us turn now to Grotius's concept of who may rightfully be attacked in war and how one may attack them.

JUS IN BELLO

Grotius's theory of *jus in bello* advocates restrictions on the lawful conduct of war in terms of the traditional topics: (1) who can be lawfully attacked; (2) what means can be used to attack them; and (3) the treatment of prisoners. Because of the extensive political and technological differences between Grotius's day and our own, it is more useful to focus on the principles that are manifested in his constraints on war, rather than the rules themselves. For example, Grotius's discussion of accepting prisoners of war as slaves rather than killing them is not relevant because the institution of slavery is defunct. But his reasons behind the prohibition against harming prisoners still apply. In fact, I believe that we may subsume all of Grotius's rules under a single principle (although Grotius does not himself attempt to do this): namely, the prohibition against intentionally harming other human beings is set aside in warfare only to the extent that combatants of opposing belligerent nations may rightfully attack one another. We will return to this momentarily.

As one commentator notes, the recognition of the innocent as a special class with certain rights comes to fruition in Grotius's *The Law of War and Peace*.[35] Grotius's argument is that war is a condition between states and that it is only "by a sort of fiction [that] the enemy may be conceived as forming a single body." He adds that "nature does not sanction retaliation except against those who have done wrong."[36] Concerning those who must be granted immunity from attack, Grotius writes,

> One must take care, so far as is possible, to prevent the death of innocent persons, even by accident . . . except for reasons that are weighty and will affect the safety of many, no action should be attempted whereby innocent persons may be threatened with destruction.[37]

Grotius includes in the class of innocents, women, children, old men, merchants, farmers, prisoners of war, and holders of religious office.[38] Women, he adds, have immunity *unless they are employed as soldiers.* He even notes that in a siege, a corridor must be left open for those who wish to escape. Still, Grotius acknowledges that some harm may befall innocents, and he adopts Vitoria's adaptation of Aquinas's double effect with "precautions." On the one hand, he recognizes that certain actions may "follow indirectly and beyond the purpose of the doer"; for example, "We may bombard a ship full of pirates, or a house full of brigands, even if there are within the same ship or house a few infants, women, or other innocent persons who are thereby endangered." On the other hand, he immediately adds,

> What accords with a strict interpretation of right is not always, or in all respects, permitted. . . . Wherefore we must also beware of what happens, and what we foresee may happen, beyond our purpose, unless the good which our action has in view is much greater than the evil which is feared, or, unless the good and the evil balance, the hope of the good is much greater than the fear of the evil. The decision in such matter must be left to a prudent judgment, but in such a way that when in doubt we should favor that course . . . which has regard for the interest of another rather than our own.[39]

Some find this consequentialist justification for overriding the sanctity of innocents troubling. In another context (reprisals), Grotius stipulates that actions must not result in either intentional *or foreseeable* deaths of innocents. Probably the best resolution of this tension between granting absolute protection for innocents and completely subordinating their safety to military objectives has been suggested by Michael Walzer.

In its military operations, the United States seems to have adopted a modification to the doctrine of double effect so that one may undertake military operations aimed at legitimate objectives or targets, even though the operations will also have foreseeable "bad" consequences. Such operations become permissible when they meet the following necessary criteria: (1) The bad effect is unintended; (2) The bad effect is proportional to the desired military objective; (3) The bad effect is not a direct means to the good effect (e.g., bomb cities to encourage peace talks); and (4) Actions are taken to minimize the foreseeable bad effects, *even if it means accepting an increased risk to combatants.*[40]

In other words, the condition of proportionality in this case refers to the acceptable upper limit of the possible bad effect; it does not absolve the agent of the duty to *minimize* the undesirable effect. This strikes me as a practical resolution that consistently recommends intuitively sound choices. It certainly prohibits direct attacks on a civilian population as a means of destroying a nation's will to fight and still recognizes that some civilians may inadvertently be harmed.

During the Vietnam War, for example, the United States adopted a policy of spreading defoliant (notably Agent Orange) on areas suspected to be enemy strongholds in order to destroy tropical vegetation and make enemy forces vulnerable to U.S. air attacks. Defoliation resulted in extensive long-term contamination of large areas of the Vietnamese countryside, contamination of water supplies, and destruction of indigenous wildlife. Setting aside the fact (presumably unknown to military planners at the time) that exposure to Agent Orange results in an increased risk of cancer, we must question whether the use of defoliants was permissible as a means of depriving enemy troops of cover and concealment based on the principle of double effect.

Even if one argues that the harm to the Vietnamese people caused by the United State's use of defoliants was unintended and not a direct means to the "good effect" of destroying the enemy's cover and concealment, the claim that the good effect was proportional to the foreseeable bad effect of long-term contamination is simply not plausible—especially given that the stated political purpose of the war was to protect the people of South Vietnam. Certainly there were other actions (burning, for example) that could have been taken to deprive the enemy of the terrain in question without the long-term threat to civilians. We can conclude that the principle of double effect does not permit the use of defoliants on land inhabited by civilian populations. Let us look at a second example.

In February 1991, U.S. Air Force bombers dropped a pair of 2,000-pound bombs on a bunker in Baghdad believed to be a military command center. The bombs resulted in the deaths of more than 300 innocent women and children who were using the bunker as an air raid shelter. Does the principle of double effect permit attacking military targets in a major city given the near certainty that civilians will sometimes be killed by mistake? In this case, it is reasonably certain that the civilian deaths were unintended and not a direct means to the desired effect of destroying Iraqi command and control centers. The question of proportionality is less clear, but given the numerous attacks against military targets and the low number of incidents of this sort, it seems reasonable to accept that the condition of proportionality was met.

Did American forces take actions to minimize the number of civilian deaths, even accepting risk to their own soldiers to do so, as required by Walzer's revision to double effect? I believe that in this case they did. The attack was made using laser-guided bombs, which are especially accurate in engaging desired targets, but the use of which places pilots at somewhat greater risk than does "fire and forget" ordinance. The problem in this instance was not that the pilots accidentally missed their target, but that they wrongly believed the target to be a command center rather than a civilian bunker. The military planners and pilots, it seems to me, took adequate care to prevent civilian casualties, even though military planners could foresee that some casualties would be inevitable if the United States continued to prosecute the war in areas populated with civilians. The revised principle of double effect permitted certain military actions, even though they resulted in the deaths of civilians.

In addition to identifying command and control centers as targets, American planners also planned to destroy much of the support infrastructure of Baghdad: namely, sewage treatment plants, water purification facilities, and electrical power generators. The destruction of these facilities affected the civilian population and its health, safety, and living standards as much, and perhaps even more, than it affected the military.[41] In this case, it seems at least questionable whether the destruction of targets of these types is permitted under the condition of double effect. None of these targets seems to meet the condition of proportionality. And attacking these types of targets certainly does not seem to meet Walzer's revision that requires planners to recognize the foreseeable bad effects and to take actions to minimize them. Surely it could have been foreseen that destruction of water and sewage treatment facilities would result in widespread illness and disease among the civilian population, long after the war had ended. In the Second Gulf War, twelve years later, the United States-led coalition was able to use extremely accurate laser and grid positioning guided bombs and missiles to attack specific military targets and limit collateral damage to a minimum.

And finally, many of those people who attempt to justify the American bombing of Hiroshima and Nagasaki during World War II take the position that fewer American lives were lost because of the bombing than would have been lost had the United States invaded.[42] Under Walzer's formulation, the most crucial statistic would be which of the many options would result in the greatest loss of *innocent lives*. Soldiers are, after all, in the business of risking their lives. It is not reasonable to argue that one must put innocents at risk for the sake of not endangering combatants when the office of the soldier is brought into existence solely for the purpose of protecting others from risk.

But even Walzer's revision to double effect does not entirely reduce the risk to innocents. As Grotius says, decisions about the extent of risk must be left to a "prudent judgment." A good rule of thumb might be that enemy civilians (innocents) should be subjected intentionally to no greater risk than that to which one is willing to subject one's own innocent population. We will return to this and other issues concerning the rules of war in much greater detail in Section III.

The last class of innocents Grotius identifies is prisoners of war. He stipulates that all who wish to surrender must be allowed to do so, and that all prisoners, regardless of whether they surrender willingly or are captured, may neither be killed nor severely punished. Only those who are personally guilty of crimes may be punished, and an "obstinate devotion to one's party" does not deserve punishment.[43] In fact, he specifies that prisoners must be released if the captor is unable to protect or guard them adequately.

It is obvious from the foregoing discussion that practices such as firing "assurance shots" at downed enemy soldiers during the assault phase of ambushes, or killing those who might jeopardize the security of long-range patrols, violate the laws of war.[44]

Perhaps we are now ready to see how each of these *jus in bello* rules might be subsumed under the principle cited earlier: *The moral prohibition against killing other human beings is overridden when they are engaged in the war effort as combatants.*

Combatants may be intentionally attacked; noncombatants may not. This principle serves as a moral bridge between the prohibition against intentionally harming innocent persons on the one hand, and the natural right each person has to defend one's self and one's community on the other hand. Because the prohibition against intentionally harming innocents is the more fundamental of the two, the natural right of self-defense is limited (only) by this principle.[45] This limitation has some interesting and significant consequences for the laws of war.

When a nation's soldiers act on behalf of their nation in carrying out policies requiring the use of force, they may be defended against. Upon capture or surrender, however, a soldier's status as a combatant is terminated, and he (or she) reverts to his (or her) former category as an innocent. Hence, prisoners of war acquire the same right to protection from harm that is afforded other innocents (the commonly used term is *benevolent quarantine*). Nevertheless, soldiers are always responsible for any crimes that they may have committed as combatants, as well as any that they might commit as noncombatants. For example, should a civilian or a prisoner kill a soldier from a belligerent nation without specific provocation, this would constitute an act of murder. Even a prisoner who kills a guard during an escape attempt is guilty of murder, because the individual's status as a combatant is terminated upon surrender or capture.[46] Thus both the authority to kill and the vulnerability to being killed are afforded to combatants only.[47]

This change in status from combatant to noncombatant can occur either because of surrender or capture, as we have seen, or because of injury. Thus when a soldier becomes incapacitated owing to injury to the extent that he or she is no longer able to participate in the war effort, his or her status as a combatant is terminated. It does not matter whether the individual surrenders, surrenders as part of a larger force, is captured against one's will, or is wounded; in each case, the soldier not only ceases to be a proper object of attack but also the soldier's care becomes the responsibility of the opposing force.

Weapons that cannot be employed in ways that discriminate between combatants and innocents are prohibited, as are those weapons that continue to cause damage after the termination of a person's status as a legitimate target, hence the oft-repeated prohibition against indiscriminate use of weapons or weapons that cause *unnecessary pain and suffering.*

Unnecessary pain and suffering continues to incapacitate or to prevent recovery after one's status as a combatant ends. For example, the prohibition against using spears with barbed tips is based on the realization that once a combatant has received an incapacitating spear thrust, that person has been rendered ineffective in the role that permitted his or her killing or being killed. While a barbed spear tip would not have any measurable effect on this, it could aggravate the injury so as to increase suffering and adversely affect recovery—and these are results that occur after the status of combatant has been terminated. This concern also explains the legal requirement that enemy wounded be given medical treatment.

The same reasoning applies to poison weapons or those contaminated with fecal matter for the purpose of causing infection. Hence, all weapons of this type are prohibited by the current laws of war. A more recent example is the prohibition against the use of ammunition containing nondetectable fragments (such as glass). The 1980 Protocol on Non-Detectable Fragments states "It is prohibited to use any weapon the primary effect of which is to injure by fragments which in the human body escape detection by X-rays."

Even military persons often misunderstand the term *unnecessary suffering.* Soldiers commonly believe that weapons such as the .50-caliber machine gun or Vulcan anti-aircraft gun cannot be used against personnel because they cause "unnecessary suffering." And in a recent textbook on Just War theory, the author confuses unnecessary suffering with proportionality.

> How does the rule against unnecessary suffering apply to nuclear or atomic weapons? If lances with barbed heads, irregularly shaped bullets, and projectiles filled with glass are forbidden, it's hard to imagine that nuclear weapons are not. They certainly cause more unnecessary suffering than projectiles filled with glass! Both the U.S. and British Manuals are coy about the matter.[48]

It is crucial to understand that the term *unnecessary suffering* refers not to the amount of destruction a weapon causes but to injuries it causes to victims after they cease to be combatants.

Indiscriminate weapons are objectionable because they cannot be employed in ways that separate innocents from combatants, hence Grotius's prohibition on poisoning drinking water "in order that the dangers of war might not be too widely extended."[49] Today for the same reason we prohibit biological weapons or the placing of mines in populated areas. Nuclear weapons, however, have always raised doubts about our ability to use them with adequate discrimination.

In his discussion, Grotius follows the principles that one must attempt to discriminate between combatants and noncombatants and that weapons that can be used in indiscriminate ways are prohibited. As a rule of thumb for what constitutes sufficient discrimination, we might use Walzer's modification of double effect with an additional stipulation: Namely, a nation's armed forces must not intentionally place the innocents among the enemy population in any greater jeopardy than that in which the same nation could reasonably place its own innocent citizens in pursuit of a political or military objective.

Now we must move from a list of examples of combatants and non-combatants to a conceptual theory that can sort other categories of persons into these two classes. From what we have discussed already, we can distinguish among soldiers, prisoners, and civilians. But how do we count civilians who are not entirely "innocent" because they contribute to the war effort through their civilian occupation? Grotius addresses this issue in a discussion of the status of third-party nations that are not directly engaged in the fighting but are indirectly involved through their trade with one of the belligerents. To determine their status, he distinguishes among three kinds of products: "Some things, such as weapons, which are useful in war; other things which are of no use in war; . . . and others which are of use both in time of war and at other times."[50] This classification of nations according to the products they supply to other nations at war forms the basis for modern identification of who among the civilian population can be regarded as combatants, even though they are not members of the armed forces. In practice, we consider only those civilians associated with the first class of goods as combatants; that is, civilians who produce goods used by soldiers in their role as soldiers (e.g., weapons, bombs, military uniforms) are combatants; civilians who produce goods used by soldiers but not *qua* soldiers (e.g., food, fuel, metals, and other products used by all human beings) are noncombatants and therefore immune from attack.

Grotius emphasizes that the distinction between combatants and innocents applies to all people, regardless of their moral or religious virtue, or their intelligence.

Some critics might object to the contention that combatants should show the same degree of care for innocents among the enemy population as they should extend to members of their own civilian population. The objection draws strength from the *jus ad bellum* condition that war be *publicly declared*. This condition, if met, might be interpreted to imply that all moral agents among the enemy population share some responsibility for the war. Why then should they not also share in the suffering that results from it?

This argument brings us back to the distinction that so troubled Vitoria between the objective justice of an act and the culpability of the agent who performs the act. The citizens of both sides are often convinced that their nation is fighting for a just cause—they are possessed of "invincible igno-rance," as far as the objective justice of the war is concerned. One need only recall the falsehoods that were perpetrated on the people of Iraq and other Middle East nations during the recent U.N.–Iraq War. The citizens of Iraq did not share in the moral culpability of the war because they never gave their informed consent to it. In such cases, the solution must be reason rather than punishment, because punishment will not change the content of one's beliefs.

Moreover, even if it is true that some of the citizens are culpable for the crime of war, certainly not all of them are; and attacks against civilians will always be indiscriminate, because there is no way to ferret out the guilty and spare the innocent.

Conclusion

Grotius's contributions to international law guiding the conduct of war are many. He argues for at least some restrictions on the autonomy of states and the authority of monarchs. He binds kings by the same moral considerations as private citizens. He ensures that political actions (specifically war) cannot be justified simply by "reason of state." He frees morality from the stifling grip of ecclesiastical judicature by insisting on natural laws that are binding on all people at all times and that "cannot be changed even by God."[51] He argues convincingly that although "reason condemns force which disrupts the har-mony of society and violates the just order, force is allowed in order to pro-tect rights and maintain order."[52] He attempts to make the conditions that justify a resort to arms so strict as to all but eliminate wars except in some cases of self-defense, and he develops the first systematic set of rules for the protection of innocents and prisoners. The principle underlying his rules of *jus in bello* (i.e., the prohibition against harming innocent persons can intention-ally be overridden only insofar as they are employed as combatants of a bel-ligerent nation) still applies to modern concepts of *jus in bello* and is manifested in existing international law.

Modern readers are not familiar with Grotius's arguments concerning the international laws of war. This ignorance in the military and political commu-nities is unfortunate. Readers will not find traditional natural law values such as life, procreation, and knowledge in Grotius's work. Instead, he defends moral rules that one could justify in Kantian or rule utilitarian terms—rules such as people have a *prima facie* duty to not harm innocents, soldiers have a duty to protect innocents from harm, and rulers must keep pacts with their constituents and other nations.

We will next turn to the topic of international law and examine why some claim that it is no more than a code of "positive morality."

Topics for Further Discussion

1. Grotius does not limit just causes for war to instances of self-defense, and he specifically includes humanitarian intervention (defense of others) as an example of a just cause. Should the United States use its military might in the international community in a constabulary role for humanitarian purposes? Should, for example, the United States intervene in the internal affairs of another nation to protect a segment of that nation's population from genocide?

2. Grotius argues that although his *jus ad bellum* criteria provide a sufficient condition for the resort to force, they do not make the use of force obligatory. Are there any conditions that would make the use of force obligatory?

3. "Advantage does not confer the same rights as necessity," Grotius warns. Develop a set of guidelines that one might use to distinguish "advantage" from "necessity."

4. In the United States, federal law severely limits involvement of military officers in political affairs. What might be the reasons for this restriction? Do you agree with it?

5. According to Grotius, the political objective for which wars are fought must be proportional to the costs associated with fighting. He goes on to add that these costs should consider not only those directly involved in the fighting, but the effect war will have on all of humankind. Provide one argument supporting the condition of proportionality, as Grotius has framed it, and one argument criticizing it. Hint: To what extent should national leaders look out for the interests of citizens of other nations?

6. Grotius argues that for a war to be just there must be a reasonable chance of success. St. Augustine discusses a nation (the Sanguntines) that chooses to fight to oblivion rather than break faith with the Roman Republic, and he implies in this discussion that honor is more important than safety (*The City of God*, Bk. XXII, chap. 6). Are there cases where a nation might reasonably choose futile resistance rather than the ignominy of capitulation? Are political decisions on behalf of others different from personal decisions in this regard?

7. In March 2003, after much debate in the United States and the United Nations, a coalition led by the United States and Great Britain invaded Iraq to force a regime change and ensure that Iraq complied with U.N. mandates. In retrospect, it seems that General Norman Schwartzkopf's statement advocating further military actions in 1991 was exactly correct (as, perhaps, was General MacArthur's forty years earlier). Explain why you believe that very senior military leaders ought (or ought not) to be more involved in strategic-level political decisions like the ones mentioned above.

8. Military officers are legally and morally obligated to carry out the political will of the nation they are sworn to defend. Does this mean they should fight wars they believe to be unjust? Is there a difference between fighting wars they believe to be unjust (a *jus ad bellum* consideration) and obeying orders they believe to be unlawful (a *jus in bello* consideration)?

9. Why is a prisoner of war who kills a guard in an escape attempt guilty of murder? Are soldiers who kill prison guards in an attack on a prison for the purpose of freeing captured comrades also guilty of wrongdoing?

Notes

1. Hugo Grotius, *The Law of War and Peace*, Dedication, (Indianapolis and New York: Bobbs-Merrill Co., 1962), pp. 4–5.
2. Ibid., *Prolegomena* 29, p. 20.
3. The issue of whether the term *rights* is the best way to speak of moral prescriptions and prohibitions is the topic of much recent debate. We can, I believe, avoid this issue by simply accepting this as an expedient way to organize and refer to certain moral rules that are themselves much less controversial. Thus we can accept a principle such as "one should not intentionally harm innocent persons" as a moral truth without using the term *rights*, even though a rights theorist would argue that such a prohibition is based on some individual right. As long as we recognize that we *need not* use the convention of "rights talk" it does not seem reasonable to avoid it in those cases where it is useful.
4. Just causes are discussed in *The Law of War and Peace*, Bk. II, chap. 1, XVI, p. 184; humanitarian intervention as a cause for war is found in Bk. II, chap. 25, VII, 2, p. 584. See also Bk. II, chap. 20, IX, I, p. 475, where Grotius discusses wars of punishment waged for "the good of mankind in general."
5. Ibid., Bk. II, chap. 20, V, p. 468. This good end may be for "either the good of the person who does the wrong, or of the persons against whose interest the wrong was committed, or of other persons in general."
6. Ibid., chap. 22, V, 1, p. 549.
7. Ibid., chap. 1, XVII, p. 184.
8. Ibid., chap. 22, VI, p. 549.
9. Ibid., chap. 23, VI, p. 560. Grotius notes that refraining from war may, on occasion, be a mistake, but engaging in war unjustly is always a crime.
10. Ibid., chap. 24, VII, p. 575.
11. Ibid., *Prolegomena*, 24, p. 18.
12. Ibid., chap. 23, II, 2, p. 558. He adds, however, that, "This course cannot be pursued where one really must do one of two things, and yet it is in doubt whether either of them is right. In that case he will be allowed to choose that which appears to him to be less wrong. . . . In a comparison of evils, the lesser evil takes the place of the good."
13. Earlier in the war, U.S. Air Force Chief of Staff General Michael J. Dugan was fired for suggesting that Iraq's president, Saddam Hussein, was himself a legitimate target of Allied air power.
14. *The Law of War and Peace*, Bk. III, chap. 11, VIII, p. 734.
15. Ibid., Bk. II, VI, pp. 573–74.
16. In another context, this principle also has important implications for tactical units. The U.S. Armed Forces Code of Conduct states, "I will never surrender of my own free will,

and I will never surrender my soldiers while they still have the means to resist." This is problematic because it seems obvious that military leaders may often have an obligation to surrender their units when the costs of continued resistance become disproportional to the tactical objectives, but this is an alternative that the Code of Conduct seems not to acknowledge. It seems obvious to me that leaders may, at times, have a moral obligation to surrender. Even if one argues that suicidal actions are a permissible alternative, they must always be an individual choice. Surely it is not plausible to hold that leaders can legitimately *order* suicidal actions.

17. Grotius divides declarations of war into conditional and absolute. The latter is for those instances where demands are not relevant, for example, when a nation must defend itself from an ongoing attack by another. In either case, the war must still be declared because it is a public act. See *The Law of War and Peace*, Bk. III, chap. 3, VII, XI, pp. 635–36, 639.

18. Ibid. Naturally, governments that routinely do not inform their constituents of public policy will fail to meet this condition.

19. Ibid., Bk. II, chap. 1, XVII, p. 184.

20. The nations whose combat power is potentially the most vulnerable to a surprise attack are those nations that depend heavily on nuclear weapons. The early warning mechanisms of the world powers, coupled with the Triad organization of nuclear forces (missile, submarine, and airplane), render a decisive surprise attack practically impossible. This was the logical basis for the incredible (now abandoned) doctrine called mutually assured destruction (MAD). If a population adopts the MAD doctrine in advance of attack, then the condition that war must be a public act is met in principle. (The larger issue of political decision making and minority rights in national policy decisions such as MAD, while relevant, are beyond the scope of this analysis.) Finally, although I have focused my discussion on nuclear war, these considerations apply to conventional war as well. Nations that are on adversarial terms maintain constant vigilance so that a successful surprise attack is equally unlikely.

21. The Senate's vote was merely a vote of support for the president and did not directly confront the issue of presidential versus congressional authority. As of this writing, the issue remains unresolved.

22. *The Law of War and Peace*, chap. 25, III, p. 579; see also chap. 23, VII–X, pp. 560–64.

23. Ibid., chap. 24, VII, p. 575.

24. Ibid., chap. 22, XVII, 2, p. 556.

25. Actually, there is a passage in Grotius that can be interpreted as presenting this as a necessary condition: "In order that wars may be justified, they must be carried on with not less scrupulousness than judicial processes are wont to be." *Prolegomena* 25, p. 18. The context of this passage indicates that it should be interpreted as a demand for recognition of the principles of *jus in bello* rather than as an additional condition for *jus ad bellum*. For a defense of just conduct in war as a *jus ad bellum* requirement, see William V. O'Brien, *The Conduct of Just and Limited War* (New York: Praeger Publishers, 1981), p. 35.

26. *The Law of War and Peace*, Bk. III, chap. 22, VII, p. 848. Recall that Plato advocated that such actions by military officers be punishable by death.

27. Michael Walzer, *Just and Unjust Wars: A Moral Argument with Historical Illustrations* (New York: Basic Books, 1977), pp. 28ff.

28. Of course, this argument does not apply to citizens who are subject to conscription, because as citizens they do have a political or *jus ad bellum* responsibility. One might argue that citizen–soldiers also have political responsibilities, but, in fact, these are limited by law (at least in this country). The underlying principle is that the use of military force is a means of political intercourse between states, and that only elected (i.e., legitimate) officials can make political decisions, hence the civilian control of the military in the United States.

29. A "bad" example is the illegal bombing mission carried out by the U.S. Air Force during the Vietnam War under the orders of Air Force General Lavelle. Some consider the use of atomic bombs on Japan also a violation of *jus in bello*.

30. *Charter of the United Nations: Commentary and Documents*, edited by Leland M. Goodrich and Edward Hambro (Boston: World Peace Foundation, 1949), pp. 101–02.

31. Ibid., p. 297. Much ink has darkened the debate between "wide" and "narrow" interpretations of these two articles. Under the wide interpretation, Art. 51 provides one example of permissible force; under the narrow interpretation, it provides the only example. For a cogent discussion of the arguments on both sides, see Yehuda Melzer, *Concepts of Just War* (Leyden: A.W. Sijthoff, 1975), pp. 17–56. For an eloquent summary, see Sheldon M. Cohen, *Arms and Judgment: Law, Morality, and the Conduct of War in the Twentieth Century* (Boulder, Colo.: Westview Press, 1989), pp. 63–71.

32. *The Law of War and Peace, Prolegomena*, 25, p. 18.

33. Ibid., p. 19.

34. Ibid., Bk. III, chap. 4, III, IV, pp. 643–44.

35. Richard Shelly Hartigan, *The Forgotten Victim: A History of the Civilian* (Chicago: Precedent Publishing, 1982), chap. VII, "The Emergence of the Civilian," pp. 93–102.

36. *The Law of War and Peace*, Bk. III, chap. 11, XVI, 2, p. 741.

37. Ibid., Bk. III, chap. 11, VIII, pp. 733–34.

38. Ibid., Bk. IX–XII, pp. 734–39. I use the terms *innocent* and *noncombatant* interchangeably, even though the innocent–guilty distinction is sometimes used to refer to one's status as determined by behavior, while the combatant–noncombatant one refers to status as determined by the role one fills. Grotius does not recognize a distinction.

39. Ibid., chap. 1, IV, p. 601.

40. Walzer, *Just and Unjust Wars*, pp. 153–55. I have used Walzer's revision of double effect in my formulation but have modified the wording of the other three traditional conditions somewhat.

41. There is a long-standing Just War prohibition against poisoning wells and water supplies, and such actions are expressly prohibited by the Hague Convention IV (Annex), Article 23, paragraph (a). If they did occur, the U.N. attacks against water treatment facilities in Baghdad seem to me to have violated both the Just War Tradition and international law. The U.S. military establishment claims that not only were no such targets attacked, none were destroyed. Iraq claims that these targets were intentionally attacked and destroyed. Clearly, in the Second Gulf War, coalition forces were successful in their efforts to avoid damaging infrastructure facilities that would impact on the quality of life of Iraqi citizens.

42. I doubt that this example from World War II represents a legitimate case of using the principle of double effect, even though the U.S. military did claim that these two cities were military/industrial targets at the time of the bombing. I include it because it points out an interesting aspect of Walzer's revision to double effect. The issue of whether the United States was justified in demanding unconditional surrender is outside of this discussion. The disjunctive of "either bomb or invade" only makes sense if one assumes that unconditional surrender is the only acceptable outcome—a contention that is, of course, always morally and pragmatically questionable.

43. *The Law of War and Peace*, XIV–XVI, pp. 739–42.

44. "Double tap" is the military expression for shooting all enemy soldiers, regardless of their condition, a second time to ensure that they are dead. Many U.S. military units routinely train soldiers to "double tap" all enemy during the assault phase of ambushes.

45. The *jus in bello* principle that the means used in fighting a war be proportional to the military objective sought is not operative here because there is no limit to the numbers of enemy I can kill in self-defense. If I am attacked by 10,000 enemy soldiers bent on my death, I am morally and legally justified in killing all of them to protect myself.

46. These examples—mine, not those of Grotius—are, I believe, deducible from his discussions of *jus in bello*.

47. This mirrors the principle behind the Roman law that stipulates that a soldier is permitted to fight only for the specific campaign for which he has received authorization from the state; and that soldiers who fight in additional campaigns without taking the proper oath are guilty of murder. See Cicero, *De Officiis*, Bk. I, XI, translated by Walter Miller (Cambridge, Mass.: Harvard University Press, 1961), p. 35.

48. Sidney Axinn, *A Moral Military* (Philadelphia: Temple University Press, 1989), pp. 77–78.

49. *The Law of War and Peace*, chap. 4, XVI, pp. 652–53.

50. Ibid., Bk. III, chap. 1, IV, 2, p. 602.

51. Ibid., Bk. I, chap. 1, X, p. 40.

52. Ibid., Bk. I, chap. 2, I, p. 33.

Chapter

7

PROBLEMS FOR INTERNATIONAL LAW

The Just War Tradition that Grotius researched and articulated so carefully in his great *corpus juris* on international law began to be formally declared as positive law in the nineteenth century. In 1862, President Lincoln directed that a code of rules be developed for the conduct of the Civil War. As a result, General Orders 100, known after its principal author as Lieber's Code, was adopted in 1863 and became the first instance since Ancient Rome of a nation adopting a formal code of law to regulate its army's conduct toward enemy soldiers. Lieber's Code also specified rules for the protection of innocents, as well as for the treatment of prisoners.

Around the same time, Henry Dunant and a group of Genevese citizens founded the International Committee of the Red Cross; and in 1864, in Geneva, Switzerland, an international conference adopted the "Convention for the Amelioration of the Condition of the Wounded Armies in the Field." Subsequent conventions held in Geneva in 1929 and 1949 addressed the treatment of prisoners, the protection of civilians, the treatment of the sick and wounded, and the status of medical persons and facilities.

In 1868, representatives of various nations met in St. Petersburg, Russia, and adopted a declaration against the use of explosive bullets. The reasoning behind this declaration is significant because it finds its way into later international documents regulating the conduct of war under the principle that prohibits "unnecessary suffering."

> The only legitimate object which states should endeavor to accomplish during war is to weaken the military force of the enemy; for this purpose, it is sufficient to disable the greatest number of men; this object would be exceeded by the employment of arms which uselessly aggravate the suffering of disabled men, or render their death inevitable; the employment of such arms would, therefore, be contrary to the laws of humanity.[1]

This was important because, unlike Lieber's Code, which was an internal document, this was an international agreement regulating the conduct of war and clearly acknowledging the principle that unnecessary harm is contrary to the "laws of humanity." Both of these documents were incorporated into the international peace conferences held at The Hague in 1899 and 1907.[2]

These agreements, to which almost every nation of the civilized world is a signatory, comprise much—but not all—of what is considered international law for the conduct of warfare. In addition to some more recent but less comprehensive agreements (which we will discuss in conjunction with relevant topics in later chapters), customary law still plays a significant role in *bellum legale,* as the Preamble to the Fourth Hague Convention of 1907 states.

> Until a more complete code of the laws of war has been issued, the High Contracting Parties deem it expedient to declare that, in cases not included in the Regulations adopted by them, the inhabitants and the belligerents remain under the protection and the rule of the principles of the law of nations, as they result from the usages established among civilized peoples, from the laws of humanity, and the dictates of public conscience.[3]

This principle is reinforced in the Geneva Convention of 1949, which does more than simply echo the 1907 agreement; it also adds that the denunciation of or withdrawal from this convention

> shall in no way impair the obligations which the Parties to the conflict shall remain bound to fulfill by virtue of the principles of the law of nations, as they result from the usages established among civilized peoples, from the laws of humanity and the dictates of the public conscience.[4]

Thus, international law has some of the characteristics of English common law in that it is grounded in custom and precedence as well as in formal rules, much the way Grotius had argued.

Given this comprehensive tradition of *bellum justum* dating back for nearly two millennia, and this impressive tradition of *bellum legale* recognized at an international level for over a century, we must inquire into the reasons why humankind's attempts to control both the initiation and the conduct of war have met with only limited success. Can it be, as Donald Wells argues, that "We have limited commitment to the laws of war precisely because of the military unwillingness to accept restrictions"?[5] Or is it some more fundamental problem with the very notion of regulating the conduct of sovereign nations, as Paul Schillp argues?

> The relations among nations with each other today can, in truth, only be characterized as anarchical. . . . This is merely another way of saying that the relations of nations with each other are *not* subject to law.[6]

The first criticism of the laws of war is an objection to the content of the law: specifically, to such caveats to the humanitarian principles of *jus in bello* as **military necessity,** or the obligation to obey superior orders. We will save our discussion of these topics for Section III. The second criticism aims at the very idea of calling a rule a law in the absence of a common power to legislate formally and enforce compliance. This is the topic we will examine in this chapter.

UNDERSTANDING INTERNATIONAL LAW

Hugo Grotius's advocacy of universal, natural laws and customs that impose legal as well as moral obligations on states continues to be highly controversial. Criticism of this view has its roots in a philosophy of law called **positivism,** which dates from the nineteenth century and is still accepted in various forms by many today.[7] Proponents of legal positivism argue that jurisprudence and ethics are unrelated disciplines and that it is simply a contingent fact that they share a common language of obligations and prohibitions. Indeed, the relationship between moral and legal rules often seems rather arbitrary. For example, there are (or have been) laws that are clearly immoral, such as those regulating slavery, apartheid, impressment, and certain religious observances and prohibitions. Likewise, there are laws that are amoral, such as those that mandate the use of seat belts, stipulate concrete vaults for burial, or require that a goat be sacrificed instead of two sheep. In certain cases, however, laws do formalize moral rules such as those that prohibit rape or murder. And, finally, there are recognized moral rules that are not regulated by law, such as tipping a waiter for good service, not cutting in line at the supermarket, informing your date if you have AIDS, and certain instances of keeping promises or telling the truth.[8]

The positivist avoids this confusion by excluding from the science of law all matters of an *a priori* or metaphysical nature, such as moral obligations.[9] Under the positivist account, **normative** questions concerning which rules of conduct should be declared *de jure* **laws** are distinct from purely analytic questions of jurisprudence proper. Individual laws that prohibit certain behaviors might be thought of as functions that link specific behaviors to punishments. Ideally, a system of law is a fully contained, logically coherent system where the role of the judiciary is analytic rather than judgmental. The requirement for a rule to be a law, then, is simply that it be declared by a duly constituted authority that has the power to enforce compliance.

We quickly see the importance of this conception of law to our enterprise. If law is understood in the positivist's way, there are no international laws of war, because rules cannot properly be considered laws when there is no recognized (or effective) common authority to enforce compliance or punish noncompliance.[10] Even treaties must be considered as prescribing moral rather than legal obligations. Obligations that cannot be enforced are not *really* laws but are mere voluntary prescriptions, like charity or friendliness. The problem is summed up in the following passage:

> It is obvious that, in the present state of the world, no civil law exists between independent states—such nations having no common superior, no common tribunal, and no common executive, can have no legal relations—in the strict sense of the word legal.[11]

Because sovereign states recognize no authority outside of their own will, they are free to adopt whatever rules they choose; and, of course, they can abrogate them whenever it is in their interests to do so. What is called "international law," proponents of this position argue, should more properly be called "international morality."

There are a number of ways jurists have responded to the positivist argument. Some claim that formal sanctions are not a necessary condition for the efficacy of laws. In primitive societies, for example, taboos may be obeyed without question for such long periods of time that their purpose is completely lost. And, as Freud notes, "Taboo is a command of conscience," where conscience is defined as "the inner perception of objections to definite wish impulses that exist in us; [and] the emphasis is put upon the fact that this rejection does not have to depend on anything else, that it is sure of itself."[12] The legal positivist would have to argue that primitive societies that have no need for and, hence, no formal sanctions also have no laws. This seems unreasonable. Grotius, quoting Plato, responds that laws can have informal sanctions that serve the same purpose as formal ones enforced by the state.

> Law, even without a sanction, is not entirely void of effect. For justice brings peace of conscience, while injustice causes torments and anguish, such as Plato describes, in the breast of tyrants. Justice is approved, and injustice condemned, by the common agreement of good men . . . [and] most true is the saying, that all things are uncertain the moment men depart from law.[13]

A second response to the legal positivist might be that there are sanctions available in the international community, even without a common authority. These include increases or reductions in such areas as foreign loans, debt structuring, tariffs, trade embargoes, foreign aid, technological innovations, scientific discoveries, and access to educational institutions. Additionally, increased information exchange and world awareness have made most nations more sensitive to world opinion now than they were only a few decades ago. Finally, there is the resort to arms.

Third, one might point out, as Roger Fisher does, that international laws are not substantially different from much of what we accept as law in our daily lives that is equally unenforceable, such as when a state or private person or corporation wins a case against the federal government.[14] In such cases, compliance by the government could not be enforced in any strict sense because there is no higher authority that can mandate compliance or impose sanctions on the federal government.

H. L. A. HART

A more recent defender of a version of positivism that accounts for these objections is H. L. A. Hart. His theory of law provides us with an excellent model for understanding some of the difficulties with international law. To begin, we will first lay out the central tenets of his position, then we will see how they are relevant to the international community.

Hart takes issue with those legal positivists who argue that the force of compliance is a necessary condition for a rule to be a law, but he denies any essential relationship between moral rules and laws.[15] According to Hart's account, the rules that are operative in primitive societies are primary or "pre-legal." These rules can be thought to constitute a legal system only after a formal structure of secondary rules is in place that governs the way primary rules are introduced, eliminated, varied, and the facts relating to their violation conclusively determined. Moreover, members of such societies often make no distinction between moral and legal obligations. As Hart puts it,

> [In a primitive society] there might be nothing corresponding to the clear distinction made, in more developed societies, between legal and moral rules. . . . When this early stage is passed, and the step from the pre-legal into the legal world is taken, so that the means of social control now includes a system of rules containing rules of recognition, adjudication, and change, this contrast between legal and other rules hardens into something definite.[16]

In "advanced" legal systems, moral questions are restricted to the secondary rules that specify procedures for how laws are recognized, adjudicated, and changed. Legal questions are strictly concerned with, "Is there a law that is relevant to this case?" Sanctions do not play the same crucial role in Hart's formulation of legal positivism (compared to earlier ones such as Austin's), because Hart believes that most group members willingly follow the group's rules. In fact, one's personal psychological identity is derived, at least in part, from membership in a community or group that is itself defined by the rules that it recognizes or that bring it into existence. These members of a community have what Hart calls an **internal point of view** toward their society's rules. This means that they view violations of the group's rules as sufficient reason for incurring punishment or group hostility—that is, the rules themselves provide a reason for behaving in certain ways and punishing those who do not because *they are my rules.* In primitive societies, such rules (taboos, in some cases) govern behavior of group members with more force than any Leviathan could.

In advanced societies, this internal point of view consists of an identification with the system of secondary rules—such as a constitution. In other words, when people derive some of their personal identity from their status as citizens of a particular nation, the rules passed in accordance with that nation's constituting document are, in a way, each person's rules. A system of secondary rules is not necessary in primitive societies because members live in an intimate relationship with the primary rules.

Those who have an **external point of view,** on the other hand, are motivated to follow the rules because of the threat of sanction; they require predictable punishment or group hostility as sufficient reason for not violating a rule.[17]

There will always be some members of a community or group, Hart notes, who will view the rules as an imposition and will follow them only when coerced. Because of their external point of view, they view the rules as "*your* rules that I must follow to avoid punishment." Hence, sanctions are necessary so that "those who would voluntarily submit to the restraints of law shall not be mere victims of the malefactors who would . . . reap the advantages of respect for law on the part of others without respecting it themselves."[18]

Hart's view has considerable appeal. It establishes an evolutionary link between morality and positive law, while at once insisting on the ideal objectivity of the latter. Moreover, Hart provides an explanation for at least a *prima facie* obligation to obey the law based on one's personal identity as a member of a group, the domain of which is defined in terms of those who view the rules as their own. Finally, Hart notes that even though there is generally a common disposition among the members of a group to obey the group's rules, sanctions are required as a guarantee that those who voluntarily obey cannot be taken advantage of by those who do not obey. Before we explore just how Hart's concept of law helps us considerably in our attempts to understand international law, let us examine critically one aspect of Hart's account that has proved problematic.

A key aspect of Hart's theory is that while the mere presence of laws tends to obligate those who are subject to them, they are void of any essential moral content. An articulate and a persistent critic of Hart's version of legal positivism has been Ronald Dworkin. Dworkin argues that the meaning of a law extends beyond a literal interpretation of the meaning of the words that express the law, much the way a literal meaning of a poem often fails to capture the poet's intent.[19] And, in fact, the legal debates that occur in appellate courts often concern this quest for "real" or intended, rather than literal, meanings. Dworkin cites a number of case examples, one of which will suffice to elucidate his point.

Elmer murdered his grandfather in order to inherit the grandfather's estate. Elmer was caught, tried, and convicted. The deceased man's daughters, who would have been entitled to the inheritance had Elmer died before his grandfather, sued. They argued that Elmer should not enjoy the fruits of his crime and that the inheritance should go to them. The will in question had been legally executed, and there was nothing in the state statutes that would allow for any deviation from the letter of the will. Nevertheless, the court upheld the suit and denied Elmer the inheritance.

Judge Earl, writing for the majority, argued thus

A thing which is within the intention of the makers of a statute is as much within the statute as if it were within the letter; and a thing which is within the letter of the statute is not within the statute, unless it be within the intention of the makers.[20]

Dworkin notes that this was not a case of altering the law, but of interpreting what legislators really meant by the law they enacted. In law, as with the other operative rules of a community, "value and content have become entangled."[21] Indeed, upon reflection, we must conclude that the decisions judges routinely make in applying legal rules rest on certain moral principles, such as fairness, equality, and so on.[22] While a literal interpretation of the rule is one important principle—and in most cases the prevailing one (i.e., that legitimate judicial expectations should be fulfilled)—other principles should (and do) sometimes override this principle.

Whatever relationship morality has to law, we can conclude that moral principles do serve as metaphysical bridges that link legal decisions to justice in those cases where the letter of the law is inadequate. In this sense, then, law cannot be separated from moral considerations as Hart would have it. Moral principles are not merely the means whereby we evaluate the law, as Hart argues, but also are interwoven in the juridical administration of the positive laws themselves. We will explain how this is relevant to our enterprise momentarily; let us first return to Hart's theory of jurisprudence.

A more palatable aspect of Hart's account (than his insistence in the absolute moral/legal separation) is that in societies where there is no secondary rule of recognition (e.g., no legislative body to formally declare laws), the operative rules must be viewed as simply a *set of individual laws* rather than as a *legal system*. In the international society of states, for example, Hart notes that "there is no basic rule providing general criteria of validity for the rules of international law, and that the rules which are in fact operative constitute not a system but a set of rules. . . ."[23] Among these rules, he adds, are those that provide for the binding force of treaties. And, in fact, according to Hart, the international community is best understood as being in a prelegal state, and international laws should be understood as primary rules, much like the rules operative in primitive societies.

Thus, Hart concludes: (1) states do not enjoy unlimited autonomy in their relationships with other states, and (2) the operative limiting rules in the international society of states should not be regarded as part of a legal system in the same sense that municipal rules are.

What is lacking in international society, Hart argues, and what keeps international society void of law in the traditional sense, is the absence of the secondary rules of recognition, adjudication, and change. Furthermore, the obligation to obey laws in the international community cannot be derived from one's identity with a system of secondary laws like it can in modern domestic societies. Nevertheless, this does not negate the binding nature of international law.

> It is a mistake to suppose that a basic rule or rule of recognition is a generally necessary condition of the existence of rules of obligation or "binding" rules. This is not a necessity, but a luxury, found in advanced social systems whose members not merely come to accept separate rules piecemeal, but are committed to the acceptance in advance of general classes of rule, marked out by general criteria of validity. In the simpler form of society we must wait and see whether a rule gets accepted as a rule or not; in a system with a basic rule of recognition we can say before a rule is actually made, that it *will* be valid *if* it conforms to the requirements of the rule of recognition.[24]

If Hart is correct, and I am convinced that he is, then even though the form that international law takes differs from that of municipal law, the content and function of international law is analogous, whether it is derived from treaties, customary practices, or legal precedents. Certainly the need for a sovereign authority to link rule infractions to punishments is less important than the requirement that members of the international community internalize the ***de facto* laws.**

Perhaps, as Hart notes, multilateral treaties can take the place of legislative enactments in the international community. In any event, the practical question is: How do we get the members of the international community to internalize the principles of the Just War Tradition? We recognize that nations cannot internalize rules because they cannot hold beliefs; this is something that can only be done by individuals. We recall that when rules are internalized this not only provides a sufficient criterion for conforming to them but also provides a sufficient justification for punishing those who break them. And if the distinction between legal and moral rules is blurred in societies that lack secondary rules, as Hart argues, then perhaps certain moral principles can be enforced as legal obligations in the absence of a duly constituted, sovereign authority.[25] Put another way, perhaps the distinction between what the law actually requires (*lex lata*) and what the law ought to require (*lex ferenda*) is less relevant to societies without secondary laws, such as the society of nations.

We can begin to address this issue by noting that certain rules (or principles) can already be said to be internalized by the majority of the civilized world. This is the idea that is embodied in the prosecution's opening statement at the Nuremberg trials, where (among other things) eight Nazi leaders were convicted of the crime of aggression.

> The real complaining party at your bar is civilization. . . . The refuge of the defendants can be only their hope that international law will lag so far behind the moral sense of mankind that conduct which is crime in the moral sense must be regarded as innocent in law. Civilization asks whether law is so laggard as to be utterly helpless to deal with crimes of this magnitude by criminals of this order of importance.[26]

This statement acknowledges the lack of distinction between moral rules and legal rules that Hart argues is characteristic of societies void of secondary rules of recognition and adjudication. The Nuremberg example establishes that there are moral rules that also can be considered legal obligations, even without a system of secondary rules of recognition, adjudicature, and change. We might debate where, precisely, the limits of acceptable behavior in the international community of nations are, but we recognize that there are limits, and that there are certain actions that violate them. This means that persons brought before the bar, as were the Nazi war criminals, are not tried *ex post facto,* but in terms of some commonly held notions of what constitutes morally and legally acceptable behavior. Clearly this way of interpreting the laws of war is the intention of the signatories of the Hague conventions when they affirm that

> Until a more complete code of the laws of war has been issued, the High Contracting Parties deem it expedient to declare that, in cases not included in the Regulations adopted by them, the inhabitants and the belligerents remain under the protection and the rule of the principles of the law of nations, as they result from the usages established among civilized peoples, from the laws of humanity, and the dictates of public conscience. [see note 3 earlier]

The obvious question to ask is, given that there exists among the peoples of the world a disposition to obey rules and punish violators even in the absence of *de jure* laws, as evidenced by the world outrage against outlaws such as Adolf Hitler, Idi Amin, and Saddam Hussein, why isn't the tradition of *jus ad bellum* considered obligatory by members of the international community? There are, after all, certain rules in the international community that have been signed and duly ratified as treaties by all of the nations of the civilized world—such as the tradition of *justum bellum,* which dates back at least to Ancient Greece and Rome.

One possible explanation is that while the tenets of Just War Tradition have been **promulgated** in the international community, they are almost virtually unknown among the population. And, as Aquinas notes,

> In order that a law obtain the binding force which is proper to a law, it must be applied to the men who have to be ruled by it. Such application is made by its being notified to them by promulgation. Wherefore promulgation is necessary for the law to obtain its force.[27]

Because the subjects of international law are states, promulgation of the laws to states is accomplished through ratification procedures. But this is obviously inadequate. As Hart has argued, the primary motive for obeying rules is "the internal point of view." In advanced societies, this is accomplished through a belief in or a commitment to the political system that formalizes the rules by the constituents of that system; in less developed systems, this consists simply in the acceptance of the rules by the group members, probably through daily exposure to them or through various types of education. Certain minimum principles of humanity, like those governing the resort to arms and the conduct of war, are good candidates for the kind of primary, international rules to which the people of the world could take an "internal point of view," as somehow identifying their status as rational members of a civilized, international community. People cannot, however, take an internal point of view toward rules that are unknown to them. Perhaps the failure of the Just War Tradition to effectively limit instances of the resort to violence can be attributed largely to the fact that the tradition is virtually unknown among the populations of the world's nations.

The problem posed by considering nations as subjects was not lost on those drafting international treaties. A requirement that the international laws of war be promulgated to citizens (the objects rather than the subjects of international law) is clearly stated in the treaties where these laws are articulated. The following passage from the Geneva Convention (IV) of 1949 on the protection of civilians is telling:

> Article CXLIV
>
> The High Contracting Parties undertake, in time of peace as in time of war, to disseminate the text of the present Convention as widely as possible in their respective countries, and, in particular, to include the study thereof in their programs of military and, if possible, civil instruction, so that the principles thereof may become known to the entire population.[28]

The nations of the world have been profoundly remiss in abiding by the requirements of this article.[29]

Promulgation of the rules of both *jus ad bellum* and *jus in bello* is perhaps the most promising method for improving their efficacy in reducing the likelihood of war and in moderating suffering when war does occur. Even though sovereign nations are notoriously contemptuous of external condemnation, the politicians who govern them are sensitive and responsive (to varying degrees) to internal pressures from the people they govern. Certainly, in the long term at least, governments reflect in many important ways the collective will of the populace. We must at least wonder if Saddam Hussein would have been able to carry out his blatant aggression against Kuwait if the people of Iraq had been educated to take an internal point of view toward the Just War Tradition.

Public conscience must dictate to rulers and government officials the parameters of acceptable behavior if we are ever to solve the problem posed by expecting normative judgments from "sovereign" abstract entities. Just as individual conscience provides a primary motive for right action in domestic society, we have to muster public judgment to provide the moral force in national decisions. Thus, the criticism that international law should properly be called "international morality" is not a criticism at all but a mandate— recognizing that it imposes legal as well as moral obligations.

Topics for Further Discussion

1. Hart argues that most people obey laws because they take an "internal point of view" toward them. What are some examples of laws (or other types of formal rules) that illustrate this?
2. The Nuremberg tribunals tried some German military and civilian leaders for "criminal acts," even though these acts were not illegal under any formal written laws. Was this simply a case of "victor's justice," or were such trials appropriate?
3. Article CXLIV of the Geneva Convention (IV) requires that the contents of the Convention be studied in the military educational programs of signatory nations and recommends that their civilian populations study them as well. How might compliance with Article CXLIV reduce the likelihood of war or ameliorate suffering when war does occur?
4. Hostilities between the Bloods and the Crips, two rival gangs with roots in Los Angeles, have persisted for years. Members of these groups are widely regarded as lawless hoodlums. Are there any rules that govern how members of these gangs treat members of the opposing gangs? Are there any rules that govern their behavior toward other members of their own gang? How might our discussion of Hart help us understand the actions of these gang members?
5. E. B. Sledge, in his brilliant personal narrative of his experiences as a marine in World War II, *With the Old Breed*, writes: "Uncommon valor was displayed so often that it went largely unnoticed. . . . War is brutish,

inglorious, and a terrible waste. . . . The only redeeming factors were my comrades' incredible bravery and devotion to each other. Marine Corps training taught us to kill efficiently and to try to survive. But it also taught us loyalty to each other—and love. That esprit de corps sustained us" (New York: Oxford University Press, 1981, p. 315). The type of loyal identification with an organization that Sledge describes is extremely positive when it reinforces beneficial norms. Likewise, such loyalty can also be dysfunctional, as when it motivates group members to cover up for one another's transgressions. Provide an example where group identity was beneficial, as well as an example where it was harmful or counterproductive.

Notes

1. "Declaration of St. Petersburg," in *The Law of War: A Documentary History*, vol. I, edited by Leon Friedman (New York: Random House, 1972), p. 192.

2. The primary purpose for The Hague peace conferences was to establish procedures for settling international disputes through arbitration rather than violence. No international agreement could be reached on this topic, however, until the Kellogg Briand Pact of 1929 (officially titled the Treaty of Paris and signed by forty-two nations). This agreement renounced war as an alternative in international relations and stated that "the settlement or solution of all disputes or conflicts of whatever nature or of whatever origin they may be, which may arise among them, shall never be sought except by pacific means." In Friedman, *The Law of War: A Documentary History*, vol. I, pp. 468–69.

3. Ibid., p. 309.

4. Ibid., p. 543.

5. Donald A. Wells, *War Crimes and the Laws of War* (Lanham, Md.: University Press of America, 1984), p. 110.

6. Paul Arthur Schillp, "International Sovereignty and International Anarchy," in *The Critique of War*, edited by Robert Ginsberg (Chicago: Henry Regnery Co., 1969), p. 152. Schillp goes on to argue that the United Nations is a "world debating society" and the World Court at The Hague has only an advisory capacity. He adds that "the very concept of 'International Law' is, therefore, in today's world situation, either a self-contradictory notion, or else an ironically humorous one" (p. 153).

7. A classic exponent of the positivist position is John Austin. See *The Province of Jurisprudence Determined*, edited by H. L. A. Hart (London: Weidenfeld and Nicolson, 1954).

8. John Stuart Mill's famous declaration that "The only purpose for which power can be rightfully exercised over any member of a civilized community is to prevent harm to others" seems to be the operative principle concerning which moral rules should be declared as law. Thus we have legal prohibitions against violence, while private issues such as beneficence and recreational sex are left largely to individual conscience. See H. L. A. Hart, *Law, Liberty, and Morality* (Stanford, Calif.: Stanford University Press, 1963).

9. This is the very antithesis of the Augustinian view where moral obligations are legal obligations. This position is still widely held among those nations where Islam is the official religion and the Koran is the state constitution and the source of municipal law.

10. Of course, there may be national laws regulating the conduct of war, such as Lieber's Code or the U.S. Uniform Code of Military Justice.

11. Nassaw W. Senior, "A Review of Henry Wheaton's *History of the Law of Nations*," published as an appendix in Henry Wheaton, *A History of the Law of Nations in Europe and America* (New York and London: Garland Publishing, 1973), p. 301.

12. Sigmund Freud, "Totem and Taboo" in *The Basic Writings of Sigmund Freud*, translated and edited by A. A. Brill (New York: The Modern Library, 1938), pp. 859–60.

13. Hugo Grotius, *The Law of War and Peace*, translated by Francis W. Kelsey (Indianapolis and New York: Bobbs-Merrill Co., 1962), *Prolegomena*, 20, 22, pp. 16–17. Of course, this "common agreement" that Grotius (and Plato) refer to is not always apparent in observed behavior because it extends only insofar as there is a consensus that justice is good; there are widely divergent views on how justice is to be understood and how it may be achieved.

14. Roger Fisher, "Bringing Law to Bear on Governments," *Harvard Legal Review* 74 (1961), pp. 1130–40.

15. H. L. A. Hart, *The Concept of Law* (Oxford, England: Clarendon Press, 1961). Hart's criticism of John Austin (see note 7 earlier) is that he (Austin) views laws primarily as functions that link certain actions to specified negative consequences. Obligations are defined in terms of the likelihood that threatened punishment will follow deviation from certain lines of conduct (Hart, p. 86). This makes the commands of the state no different from "the case of the gunman who says to the bank clerk, 'Hand over the money or I will shoot'" (Hart, p. 19). This implies an adversary (external) relationship between the lawmaker and subjects; while in practice, most subjects routinely conform to laws irrespective of the threat of punishment (i.e., they have an internal relationship to the lawgiver). Moreover, while predictability of punishment is one important aspect of some legal rules, it is not a factor in laws that "facilitate" social harmony, such as those defining ways in which valid wills or contracts or marriages are made (Hart, p. 27). We will discuss Hart's own theory of jurisprudence momentarily.

16. Ibid., p. 165. This would correspond to the early Christian position, which did not distinguish between the legal and moral rules we discussed in chapter 2. Interestingly, some modern Islamic nations that recognize the Koran as the source of all law seem to meet Hart's description of a state with just primary rules.

17. Ibid., pp. 86–88. Hart summarizes: "At any given moment the life of any society which lives by rules, legal or not, is likely to consist in a tension between those who, on the one hand, accept and voluntarily cooperate in maintaining the rules, and so see their own and other persons' behavior in terms of the rules, and those who on the other hand reject the rules and attend to them only from the external point of view as a sign of possible punishment. One of the difficulties facing any legal theory . . . is to remember the presence of both these points of view and not to define one of them out of existence. Perhaps all our criticisms of the predictive theory of obligation [i.e., John Austin's] may be best summarized as the accusation that this is what it does to the internal aspect of obligatory rules" (p. 88).

18. Ibid., p. 213; see also p. 193.

19. Ronald Dworkin, *Law's Empire* (Cambridge, Mass.: Harvard University Press, 1986). The notion of interpretation is introduced on pp. 16–20 and is discussed in detail in chapter 2.

20. Ibid., pp. 15–20. Dworkin cites the case of Elmer and his grandfather as *Riggs v. Palmer*, 115 N.Y. 506, 22 N.E. 188 (1889). The same point is made by Roscoe Pound, who also chooses a case where an heir commits murder in order to inherit (*Perry v. Strawbridge*, 209 Missouri 621, 628–29). In overturning a lower court ruling, Judge Graves stated, "We do not believe that these courts have fully applied and used the canons of statutory construction which we have the right to use and ought to use to avoid a result so repugnant to common right and common decency. The construction as has been given such statutes

bruises and wounds the finer sensibilities of every man. . . . To us this seems abhorrent to all reason, and reason is the better element of the law."

Pound goes on to add, "However much the analytic theory of 'genuine interpretation' may purport to exclude the moral ideas of the judge, and to insure a wholly mechanical logical exposition of a logically implied content of legal precepts, two doors are left open. The court must determine whether the criteria of the literal meaning of the words and of the text read with the context yield a 'satisfactory' solution. If he holds that they do not, he must inquire into the 'intrinsic merit' of the competing interpretations. 'Satisfactory' will almost always mean in practice, morally satisfactory. 'Intrinsic merit' will always tend to mean intrinsic ethical merit." Roscoe Pound, *Law and Morals* (London: Oxford University Press, 1926), pp. 52–53.

21. Dworkin, *Law's Empire*, p. 48.
22. In the cases cited earlier, the operative principle is that persons should not profit from their criminal actions. This principle can be traced to Elijah's condemnation of Ahab, who murders Naboth and then inherits his property, as recounted in the Talmud (1 Kings 21: 19–20).
23. Hart, *The Concept of Law*, p. 231.
24. Ibid., p. 229.
25. Hart is not entirely consistent on this point. On the one hand, he compares international law to a prelegal society where the distinction between moral and legal rules is not clear because it lacks secondary rules. On the other hand, he argues that there is a clear distinction between moral and legal rules in international society. The point is less important in light of Dworkin's argument that no such clear distinction is possible.
26. *Trial of the Major War Criminals Before the International Military Tribunal* (Nuremberg, Germany, 1947), transcript of 21 Nov. 1945, p. 155 (chief prosecutor Jackson speaking).
27. Thomas Aquinas, *Summa Theologica*. I–II, Q. 90, A. 4, p. 9. Grotius, too, notes that some laws are binding only insofar as they are known. See *The Law of War and Peace*, Bk. I, chap. 1, XV, p. 45.
28. Friedman, *The Law of War: A Documentary History*, vol. 2, p. 689.
29. This criticism is especially pertinent in the United States where Article 6(2) of the Constitution states that "all Treaties made, or which shall be made, under the Authority of the United States, shall be the supreme law of the Land; and the Judges in every State shall be bound thereby, anything in the Constitution or Laws of any State to the contrary notwithstanding.

SECTION

III

MORAL ISSUES IN WAR

In the last chapter I argued that if the Just War Tradition and the laws that formalize parts of it are going to ameliorate the tragedy of war, there will have to be an increased emphasis on promulgating the prescriptions and prohibitions contained in these laws. In this section I will argue that the rules, as written, afford so many opportunities for mitigation and extenuation after crimes are committed that they can make distribution of fair and equitable punishment for transgressions seem capricious. Additionally, even if all soldiers obeyed all of the rules of war as they are presently recognized in international law, either because they identified with them (the internal point of view) or because of the fear of sanctions (the external point of view), there still would be serious difficulties with what the rules prescribe and permit. A brief sampling of actual cases from the last century points to the inefficacy of sanctions for war crimes and highlights the extent of the problems with enforcement.

In 1901, following the Philippine War, Lieutenant Preston Brown was found guilty of willfully murdering an unarmed prisoner of war. His sentence was forfeiture of one-half month's pay per month for nine months.[1] Brigadier General Jacob Smith was tried in 1902 and was found guilty of ordering his subordinates to "take no prisoners" and to kill all persons over ten years old in an attack on the island of Samar. His punishment was an official admonition. During the same year, Major Edward Glenn was convicted of having tortured a POW and was fined fifty dollars.[2]

At the close of World War I, the Allies were unsuccessful in their attempts to bring to trial 896 Germans who were alleged to be war criminals. German officials insisted that Germany conduct its own trials, but ended up prosecuting only 12 of the 896. Of these, six were convicted. Major Benno Crusius was found guilty of ordering the murder of wounded POWs and was sentenced to imprisonment for two years. The stiffest penalties were given to two German submarine officers who sank a British troop ship and ordered their crew to surface in order to machine-gun the helpless survivors. They were sentenced to four years each, but were soon allowed to escape.[3]

The high-water mark for accountability for war crimes came following World War II. The International Military Tribunals established by the Allied Powers at Nuremberg and in the Far East were the first international courts formed to try war criminals.[4] For decades, the Nuremberg and associated trials conducted in the aftermath of World War II were an anomaly, brought on perhaps by the stark-naked predation and undisguised evil of the Nazi regime. After this flood of prosecutions, the enthusiasm for trying war criminals dried up. This has given rise to charges of "victor's justice" and *ex post facto* laws in referring to the post–World War II trials.

Nearly fifty years passed before an international tribunal was formed to address war crimes and crimes against humanity. In 1991, the UN Security Council determined that the fighting in the former Yugoslavia posed a threat to international peace, which thereby authorized the use of force under Chapter VII of the United Nations Charter. In May 1993, the International Criminal Tribunal for the former Yugoslavia was established by the UN Security Council, and on May 7, 1997, the Tribunal convicted Dusan Tadic on eleven counts of crimes against humanity and war crimes. On July 14, 1997, the presiding judge, Gabrielle Kirk McDonald of the United States, sentenced Tadic to twenty years in prison. Some significant political figures have also been arrested and indicted, including former Yugoslav President Slobodan Milosevic and former Bosnian Serb President Bijana Plavsic. Other Bosnian Serbs convicted of murder have been sentenced to five years in prison. Scores of others have been indicted for war crimes but, as of this writing, many are still at large.

During the Korean War, General Douglas MacArthur established a war crimes commission that conducted extensive investigations and compiled detailed evidence on war crimes committed by North Korean and Chinese soldiers. An interim report issued by the Korea War Crimes Division of the Judge Advocate General's office in June 1953 listed numerous cases that were ready for referral to an international tribunal. Records of atrocities—some involving the torture and subsequent murder of thousands of prisoners—included pictures, statements by witnesses, and signed confessions. Nevertheless, no trials were ever held.[5]

Only a few members of the U.N. forces were tried for war crimes. In one case, *U.S. v. Kinder,* a soldier was tried and convicted of executing a Korean prisoner, despite his claim that he was directly ordered to do so by his commanding officer. He was sentenced to life, but the convening officer reduced this sentence to two years.[6]

During the Vietnam War, the attempted cover-up of the illegal, immoral, unnecessary, cowardly, counterproductive, and profoundly stupid atrocities of

My Lai, and the farcical, token admonishments meted out to the guilty parties by the U.S. Army, are often cited as evidence for the sterility of the laws of war. Lieutenant William Calley, a platoon leader at My Lai, was tried and convicted of the premeditated murder of numerous Vietnamese civilians. He served a total of five years on house arrest, where he was allowed various amenities, including pizza deliveries and frequent unsupervised visits with his girlfriend. Of the other two dozen individuals charged in the incident, five were tried and acquitted and charges were dropped on the remainder (although some had their awards for valor rescinded or received administrative reprimands).[7]

In a more recent case (1991), members of the Iraqi army, while occupying cities in Kuwait, pillaged, raped, tortured, and murdered innocent noncombatant Kuwaiti citizens. Additionally, prior to withdrawing from Kuwaiti territory, Iraqi soldiers opened oil wells along the coast in order to foul Saudi Arabian water treatment facilities and ignited hundreds of oil wells inland in a gesture of malicious destruction aimed at polluting the atmosphere, contaminating the soil, and destroying the oil. It is almost certain that these intentional, vengeful attacks against both Kuwaiti oil and regional ecosystems were personally ordered by Saddam Hussein, and it is likely that he personally approved at least some of the atrocities carried out against the citizens of Kuwait as well—certainly he knew of them, and his inaction constituted tacit approval. Nevertheless, until a coalition led by the United States and Great Britain invaded Iraq in 2003, there was no international initiative whatsoever to hold Saddam Hussein or any members of his armed forces culpable for these crimes.

In this section we will explore (1) why the United States has not been more vigorous in its enforcement of the *jus in bello* rules, and (2) those factors in the way the laws are formulated that impede consistent enforcement. I believe that these issues must be addressed in some satisfactory way if the Just War Tradition and the laws of war are going to be a viable force in future conflicts.

We will approach these problems from two related perspectives. The first concerns how the military virtue of following orders or obedience can interfere with determining the culpability for war crimes after they are committed; this will be the topic of chapter 8. The second perspective concerns certain caveats built into the laws of war—military necessity and reprisals—that permit overriding the humanitarian principles of *jus in bello* for the sake of military objectives. These will be the subjects of chapters 9 and 10.

Chapter

8

THE RESPONSIBILITY FOR WAR CRIMES

H. L. A. Hart notes that even though it is the internal point of view rather than sanctions that provides the primary motive for obedience to laws, sanctions are still necessary to motivate into conformity those who take an external point of view toward laws and do not view them as their laws. The imposition of sanctions, however, becomes problematic when the rules are vague or widely ignored. This is particularly important to our study because sanctions are a crucial aspect of the humanitarian laws of war for at least two special reasons. First, as I argued in the last chapter, nations have been remiss in promulgating these laws to their armed forces in ways that allow soldiers to take an internal point of view to them. This increases the need for effective sanctions as a deterrent.

Second, before sanctions can be imposed, there must be a means for establishing culpability. This has often been problematic in the military, because one characteristic specific to the military profession—and one that all soldiers understand clearly—is that the orders one receives from a superior inherently bear with them the force of law. Because obedience to orders is emphasized during all phases of a soldier's service—in peacetime and in combat—and is an integral part of the indoctrination each recruit receives in Basic Combat Training or "boot camp," instant and unquestioning obedience to superior orders soon becomes a rule toward which soldiers almost invariably take an internal point of view. When one considers that the rule of instant obedience is one that soldiers understand the reasoning behind, accept as important to their own interests, and know the punishment for violating, it is not surprising that they have often committed war crimes when directed to do so by their superiors, especially since many of the laws and sanctions associated with these crimes are vague or ambiguous. Moreover, the units to which soldiers are assigned soon become *their units*, and the officers and noncommissioned officers of these units become *their leaders* (i.e., those who will look out for their welfare). This increases even further a soldier's disposition to obey, without question, orders received from superiors. The military principle (MP) of obedience, then, might be stated in the following way:

MP₁ Soldiers have a legal duty to always obey the orders of their superiors.

Even if MP₁ is true (we will return to it momentarily), there remains the additional question of whether soldiers have a *moral duty* to always obey the orders received from superiors. We might formulate this as a principle in the following way:

MP₂ Soldiers have a moral duty to always obey the orders of their superiors.

Of course, if soldiers have a moral duty to always obey the orders of their superiors, then this would severely limit their moral agency in those cases when they are acting under such orders. This seems to be reinforced by a third military principle, recognized by virtually all nations, that holds commanders legally responsible, at least to some extent, for the actions of their subordinates. This might be formulated in the following way:

MP₃ Commanders are legally responsible for any actions performed in accordance with their orders.

There are a number of reasons why these principles warrant rigorous scrutiny. As the cases in our introduction to this section demonstrate, commanders accused of ordering or overlooking criminal acts have frequently been excused or received only token punishments because they did not commit the acts themselves. On the other hand, those who have executed war crimes have often claimed superior orders as a justification or excuse for their actions. In many cases, the result of this "who is responsible?" shell game has been either that no one has been held accountable for war crimes, or that the extent of culpability has been so mitigated as to seem ridiculous, as the historical evidence shows.

Without clear, established criteria for delineating individual responsibilities for war crimes, the issue of sanctions becomes moot. And without sanctions, the *jus in bello* rules found in national and international laws of war might be interpreted as ideals to be followed only when expediency permits, rather than legal prescriptions grounded in moral principles.

We will now examine these three military principles more closely and explore ways that the difficulties each presents might be resolved.

OBEDIENCE AS A LEGAL OBLIGATION

Prior to World War II, the lack of consensus concerning a subordinate's responsibility to always obey superior orders was reflected in the divergent laws that various nations adopted concerning this issue (referred to by lawyers as *respondeat superior*). The English military code of 1749 specified that soldiers had to obey only those orders that were *lawful*. Lassa Oppenheim's classic, *International Law*, first published in 1906, however, states that members of the armed forces who violate the laws of war under orders from superiors are not war criminals and may not be punished by the enemy. This probably influenced the British and U.S. World War I army manuals that absolved from culpability those who violated the laws of war under orders from their superiors.

The 1914 edition of the U.S. Army's *Rules of Land Warfare* enumerates all of the acts that are prohibited in war, and adds, "Individuals of the armed forces will not be punished for these offenses in case they are committed under the orders or sanction of their government or commanders."[8] During World War II, however, both Great Britain and the United States adopted variations of Article 47 of the German Military Code of 1872, which states that a subordinate "is liable to punishment as an accomplice if he knew that the order involved an act the commission of which constituted a civil or military crime or offense."[9] Unfortunately, neither the Geneva Convention nor the Hague Convention addresses the subject of superior orders.

In the armed forces of the United States, disobeying a lawful order can be prosecuted as a felony under the Uniform Code of Military Justice. In their oath of enlistment, for example, U.S. military personnel swear to obey the lawful orders of their officers and those legally appointed over them.[10] This is in consonance with present U.S. doctrine on obedience to superior orders, as discussed in Field Manual 27–10, *The Law of Land Warfare*, which states that "members of the armed forces are bound to obey *only lawful orders*"[11] [italics added]. Thus, even though most orders carry with them the force of law, there are certain laws that are more fundamental and that take precedence over orders. Lawful orders, we may presume, are those given by a duly appointed authority that prescribe lawful acts; unlawful orders are those that either originate with an improper authority or that command acts that are illegal. Perhaps we are ready to alleviate part of the difficulty with the legal obligation of obedience by rewording our principle so that obedience is required only in response to lawful orders.

MP$_{1a}$ Soldiers have a legal duty to obey the lawful orders of their superiors.

This formulation seems to address some of the difficulties with MP$_1$ because it provides for limitations to the rule of obedience by making certain legal prescriptions more fundamental than others. In other words, superior orders carry with them the force of law, provided that they do not prescribe criminal acts.[12] Now, however, although we have limited the domain of actions into which superior orders may take subordinates by excluding those that are illegal, we are faced with the practical question of how recipients of orders are going to be able to distinguish between legal and illegal acts. This is particularly problematic because in war the boundaries between legal and illegal behavior are drastically different from those recognized in peacetime. Consider the distinction between criminal acts for which soldiers are culpable, and lawful acts of war for which they are not, as explained by Telford Taylor, the chief American counsel at the Nuremberg trials.

> War consists largely of acts that would be criminal if performed in time of peace—killing, wounding, kidnapping, destroying or carrying off other peoples' property. Such conduct is not regarded as criminal if it takes place in the course of war, because the state of war lays a blanket of immunity over the warrior. . . .
>
> But the area of immunity is not unlimited, and its boundaries are marked by the laws of war. Unless the conduct in question falls within those boundaries, it does not lose the criminal character it would have should it occur in peace time circumstances. In a literal sense, therefore, the expression "war crime" is a misnomer, for it means an act that remains criminal even though committed in the course of war, because it lies outside the area of immunity prescribed by the laws of war.[13]

A difficulty arises when we attempt to determine just how far the "blanket of immunity" extends. Taylor argues that its limits are "marked by the laws of war," but the laws of war are often themselves unclear. For example, international law permits reprisals against the enemy as a legitimate means of responding to violations of *jus in bello* when other efforts to curb criminal actions fail. In other words, as a means of deterrence, one side can legally violate many of the rules of war in response to enemy violations. This means that soldiers may be legally ordered to commit acts that would otherwise be war crimes as reprisals. As one jurist, commenting on the trial of General Falkenhorst, commander in chief of the German armed forces in Norway during World War II, notes,

> Possibly there is no more difficult subject in the ambit of the law relating to war crimes than a correct application of the principles in a case where reprisal and superior orders are raised by the defense in respect of one and the same order which the defendant is alleged to have carried out.[14]

Moreover, it is not only reprisals that can cause such difficulties: Almost every humanitarian law that is articulated in either the Geneva and Hague Conventions or the Nuremberg Principles specifies that certain actions are prohibited *unless required by military necessity.* (We will return to reprisals and military necessity in greater detail in the next two chapters.) And, of course, all of this complexity is compounded by the extreme stress of combat situations where such decisions are generally made. As a German court noted in convicting two submarine officers who had sunk a British troopship and, afterwards, under orders from their captain, surfaced to destroy the survivors in lifeboats with machine-gun fire, "A refusal to obey the commander on a submarine would have been something so unusual that it is humanly possible to understand that the accused could not bring themselves to disobey."[15]

Given these overriding considerations that are built into the international laws of war, the boundaries of the "blanket of immunity" are not as obvious as they might initially seem. Because soldiers *routinely* perform acts at the direction of their superiors that would be crimes under peacetime conditions, it seems unreasonable to require soldiers to distinguish between acts that are illegal in peacetime but legally obligatory in war from those that are illegal in peacetime and in war—especially when this latter group can change entirely depending on the circumstances. As one author, commenting on his World War II experience, observes,

> To be sure, since the Nuremberg trials, Western nations have officially denied the soldier's right to obey orders that involve him in crimes. He must distinguish between illegitimate orders and those that are in line with his duty as a soldier. Presumably, the distinction is always clear according to official pronouncements, but in reality under the conditions of total war few things are more difficult to distinguish. Our age is caught in a painful contradiction for which there is no resolution other than the renunciation of wars or at least of the way we have been waging them in this generation.[16]

The difficulties inherent in requiring soldiers to distinguish between lawful and unlawful orders in light of the situational aspects of the laws of war have not been lost on those in charge of defining U.S. military doctrine. The previous passage cited from U.S. Army Field Manual 27–10, *The Law of Land Warfare*, is prefaced with the following discussion:

> In considering the question of whether a superior order constitutes a valid defense, the court shall take into consideration the fact that obedience to lawful military orders is the duty of every member of the armed force; that the latter cannot be expected, in the conditions of war discipline, to weigh scrupulously the legal merits of the orders received; that certain rules of warfare may be controversial; or that an act otherwise amounting to a war crime may be done in obedience to orders conceived as a measure of reprisal. At the same time it must be borne in mind that members of the armed forces are bound to obey only lawful orders.[17]

This passage reinforces a number of concerns. On the one hand, it acknowledges that soldiers cannot "weigh scrupulously the legal merits of the orders received" and that certain acts of war may be criminal under some circumstances and legal under others. On the other hand, however, it enjoins soldiers to obey "only lawful orders." It seems, then, that soldiers should always obey military orders unless they know such orders to be unlawful; but because what is lawful can change dramatically depending on the circumstances, it often will be impossible for soldiers to *know* with any reasonable degree of certainty whether or not certain orders are unlawful.[18] In other words, the relevant military manual advises soldiers to obey only lawful orders, while at the same time acknowledging that they often will be unable to tell lawful orders from unlawful ones! With this in mind, it is not surprising that the imposition of sanctions on soldiers who have violated the laws of war under orders has been minimal.

So far we have identified two serious problems for the Just War Tradition that are associated with a soldier's legal obligation to obey lawful orders. The first is that soldiers often view the rule of obedience to superior orders as being more fundamental than other relevant rules such as those associated with the humanitarian principles of *jus in bello*. In most cases, this may be attributed to soldiers taking an internal point of view to the former and an external point of view to the latter. The second problem is with the formulation of the rules themselves. Soldiers cannot reasonably be expected to conform to rules that require them to choose between alternative courses of action based on information that they will frequently not know, as required by MP_{1a} and the existing laws of war.

Unfortunately, these two difficulties present for us a case where developing an acceptable solution may be as challenging as explicating the nature of the problem and understanding its causes. One possibility is to modify the laws themselves by reducing the situational aspects of caveats such as military necessity and reprisals. This topic is best postponed until our detailed discussion of these doctrines in the next two chapters. A second solution might be to question the merits of obedience as a central military virtue. We might ask, for example, whether obedience to orders is of sufficient importance to the military profession in terms of expediency to justify its codification into laws and enforcement through sanctions in light of the difficulties we have identified. And if obedience as a military virtue is crucial to military methods and purpose, we might ask, How can the rules that reflect this principle be modified so that soldiers can reasonably be expected to distinguish between those orders that they have a legal obligation to obey and those that they have a legal obligation to disobey? Similarly, we might establish the relationship of the principle of obedience to other relevant principles, such as those that are reflected in the *jus in bello* tradition.

These are questions of how the law should be, and we can proceed in this direction by examining the moral and prudential considerations that motivate the military emphasis on obedience as a legally obligatory and morally praiseworthy requirement. If we can determine where the moral boundaries of the principle of obedience lie, then perhaps we can better ascertain its relationship to other relevant principles and modify the legal rules accordingly.

OBEDIENCE TO ORDERS AS A MORAL DUTY

In the widely read *The Soldier and the State,* Samuel Huntington argues that obedience to *legal orders* is the paramount virtue of soldiers; that is, soldiers have a moral duty to follow the legal orders of their superiors. Huntington provides the following rationale:

> For the [military] profession to perform its function, each level within it must be able to command the instantaneous and loyal obedience of subordinate levels. Without these relationships military professionalism is impossible. Consequently, loyalty and obedience are the highest military virtues. . . . When a military man receives a legal order from an authorized superior, he does not argue, he does not hesitate, he does not substitute his own views; he obeys instantly. He is judged not by the policies he implements, but rather by the promptness and efficacy with which he carries them out. His goal is to be an instrument of obedience; the uses to which that instrument is put are beyond his responsibility.[19]

Huntington's position is that as long as an order is lawful, soldiers have a moral obligation to obey it. He concludes that soldiers carry no moral responsibility for war crimes committed in response to superior orders.[20] This can be summarized with the following principle:

MP$_{2a}$ Soldiers have a moral obligation to obey lawful orders.

One might object to this principle on the grounds that it is impossible to determine lawful orders from unlawful ones, as we noted in our earlier discussion. Huntington could respond, however, that the assumption always favors obedience and that soldiers are morally obligated to obey, except in those cases where they have reasonable evidence to believe that an order is unlawful.[21] We can incorporate this into our principle in the following way:

MP$_{2b}$ Soldiers have a moral obligation to obey all orders, except in cases where they have reasonable evidence to believe the orders to be unlawful.

We turn now to the reasons that Huntington provides to support his claim.

Huntington argues that without complete and unquestioning obedience, military units will be unable to perform their functions. (We define "function" as defeating the enemy with minimum loss of life.) Of course, we can all think of examples where this claim would be false. Soldiers or even entire units might disobey orders when they become aware of information that the person issuing the orders does not have, and disobedience under such circumstances could possibly produce better results than obedience.

Surely, however, Huntington recognizes this **act utilitarianism**-based objection to his position. If so, then it is difficult to understand just what his justification might be for advocating instant and unquestioning obedience. Perhaps he means that in the long run, better performance of soldierly functions will follow from all soldiers conforming to the rule of obedience all the time than would follow from conformance to any alternative rule(s). The very idea of a military *unit*, he might argue, requires that various roles be assigned to individual group members and that each member perform his (or her) role as efficiently as one can with the conviction that others will do likewise. The role of decision maker is reserved for the commander. It certainly would not do to have each individual soldier deciding which orders to obey and which to ignore. Moreover, the commander is in a better position to make decisions on behalf of the members of the unit—even those with moral impact—because the commander is often the only one who has access to all of the information relevant to such decisions.

Understood this way, the principle of obedience isolates the culpability for war crimes with those commanders who initiate such orders, rather than extending it to those who simply execute them. Better results, one might argue, both in terms of overall conformity to humanitarian principles as well as achieving military objectives, can be obtained by isolating the responsibility and culpability for war crimes in commanders who are better educated and have access to the crucial information needed to make tactical decisions.

Although this **rule utilitarianism** argument initially seems appealing, it is not without difficulties. One might challenge the consequential aspects of Huntington's claim by examining the relationship between defeating the enemy and obeying orders. For example, is instant and unquestioning obedience to orders really as crucial to military success as Huntington maintains, or might there often be cases where acts of disobedience would contribute to military success? We can address this question by first considering some possible reasons why a soldier might refuse to obey orders, and then speculating how such behavior might affect the "military function." As we pursue this, our goal will be to distinguish those cases where instant and unquestioning obedience is crucial to military efficiency from those where disobedience would not have a significant negative affect on performance, so that we will later be able to modify the rules of obedience to reflect these differences. We will attempt to fine-tune the rules of obedience in ways that preserve the consequential considerations that Huntington raises without negating the moral agency of individual soldiers.

I can imagine three types of reasons why a soldier would not have an obligation to obey an order. First, suppose that after having received lawful orders to perform some action (A_1), a soldier concludes that there is an alternative course of action available (A_2) that is better in terms of achieving the military objectives than the one prescribed. Let us call this the *prudential argument.* Second, one might believe that by following orders there is a greater chance of coming into harm's way than there is by not following orders (the soldier is afraid). We will refer to this as the self-interest argument. Finally, one could believe that the order received dictates actions that are either morally or legally wrong. We will call this the *moral objection argument.* Let us see whether any of these pose a problem for the obedience principle.

The prudential argument advocates that disobedience may sometimes be morally justified based on expediency. The very nature of rules is such that they often cannot take into consideration all of the relevant aspects of particular situations. And if one discovers a better way of accomplishing an objective than the one decreed by one's superiors, then it would seem foolish not to adopt it. This point is developed by Plato in a discussion concerning the shortcomings of civil laws, but it seems equally applicable to our discussion because soldiers are legally bound to obey lawful orders.

> Laws can never issue an injunction binding on all which really embodies what is best for each; it cannot prescribe with perfect accuracy what is good and right for each member of the community at any one time. The difference of human personality, the variety of man's activities, and the inevitable unsettlement attending all human experience make it impossible for any art whatsoever to issue unqualified rules holding good on all questions at all times. But we find practically always that the law tends to issue just this invariable kind of rule. It is like a self-willed, ignorant man who lets no one do anything but what he has ordered and forbids all subsequent questioning of his orders even if the situation has shown some marked improvement on the one for which he originally legislated. (294b–c)[22]

Plato's criticism is that laws are never completely universalizable; they must inevitably admit of exceptions. Military orders given by commanders in combat, however, are legal prescriptions that are not subject to this criticism because they are particular judgments aimed at specific situations. It follows that they should take precedence over more general rules that are written to cover general scenarios.[23] If so, then individual action should take precedence over superior orders, which would take precedence over standing orders, and so on. Of course, if conflicts in orders are to be resolved at the lowest level, then individuals will always be permitted to set aside orders received, based on their own individual assessment of the alternatives.

The distinct aspect of military operations that makes Plato's observation unconvincing when applied to military orders and thereby favors the rule of obedience in such cases is the importance of coordinated action to military tactics and strategy. Even if there is a better way (call it A_2) of accomplishing a particular objective than the one delineated in an order (call it A_1), the importance of unison of action is crucial enough to combat operations to almost always override this as an argument for disobedience.[24] In other words, because the success of military operations depends on coordinated efforts, alternative A_2 is better only if everyone were to adopt it in place of A_1. But it does not follow from the fact that a better outcome would result if everyone were to adopt A_2 that one individual should refuse to obey an order to do A_1 in order to adopt A_2 on his or her own. And even if we grant uniform disobedience in some cases (a rout, for example), proponents of obedience can still respond that rules must be evaluated against types of cases rather than particular ones.[25] The prudential argument, then, does not cause serious problems for MP_{2b}, and in fact seems to support it.

The second possible explanation for disobeying superior orders, the self-interest argument, also seems to support rather than cast doubt upon MP_{2b}. When one chooses to disobey lawful orders for the sake of one's own welfare or safety during combat, it is called "cowardice in the face of the enemy," and it is a felony punishable by death. Nor can the self-interest argument be defended against the rule utilitarian position by appealing to another generally acceptable moral theory (either teleological or deontological) because such theories invariably require that the interests of others be given the same importance as one's own interest.[26] While self-interest might provide an explanation for immoral behavior in the same way greed or hatred might, it does not serve as an adequate justification.

In addition to the prudential and self-interest arguments, another possible objection to MP_{2b} is the argument that soldiers have a moral duty to disobey legal orders if they believe such orders are immoral. For example, one might argue that while it is considered virtuous for soldiers to be obedient, there are nevertheless more fundamental *human* principles that are always operative, regardless of the role one occupies. Perhaps the difficulty this raises for Huntington's position can be made more apparent if we imagine that the process of obeying an order involves two components: the obedience of an order, and the performance of that which is entailed by the order received. Huntington's position blurs this distinction by describing those who carry out commands as mere "instruments"; and, of course, the responsibility for the uses to which an instrument is put rests entirely with the user of the instrument. But obedience, like courage, perseverance, and genius, cannot be judged independently of the ends toward which it is directed. Certainly we can imagine a murderer whose courage, perseverance, and intellect assist him in accomplishing heinous injustices. And while we might generally regard courage as virtuous, it is only contingently so because in the final analysis it takes its character from the end toward which it is directed.

Huntington's argument would make obedience the fundamental principle, regardless of the evil nature of the ends one may knowingly bring about under the rubric of obeying. We can best point out the difficulties with this line of reasoning if we digress for a few moments and reflect on the derivation of certain special rights and duties normally associated with particular roles, the way that obeying orders or attacking enemy combatants is associated with soldiering.

In domestic society, for example, the right to punish others for attacks upon one's person or property, or to seek redress for wrongs received, is located in the office of the magistrate. The community has, through its system of secondary laws, assigned certain individual rights to various roles, and the persons filling these roles, by proxy, act on behalf of the community's members—indeed, they have a duty to so act. As Grotius puts it, according to natural law, "every man has the right to punish wrongdoers"; but in civil society, the rights of preventing and punishing wrongdoers are restricted to particular offices. Only in those places where there is no such civil authority, Grotius adds, "do the old natural liberties remain."[27] It is not the case, therefore, that wrong acts become right when condoned by a legitimate authority, but rather that acts that were permissible for everyone in precivil society have become restricted to those legally endowed with the public authority for such acts.

We can conclude, then, that the power of the magistrate is not unlimited, because no rights can be assigned to an office that do not exist in the population in the first place.[28] Likewise, the rights that individual members of a family or community have to protect themselves, their fellows, and their property from foreign attack, as well as to seek redress for wrongs suffered, are collected in the role of the military for reasons of expediency.

It is not because a "blanket of immunity" is spread over certain actions that would otherwise be crimes that soldiers are permitted to inflict harm on other human beings, as Telford Taylor argues (earlier), but because certain natural, universal rights intrinsic to all human beings have been given up by the population at large and assigned to those filling the role of soldier. Understanding the role of the soldier in this manner is consistent with the Roman practice (discussed in chapter 1) of commissioning military leaders to fight in specific campaigns; those who fought in campaigns other than the ones for which they were commissioned could be charged with murder for any deaths they caused during their unauthorized combat.

As in the example of the magistrate, soldiers at the very most acquire only those rights that are inherent in individual persons who do not have recourse to a higher authority (e.g., in precivil society). Actions that would be illegal or immoral for individuals (acting alone or collectively as members of a community) to engage in—torture, mutilation, intentional harming of innocents—cannot ever become permissible for a person based on a "blanket of immunity" or a particular role, because actions that are morally wrong cannot become permissible by fiat. It follows that the duty to obey orders is not unlimited—and certainly the principle of obedience is at least limited to the extent that no person can ever incur a moral obligation to obey an order that prescribes actions that would always be immoral for one to perform if no civil authority were to exist.

In other words, imagine that the office of personhood is a natural, inalienable one that all human beings hold; it is always more fundamental than other offices that individuals might occupy concurrently, such as that of soldier (or judge, or police officer). In this respect, obedience to military orders is a second-order principle that acquires its character from the ends at which it aims. This is not to deny that soldiers have a *prima facie* duty to obey lawful orders; it is simply that this is not their most fundamental duty, as Huntington would have it.

Another closely related difficulty with the rule utilitarian argument for obedience is that it absolves soldiers from any moral responsibility for actions done at the direction of superiors. Recall that according to rule utilitarianism, acts are morally right if they are in accordance with a prescribed rule that, if followed universally, would produce better results (i.e., utility) than any alternative rule would if followed in a like manner. If rule utilitarianism is true, and one of the rules is that *soldiers must always obey lawful orders,* then soldiers are only morally responsible insofar as they do what they are told, regardless of the consequences of any specific case. Even if an order prescribes an immoral act, under this formulation, we could condemn the act and still praise the agent who carried it out. Put in Augustinian terms, the soldier's intention is to obey the legal orders received; the act inherent in this obedience is beside the intention.

This view, which makes obedience to orders the most fundamental rule for soldiers, harks back to previous discussions concerning obedience to unjust laws. Only if we view law as originating entirely by fiat through a lawgiver (e.g., Jehovah to Moses, Allah to Mohammed, Sun-god to Hammurabi, philosopher-king to subjects) as Augustine does, can its domain be considered ubiquitous, timeless, and sacrosanct. As we have seen, Aquinas (and Aristotle) reject this notion and conclude that, as rational agents, individuals are always responsible for their actions unless the acts are done out of ignorance or under duress.[29]

Both our experience and our reasoning tell us that not only is no set of rules completely universal, but that the means whereby rules are formulated are often corrupt, biased, or influenced by false beliefs. The historical existence of immoral and unnecessary orders issued by both heads of state and military leaders is irrefutable. Two orders issued by Hitler will suffice as examples. The first passage is taken from the Commissar Order, issued on June 6, 1941.

1. In this fight [against Russia], leniency and considerations of international law are out of place in dealing with these elements. . . .

2. The originators of barbarous Asiatic methods of warfare are the political commissars. They must therefore be dealt with most severely, *at once*

and summarily. Therefore, they are to be liquidated at once when taken in combat or offering resistance.

***

1. (2) Political commissars as *organs of the enemy troops* are recognizable by special insignia—red star with interwoven gold hammer and sickle on the sleeves. They are to be segregated *at once,* e.g., still on the battle-field, from the prisoners of war. . . . The protection of prisoners of war by international law does not apply to them. They will be liquidated after segregation.[30]

The second quotation that follows is from the infamous Commando Order, issued by Hitler on October 18, 1942:

3. From now on all enemies on so-called commando missions in Europe or Africa challenged by German troops, even if they are to all appearances soldiers in uniform or demolition troops, whether armed or unarmed, in battle or in flight, are to be slaughtered to the last man. . . . Even if these individuals, when found, should apparently be prepared to give them-selves up, no pardon is to be granted them on principle. . . .

4. If individual members of such commandos, such as agents, saboteurs, etc., fall into the hands of the military forces by some other means, through the police in occupied territories for instance, they are to be handed over immediately to the SD. Any imprisonment under military guard, in PW stockades for instance, etc., is strictly prohibited, even if this is only intended for a short time. . . .

6. I will hold responsible under military law, for failing to carry out this order, all commanders and officers who either have neglected their duty of instructing the troops about this order, or acted against this order where it was to be executed.[31]

While we might accept the claim that soldiers should generally obey superior orders, numerous examples of abuses, some with catastrophic conse-quences, clearly demonstrate that there cannot be a universal prescription that all orders must always be obeyed. At a minimum, soldiers have a moral responsibility to refuse to obey orders that patently violate the traditions of *jus in bello* and cannot be justified by *military necessity.* Rommel's burning of Hitler's Commando Order provides a good example of a military leader exer-cising this judgment.

One need only recall the defense of war criminals such as Adolf Eichmann. "I could feel that the guilt was not mine, since . . . the men at the top, the elite, the popes of the empire, laid down the laws. And I? I had only to obey."[32] Or statements by Nazi officers like Rudolf Hess. "I commanded Auschwitz until 1 December 1943, and estimate that at least 2,500,000 victims were executed and exterminated there by gassing and burning, and at least another half million succumbed to starvation and disease." His explanation?

"The only one and decisive argument was the strict order and reason given for it by the *Reichsfuhrer* Himmler."[33] Such examples make Huntington's rule utilitarianism justification for obedience indefensible.

Moreover, the Nuremberg trials clearly establish the precedent that legal considerations are subordinate to moral ones when considering the issue of obedience. The most common defense of the Nazi criminals was that their first duty was to their national laws—that there can be no higher authority than the sovereign state. The International Tribunal, however, ruled that the very essence of the Nuremberg Charter is that "individuals have international duties which transcend the national obligations of obedience imposed by the individual state. He who violates the laws of war cannot obtain immunity while acting in pursuance of the authority of the state, if the state in authorizing action moves outside its competence under international law."[34]

Soldiers are judged twice. They are judged based on the compatibility of their actions with the common good of their unit or nation; this is an assessment of how well they perform the duties inherent in their role as combatant; but also, and even more importantly, they are judged based on the compatibility of their actions with universal moral truths. Thus soldiers have a moral responsibility to disobey orders—*even legal orders*—when they prescribe immoral acts.

Nor can duress be used as a defense for obeying illegal or immoral orders, unless it can be shown that there was a direct and immediate danger to one's safety. In the trial of German military officers of the German High Command by the Nuremberg tribunal, the court noted

> The defendants in this case who received obviously criminal orders were placed in a difficult position, but servile compliance with orders clearly criminal for fear of some disadvantage or punishment not immediately threatened cannot be recognized as defense. To establish the defense of coercion or necessity in the face of danger there must be a showing of circumstances such that a reasonable man would apprehend that he was in such imminent physical peril as to deprive him of freedom to choose the right and refrain from the wrong.[35]

And although both the Geneva and Hague Conventions are silent on the subject of superior orders, the Nuremberg Charter and Nuremberg Principles are not. The Nuremberg Charter states

> *Article 8.* The fact that the Defendant acted pursuant to order of his Government or of a superior shall not free him from responsibility, but may be considered in mitigation of punishment if the Tribunal determines that justice so requires.[36]

We must conclude that soldiers are obligated to only obey orders that are lawful and that prescribe acts that would be permissible for individuals to do *in principle* (e.g., defense of self or community), were there no legitimate civil authority. The questions that were unsettled prior to World War II concerning a soldier's culpability for crimes committed under orders should have been settled at Nuremberg. One commentator, after citing current U.S., British, German, and Soviet laws on obedience to superior orders and, "after surveying the relevant provisions of many other national military codes," concludes that "the principle of unconditional obedience and of complete freedom from responsibility for superior orders has all but disappeared today."[37] The acceptance of this principle by most nations, as evidenced by their having incorporated it into their national laws, is sufficient to give it status as customary law in the international community.

The debate that occurred during the Nuremberg trials—that there can be no punishment for crimes in the absence of laws (*nullum crimen sine lege, nulla poena sine lege*)—could not now be successfully used as a defense—even by members of a nation having national laws that require universal obedience to all orders.

Obviously this places a greater personal responsibility on individual officers and soldiers to be able to determine where the moral and legal boundaries are in various wartime circumstances. This mandates that the international laws of war must be promulgated and understood by those soldiers who are subject to them so that they can make the kind of moral decisions that the laws of war require.

Up to this point, our discussion of obedience has addressed only *jus in bello* considerations. We must take care that we do not too hastily extend our conclusions concerning a soldier's obligation to disobey orders he or she believes to be immoral under *jus in bello,* with his or her *jus ad bellum* responsibility to carry out the political will of the nation the soldier represents. Determining when a nation should resort to the use of force is a difficult matter involving human judgments and political processes. Wars fought in accordance with these judgments and processes are **formally just.** It is as though professional soldiers have taken the following oath: "Recognizing that I may never know in advance whether the use of force being contemplated is **objectively just,** I swear to respond as a soldier on behalf of my nation to all wars that are formally just." Soldiers agree to accept as just all wars declared in accordance with a predetermined decision-making procedure. Thus, Grotius discusses his *jus ad bellum* conditions not as rules for international law but as a checklist for leaders who wish to make moral decisions in the international arena. Under the Just War Tradition, the responsibility for applying this checklist rests with the legitimate political body.

War is a public act, and decisions concerning when to use force are political rather than military. Such decisions can only justly be made by political leaders who speak with the political will of their constituents. All acts of violence done by individuals or groups that do not represent the will of a formally established legal political body are crimes.[38] Military leaders are guilty of violating *jus ad bellum* if they initiate acts of violence against another nation without a political mandate passed in accordance with the accepted formal procedures of the nation they represent.

Professional soldiers who refuse to fight in wars that are formally just are guilty of a much greater crime than conscripts who choose civil disobedience rather than fight in wars they believe are unjust. While the conscript may have some implied obligation to the state of which he or she is a member, the professional military person has willingly agreed to fight in wars that are declared just by a legally constituted body in accordance with a formal procedure.[39] Therefore, it is morally reprehensible for professional soldiers to refuse to fight on behalf of their nation when ordered to do so by their legitimate political body, or to initiate armed conflict without a legitimate political sanction. Soldiers have a different responsibility under *jus in bello* because the actual prosecution of combat is specifically a military responsibility. We will return to this topic in greater detail in chapter 14.

COMMAND RESPONSIBILITY FOR WAR CRIMES

The question we must now answer is, "To what extent are commanders responsible for the illegal actions of their subordinates?" This is the inverse case to the defense of superior orders discussed earlier. In the case of a subordinate carrying out a war crime at the direction of a superior, the only act the order giver performs is that of giving the order. The subordinate, on the other hand, has two components with which to contend: obedience to the order and the act that is prescribed by the order; and in such cases it is the latter that forms the basis for our moral judgments. This might lead us to conclude that orders are themselves morally irrelevant—that it is the performance of the act itself regardless of the existence of an order that provides the basis for judging the agent. Understood this way, it would seem that a commander's responsibility for actions performed by subordinates is severely limited.

Others might argue that the purpose of prohibiting superior orders as a defense is not to shift the focus downward from those who issue the order to those who execute it; rather, it is to implicate all of the parties involved in the commission of criminal acts. Recall that we previously formulated this as a principle, thus,

MP₃ Commanders are morally and legally responsible for any actions performed in accordance with their orders.

Grotius argues that "to participate in a crime a person must not only have knowledge of it but also have the opportunity to prevent it."[40] He adds, however, that "we may presume that acts which are conspicuous, or frequent, are easily known, for none can be ignorant of what is done by many."[41] This implies a revision of MP3 that would extend command responsibility for crimes performed by subordinates to include those who either fail to initiate positive action to stop crimes from occurring or who do not take corrective action when they become aware that crimes have occurred.

Before we attempt to revise MP3, let us examine some actual cases. Two divergent legal precedents are available to work with here, both of which seem to be based on different interpretations of Grotius.

In December 1945, Japanese General Tomoyuki Yamashita was tried for crimes committed by his soldiers (particularly those who had occupied Manila) while defending the Philippines during the U.S. reinvasion. The prosecution charged that General Yamashita did not adequately perform his duties as a commander, in that he failed to initiate positive measures that would have prevented illegal actions by those assigned to his command. The court's decision noted

> Assignment to command military troops is accompanied by broad authority and heavy responsibility. This has been true in all armies throughout recorded history. It is absurd, however, to consider a commander a murderer or rapist because one of his soldiers commits a murder or a rape. Nevertheless, where murder and rape and vicious, revengeful actions are widespread offenses, and there is no effective attempt by a commander to discover and control the criminal acts, such a commander may be held responsible, even criminally libel, for the lawless acts of his troops.[42]

General Yamashita was not charged with personally participating in any acts of atrocity, or even of condoning them; in fact, *it is unlikely that he was even aware that the atrocities occurred.* Nevertheless, because the acts were so conspicuous and widespread, the court believed that *he should have known about them.* He was therefore convicted of failing to provide effective control of his troops, and he was hanged.[43] Based on this case, MP3 might be revised in the following way:

> MP3a Commanders are responsible for war crimes committed by members of their command in cases where they have not taken positive action to prevent the occurrence of such crimes, *or* they have not attempted to uncover and investigate any that they have reason to believe might have occurred, *or* they have not taken appropriate action against those known to have committed such crimes.

The second case we will examine is the court-martial of Captain Ernest Medina, which occurred in September 1971. Soldiers and officers under Captain Medina's command committed numerous atrocities during assaults on Vietnam villages. In one village, My Lai, hundreds of unarmed civilians were murdered and numerous persons were raped or mutilated by members of Medina's company. The prosecution argued that Medina was in and around the village of My Lai and in continual radio communication with his subordinate elements during the time the atrocities were committed, and that he failed to take proper actions to control his men. Moreover, there was conflicting evidence about whether Medina had actually directed that his men destroy everything in the village, or that he himself had intentionally murdered at least one unarmed woman and specifically ordered the killing of another.[44] At a minimum, it is certain that he did not take any positive action to prevent violations of the laws of war by his subordinates, either in advance or during the operation, even though he knew that they were operating in a civilian community. Nevertheless, despite the Yamashita precedent, the military judge provided the following instructions to the jury:

> [A commander is responsible] if he has *actual* knowledge that troops or other persons subject to his control are in the process of committing or are about to commit a war crime and he wrongfully fails to take the necessary and reasonable steps to insure compliance with the laws of war. You will observe that these legal requirements placed upon a commander *require actual knowledge plus a wrongful failure to act.* Thus mere presence at the scene without knowledge will not suffice. . . . [italics added][45]

Based on this guidance, Medina was acquitted.[46] This case implies a principle somewhat different from MP$_{3a}$.

> MP$_{3b}$ Commanders are responsible for war crimes committed by their subordinates in cases where they know such crimes have occurred and take no action to investigate them and act appropriately against those responsible.

Clearly, the same standard was not applied in each instance. In the case of Yamashita, it is unlikely that he knew of the atrocities committed by his troops; nevertheless, he was convicted because *he should have known,* and therefore he should have initiated positive measures to prevent or stop them. In the case of Medina, it is likely that he knew of the atrocities, and it is certain that he should have known; nevertheless, it was not demonstrated to the court's satisfaction that *he must have known* of the crimes committed by his officers and men. The mere possibility that he did not know of the widespread atrocities was enough for acquittal.

Oppenheim's *International Law* states that commanders may share the responsibility for atrocities committed against civilians and prisoners. It continues, "Such responsibility arises, directly and undeniably, when the acts in question have been committed in pursuance of an order of the commander concerned, or if he has culpably failed to take the necessary measures to prevent or suppress them."[47] The U.S. interpretation of international law concerning the responsibility that commanders have for subordinate actions follows the Yamashita precedent.

> When troops commit massacres and atrocities against the civilian population of occupied territory or against prisoners of war, the responsibility may rest not only with the actual perpetrators but also with the commander. . . . The commander is responsible if he has actual knowledge, or *should have knowledge*, through reports received by him or other means, that troops or other persons subject to his control are about to commit or have committed a war crime and he fails to take the necessary and reasonable steps to insure compliance with the law of war or to punish violators thereof. [italics added][48]

Other nations have adopted similar rules. Following Grotius's argument that one cannot claim ignorance of widespread crimes, the Canadian War Crimes Regulations state, "Where there is evidence that more than one war crime has been committed by members of a formation . . . the court may receive that evidence as *prima facie* evidence of responsibility of the commander for those crimes."[49] It seems, then, that the Yamashita case and MP$_{3a}$ best represent the degree of responsibility that commanders should have for the actions of their subordinates.[50]

Unfortunately, Captain Medina was not tried for violations of war crimes under either the Nuremberg Principles or international law. He, like other members of the U.S. military who have committed war crimes, was tried by a military court for violations of the Uniform Code of Military Justice (UCMJ). This is in keeping with the Geneva Convention, which states that because there is not an international court, nations may either bring those guilty of war crimes before their own courts, or hand them over to another nation for prosecution.[51]

I am not convinced that it is hopeless to expect the military community to prosecute vigorously their own members for crimes against "outsiders" (i.e., enemy soldiers and civilians), but certainly the procedure is suspect. Perhaps such cases could be handled with less bias by a federal court established for that purpose.

In any case, the fact that war crimes are committed is not an indictment of the laws of war. The failure to seek out and punish criminals is, however, a serious indictment of those responsible for maintaining the laws. In the case of Captain Medina and My Lai, the military and political systems failed. The extent of responsibility that commanders have for enforcing the laws of war is summed up well in General Douglas MacArthur's rejection of General Yamashita's appeal.

> Rarely has so cruel and wanton a record been spread to the public gaze. Revolting as this may be in itself, it pales before the sinister and far-reaching implication thereby attached to the profession of arms. The soldier, be he

friend or foe, is charged with the protection of the weak and unarmed. It is the very essence and reason for his being. When he violates this sacred trust he not only profanes his entire cult but threatens the very fabric of international society. The traditions of fighting men are long and honorable, based upon the noblest of human traits—sacrifice. This officer . . . entrusted with a high command involving authority adequate to his responsibility, has failed this irrevocable standard; has failed his duty to his troops, to his country, to his enemy, and to mankind; he has failed utterly his soldier faith.[52]

If protection of the innocent is one of the fundamental responsibilities of soldiers, then it is not enough for a commander to simply react to violations of the laws of war; the commander also must take positive steps to prevent violations before they occur. Based on the detailed prohibitions against acts that would harm or endanger innocents, which comprise the bulk of the Geneva and Hague Conventions, it is reasonable to conclude that ensuring their protection is one of the primary responsibilities of commanders under international law. Moreover, the references to chivalry in both U.S. Army and U.S. Air Force documents pertaining to the law of war provide additional emphasis for this as a primary responsibility of U.S. military officers.

We can conclude that commanders who do not take action to prevent war crimes from occurring, or to apprehend and punish those who commit war crimes, themselves share in the culpability for such crimes.

Topics for Further Discussion

1. Telford Taylor argues that acts routinely performed in wartime—killing, wounding, kidnapping, destroying property—are not regarded as criminal because war lays a "blanket of immunity" over the warriors who perform such acts. What is wrong with Taylor's account?

2. Army Field Manual 27–10, *The Law of Land Warfare,* advises soldiers to only obey lawful orders while at the same time conceding that soldiers will often not be able to determine whether given orders are lawful or not. Either defend the way this is presently written or offer some alternative guidance on how the principle of obedience should be communicated in army manuals. As a military leader, what would you tell your subordinates about obedience to your orders?

3. In a passage quoted from the *The Statesman* (page 149), one of Plato's interlocutors argues that because of the nature of human beings and their complex social relationships, it is impossible to develop unqualified rules for every situation. Is this an indictment of our own legal system? How might a proponent of our justice system respond?

4. Philosophers generally hold that moral rules override other types of rules such as legal rules, religious rules, and rules of etiquette. Can you think of any cases when legal rules should override moral ones?

5. Field Marshal Rommel burned Hitler's Commando Order rather than pass it on to his subordinate commanders. Other German commanders did not. Do you believe that those German commanders who passed along Hitler's Commando Order to subordinates committed a crime by doing so, or do you believe that Rommel's act of disobedience was **supererogatory?**

6. Lieutenant Colonel Oliver North secretly orchestrated acts of war against other nations without congressional approval. In his defense, he argued that he was carrying out the orders of the president of the United States that were passed on to him through his superiors. Independent of the issue of whether he lied to Congress, why were North's actions a clear violation of the Just War Tradition?

Notes

1. *The Law of War: A Documentary History*, vol. I, edited by Leon Friedman (New York: Random House, 1972), pp. 820–29.
2. Ibid., pp. 799–813.
3. Ibid., p. 777.
4. Twenty-two members of the German government were tried, nineteen convicted, and twelve sentenced to death by this tribunal. Of these, eight were convicted of "crimes against peace" (i.e., aggression). Additionally, military courts of the occupying powers conducted numerous additional trials of German military and government officials. For example, Great Britain prosecuted 937 Germans, and of these, 230 were sentenced to death; France tried 2,107 and executed 104. At the same time, in the Far East, an international military tribunal tried twenty-five senior Japanese citizens, convicted twenty-three, and imposed the death penalty on seven. See ibid., pp. 779–81.
5. North Korean and Chinese soldiers were not tried because it was feared that this would interfere with repatriation. A summary of the cases that were prepared and ready for trial is contained in *Extract of Interim Historical Report*, Korea War Crimes Division, cumulative to June 30, 1953, U.S. Army Korea Communications Zone.

   It is significant that there were very few substantive charges of war crimes brought against U.N. forces during the Korean War. North Korea, China, and the Soviet Union claimed that the United States was guilty of employing bacteriological weapons and killing eighty-two prisoners at Pongam. Upon examining the evidence, the United Nations determined that the prison deaths all occurred as a result of attacks on prison guards during a mass riot, and formally rejected the charges of criminal actions. At the request of the United States, the United Nations appointed a five-nation group to investigate the use of bacteriological weapons, but China and North Korea refused to participate in or cooperate with any investigation. The U.N. General Assembly took this as sufficient evidence that the charges were false.

6. See L. C. Green, "Superior Orders and the Reasonable Man," in *Essays on the Modern Laws of War* edited by L. C. Green (New York: Transnational Publishers, 1985), p. 68. The strong regard that the multinational U.N. forces showed for the laws of war can probably be attributed to the influence of the commander of the U.N. forces, General MacArthur, who also served as the convening authority for the International Tribunal of the Far East, which prosecuted war crimes after World War II. In upholding the death sentence for a Japanese general officer whose men had committed atrocities without his knowledge, MacArthur had noted that military commanders are responsible for the actions of their subordinates even when they do not know about them. The behavior of U.N. forces, especially in light of the atrocities committed by the opposing side, is a good indication of the extreme influence commanders can have on their subordinates. We will return to this topic in greater detail in a later discussion.

7. For a good analysis of the entire My Lai affair, see Joseph Goldstein, Burke Marshall, and Jack Schwartz, *The My Lai Massacre and Its Cover-Up* (New York: The Free Press, 1976). This work also reproduces the U.S. Army's own investigation into My Lai, "The Peers Commission Report."

    Referring to the U.S. handling of the case, Telford Taylor (who served as the chief U.S. prosecutor at the Nuremberg trials) writes, "As in the United States in 1902, as in Germany in 1921, the criminal consequences of My Lai were 'almost farcical' . . . many inferential lessons might be drawn from these events. One of them is that American and German military establishments are alike in that neither can be counted on for diligent enforcement of the laws of war against its own men. Another conclusion, readily to be drawn from the events in the world around us, is that many other national military establishments do not make the slightest effort to ensure internal compliance with the rules of war." See Friedman, *The Law of War: A Documentary History*, vol. 2, pp. xxiv–xxv.

    Despite the My Lai tragedy, the United States tried more of its own soldiers for war crimes during the Vietnam War than any government ever has before. Nevertheless, although we might conclude that there has been an increased commitment to the laws of war, this should not be construed to mean that there is now sufficient commitment. We should not forget that after two marines involved in killing five women and eleven children were convicted of murder, 160,000 citizens of Oklahoma signed a petition and sent it to the commandant of the Marine Corps requesting the release of these "unjustly confined men." Moreover, within months of Lieutenant Calley's conviction for the premeditated murder of not less than twenty-two innocent civilians, President Richard Nixon received 15,000 letters critical of the conviction. See Guenter Lewy, *America in Vietnam* (New York: Oxford University Press, 1978). The aforementioned statistics are taken from pp. 356–57 of Lewy's book. We should note that military training has become significantly more focused on legal and moral issues since Vietnam. The more specific rules that have been adopted by the United Nations and promulgated in international agreements have begun to find their way into military education programs, and are often summarized and emphasized as Rules of Engagement.

8. *Rules of Land Warfare* (Washington, D.C.: U.S. War Department, Office of the Chief of Staff, 1914), para. 366, p. 130.

9. Article 47 of the German Military Code is discussed in "The High Command Case," Nuremberg, October 1958, in Friedman, *The Law of War: A Documentary History*, vol. II, pp. 1431–32.

    In chap. 2 of *Nuremberg and Vietnam: An American Tragedy* (Chicago: Quadrangle Books, 1970), Telford Taylor cites other (earlier) legal precedents, notably the trial of Major Henry Wirtz, commandant of the Andersonville Prison Camp during the U.S. Civil War. Wirtz was hanged for his treatment of prisoners despite his claims (which were verified) of superior orders. For a summary of the case, see Friedman, *The Law of War: A Documentary History*, vol. I, pp. 783–98.

10. The oath for officers is different. Officers swear to support and defend the Constitution of the United States against all enemies, foreign and domestic.

11. U.S. Department of the Army *Law of Land Warfare*, Field Manual 27–30 (Washington, D.C.: U.S. Government Printing Office, 1956), para. 509, pp. 182–83.

12. I am dealing with only one of two broad types of unlawful orders: those that prescribe criminal acts. There can be unlawful orders that do not prescribe criminal acts, such as when I tell one of my soldiers to wash my car.

13. Telford Taylor, *Nuremberg and Vietnam: An American Tragedy*, reprinted as chap. 25, "War Crimes," in *War, Morality, and the Military Profession*, edited by Malham M. Wakin (Boulder, Colo.: Westview Press, 1979), pp. 415–16.

14. "Trial of Generaloberst Nickolaus von Falkenhorst," dated July 1946, in Friedman, *The Law of War: A Documentary History*, p. 1564. The aforementioned quotation is from an extract of the trial's transcript.

15. In this case the court ruled, however, that superior orders did not constitute an adequate justification in those cases where "an order is known to everybody, including the accused, to be without any doubt whatsoever against the law." The excuse of superior orders was considered in mitigation. "The Landovery Castle Case," Leipzig, July 1921, in Friedman, *The Law of War: A Documentary History*, vol. 2, pp. 868–82.

16. J. Glenn Gray, *The Warriors: Reflections on Men in Battle* (New York: Harper & Row, 1970), p. 182.

17. U.S. Department of the Army *Law of Land Warfare*, Field Manual 27–10 (Washington, D.C.: U.S. Government Printing Office, 1956), para. 509, pp. 182–83. Interestingly, this paragraph from the Army manual is taken almost verbatim from the discussion of this topic in the eighth edition of Lassa F. Oppenheim's *International Law*, edited by H. Lauterpacht (New York: David McKay, 1952), pp. 568–69. In a footnote, Lauterpacht notes that previous editions of Oppenheim's work absolved soldiers from responsibility, as did earlier U.S. military manuals. One is tempted to conclude that military officers assigned to write manuals are greatly influenced by works such as Oppenheim's.

18. My use of "know" in this context refers to a soldier's ignorance of relevant empirical data rather than to an ignorance of the relevant law.

19. Samuel P. Huntington, *The Soldier and the State* (Cambridge, Mass.: The Belknap Press of Harvard University, 1957), reprinted as chap. 3, "The Military Mind: Conservative Realism of the Professional Military Ethic," in *War, Morality, and the Military Profession*, 2d ed., edited by Malham M. Wakin (Boulder, Colo.: Westview Press, 1986), pp. 47–48.

20. To his credit, Huntington is uncomfortable with all of the consequences of his own argument. He notes that his position places the principle of obedience into conflict with "basic morality." He writes, "For the officer this comes down to a choice between his own conscience on the one hand, and the good of the state, plus the professional virtue of obedience, upon the other. As a soldier, he owes obedience; as a man, he owes disobedience. Except in the most extreme instances it is reasonable to expect that he will adhere to the professional ethic and obey" (Ibid., p. 44). This brief paragraph at the conclusion of his discussion of the topic of obedience seems to retract much of what he said about obedience up to that point. Furthermore, note that by not stipulating any of the considerations that might make disobedience permissible (or obligatory) his position becomes almost useless as a practical guide.

21. I omit from discussion the type of mindless, bureaucratically enforced, trivial orders that are endemic to military life and most often imposed by overly paternalistic, well-meaning, unimaginative leaders, such as keep off the grass, wear your hair short, fasten seat belts on

post, do not wear headphones while jogging, wear long sleeves when riding motorcycles, and so on, *ad infinitum.*

22. Plato, *The Statesman,* in *The Collected Dialogues of Plato,* edited by Edith Hamilton and Huntington Cairns (Princeton, N.J.: Princeton University Press, 1982), p. 1063.

23. Of course, formulated this way, the rule that particular orders should always take precedence over general orders would itself be subject to exceptions. Presumably this is the intention behind the caveat that soldiers obey only lawful orders. Thus the limits of the exceptions are specified.

24. I say that the requirement for coordinated action *almost* always prohibits disobedience, because there could be isolated situations where individual initiatives do not affect other elements. Suppose that a small military unit is moving along a prescribed route to an objective and encounters an obstacle. Should members of the unit modify the route to bypass it, attempt to traverse it, or wait for additional orders? The format for military orders in the U.S. Army has recently been modified to allow for such contingencies by requiring commanders to include a discussion of their intention. This permits soldiers some latitude in modifying methods in rapidly changing scenarios characteristic of combat with the purpose of remaining focused on the intention of the action rather than the method.

25. While this objection to the principle of obedience does not persuade us to reject the principle, it might provide a good argument against the instant and unquestioning obedience that Huntington advocates. There is considerable difference between suggesting an alternative to a legal order and then performing the same order when it is reaffirmed, and simply disobeying an order. In other words, one might argue that more utility would result from a rule that allowed for the possibility of an open exchange of suggestions followed by compliance than would result from a rule requiring instant, unquestioning compliance without such a possibility.

26. Utilitarianism calculations, for example, require that the consequences of alternatives be calculated in a manner that gives equal weight to all persons affected. Likewise, Kantian respect for persons prohibits anyone from giving preference to his or her own ends over the ends of others; or, put another way, actions should always be in accordance with rules that can be universalized without resulting in preferential treatment for anyone. In each case, these moral theories support MP_2 over disobedience based on selfish motives.

27. Hugo Grotius, *The Law of War and Peace,* translated by Francis W. Kelsey (Indianapolis and New York: Bobbs-Merrill Co., 1962), Bk. II, chap. 20, IX, pp. 473–76. See my earlier discussion of this in chapter 4, esp. note 31.

28. The magistrate also may impose requirements and restrictions on the populace as a means of accomplishing legitimate ends that the magistrate has been assigned the authority to bring about, such as collecting taxes, for example. What limitations should be placed on these means, and how, will be a crucial political question for our nation in the twenty-first century in light of our geometrically expanding political structure.

29. Kant, inspired by Hume, argues that the fact that God wills us always to follow rule *R* is sufficient reason for always following *R* only if we add the additional premise that whatever God commands is unequivocally, objectively good; and even then it would have to be verifiable or at least compatible with our reason. Rules made by transitory political entities and their agents, however, are not unequivocally good; and rules that are situational in their content—like the one requiring obedience—are extremely suspect. See R. M. Hare, *Applications of Moral Philosophy* (Berkeley, CA: University of California Press, 1972), pp. 1–8. The discussion is reprinted in Wakin, *War, Morality, and the Military Profession,* chap. 27, pp. 443–50.

30. Friedman, *The Law of War: A Documentary History,* vol. II, pp. 1438–39.

31. Ibid., p. 1445.

32.   "The Eichmann Trial," in Friedman, *The Law of War: A Documentary History,* vol. II, p. 1646.

33.   *Trial of the Major War Criminals Before the International Military Tribunal,* vol. XI (Nuremberg, Germany, 1947), Transcript of the Proceedings of April 15, 1946, pp. 401, 415.

34.   "The Nuremberg Judgment," ibid., p. 941.

35.   Ibid., p. 1431.

36.   Friedman, *The Law of War: A Documentary History,* vol. I, p. 887. Principle IV of the Nuremberg Principles, prepared by the International Law Commission for the U.N. General Assembly, states, "The fact that a person acted pursuant to order of his Government or of a superior does not relieve him from responsibility under international law, provided a moral choice was in fact possible to him." Yehuda Melzer, *Concepts of Just War* (Leyden: A. W. Sijthoff, 1975), p. 61.

37.   Guenter Lewy, "Superior Orders, Nuclear Warfare, and Conscience," in *War and Morality,* edited by Richard A. Wasserstrom (Belmont, Calif.: Wadsworth Publishing Co., 1970), p. 124.

38.   This is a minimum conception. Other acts of violence that do represent the political will of a people may be crimes as well if they are not carried out in accordance with the *jus in bello* rules.

39.   One might claim that citizens in general have an *imperfect duty* to defend their nation, while professional soldiers have a *perfect duty* to do so because of the role they have freely chosen for themselves.

40.   Hugo Grotius, *The Law of War and Peace,* Bk. II, chap. 21, II, 4, p. 524.

41.   Ibid., 6, p. 526.

42.   "The Yamashita Case," in Friedman, *The Law of War: A Documentary History,* vol. II, p. 1597.

43.   General Yamashita's conviction remains controversial. In a dissenting opinion, Justice Murphy noted, "Read against the background of military events in the Philippines . . . these charges amount to this: 'We, the victorious American forces, have done everything possible to destroy and disorganize your lines of communication, your effective control of your personnel, your ability to wage war. In those respects we have succeeded. We have defeated and crushed your forces. And now we charge and condemn you for having been inefficient in maintaining control of your troops during the period when we were so effectively besieging and eliminating your forces and blocking your ability to maintain effective control. . . . We will judge the discharge of your duties by the disorganization which we ourselves created in large part.'" There were also other issues, such as the excessively hasty trial (three weeks). Ibid., pp. 1596–1623. Numerous books are available on the details of the trial.

44.   Medina admitted killing a wounded female but pleaded self-defense in that he thought she was armed with a grenade. He also admitted to ordering one of his men to shoot a child, but claimed that it was in the heat of battle and that he quickly attempted to retract the order, but that it was too late.

45.   "Court Martial of Ernest L. Medina," in Friedman, *The Law of War: A Documentary History,* vol. 2, p. 1732.

46.   There are other problems with the Medina case. The Peers Commission Investigation conducted at the direction of General William Westmoreland and the Secretary of the Army reached the following conclusions (among others) relevant to this case: "(1) The massacre resulted primarily from the nature of the orders issued by persons in the chain of command. . . . (2) On 16 March, soldiers at the squad and platoon level, within some elements of Task Force Barker, murdered noncombatants while under the supervision and control of their immediate supervisors. (3) Part of the crimes visited on the inhabitants of Son My [My

Lai] Village included individual and group acts of murder, rape, sodomy, maiming, and assault on noncombatants and the mistreatment and killing of detainees. (4) The commanders of Task Force Barker and the 11th Brigade had substantial knowledge as to the extent of the killing of noncombatants.... (5) At every command level within the Division, actions were taken, both wittingly and unwittingly, which effectively suppressed information concerning the war crimes committed at Son My Village. (6) At the company level there was a failure to report the war crimes which had been committed."

Concerning Captain Medina personally, the Peers Commission reached the following conclusions: "(1) He planned, ordered, and supervised the execution by his company of an unlawful operation against inhabited hamlets in Son My Village which included the destruction of houses by burning, killing of livestock, and the destruction of crops and other foodstuffs, and the closing of wells; and impliedly [*sic*] directed the killing of any persons found there. (2) There is evidence that he possibly killed as many as three noncombatants in My Lai. (3) He probably conspired with Lieutenant Colonel Barker and others to suppress information concerning the killing of noncombatants.... (4) He actively suppressed information.... (5) He failed to report the killings.... (6) He obstructed an inquiry in the killings of civilians.... (7) He failed to prevent the killings of suspects.... (8) He gave false testimony...."

The Peers Commission Report can be found in Goldstein, Marshall, and Schwartz, *The My Lai Massacre and Its Cover-Up.* The aforementioned findings are on pp. 314–40 of this source.

Finally, Mary McCarthy notes that the acquittal party held in F. Lee Bailey's (the defense counsel) suite after the trial was attended by the military judge and one of the prosecuting attorneys. See Mary McCarthy, *Medina* (New York: Harcourt Brace Jovanovich, 1972), p. 81.

47. Lassa F. Oppenheim, *International Law,* 7th ed., edited by H. Lauterpacht (New York: David McKay, 1952), p. 572.

48. U.S. Department of the Army, *Law of Land Warfare,* Field Manual 27–10 (Washington, D.C.: U.S. Government Printing Office, 1956), para. 501, pp. 178–89.

49. Oppenheim, *International Law,* p. 573, n. 2.

50. An important issue that I have not addressed is whether commanders are guilty if they order crimes and their orders are not carried out.

51. Geneva I, Art. 49, Geneva II, Art. 50, Geneva III, Art. 129, and Geneva IV, Art. 146, in *Documents on the Laws of War,* edited by Adam Roberts and Richard Guelff (New York: Oxford University Press, 1982), pp. 189, 210, 267, 323, respectively.

52. Friedman, *The Law of War: A Documentary History,* vol. II, p. 1598.

Chapter

9

MILITARY NECESSITY

In our previous discussions we noted that part of the reason why nations have been remiss in prosecuting those who commit war crimes is that the laws prohibiting certain actions in war—such as those against intentional killing of noncombatants—contain so many caveats that it is often impossible for soldiers to determine whether such acts are crimes in particular situations. The two issues that create the most difficulty in this regard are military necessity and reprisals. In this chapter we will examine the first of these doctrines to determine how it might reasonably be modified so that soldiers acting under orders will be able to distinguish illegal acts from legal ones.

MILITARY NECESSITY

There is a tension between what the Germans call *Kriegsraison*, or the logic of war, and *Kriegsmanier*, or the customs of war. Sometimes this tension is referred to as a dialectic between military objectives on the one hand and humanitarian principles or the demands of civilization on the other hand. We have been referring to these opposites as *jus in bello* principles and military necessity. Historically, the tension has always yielded to military necessity.

"Military necessity" should not be confused with "necessities of war." The latter refers in a more general way to the suffering and hardship—in both the military and civilian populations—that is an inevitable by-product of the resort to force as a means of resolving political issues. In this sense it is a descriptive expression that reflects an inevitable aspect of the use of force. "Military necessity," on the other hand, is a formal term that specifically addresses the tension inherent in attempting to minimize suffering through rules, while at the same time employing a method (violence) that necessarily causes the suffering of innocent people.

We previously noted briefly the distinction between the necessities of war and military necessity found in the work of Francisco de Vitoria. Recall that in his discussion of the protection of innocents, Vitoria added the caveat that "it is right, in virtue of collateral circumstances, to slay the innocent . . . [otherwise] war could not be waged against even the guilty." Hugo Grotius's formulation of the issue places greater emphasis on the protection of innocents, and he argues that care must be taken to prevent the death of innocents "except for reasons that are weighty and will affect the safety of many."

More recently, military necessity has been used to refer to a justification for setting aside or overriding the *jus in bello* principles found in the laws of war for the sake of military objectives. In Lieber's Code, for example, expediency receives considerable emphasis under the rubric of military necessity as a justification for violating the sanctity of innocents. Lieber writes, "Military necessity does not admit of cruelty . . . and does not include any act of hostility which makes the return to peace unnecessarily difficult."[1] In every instance where Lieber addresses the protection of the innocent, however, he includes a caveat.

> The principle has been more and more acknowledged that the unarmed citizen is to be spared in person, property and honor *as much as the exigencies of war will admit.*
>
> The inoffensive individual is as little disturbed in his private relations *as the commander of the hostile force can afford to grant in the overruling demand of a vigorous war.*
>
> Military necessity admits of all direct destruction of life or limb of armed enemies, *and of other persons whose destruction is incidentally unavoidable* in the armed contests of war. [italics added][2]

These passages—which seem to relegate humanitarian principles to the status of ideals—were influential in the development of subsequent international documents.[3] The Preamble to the 1907 Hague (IV) Convention states that signatories shall abide by "these provisions, the wording of which has been inspired by the desire to diminish the evils of war, *as far as military requirements permit.*"[4] Even the Nuremberg Principles, formulated by the International Law Commission at the request of the United Nations General Assembly, include a similar caveat in its discussion of what constitutes a war crime.

> VI(b) War Crimes: Violations of the laws or customs of war which include but are not limited to, murder, ill-treatment or deportation to slave-labor or for any other purpose of civilian population of or in occupied territory, murder or ill-treatment of prisoners of war or persons on the seas, killing of hostages, plunder of public or private property, wanton destruction of cities, towns, or villages, or devastation *not justified by military necessity.* [italics added][5]

In the absence of any specific criteria for assessing when military necessity might legitimately be invoked, Grotius's emphatic declaration that "Advantage does not confer the same right as necessity" might be interpreted as a plea rather than a mandate; and, in any case, it is certainly too vague to serve as a practical guide. Under existing international and national laws the prohibition against harming innocents may be subjectively overridden for the purpose of *military advantage,* or even military convenience. Moreover, no distinction is made between military necessity in terms of tactical, strategic, or political objectives. Understood this way, military necessity amounts to a claim that certain blatantly immoral acts are justified on no other basis than that they might contribute in some way to military objectives. When this is considered in light of our earlier discussion concerning a soldier's responsibility to obey lawful orders and to disobey unlawful ones, the problem becomes even more profound, because almost any action imaginable might on some occasion be lawful based on military necessity. And as we noted in the last chapter, this makes it virtually impossible for soldiers to know with any surety whether certain orders they might receive are lawful or not. This is inadequate. If the Just War Tradition is going to function as a viable set of legally enforceable rules, the principle of military necessity must be more precisely defined and its relationship to other principles clearly articulated in law.[6]

Our mission, then, is twofold. We must examine the notion of military necessity to determine those conditions where it might provide sufficient justification for overriding certain humanitarian laws. Second, we will want to specify which, if any, *jus in bello* principles are indefeasible even in light of military necessity. Our objective is to mark the boundaries where military necessity may legitimately be invoked with vivid, patently identifiable borders that can serve as guideposts for soldiers and officers who subjectively perceive themselves to be fighting the battle of Armageddon. These *legally enforceable* guidelines must spell out specific, objective criteria for determining when instances of military necessity obtain.

The most problematic aspect of the tension between military necessity and the just conduct of war, and the one on which we will focus our discussion, is the question of when innocent persons may be killed or endangered in order to achieve some military objective. This is not simply an examination of when innocents can be endangered under the aegis of double effect. Rather, we will attempt to determine when, if ever, innocents can be *intentionally targeted.* We know, of course, that innocents often have been intentionally targeted in recent wars. Iraq's Saddam Hussein fired long-range missiles at Israeli cities in an attempt to disrupt the coalition forces arrayed against him during the Persian Gulf War; "civilian" targets such as waste treatment plants and water purification facilities in Baghdad were bombed by members of the U.N. coalition; the United States bombed Hanoi in order to force North Vietnam to negotiate an end to the Vietnam War; Great Britain and Germany engaged in regular bombing attacks against each other's cities in World War II; the United States used fire bombs against German and Japanese cities in World War II and employed nuclear weapons against Hiroshima and Nagasaki in order to "break the will of the [Japanese] people"; and finally, in 1992, only after the breakup of the Soviet Union did the president of the Russian republic, Boris Yeltsin, announce that the Soviet/Russian nuclear missiles would no longer be targeted at American cities.

I will proceed under the assumption that human beings have a *prima facie* obligation not to intentionally harm innocent persons. The issue facing us is to determine when, if ever, military objectives or soldierly duties override this obligation. If we can determine the necessary and sufficient conditions for when innocents may intentionally be attacked and perhaps killed, based on military necessity, we will have addressed the most problematic and extreme case. Let us begin, then, with a brief review of who might be considered "innocent" in war, as well as the basis for distinguishing innocents from other categories of persons such as civilians, combatants, and noncombatants.

During wartime, combatants are those who are either directly or indirectly involved in attacking one belligerent nation's constituents on behalf of another nation or political group. The term *combatants* refers primarily to members of the armed forces, but can include certain political leaders who are engaged in planning and carrying out the war effort as well as civilians who are working on behalf of the military. Shopkeepers, farmers, and other members of what Grotius refers to as the "peaceable population" are not considered combatants, although they may pay taxes and even approve of the belligerent actions of their government. Any civilians directly involved in the war effort, on the other hand, such as those working in munitions factories or manning radar sites, are considered combatants and are subject to being attacked, even though they have not performed any action that might cause them to be considered guilty for having committed some wrong.

Nor can soldiers be considered guilty simply for fighting on behalf of their nation, even if the war itself is an unjust one, because (as we concluded in chapter 6) soldiers are always presumed to be shrouded in invincible ignorance as far as *jus ad bellum* is concerned. Nevertheless, it seems obvious that combatants are subject to attack by opposing combatants. The justification, then, for soldiers intentionally inflicting harm on one another cannot be based on their mutual guilt; it must derive from some other basis.

Likewise, the conventional use of the term *innocent* (i.e., anyone who is not guilty is innocent) is problematic when applied to soldiers because it is generally accepted that there is *at least* a *prima facie* obligation not to intentionally harm innocents. One might argue that if soldiers are not guilty, then they are innocent; and if they are innocent, then they should not be intentionally harmed. But, of course, it is permissible to harm enemy soldiers intentionally. Thus we must conclude that the *prima facie* obligation not to intentionally harm those who are innocent (where all those who are not guilty are innocent) is inappropriate when applied to soldiers.[7] We will return to the reasons for this shortly.

But while notions of guilt and innocence are not applicable to soldiers carrying out public policy—although such notions might apply to officials formulating such policies—soldiers can be guilty or innocent in terms of the means they use in performing their soldierly duties. For example, soldiers can be guilty of war crimes when they violate the laws governing the means that can legally be employed in warfare. Nevertheless, neither "guilt" nor "innocent" seems to be a suitable term to use in discussing the combatant–noncombatant distinction. Perhaps if we can determine the justification for combatants intentionally harming one another it will help us distinguish those who are legitimate targets from those who should not be attacked.

Recall from our discussion of Grotius that a state's right to engage in hostilities is grounded in the fundamental individual right to defend one's own person, one's property, and one's family or communal group from unjust predation. (Grotius would argue that this right is derived from the social aspect of human nature; we will simply accept it as a moral truth.) From this individual right of self-defense, it follows that it is permissible for members of communities and states to collectively employ force in self-defense against other groups, and many nations have fixed the responsibility for doing so in the office of the soldier. Soldiers act as agents of their state in exercising the state's right of self-defense. Because a state's right to self-defense is derived from the rights of individual citizens and families, soldiers cannot perform any action on behalf of their state that would be wrong for an individual to perform in his or her own defense. In other words, the principle of self-defense is not unlimited—at a minimum, it is limited by the prohibition against intentionally harming innocent bystanders in order to protect oneself. And because it is defense that is the basis for violence done in wartime, there is no justification for intentionally harming those who are not involved in attempting to harm others.[8] With these considerations in mind, it is more appropriate to refer to the distinction between those who may be attacked and those who are protected under the humanitarian laws of war as a distinction between combatant and noncombatant, rather than between guilty and innocent.[9]

Furthermore, it is important to note that these are wartime distinctions; the role of combatant comes into existence simultaneously with a state of war. During peacetime, even professional soldiers are not properly considered combatants because they are not imbued with the authority to act on behalf of their society in inflicting harm on others. A soldier acquires the right to use violence on behalf of the members of his or her community only by political authority; indeed, a soldier has the duty to do so for the safety of constituents.

Despite these considerations, favoring the use of the terms *combatant* and *noncombatant* in wartime, many commentators, some whose work we will discuss later, use the term *innocent* to refer specifically to any persons protected from attack under the *jus in bello* tradition. Additionally, prisoners of war and "protected persons," although they represent distinct categories in that they are not considered either combatants or noncombatants under international law, are often referred to as noncombatants or innocents in the literature. For purposes of our discussion, then, we will only make a single broad distinction: We will use the term *combatant* to refer to those opponents who can justifiably be attacked in wartime, and the terms *innocent* and *noncombatant* interchangeably to refer to all of those categories of persons who are protected from attack under international law. What we will *not* presume, however, is that all who are not guilty are innocent, because soldiers are both not guilty and still subject to attack. Where special considerations are required, such as in discussions that rely on the particular rights afforded to prisoners of war, I will specify the category of noncombatants under discussion and the relevant rights particular to that group under international law.

Finally, before we tackle military necessity, I want to identify two moral truths or precepts that seem to be at the heart of both *jus ad bellum* and *jus in bello*. I am going to refer to these as moral truths because they seem more specific than moral principles such as "all people deserve respect" and "human suffering ought to be minimized," and yet they also seem too timeless and universal to be called rules or laws. Some of the philosophers whose work we have discussed (e.g., Cicero, Aquinas, Grotius) might consider these either examples of natural laws proper or dispositions derived from natural laws. In any case, I believe that these two humanitarian precepts do identify universal human dispositions, and I will refer to them as "Moral Truths."

MT$_1$ It is wrong to intentionally harm innocent persons.

MT$_2$ One is sometimes obligated to protect innocent persons from harm.

Of course, those who simply violate MT$_1$ are not innocent and may be harmed in self-defense or in retribution. The more interesting and problematic case is when MT$_1$ and MT$_2$ come into conflict, as they do in wartime. It is useful to understand military examples in terms of a conflict between these two moral truths because enemy soldiers are presumed to be possessed of "invincible ignorance" as far as *jus ad bellum* is concerned—that is, even though soldiers know that they are inflicting harm on others, including collateral damage to peaceful members of the civilian population, they always believe that they are justified in doing so. Therefore, soldiers do not attempt to harm enemy combatants because they believe they are guilty, but because they believe enemy combatants must be stopped in order to protect innocent members of their own community.[10]

Even political leaders who order their armed forces into combat are usually presumed to be motivated by a desire to protect their own innocent constituents rather than to harm others. The very act of declaring a state of war begins a chain of events that involves changing the status of active-duty soldiers, citizens who are reserve soldiers, and possibly potential conscripts or enlistees, from innocents or noncombatants to combatants who are subject to attack. Thus the act of declaring war entails intentionally putting certain innocent members of one's own community in harm's way, thereby violating MT_1, in order to protect other innocents, thereby conforming to MT_2. We will next discuss various versions of military necessity and how they relate to MT_1 and MT_2.

MILITARY NECESSITY AND REDUCING RISKS

Sheldon Cohen proposes certain guidelines for military necessity. He writes, "The notion of 'military necessity' lends itself to abuse, but every use of it is not abusive. It is not being abused if the alternative is to ask more of troops than we have any right to ask of anyone or than anyone can deliver."[11] The limits he proposes are best understood in terms of his own example.

> The law of war implies that soldiers are not obliged to raise their already high risks to even higher levels in order to lower further the risk to innocents in combat zones. . . . The rights of innocents are defeasible when honoring those rights would push the soldiers' risk beyond what it is reasonable to expect any group to endure. The rule is, I suggest, that the attacker may, given the presence of innocents in a combat zone, do anything that it would be permissible to do if there were no innocents there—subject to the restrictions entailed by the principle of proportionality. This rules out discriminatory (selective) attacks on innocents but allows the indiscriminate shelling or bombing of defended areas containing innocents.[12]

Cohen wants to set limits on the amount of risk it is reasonable to expect a soldier to take, and he is willing to increase the risk to civilians in order to do so. He sees limiting a soldier's risk as the criterion for when military necessity might be invoked to justify setting aside the laws of war, as long as the risk to soldiers is proportional to the risk to innocents. Stated as a conceptual theory, Cohen's position on military necessity seems to read,

> MN_1 A particular action is justified by military necessity if and only if:
>
> (a) its performance will reduce the risk to one's own soldiers' lives;
>
> (b) no alternative action will result in less risk to their lives; and
>
> (c) the amount of increased risk to noncombatants is proportional to the amount of reduced risk to soldiers.

One difficulty with this account is that it does not acknowledge that part of what it means to be a soldier is taking risks. Perhaps the problem with MN_1 is best understood in terms of an example.

During the Korean War (and more recently in the Second Gulf War), enemy combatants would hide among groups of civilian women and children and force them at bayonet point to advance toward American positions.

American conscripts manning the forward positions saw themselves faced with two alternatives: attack the soldiers using either artillery or small arms fire, or withdraw from their positions. The former choice would result in numerous civilian deaths; the latter, the loss of key defensive terrain. Certainly any other action would substantially increase the risk to American troops.

In this case, if the defensive positions were crucial to the mission, one might reason that military necessity justified an artillery barrage against the enemy troops. Any civilian casualties, one could argue, would be the fault of those who placed them in harm's way to begin with.[13]

The problem with this line of reasoning is that both alternatives are based on the assumption that no action should be taken that would "unnecessarily" increase the risk to American soldiers' lives. To appreciate the more reasonable alternatives, we need only remove the assumed premise concerning the sanctity of soldiers' lives. Once we accept that it is part of the ethos of the soldier to behave courageously and to protect innocents, even at the risk of one's own life, then it becomes clear that it is the civilians' lives that must be safeguarded, not the lives of soldiers. In this case, for example, the men could assault the enemy/civilian formation and use bayonets to engage the combatants.

The requirement to assume great personal risk in the performance of one's duty has always been a fundamental aspect of the office of soldier, although one seldom finds it bluntly articulated. Nevertheless, the values identified and discussed in the U.S. government publications on the Profession of Arms—courage, selfless service, candor, compassion, commitment—capture the expectation that soldiers should be prepared to sacrifice their own well-being as part of their duties.[14]

While all widely accepted moral theories require some degree of impartiality or objectivity in choosing among alternatives, the risk to the lives of combatants should not be weighed equally against the risk to the lives of noncombatants, because it is in the nature of the soldier to take risks—risking one's life is part of what it means to be a soldier. Taking the position that minimizing the risk to soldiers is the basis for choosing among alternatives undermines the very notion of distinguishing between combatants and noncombatants. An analogous domestic example might be to hire a police officer to prevent crime and to limit her duty to times or places where there was little crime so that she would not be put at risk; or to hire a bodyguard for protection in the city and then to stay home so that the bodyguard would not be endangered.

Still, the principle of impartiality applies *within* the class of noncombatants. Although soldiers do not have the same positive duty (MT_2) to protect innocents among the enemy population as they have to protect their own population, they most certainly do have the same obligation not to intentionally harm innocents, regardless of their national affiliation. This is because all human beings—including soldiers—have a moral duty not to intentionally harm innocent people (MT$_1$). No similar universal moral duty obligates all persons to risk their lives to protect innocents. Soldiers, however, do have a duty to protect others, and because they acquire this duty from the individual right of self-defense that is assigned to them from the members of the society they are defending, the duty (MT$_2$) obligates only on behalf of the constituents of that society. As Augustine noted, humans have some duties in virtue of their personhood, and some in virtue of their societal roles.

In sum, all soldiers have a moral duty to refrain from intentionally harming innocents (MT$_1$), regardless of nationality, and they also have a moral duty to protect the members of that society that is the *raison d'être* for their being soldiers (MT$_2$). Of these, the former is the more fundamental duty because it is a universal duty common to all humans. When one assumes the role of soldier, one does not relinquish one's fundamental human obligations. Moreover, social roles are merely expedients whereby individual rights and duties are collected in particular individuals by virtue of their office. It follows that the parameters of permissible behavior that are acquired in conjunction with assuming a particular office can never exceed the individual rights and duties of those that bring the office into existence. In other words, a nation's citizens cannot assign rights to soldiers that the citizens themselves do not have in the first place. In this case, because the right to self-defense is limited, in that one cannot sacrifice innocents to protect oneself, the soldier must function under a similar constraint.

Undoubtedly, the most controversial aspect of this argument is the premise that no distinction should be made between one's own innocents and the innocent citizens of an enemy nation in terms of MT$_1$. One might, after all, object that the domestic analogy justifies preferential treatment for the members of one's own community in the same way that it is reasonable for a person to give preferential treatment to one's family. However, while this is undoubtedly true as a positive duty, there is an important difference between preferential treatment for one group over another, and sacrificing one group to save another. As we noted in an earlier discussion, a parent attacked by a wild beast might well protect her family first, even though this would mean leaving others unprotected. She would not be justified, however, in throwing the members of another family to the beast in order to keep the beast away from her own.

One troubling aspect of MN$_1$ is that the soldier's right to safety becomes more fundamental than anyone else's, including the very individuals the office of soldier was created to protect! The following example points to the ludicrous consequences that are possible, given this formulation: Imagine that you are a member of an infantry rifle squad that is surrounded, low on ammunition, and under siege by an overwhelmingly superior force. Suppose that the only way to escape is to force a nearby group of innocent women and children to act as a shield and to lead you and your men through a minefield to safety at gunpoint. Suppose, further, that there is reason to believe that if you surrender you will be murdered. Does military necessity excuse endangering civilian lives to facilitate your escape?[15] Using Sheldon Cohen's reasoning, a soldier might conclude that he is justified in reducing the danger to his own life by transferring that danger to a civilian.

Note that in our example the distinction between military necessity and military advantage cannot be determined from the soldier's point of view, primarily because combat is characterized by scenarios that are life threatening and extraordinary. Let us provide a few more details about the aforementioned situation that help point this out.

Let us now suppose that the scenario I have just described is taking place in Virginia, and that the innocent women and children, as well as the soldiers who are surrounded, are all American citizens. In this context, Sheldon Cohen's argument would justify American soldiers putting the lives of U.S. citizens at risk in order to reduce the risk to their own lives. But this is, of course, contrary to the very purpose for which military forces are maintained, which is to protect the civilian population. As Grotius reminds us, while the basis for the resort to arms is self-defense, this is not an absolute right—one does not have the right to kill innocent people in order to preserve oneself. There is, after all, no good argument for distinguishing between innocents, all of whom are the victims of war, on the basis of their nationality. Because Cohen does not pay sufficient attention to the logical basis for the resort to force, he fails to recognize the limits of the amount of force that may reasonably be employed. Hence his argument that military necessity may be invoked to reduce risk to combatants improperly subordinates the humanitarian principles of *Kriegsmanier* or *jus in bello* to tactical considerations. MN₁ must be rejected.

MILITARY NECESSITY AND THE NECESSITY OF SUCCESS

Telford Taylor attempts to solve the problem of when soldiers may invoke military necessity by subordinating *jus in bello* to military objectives. Referring to the humanitarian aspects of the laws of war, he writes,

> These requirements [the laws of war] are followed more often than not, and for that reason millions are alive today who would otherwise be dead. But they are not infrequently violated; the rules read like absolute requirements, but circumstances arise where military necessity, or even something less, cause them to be disregarded. In the heat of combat, soldiers who are frightened, angered, shocked at the death of comrades, and fearful of treacherous attacks by enemies feigning death or surrender, are often prone to kill rather than capture. Under quite different circumstances, the killing may be done in cold blood, by order of humane commanders. Small detachments on

special missions, or accidentally cut off from their main force, may take prisoners under such circumstances that men cannot be spared to guard them or take them to the rear, and that to take them along would greatly endanger the success of the mission or the safety of the unit. *The prisoners will be killed, by operation of the principle of military necessity, and no military or other court has been called upon, so far as I am aware, to declare such killing a war crime.* [italics added][16]

Taylor provides two independently sufficient reasons for setting aside the *jus in bello* rules: safety and success. Since our previous discussion has already determined that the safety of one's soldiers is not a sufficient justification for setting aside the rules of war, it remains for us to examine the second of Taylor's criteria: mission success. Taylor's "necessity of success" principle might be stated in the following manner:

MN$_2$ An action is justified by military necessity if it will contribute significantly to the success of the mission.

One interesting aspect of Taylor's position is that he does not offer any arguments on behalf of military necessity. Instead, he assumes that military necessity should always override the laws of war, and he presents arguments concerning why we should continue to accept and promulgate the laws of war in light of their sterility. He states that, although the laws of war are frequently violated, and even though such violations are justified based on either military necessity or simply the awful realities of combat, the laws of war are still useful for two reasons. It is worthwhile for us to examine these two justifications for the laws of war because they provide us with insights into how Taylor understands the relationship between these laws and military necessity. In his own words,

Violated or ignored as they often are, enough of the rules are observed enough of the time so that mankind is very much better off with them than without them. . . . If it were not regarded as wrong to bomb military hospitals, they would be bombed all of the time instead of some of the time . . . [and the laws of war] are necessary to diminish the corrosive effect of mortal combat on the participants. . . . Unless troops are trained and required to draw the distinction between military and nonmilitary killing, and to retain such respect for the value of life that unnecessary death and destruction will continue to repel them, they may lose the sense for that distinction for the rest of their lives. The consequence would be that many returning soldiers would be potential murderers.[17]

The latter of Taylor's two consequential justifications for the laws of war is that they are necessary so soldiers will be able to distinguish legal killing on behalf of the state from illegal killing done for selfish reasons. This seems troublesome, however, in light of Taylor's earlier discussion (quoted on the previous page) of acceptable excuses for violating the laws of war, which included the heat of combat, fear, anger, and shock, as well as military necessity. If one is not culpable for violating national and international laws as a result of such reasoning in wartime, this would seem to encourage violations of similar laws for similar reasons in peacetime. Indeed, almost any alternative would support Taylor's consequence of reducing the "corrosive effect of mortal combat" more than the one he defends. For example, it would be more persuasive to argue either that in wartime the laws operative in civil society cease to apply and a different set of absolute laws is in effect, or that war is characterized by the absence of rules, than it is for Taylor to argue that in wartime there are rules against certain actions (such as intentionally killing innocents) but that these can be overridden on the basis of anger, fear, the heat of battle, mission success, or the safety of friendly soldiers. I cannot imagine any policy that would be more pervasive to a wanton disregard for the law than the one Taylor justifies by appealing to a need to teach respect for the law. Indeed, Taylor's own consequentialist argument supports a much stronger regard for the laws of war than the one he advocates.

His second justification for the laws of war is that they reduce suffering. If there were no such laws, he argues, there would be increased suffering. Nevertheless, he makes it clear that *any* suffering that contributes significantly to military success is justified. The only suffering, then, that is prevented by the laws of war, according to Taylor, is that which does not significantly contribute to military success. But even this seems questionable, given Taylor's earlier contention that the laws of war may often be ignored because of anger, fear, the heat of battle, and so on. This would seem to make the humanitarian dimension of the "laws" of war not laws at all but merely a set of voluntary guidelines. Moreover, it is difficult, given Taylor's perspective, to distinguish between military necessity and military advantage. In fact, his discussion seems to make the humanitarian dimension of the laws of war entirely defeasible in the name of military advantage.

This view is especially troublesome in light of Taylor's background as the chief U.S. prosecutor at the Nuremberg trials. Before we explore some additional difficulties with Taylor's position, we should perhaps note that the view I have attributed to him is one that has often been defended in the aftermath of the Vietnam War, and that the text from which I have taken the earlier quotations is Taylor's critical analysis of American actions in Vietnam. This is relevant to our discussion, because the Vietnam War was characterized by a lack of distinction between friendly and enemy territory and between combatants and noncombatants. Many U.S. military and political leaders believed that the rules that had worked in the wars of Europe and Korea—wars where enemy and friendly forces and territory were clearly delineated—were no longer practical in a guerrilla war, and they blamed this on the guerrillas. Another well-known commentator on the Vietnam War notes the many problems for the *jus in bello* tradition that resulted from the new tactics and concludes,

> U.S. violations of the *jus in bello* were in substantial measure the result of deliberate Communist policies of using the populations as a shield. Often it was impossible to get at the enemy without risking disproportionate indiscriminate actions.[18]

And Paul Ramsey, specifically addressing U.S. actions in Vietnam, argues that guerrillas who fight between and behind women and children are themselves responsible for any innocent deaths, not the counterguerrillas who have no choice of battlefield. He goes on to note, "To draw any other conclusion would be like, at the nuclear level, granting an enemy immunity from attack because he had the shrewdness to locate his missile bases in the heart of his cities."[19]

In each case these writers are proposing that the military community had no choice but to deemphasize (or override) the principles of *jus in bello* on the basis of military necessity. Their argument is that if winning requires us to set aside the humanitarian principles of *jus in bello*, then we should set them aside. Each of these writers seems to advocate a version of the necessity of success argument in MN_2. Now let us see why MN_2 provides a poor justification for overriding the laws of war.

There are certain difficulties inherent in MN_2, simply because of the various ways one might define success. For example, one might argue that there is a correlation between the likelihood of success and the number of friendly casualties. The fewer soldiers one side loses in a mission relative to enemy losses, the greater is that side's chance of success. This, however, takes us back to the previous argument that any actions that reduce the risk to American lives are justified under military necessity—a position we have already shown to be untenable.

The most problematic aspect of this ambiguity is that success can be defined in terms of tactical, strategic, or political objectives. Thus the necessity of success principle would allow soldiers at every level to ignore the rules of war in order to be successful. But as we noted in earlier discussions, it is unlikely that soldiers have the rightful authority to condemn innocents to death under any circumstances, and certainly not on behalf of some tactical objective that is only contextually "necessary." Permitting soldiers at each level to override the rules because of a subjective assessment of how doing so might contribute to success is almost the same as doing away with the rules altogether. The oft-quoted remark by an Army officer after U.S. Air Force raids had destroyed the Vietnamese village of Ben Tre with heavy civilian casualties—"It was necessary to destroy the town to save it"—exemplifies the logical consequences of "necessity of success" reasoning.[20]

One of the most serious problems for the prosecution of the Vietnam War was that military success was often defined entirely in terms of "body count," without any relationship to the political objectives that prompted the resort to violence in the first place. This is especially troublesome in light of the moral truths that dictate the parameters of a soldier's charter. Certainly soldiers have a duty to protect those innocents on behalf of whom they are fighting. In the Vietnam War these were the people of South Vietnam. In fact, it seems obvious to me that American soldiers in Vietnam had the same obligation to protect South Vietnamese innocents (MT_2) that they would have had to protect U.S. innocents had they been fighting in the United States.

Second, American soldiers in Vietnam had the same obligation to not harm any innocents intentionally—friendly or "enemy"—that they would have had if they had been fighting in the United States or in any friendly country in Europe or the Western Hemisphere (MT_1). In view of these precepts, it is certain that for commanders and platoon leaders and squad leaders, success must be defined in terms of both the military objectives *and the means employed to attain them*. And of these two, the military objectives and the means, it is the latter that is the more fundamental at the tactical and even strategic level, because these principles provide the basis for creating the office of soldier in the first place. It is contradictory to create the office of soldier in order to enforce certain moral prescriptions and prohibitions, and then to permit those filling this office to violate these same prescriptions and prohibitions as their means of enforcing them!

Yet another problem for the necessity of success view is that if we accept the argument that success justifies setting aside the humanitarian laws of war, then in every battle of every war only one side—the winning side—will be obligated by these laws! The losing side will always be justified in invoking military necessity under Taylor's necessity of success account. This is ridiculous. We have no choice but to conclude that soldiers do not have the authority to harm innocents intentionally. Hence, MN_2 will not suffice as a theory for military necessity.

Another way to understand the relationship of the laws of war to military objectives is to view the laws as absolute prescriptions that are never defeasible (capable of being voided). Let us examine the arguments of one well-known philosopher who defends this view.

THE ABSOLUTIST POSITION

Thomas Nagel, in defending an absolutist argument for the principles of *jus in bello*, describes the dilemma as a "moral blind alley," and he rejects military necessity as a justification for setting aside the rules.

> In situations of deadly conflict, particularly where a weaker party is threatened with annihilation or enslavement by a stronger one, the argument for resort to atrocities can be powerful, and the dilemma acute. There may exist

principles, not yet codified, which would enable us to resolve such dilemmas. But then again there may not.[21]

Nagel's frustration at the "dilemma" is reminiscent of Augustine's lamentation that we are often faced with alternatives, each of which seems to entail evil consequences. Grotius, too, notes that there are situations where evil may result, no matter what one does. But where Augustine counsels that moral agents keep their intentions pure and answer their calling, and Grotius advises that in such situations the lesser evil assumes the character of the good, Nagel balks: "It is naive to suppose that there is a solution to every moral problem with which the world can face us. We have always known that the world is a bad place. It appears that it may be an evil place as well."[22]

We might liken Nagel's assessment that the world is an evil place to Marcellus's lamentation in *Hamlet,* that there is something rotten in the state of Denmark, and although we may sympathize with Nagel's assessment of the difficulty with moral choices in such a world, it is likely that his solution would fare as poorly in wartime as Hamlet's does in Shakespeare's play. Certainly the moral principles that are manifested as rules in the laws of war represent key, even crucial, terrain; and it may very well be that we should often defend them to the death. Nevertheless, there may arise situations where this terrain must be abandoned in order to defend other important positions—positions that could affect the safety of thousands of innocents.

It is just this type of assumption that justifies the resort to war in the first place, an assumption that Nagel seems to accept. Once one accepts that there may be scenarios where the outcome is so important, the alternatives so heinous, that the intentional expenditure of human life is justified in order to gain a particular result, then one has already committed oneself to some type of consequentialist analysis.

Nagel argues that it is naive to believe that there is a solution to every moral problem; what he means is that in human affairs there is not a *perfect* solution to every problem. But that is not a good reason to "dig in" behind a Maginot Line of absolute moral principles and contend that the principles are inviolate, especially since his commitment to the resort to arms in the first place has already shown that he accepts some justifications for intentionally setting aside these same principles. Consider this: The decision to resort to arms entails a decision that certain noncombatants become combatants for the sake of some political objective. In other words, a declaration of war is a declaration that the requirements of justice are so great that the innocent lives of one's own citizens must intentionally be put at extreme risk for the sake of some worthwhile end.

Just as the resort to force is sometimes the *best* solution among a number of repugnant alternatives, so might certain actions in warfare that are normally prohibited "assume the character of the good" based on the available alternatives.[23] When multiple "absolute" principles conflict with one another in such a way that all available alternatives entail violating the same principle or ones that are equally weighty, we have no choice but to decide on the basis of a comparison of probable consequences. Refusing to choose alternatives in such circumstances is, after all, a form of choice.[24]

Because the resort to force as a legitimate means of achieving political objectives must always be a political decision, perhaps this is a reasonable perspective from which to invoke military necessity as a means of realizing objectively important ends. Let us consider one author who only accepts military necessity as a political decision.

POLITICAL NECESSITY

Michael Walzer presents a thoughtful, provocative attempt at providing some guidelines for determining when military necessity would justify setting aside the laws of war.[25] According to his argument, the laws of war must be obeyed "until the heavens fall." He calls such a calamity a *supreme emergency,* and he uses Nazi Germany's early successes in World War II as an example of a supreme emergency for Great Britain.

Walzer argues that only in the case of imminent defeat, with "backs to the wall," facing an enemy so heinous and fearful that the very idea of restraint seems ludicrous, may a nation set aside the principles of *jus in bello.* He concludes that the Western Allies may have been justified in bombing German population centers because of military necessity, although only during the early part of the conflict when the outcome of the war was extremely doubtful.

For Walzer, then, "military necessity" could more appropriately be called "political necessity": Supreme emergencies, as he has defined them, do not exist at the tactical or unit level. Applied to the soldier in the foxhole or the lieutenant general in a corps command center, Walzer's interpretation makes the humanitarian principles of *jus in bello* absolute prohibitions. According to his argument, only in cases where a nation is faced with imminent, disastrous defeat—a defeat that would likely result in enslavement or genocide—may military necessity be invoked. But this seems too restrictive.

One rule that might serve as a practical guide is that if the situation is grave enough to justify killing or putting at risk one's own citizens to accomplish military objectives, then military necessity may also justify the same risk to other "non-friendly" noncombatants. In other words, no factor analysis is permitted that gives a greater weight to those innocents that will be put in harm's way because of their nationality. This, it seems to me, is similar to what occurs when a nation decides to employ force as a means of seeking some political objective because, as we noted earlier, the decision to resort to arms entails a decision that certain of one's own innocent citizens be put at risk. Perhaps we can now identify our guidelines for deciding when military necessity may be invoked as a justification for attacking innocents.

The only justification for setting aside MT_1 is to satisfy MT_2. Because doing this is such an extraordinary step, it is important to establish a set of clearly defined and objective conditions that must be met to ensure the efficacy of the circumstances and to prevent abuse. The same *jus ad bellum* criteria that justify the resort to force in the first place, it seems to me, would satisfy the conditions for when military necessity might be invoked, because both cases involve violating MT_1 for the sake of MT_2. In this regard, it must always be a political rather than a military decision. Moreover, the decision to invoke military necessity and the specific rules that will be set aside by doing so must be publicly declared by a lawful authority.[26]

Additionally, the importance of the end sought must be proportional to the amount of human suffering that will be incurred in achieving it. In other words, if the cost is measured in terms of innocent lives, decision makers would be just as willing to exchange the same number of lives of their own citizens in order to achieve it. We generally call this criterion *proportionality*, although it usually has not been framed in this context.

Finally, the means used must be both necessary and sufficient to attain the desired end—necessary because overriding the prohibition against intentionally attacking innocent people must always be truly a last resort, and sufficient because the total means that one is willing to employ must be weighed against the outcome. Put another way, the limits of the means to be used must be specified in advance. For example, one must not argue that bombing a city is justified to achieve a specific objective and then argue later, after the initial bombing has failed to achieve the desired outcome, that the bombing of a second city is justified to achieve the same objective, and so on *ad infinitum*. This does not preclude the sufficient conditions from including a graduated response in advance; it merely requires that this be part of the decision-making process so that these means are not weighed against the outcome in a piecemeal fashion.

Of course, meeting these criteria is not impossible, as it is precisely what is done when a nation resorts to force in the first place—that is, when it decides to "spend" the lives of its own citizens (as soldiers) in order to achieve some political objective.

If followed, the criteria I have suggested would eliminate military necessity as a tactical decision and would severely limit the occasions where military necessity might be invoked as a national or strategic decision. This would eliminate the ambiguity inherent in the international laws of war without eliminating military necessity altogether. The *jus ad bellum* criteria that provide the key for unleashing the dogs of war will also open the door to military necessity on those rare occasions where it is justified.

Topics for Further Discussion

1. In this chapter we discussed a scenario where enemy soldiers seized innocent women and children and used them as a shield to advance on friendly positions. Imagine that you are a soldier faced with such a situation: Should the nationality of the civilians (they could be members of your nation, members of an allied nation, citizens of a neutral nation, or citizens of the enemy nation) make any difference to you in determining your course of action? Why or why not?

2. Telford Taylor argues that long-range patrols behind enemy lines might justifiably execute enemy prisoners rather than endanger the success of a patrol's mission. International law, however, expressly prohibits killing or mistreating prisoners of war. Can you think of a scenario where killing prisoners might be justified? If you were a commander sending out such a patrol, what guidance concerning prisoners would you give the patrol members?

3. The United States Code of Conduct for members of all of the armed forces states, *I will never surrender of my own free will; if in command, I will never surrender my subordinates while they still have the means to resist.* Can you imagine a combat scenario where surrender would be permissible? Do you believe that military leaders might face situations where surrender would be obligatory? What should a leader do if he decides that surrender is the only reasonable alternative and one of his subordinates, citing the Code of Conduct, refuses to lay down his arms, thereby endangering the safety of the other members of the unit? Can you think of any situations where a leader might reasonably order subordinates to fight to the death, regardless of the circumstances?

4. As an officer in an enemy POW camp, how would you deal with a fellow prisoner who kills a guard during an escape attempt? As a commander of a POW camp, how would you deal with an enemy prisoner who kills one of your soldiers while trying to escape?

5. Because prisoners are no longer considered combatants, they can no longer be harmed, nor can they intentionally harm others. International law grants prisoners of war "benevolent quarantine" for the duration of hostilities. Are soldiers who are taken prisoner but who have never surrendered (e.g., they were captured while wounded or unconscious) under any different obligation toward their captors than those who actually surrender?

6. A few hours before you are scheduled to cross the Line of Departure signifying the beginning of a major offensive operation, your commander tells you that you must be ready to pursue the enemy after the objective is secure and that you will not be able either to take prisoners along or

to spare any soldiers to guard them. He concludes by suggesting that if you do not take any prisoners the "problem" of what to do with them goes away. What should you tell your subordinates about prisoners? Do you have any additional responsibilities?

7. During a training exercise for ambushes, you hear one of your senior sergeants explaining the practice of "double tap" to his subordinates. He tells them the following:

> After the ambush has been triggered and all the enemy has either been shot or has fled, we will send one squad across the ambush site to set up security on the far side so that the second squad can search the enemy dead without the threat of a counterattack. As the security team moves across the ambush site they are to fire "insurance" rounds into each enemy just in case any are "playing possum" or just superficially wounded.

When you question this sergeant later, he tells you that "double-tapping" downed enemy during ambushes is an accepted practice and that anything else will unnecessarily endanger the lives of soldiers. What are some of your options for dealing with this scenario? How would you handle it?

8. The Rules of Engagement pocket card issued to coalition forces during the 1991 Gulf War (Desert Storm) reads:

> "ALL ENEMY MILITARY PERSONNEL AND VEHICLES TRANS-PORTING THE ENEMY OR THEIR SUPPLIES MAY BE ENGAGED SUBJECT TO THE FOLLOWING RESTRICTIONS:
>
> **A.** Do not engage anyone who has surrendered, is out of battle due to sickness or wounds, is shipwrecked, or is an aircrew member descending by parachute from a disabled aircraft.
> **B.** Avoid harming civilians unless necessary to save US lives. Do not fire into civilian populated areas of buildings which are not defended or being used for military purposes.
> **C.** Hospitals, churches, shrines, schools, museums, national monu-ments, and any other historical or cultural sites will not be engaged except in self-defense.
> **D.** Hospitals will be given special protection. Do not engage hospitals unless the enemy uses the hospital to commit acts harmful to US forces, and then only after giving them a warning and allowing a reasonable time to expire before engaging, if the tactical situation permits.
> **E.** Booby traps may be used to protect friendly positions or to impede the progress of enemy forces. They may not be used on civilian personal property. They will be recovered or destroyed when the military necessity for their use no longer exists.

    F. Looting and the taking of war trophies are prohibited.

    G. Avoid harming civilian property unless necessary to save US lives. Do not attack traditional civilian objects, such as houses, unless they are being used by the enemy for military purposes and neutralization assists in mission accomplishment.

    H. Treat all civilians and their property with respect and dignity. Before using privately owned property, check to see if publicly owned property can substitute. No requisitioning of civilian property, including vehicles, without permission of a company level commander and without giving a receipt. If an ordering officer can contract the property, then do not requisition it.

    I. Treat all prisoners humanely and with respect and dignity.

    J. Rules of Engagement Annex to the Operations Plan provides more detail. Conflicts between this card and the Operations Plan should be resolved in favor of the Operations Plan.

REMEMBER

    1) FIGHT ONLY COMBATANTS.
    2) ATTACK ONLY MILITARY TARGETS.
    3) SPARE CIVILIAN PERSONS AND OBJECTS.
    4) RESTRICT DESTRUCTION TO WHAT YOUR MISSION REQUIRES."

    a. How do these guidelines differ from what you know about U.S. actions in Vietnam?

    b. Which rules might cause the most difficulty for mission accomplishment?

    c. How would you change these rules?

9. During the Second Gulf War, Iraqis attacked and killed U.S. forces by driving vehicles loaded with explosives into U.S. positions while waving a white flag. What guidelines would you give your soldiers to protect them from such attacks?

Notes

1. Richard Shelly Hartigan, ed., *Lieber's Code and the Law of War* (Chicago: Precedent Publishing, 1983), p. 48.

2. Ibid., pp. 48–49.

3. For later examples of references to military necessity, see Hague IV (1907), Article XXII, and Geneva IV (1949), Article CXLVII, in *The Law of War: A Documentary History*, vol. I, edited by Leon Friedman (New York: Random House, 1972), pp. 318, 690, respectively.

4. Ibid., p. 309.

5. "Principles of International Law Recognized in the Charter of the Nuremberg Tribunal and in the Judgment of the Tribunal," reproduced and discussed in Yehuda Melzer, *Concepts of Just War* (The Netherlands: Leyden: A.W. Sijthoff, 1975), pp. 88–93.

6.   Colonel Anthony Hartle argues that there are two humanitarian principles reflected in the laws of war. The first, a deontological principle (HP1) states that "individual persons deserve respect as such." The second, a consequentialist principle (HP2), states, "Human suffering ought to be minimized." Hartle argues that in international law HP1 is more fundamental than HP2 (i.e., only when the first is satisfied will the second be applied). I am convinced that Colonel Hartle is entirely correct. My analysis differs from his in that his analysis concerns the operative considerations inherent in the humanitarian principles, while my concern is the relationship between humanitarian principles and military objectives. See Colonel Anthony E. Hartle, "Humanitarianism and the Laws of War," *Philosophy* 61 (1986): 109–15.

7.   This point is made persuasively and discussed in detail by Jeffrie G. Murphy, "The Killing of the Innocent," in *The Monist* 57, no. 4 (1973), reprinted in *War, Morality, and the Military Profession,* edited by Malham M. Wakin (Boulder, Colo.: Westview Press, 1979), pp. 343–69.

8.   Grotius argues that a sovereign's authority over his subjects is limited in that he cannot perform or order any actions that violate natural law. John Locke develops the same idea more precisely. In his discussion of the "extent of legislative powers," he argues that "it is not, nor can possibly be absolutely arbitrary over the lives and fortunes of the people. For it being but the joynt power of every member of the society given up to that person, or assembly, which is legislator, it can be no more than those persons had in a state of nature before they enter'd into society, and gave up to the community. For no body can transfer to another more power than he has in himself; and no body has an absolute arbitrary power over himself, or any other . . . having in the state of nature no arbitrary power over the life, liberty, or possession of another, but only so much as the law of nature gave him for the preservation of himself and the rest of mankind; this is all he doth, or can give up to the commonwealth . . . so that the legislative can have no more than this." *Two Treatises of Government,* with an introduction and notes by Peter Laslett (New York: New American Library, 1963), Bk. II, 135, pp. 402–03.

9.   Jeffrie Murphy notes that it is not necessary that enemy combatants be *sincerely* engaged in trying to kill an opponent in order to justify self-defense; it is reasonable to *believe* that individual enemy combatants are so engaged, and that is sufficient grounds to kill them in self-defense. The domestic example that parallels this is the police officer who shoots a person in self-defense, only to find out that the weapon the victim was brandishing was a fake. Murphy, "The Killing of the Innocent," in Wakin, *War, Morality, and the Military Profession,* p. 347.

10.   Imagine that a construction worker is about to dump a quantity of enormous slabs of granite into a narrow pit. From your vantage point you see that a large group of students on a field trip has inadvertently entered the pit and is exploring it. You conclude that many of them are sure to be crushed unless you stop the worker, who knows nothing of the students' presence. The only means available to you is to shoot the worker using a small caliber rifle you have in your pickup, thereby wounding her before she carries out her task. You cannot simply execute a near-miss because there is so much noise that the worker will not be aware of the shot unless it hits her.
          The salient features of the example are that the person (the construction worker) doing the harm to the innocent students does not know that she is doing it, and if you conform to MT$_1$ you violate MT$_2$ and vice versa. Perhaps one could draw a better parallel to a wartime example by constructing a case where the person who is inflicting harm knows he is harming others but nevertheless believes it to be necessary and justified. Perhaps a primitive tribe that is about to sacrifice a group of sociologists at the command of their local gods might be stopped by shooting one of the tribal leaders, and so on.

11.   Sheldon M. Cohen, *Arms and Judgment: Law, Morality, and the Conduct of War in the Twentieth Century* (Boulder, Colo.: Westview Press, 1989), p. 32.

12. Ibid., p. 33.
13. One might argue that the principle of double effect could be used to excuse the civilian deaths. This seems questionable because the argument that the civilian deaths are inadvertent, unintended, and proportional, as required by the principle of double effect, does not seem plausible, given the circumstances I have described.
14. According to U.S. Army manuals, the Professional Military Ethic consists of four "social" values—loyalty, duty, selfless service, and integrity—and four "individual" values—courage, candor, commitment, and competence. U.S. Department of the Army, *The Army, Field Manual 100–1* (Washington, D.C.: U.S. Government Printing Office, 1986), pp. 21–24.
15. One's belief that the enemy will behave criminally is not relevant to the case. The possibility that another will act criminally toward you does not justify your criminal actions toward a third party.
16. Telford Taylor, *Nuremberg and Vietnam: An American Tragedy* (Chicago: Quadrangle Books, 1970), reprinted as chap. 24, "War Crimes," in Wakin, *War, Morality, and the Military Profession,* p. 426
17. Ibid., p. 429.
18. William V. O'Brien, *The Conduct of Just and Limited War* (New York: Praeger Publishers, 1981). This brief quotation from p. 123 does not reflect the detailed and insightful analysis of the Vietnam debacle that O'Brien provides in this work.
19. Paul Ramsey, *The Just War: Force and Personal Responsibility* (New York: Charles Scribner's Sons, 1968), p. 437.
20. Quoted by Telford Taylor in *Nuremberg and Vietnam,* p. 169. Taylor cites the February 7, 1968, edition of the *New York Post* as the source for this quotation.
21. Thomas Nagel, "War and Massacre," in *War and Moral Responsibility,* edited by Marshall Cohen, Thomas Nagel, and Thomas Scanlon (Princeton, N.J.: Princeton University Press, 1974), p. 23. Perhaps the position I develop in the following discussion is more "absolute" than Nagel intends. In a recent lecture to a group of prospective army officers at the United States Military Academy, Professor Nagel advised his audience that often there are no rules to which one can always turn for the right guidance in troublesome situations. Once all of the considerations on all sides of a difficult choice have been identified, the final decision will still amount to a matter of judgment. He is, of course, absolutely right.
22. Ibid., p. 24.
23. R. M. Hare offers a clear, commonsense analysis of the tension between military necessity and humanitarian principles. In discussing the practical considerations of the problem, he writes, "On the one side, there is the danger that a too rigid adherence of the standard general principles will lead us to disregard special features of the situation which ought to make a difference to our appraisal of it. On the other side, there is the danger that, if we once allow ourselves to question the general principle, our lack of knowledge and our partiality to our own interests may distort our reasoning." His solution is to treat the humanitarian principles as practical guides, habituated by training and education, but not sacrosanct. In certain extraordinary situations that call for special considerations, they may be criticized, justified, or even rejected. The problem with Hare's view is that combat is characterized by extraordinary situations just like the kind Telford Taylor mentions: heat of battle, death of comrades, fear, and so on. See "Rules of War and Moral Reasoning," in Cohen, Nagel, and Scanlon, *War and Moral Responsibility,* pp. 46–61.
24. In an essay titled "Utilitarianism and the Rules of War," R. B. Brandt responds to Nagel's absolutism by suggesting a version of John Rawls's rule utilitarianism (i.e., rules that enlightened, rational agents might contract to from behind a veil of ignorance). Brandt incorporates, however, a form of military necessity into these utilitarian rules: "The rules of war, then, subject to the restriction that the rules of war may not prevent a belligerent from using all the power necessary to overcome the enemy, will be ones whose authorization

will serve to maximize utility. . . . This restriction, incidentally, itself manifests utilitarian considerations, for a nation is limited to the use of means necessary to overcome an opponent." This "solution," however, is simply a restatement of the problem of military necessity as being more fundamental than the rules of war. The interesting question which Nagel attempts to answer (i.e, "never") and Brandt sidesteps is, "When should military necessity override humanitarian principles?" For Brandt to advise one to use only the means necessary to ensure victory is as complete a subordination of the humanitarian principles to military necessity as Nagel's is a denial of military necessity. See Cohen, Nagel, and Scanlon, *War and Moral Responsibility*, pp. 25–45.

25.   Michael Walzer, *Just and Unjust Wars: A Moral Argument with Historical Illustrations* (New York: Basic Books, 1977), pp. 251–68.

26.   I pass over any discussion of the methods whereby political decisions are made (even though it is obviously crucial), except to note that truth and freedom of information are necessary conditions for a government to "legitimately" represent a people. A government that deliberately deceives its constituents cannot legitimately represent its people.

Chapter

10

REPRISALS

Like military necessity, the doctrine of reprisals can provide a justification for setting aside the protection that is normally afforded to innocents under the international laws of war. Reprisals constitute the traditional remedy for belligerents against whom war crimes have been committed. Reprisals are conducted either to deter further occurrences of the crimes or to force one's opponent into offering redress for those crimes already committed. In the parlance of contemporary international law, reprisals are acts that would normally be violations of the laws of war but that are exceptionally permitted as a means of compelling a lawless enemy back into conformity with the law. There is no requirement that reprisals reflect the type of violation that they seek to stem. If, for example, one nation uses a certain type of illegal weapon (say a viral or bacteriological agent), the nation against which it is employed can *legally* employ another type of "illegal" weapon (say a chemical agent) in reprisal. The form that reprisals may take is left entirely to the discretion of the party initiating them. The important point is that reprisals be motivated by a desire to force obedience to the law rather than by a desire for revenge. This type of belligerent reprisal is not to be confused with our previous discussion of reprisals in chapter 4. The earlier discussion addressed reprisals conducted outside of or in lieu of war; here we will focus on reprisals that are conducted by belligerents during war as a legal remedy for another party's illegal actions, although both types are undoubtedly similar in many respects.

When the doctrine of reprisals is coupled with the current doctrine regarding military necessity, the potential for "lawlessness" becomes disturbing. If one warring faction, the one losing the war, invokes military necessity to justify violating the laws of war, then the opposing side is then justified in violating the same or other laws in reprisal. And because under current international law one side will always be justified in invoking military necessity, and the other will always be justified in conducting reprisals (and counterreprisals, etc.), there can never be a war in which the humanitarian laws are anything but ideals to be followed just in case you are winning and your opponent continues to follow them, even though he (or she) is losing.

171

The status of reprisals as a legitimate means of enforcing the laws of war has long been an issue of contention. In 1874, the Russian delegation fought to get a variation of Lieber's restrictive use of reprisals written into the Brussels documents, and when they were unsuccessful, F. F. Martens, a Russian jurist and president of the 1899 Hague Convention, noted,

> I regret that the uncertainty of silence is to prevail with respect to one of the most bitter necessities of war. If the practice could be suppressed by this reticence, I could but approve of this course. But if it is still to exist, this reticence may, it is to be feared, remove any limits to its exercise.[1]

Neither the members of the Brussels Conference of 1874 nor the Hague Conferences of 1899 and 1907 were able to reach any agreement on the topic, and the issue of reprisals does not appear in international documents until the Geneva Convention of 1929.

Reprisals against prisoners of war are expressly prohibited by Article 2 of the Geneva Convention of 1929 and Article 13 of the Geneva Convention (III) of 1949.[2] Other limitations in international law on the conduct of reprisals include prohibitions against harming the wounded, sick or medical personnel or equipment, shipwrecked persons, and all persons under the protection of the nation contemplating reprisals.[3]

In spite of these restrictions, of the examples I have chosen for our discussion several concern reprisals against prisoners. I have included them primarily because they are widely discussed cases, but also because the interesting aspects of the issue of reprisals are identical, whether one postulates prisoners of war or civilians as the victims.

During the American Revolutionary War, General Washington, angered by the British refusal to respond to his inquiries concerning the death of a New Jersey militia captain, ordered the designation of a British prisoner (Captain Asgill) to be executed in reprisal. After Washington had designated the time and place of the execution, the British responded with an explanation, Washington was satisfied, and the "terrible alternative" was avoided.[4]

My second example is taken from Telford Taylor's discussion of reprisals in *Nuremberg and Vietnam: An American Tragedy.*

> In 1864, the Union General David Hunter burned many Virginian homes during his advance in the Shenandoah Valley. The Confederate General Jubal Early drove Hunter's forces back across the Potomac and, when Confederate troops reached Chambersburg, Pa., Early ordered the town burned by way of reprisal. The regimental commander in Chambersburg, Colonel William E. Peters, refused to obey Early's order, and was relieved of his command and placed under arrest, while others did the burning.[5]

Our third example occurred during World War II when the French Forces of the Interior continued to fight German occupation forces in France. Germany refused to treat members of the French Resistance as combatants—even though they wore insignia, carried their arms openly, and were in touch with both the Allies and the French Provisional Government in Algeria—and subjected them to summary execution despite formal protests by the Provisional Government. The French Forces of the Interior threatened reprisals, and when the executions did not stop, they shot eighty German prisoners under their control.[6]

Finally, in 1965, the National Liberation Front (Vietcong) executed three American prisoners (one officer and two noncommissioned officers) in reprisal for South Vietnamese executions of three captured Vietcong "terrorists."[7]

The consequentialist logic of such cases is manifest. By conducting reprisals, the harm suffered by one's own soldiers or civilians is less than if reprisals are not conducted. And, of course, the assumption—undoubtedly true in some cases at least—is that no alternative method will yield the same desirable results.

Sheldon Cohen has recently used variations of the consequentialist argument to defend the doctrine of reprisals. I am not sure that he is really as committed to reprisals as he seems to be, or to what extent he would defend the arguments I develop in the following discussions. Nevertheless, I will refer to Cohen's arguments and will use them to underscore some difficulties for the doctrine of reprisals, as it is currently manifested in international law and practiced.

After discussing the earlier example concerning Germany and the French Forces of the Interior, Cohen writes,

> The French had an obligation to their own fighters and to their own cause, which would be harmed if every would-be volunteer had to mull over the fact that he would be executed if he were captured. The execution of the German prisoners was a terrible act, but when the Germans did not reply to the French protests, nor to the French threats for taking reprisals on captured Germans, the responsibility for those deaths passed to the Germans, who had left the French with no other effective means of ending the executions. . . . The eighty dead Germans should be added to the eighty dead Frenchmen as the result of German decisions. When a criminal act by one belligerent leaves the other no effective means of compelling the first to desist except another act of the same kind, responsibility lies, not in the hands of those who have been placed in the dilemma, but of those who created it.[8]

Cohen's argument is that "the French had an obligation to their own fighters and their own cause," and that fulfillment of this obligation was being impeded because prospective soldiers had second thoughts about joining the Resistance in light of the German policy. Moral dilemmas are invariably questions of competing obligations. In this case, Cohen provides two obligations that he believes override the obligation that belligerents have not to harm prisoners of war. The first is that the French cause is of greater importance than the prohibition against murdering prisoners. The second is that the French

Resistance had a responsibility to protect those of their forces who had fallen into enemy hands, and that this obligation was greater than their responsibility not to execute enemy soldiers under their own control. Let us take the arguments one at a time.

Even if, for the sake of discussion, we concede Cohen's contention that the importance of the French cause justifies intentionally executing innocents, he must also convince us that there is a correlation between the German policy of murdering partisans and the French cause. Cohen suggests that some patriots who would otherwise volunteer to fight the German soldiers occupying their country might be deterred because of the German policy. If so, then this would hurt the French cause. Put this way, we can recognize this argument as a veiled appeal to military necessity as the justification for conducting reprisals. But this appeal to necessity seems highly questionable. Surely patriots who voluntarily enlist to fight in a guerrilla war against a world power like Germany are profoundly aware of the possibility that they may be killed. For Cohen's argument to persuade, we would have to imagine a prospective volunteer who is ready to join the resistance against the Germans despite the realization that he (or she) may very well be killed in battle, but who decides not to join because of the possibility that he or she will be captured and then killed. This seems too far-fetched to be plausible. And even if we grant that this dubious line of reasoning may have been taken by some French patriots, it is too much of a concession to presume that they would be of sufficient number to "hurt the French cause." If anything, the German policy made the French partisans fight with even more tenacity, realizing as they did that surrender meant execution. Put this way, the German policy may have actually helped the French cause rather than hurt it, as Cohen argues.

Cohen's second justification for the French reprisals is somewhat more plausible. Here Cohen maintains that if one side can prevent the murder of its soldiers who are in enemy hands by murdering enemy prisoners in their hands, then it has an obligation to do so. The conflict is between the negative duty not to harm innocents intentionally (MT_1) on the one hand, and the positive duty to prevent others from intentionally harming innocents (MT_2) on the other hand. One could, of course, respond that the former is more fundamental, as we concluded in the last chapter; but some might argue that this is heavy-handed, especially since military leaders have a special obligation to care for the welfare of their own soldiers.

It is reasonable for Cohen to assert that the positive and negative duties associated with the prohibition against harming innocents are equally weighty, at least in this case. Granting this, one can furthermore argue that in those cases where the alternatives are governed by the same or equal principles, it is reasonable to resort to a comparison of consequences as a means of choosing between them. Applying this line of reasoning to the case at hand, Cohen can argue that, given that the Germans have executed eighty French prisoners, the

French are faced with only two alternatives: either not retaliate and expect more French prisoners to be executed; or retaliate and make it in the Germans' interests to stop executing French prisoners in order to protect their own soldiers. The alternatives might look something like the following:

A$_1$ *The French do not conduct reprisals* and the Germans continue to execute n number of French prisoners: total innocent deaths: 80 plus n.

A$_2$ *The French conduct reprisals,* kill 80 German prisoners, and the Germans stop executing French prisoners: total innocent deaths: 160.

One might object that, whereas the two alternatives presented in the example are exhaustive (i.e., either conduct reprisals or not conduct them), the consequences that are presumed to follow each course of action (integrated into A$_1$ and A$_2$ with a conjunction) are not so certain. This argument, one might object, only justifies reprisals when they are successful; that is, for A$_2$ to be justified on a purely objective, consequentialist evaluation, one would have to assume that $n > 80$. And since it is impossible to say with any assurance that any particular act of reprisal will be successful (e.g., that $n > 80$), it will always be a question of committing a known wrong for a possible good.

Moreover, objectors might add, if one is going to use a consequentialist argument to justify making exceptions to the most fundamental, universal prohibitions—such as the one against intentionally executing innocent people—then the consequentialist must live with the results when one is not successful. In those cases, then, where one side intentionally executes innocent people in an *unsuccessful* effort to deter like actions by the other side, those who perpetrate the crimes are guilty of premeditated murder, regardless of their worthy motives. And, in fact, my earlier examples notwithstanding, the arguments supporting reprisals based on consequences are not convincing because the empirical evidence is that reprisals tend to lead to counterreprisals and an eventual denegation of all restraints in the conduct of war. As Telford Taylor notes in his discussion of this topic: "Reprisals . . . are not much used today, partly because they are generally ineffective, and partly because the resort to crime in order to reform the criminal is an unappetizing method."[9] Another well-known commentator on the laws of war writes: "The doctrine of reprisals in its present somewhat obscure and undefined state provides the chief loophole for the evasion, violation, and nullification of the laws of war."[10]

One good example of an attempt at abusing the doctrine can be found in the opening sentence of Hitler's Commando Order: "For some time our enemies have been using in their warfare methods which are outside the international Geneva Conventions."[11] Hitler used this as his justification for ordering the summary execution of all Allied forces found behind German lines.

One way to avoid the difficulty with this consequentialist argument as I have constructed it is to give special weight to the deaths of one side over the other. One may believe, for example, that because the Germans are guilty both of starting the war and violating the laws of war that they have forfeited their right to protection under the law. This line of reasoning would allow one to conclude that the execution of eighty guilty Germans is justified, regardless of whether it prevents the deaths of more innocent Frenchmen.

This will not do, however, because, as Grotius reminds us, it is fiction to imagine that an entire people share in the guilt of a crime perpetrated by a few. Soldiers are subject to attack because of their status as combatants, not because of their guilt. And in this case, the German soldiers in question were innocent, in terms of both *jus ad bellum* and *jus in bello,* and their status was that of prisoner of war rather than combatant. The execution of eighty Germans based on this line of reasoning would be motivated more by retaliation or revenge than by a desire to enforce the law, and such action is both morally wrong and expressly prohibited by international law.

Perhaps these consequential formulations are not Cohen's arguments at all. Perhaps he believes that the laws of war are grounded in a contractual obligation wherein each article of the agreement is binding only on one side insofar as it is observed by the other side. Some justification for this argument may be found in Article II of the Geneva Conventions of 1949, which states that parties shall remain bound by the provisions of the present convention if the other parties thereto "accept and apply the provisions."[12]

This argument seems reasonable when applied to the use of certain strategies or weapons systems that might give one side a potentially decisive military advantage. Suppose, for example, that one side could gain a military advantage by violating rules concerning the use of chemical weapons. In such cases, a policy of reprisals might be an effective means of compelling compliance with the prohibitions against those weapons. One stipulation that would have to be met before reprisals could be conducted based on this line of reasoning would be that the initial violation constitute a policy decision, rather than simply an irresponsible action by some individual. If, for example, Saddam Hussein ordered the use of chemical weapons against U.N. forces during the Gulf War, then the United Nations might have been justified in using chemical weapons in reprisal. The same would not hold true if an irresponsible field commander ordered the use of chemical weapons contrary to national policy. (In the next chapter we will examine why chemical weapon reprisals might be justified, while reprisals using biological weapons would not.)

This type of reprisal involving an illegal weapon system does not seem to create the same sense of injustice as the one involving the execution of prisoners. The difference between the prisoner case involving the French Forces of the Interior and the example of an outlawed weapon system is that the initial and subsequent use of illegal weapons in the latter example is directed at combatants who are the proper targets of attack, whereas in the prisoner examples, the reprisals are directed against innocent prisoners who have surrendered with the understanding that they would be safe from harm. Reprisals that are conducted in response to crimes conducted as the result of an intentional policy decision and that are directed solely against combatants seem to me to be justifiable, because combatants are legitimate objects of attack. It still remains for us to determine whether reprisals against innocents are ever justified.

An alternative to accepting the legitimacy of reprisals against innocents might be to argue that violence and punishment must always be directed either at combatants or the guilty, and that the thread of guilt between national policies and individual citizen responsibility is a tenuous one, especially in nations where the government owns the franchise on the information media. Perhaps an analogy with a domestic example will be instructive.

Imagine a young man who is a murderer and fugitive. He is positively known to be guilty, the authorities believe that he is likely to kill again, and his whereabouts are unknown. Government officials are convinced that one way to get this criminal to turn himself in, or at least to cease his criminal activity, would be to execute members of his family in reprisal for any future crimes. As Cohen would put it, "Add the death of your siblings to the crimes you've already committed."

Of course, it would be outrageous to kill an innocent person on the basis of such reasoning. Wartime reprisals only *seem* more palatable because we project some modicum of guilt on the enemy population in general. As we noted previously, however, this is fiction. Recall that the argument we are attributing to Cohen claims that because the Germans abrogated their responsibility to French prisoners, the French were released from their responsibility toward German prisoners. The problem with this line of reasoning is that it assumes that the legal obligation not to harm prisoners is based purely on the contractual agreement between the parties. Because one side has broken the agreement, the other party is no longer bound by it. But while this may be true of conventions concerning certain types of weapons that combatants may use against one another, the argument is not persuasive if we believe that there is a moral principle behind the prohibition against intentionally killing innocents. If so, then the act of killing innocent people is morally wrong, unless it is done for the purpose of protecting other innocent persons. And even when this is the case, it would have to be a political decision that meets the same set of *jus ad bellum* criteria that we determined was required to justify military necessity.

Michael Walzer addresses the issue of reprisals and, discussing the case of the French Forces of the Interior, reaches a conclusion opposite to that of Cohen.[13] His approach is to deny the premise that reprisals are ever the only alternative. In his discussion of the Germans and the French Resistance, Walzer suggests that the French could have conducted raids on German prison camps, published the names of the Germans who would be tried as war criminals after cessation of hostilities, or merely claimed to have conducted reprisals without actually doing so. In any event, he argues, the "last resort" must always be something short of attacks on innocent persons.[14]

Suppose, for example, that reprisals are directed at a civilian community. This seems to have been the basis for the NATO/Warsaw Pact policy of mutually assured destruction (MAD). If, during a conventional war in Europe, one of the belligerents attacked a major city using a strategic nuclear weapon, would the nation so attacked be justified in a reprisal against a city in the attacker's territory? Obviously, the targets of both attacks would be innocent citizens.[15]

Article 51(6) of the 1977 Protocols to the Geneva Conventions of August 12, 1949, states that "Attacks against the civilian population or civilians by way of reprisals are prohibited."[16] This article was hotly debated prior to its inclusion in the Protocols. Those who opposed it argued that civilian populations of belligerent nations were not entirely innocent when it came to the political actions of their count.[17] At some point, they maintain, a nation's citizens must shoulder some responsibility for their government's actions. One can certainly sympathize with their logic, "Are we to let the enemy reduce our cities to ashes without striking back when we have the means?"

If one adopts our formulation of the doctrine of reprisals, the cases where they might legitimately be conducted can be subsumed under the doctrine of military necessity. If so, then reprisals might be justified using the same criteria that we used to justify military necessity. That is, reprisals are not a military option, but a political one subject to the same *jus ad bellum* conditions as the initial resort to force. In no case may reprisals be authorized as a tactical or an operational decision.

Given the circumstances where a belligerent nation employs, as a matter of policy, actions that are illegal *and* immoral, the nation against whom such actions are perpetrated may employ the same or other illegal/immoral actions in reprisal, provided that such action is a political decision reached in accordance with the traditional *jus ad bellum* criteria. When a nation violates, as a matter of policy, part of the war convention that has legal but not moral foundations (such as the prohibition against chemical weapons, discussed in the next chapter), such action simply invalidates the treaty obligation by the opposing side to refrain from the same type of action. In other words, restrictions based solely on contractual obligations amount to restrictions against first use only. Although both sides have a moral obligation to adhere to the terms of a treaty (Grotius calls this a form of promise keeping), once one party (Nation A) breaks the agreement, the second party (Nation B) is no longer bound to adhere to those aspects of the agreement that have been violated by Nation A in its dealings with Nation A. Nation B is, however, still bound by all of the terms of the treaty in its intercourse with other signatory nations, and is still bound to follow the other terms of the treaty (those Nation A did not violate) in its dealings with Nation A.

In the last two chapters we have examined some of the more controversial aspects of the rules of war and made some modest efforts at clarifying ambiguities. In the two chapters we will examine special problems associated with when and how some attempt to use force to achieve political objectives.

Topics for Further Discussion

1. F. F. Martens, who headed the 1899 Hague Convention, called reprisals "one of the most bitter necessities of war." If they are as awful as he claimed, why do you suppose he believed them "a necessity"?

2. Imagine that you are a military commander and that you discover incontrovertible information that enemy soldiers have been torturing and executing captured members of your unit. Your own soldiers are infuriated by the evidence, and you suspect that they may attempt reprisals against any enemy that fall into their hands. How should you respond to this information? At a political level, what might be an appropriate response?

3. As a corps commander, you receive information that an enemy force operating in friendly territory has been executing innocent civilians in reprisal for sabotage attacks against their reserve armor and artillery units. What military actions do you think might constitute an appropriate response? What political actions?

4. In September 1997, eighty-nine countries approved a ban on antipersonnel land mines. The United States, along with Russia, China, Vietnam, India, Pakistan, Iran, Iraq, and Israel, rejected the ban. Would those countries that approved the ban be bound by it if they were engaged in hostilities with a country that did not approve it—the United States for instance—or does the ban only obligate when both parties agree to it?

5. Are you satisfied with what the laws of war presently prohibit and permit under the doctrine of reprisals? Why or why not?

6. During the Second Gulf War, U.S. special operations forces were widely used to infiltrate populated areas and military bases in order to gather intelligence. Did these forces violate the international law requirement that combatants "wear distinctive insignia and carry their arms openly?" Were Iraqi military and paramilitary justified in disguising themselves as civilians in response to the actions of U.S. special operations teams?

Notes

1. Quoted in Geoffrey Best, *Humanity in Warfare* (New York: Columbia University Press, 1980), p. 172.

2. The 1929 Convention states, "Prisoners of war are in the power of the hostile Power, but not of the individuals or corps who have captured them. They must at all times be humanely treated and protected, particularly against acts of violence, insults, and public curiosity. Measures of reprisal against them are prohibited." In *The Law of War: A Documentary History,* edited by by Leon Friedman (New York: Random House, 1972), vol. I, p. 494. The Geneva Convention (III) of 1949 reiterates this prohibition, ibid., p. 594.

3. The restrictions may be found in the following 1949 conventions: Geneva I, Art. 46, Geneva II, Art. 47, and Geneva IV, Art. 33. See *Documents on the Laws of War,* edited

by Adam Roberts and Richard Guelff (New York: Oxford University Press, 1982), pp. 188, 209, 284, respectively. Additional restrictions may be found in the Protocols (not ratified by the United States) of 1977.

4. I have taken this example from Best, *Humanity in Warfare*, p. 168. Best cites Charles de Martens, *Causes celebres du droit des gens* (Leipzig, 1827), vol. 2, pp. 169–82, as the source for this case.

5. Taylor notes that Colonel Peters was never tried for his refusal to obey superior orders. See Telford Taylor, *Nuremberg and Vietnam: An American Tragedy* (Chicago: Quadrangle Books, 1970), p. 55. Taylor refers the reader to General John B. Gordon's "Reminiscences of the Civil War" (1903) for a more detailed account of the incident.

6. Frits Kalshoven, *Belligerent Reprisals* (Dordrecht, The Netherlands: Martinus Nijhoff Publishers, 1971), pp. 193–200.

7. In April 1965, a South Vietnamese court sentenced a Vietcong prisoner to death. The Vietcong immediately named a captured American officer who would be shot in reprisal if the execution was carried out. On June 22, 1965, a Vietcong prisoner was executed by the South Vietnamese government after being convicted by a military court. The Vietcong immediately executed an American sergeant being held as a POW in reprisal. On September 22 of the same year, three Vietcong prisoners were executed after being tried, convicted, and sentenced to death. On September 26, the Vietcong executed two American POWs, a captain and a sergeant, in reprisal. No more Vietcong prisoners were executed (at least officially) by the South Vietnamese. See Kalshoven, *Belligerent Reprisals*, pp. 295–305. Kalshoven cites the June 22, June 26, and September 28, 1965, issues of the *New York Times* as sources for some of this information.

8. Sheldon M. Cohen, *Arms and Judgment: Law, Morality, and the Conduct of War in the Twentieth Century* (Boulder, Colo.: Westview Press, 1989), p. 39.

9. Taylor, *Nuremberg and Vietnam*, p. 54.

10. Morris Greenspan, *The Modern Law of Land Warfare* (Berkeley and Los Angeles, CA: University of California Press, 1959), p. 408.

11. Friedman, *The Law of War: A Documentary History*, vol. II, p. 1444.

12. Ibid., vol. I, p. 525.

13. Michael Walzer, *Just and Unjust Wars: A Moral Argument with Historical Illustrations* (New York: Basic Books, 1977), pp. 207–16.

14. Ibid., p. 215. Walzer condemns reprisals as being morally wrong, but he still argues for a moral distinction between those who commit the wrong acts initially, and those who do so as a response in order to force the transgressors back into conformity with the law. He notes, "I don't know how to measure the difference between them; perhaps it isn't great; but it is worth stressing that there is a difference, even as we give their crimes a common name" (p. 215).

15. H. L. A. Hart argues that proliferation of nuclear weapons worldwide might give nations enough equality (in terms of the ability to harm each other) that the fear of reprisal would recreate a kind of atomistic, Hobbesian state of nature in the international society of states and would thereby deter war.

16. Roberts and Guelff, *Documents on the Laws of War*, p. 416. Other restrictions on reprisals in this document include prohibitions on attacks against civilian objects (Art. 52(1)), against cultural objects and places of worship (Art. 53(c)), against the natural environment (Art. 55(2)), against objects indispensable for the survival of the civilian population (Art. 55(4)), and against the works and installations containing dangerous forces (Art. 56(4)). The United States has not ratified the 1977 Protocols as of this writing, and there appears to be no interest in doing so anytime soon.

17. Frits Kalshoven, *Constraints on the Waging of War* (Dordrecht, The Netherlands: Martinus Nijhoff Publishers, 1987), p. 103.

Chapter

11

TERRORISM AND WAR

Terrorism is an inflammatory term used pejoratively to label certain acts of violence as morally reprehensible. Terrorists dress themselves in a variety of cultural, political, and religious garbs. Examples of violence directed against innocent people in domestic societies, such as chemical agents released in public transportation facilities, bombs delivered through the mail to those involved in technological advances, the spread of biological agents in government mailrooms and offices, attacks against medical research facilities by animal liberation groups, and violence perpetrated against abortion clinics, physicians, their staffs, and their clients, are all examples of what most would consider terrorism.

In international society, examples of terrorism include attacks against Olympic athletes; the murder and mutilation of those of different religions or tribes; bombs detonated to kill soldiers, sailors, police officers, and government leaders in their homes or when off duty; bombs exploded in crowded stores, malls, and other gathering places; destruction of airplanes, trains, and busses (some of them carrying schoolchildren); and hundreds of other examples too varied to enumerate. For this reason, defining what, precisely, counts as a terrorist act has proven to be extremely difficult, even though there has been no shortage of efforts by scholars, political leaders, and committees.

One might respond with the old adage, "I may not be able to define terrorism, but I know it when I see it." But surely this is inadequate. The problem is that not all those involved in terrorist activities are mentally challenged or sick. Many—perhaps most—believe deeply and sincerely that the cause they are pursuing is just and the methods they are using are justified. Some are well-educated people with strong moral convictions. Those who commit and support terrorist acts are more likely to refer to themselves as "freedom fighters" or "warriors for justice," than as terrorists. Even the most blatant and seemingly uncontroversial instance of terrorism, the September 11, 2001, attack on the World Trade Center, is not universally condemned as morally reprehensible. In fact, many groups and individuals have praised this as an act of courage against an evil society.

Our challenge is both to understand the reasoning that forms the basis for such widely divergent moral judgments and to evaluate the moral arguments objectively. Condemning those who attack our neighbors and allies is all too easy if we don't take the time to provide an objective moral grounding for our condemnation—one that acknowledges the position of those with whom we disagree and addresses the basis for their beliefs as well as the basis for our condemnation. We must acknowledge that not all who support or commit terrorist acts are intellectually challenged or unstable. Certainly those who are willing to sacrifice their lives on behalf of a cause must be single-mindedly sincere in their commitment to that cause. Understanding the rationality for this type of behavior is crucial if we hope ever to change the moral landscape.[1] History informs us that sheer power will seldom suffice; in order to change belief systems we must appeal to reason as well.[2]

DEFINING TERRORISM

Having stated that developing a conceptual definition for terrorism that will satisfy all may be close to impossible, we must nevertheless begin by agreeing on a definition to guide us in our investigation. I propose that we proceed with a working definition that is comprehensive enough to facilitate our discussion, while making no claims to fulfill all requirements of a conceptual theory. If during our exegesis, we encounter difficulties that stem from inadequacies in our working definition, we will attempt refinements at that time.

> Terrorism: Any act that involves the illegal and intentional threat or use of random violence against innocent people for the purposes of instilling fear in others to bring about a political agenda.

This definition is admittedly vague, but it does capture at least some of the necessary conditions for an act to be considered an example of terrorism.[3]

Notice that according to this definition, the violence unleashed against the victims is not the purpose of the attacks, but serves only as a means to the terrorist's goal. These victims are merely used or, as one commentator puts it, "used up" for propaganda purposes.[4] In sum, there is no direct correlation between the victims of a terrorist attack and the purpose for which the attack is carried out other than their membership in a group that is somehow related to the terrorist's political agenda. The fact that the victims are arbitrarily chosen by the terrorist is what serves to instill terror in others because they recognize that anyone identified with a particular group could become a victim regardless of what that person may or may not have done. Indeed, the more innocent the victims and arbitrary their selection, the greater the impact of the terrorist attack.

The arbitrariness of the victims forms the basis for the most commonly voiced criticism of terrorism. Many pass judgment on terrorist activities by distinguishing between force and violence. According to this view, in domestic society force is a legitimate means of maintaining the social order in accordance with the law; violence is hostile, harmful behavior that is outside the law. In the international society of states, force is a legitimate means of addressing grievances between sovereign groups provided it is employed in accordance with the United Nations Charter and the Just War Tradition. Because both domestic and international terrorists operate outside the boundaries of both positive and natural law, their violent methods are always criminal in nature and elicit the legal (and legitimate) use of force in response.

Unfortunately, even though this line of reasoning may seem persuasive from the victim's standpoint, it does not address the terrorist's perspective. As we noted previously, most terrorists consider their actions to be a legitimate means of ending what they perceive as intolerable injustices in the existing social order. International terrorists might invoke military necessity or reprisals as an excuse for their methods. Both reprisals and military necessity provide a long-standing excuse for setting aside the Just War Tradition based on the exigencies of particular circumstances.

In domestic society, terrorists might claim (in the tradition of St. Augustine and Martin Luther King) that unjust laws are not laws at all and ought to be disobeyed. As one commentator puts it:

> Terrorism is always a response to institutional terror. It is an evasion to label some acts as terrorism, while ignoring the institutional terror which underlies this form of protest. . . . The amount of terror inflicted by "terrorists," no matter how dreadful, is a thimbleful compared to official, legally sanctioned terror.[5]

Rather than debate the views of commentators such as this one, or attempt to evaluate various political agendas, I propose that we assume that terrorists sincerely believe their cause to be just, and that given a belief in a just cause, we must determine when, if ever, it is morally permissible to attack innocent people intentionally in order to generate terror as a means of coercing others into accepting a political agenda.

Notice also that the political agendas of the terrorists distinguish them from those who commit violence merely because they are deranged people, or social malcontents, or profiteering criminals, or other nefarious sorts who do not even pretend to be motivated by a just cause. These individuals do not concern us here. While some of these agents of evil may seem like terrorists, and are often referred to as such in the media, they differ in that they are not acting on behalf of what they believe to be a just cause, even though their methods and the outcomes of their actions might be similar to those of the terrorists.

MAKING MORAL JUDGMENTS

Moral judgments regarding those who harbor different—but sincere—beliefs can be devilishly slippery because there is no single universally accepted ethical theory on which to base such judgments. Some condemn terrorist acts because they cause harm to innocent people. These critics subscribe to the principle that "it is always wrong intentionally to harm innocent people," but such universal judgments are problematic because under other circumstances societies engage in acts whereby the innocent are harmed—such as the bombing of inhabited areas during war and the storming of nonmilitary buildings in law enforcement.[6]

If terrorist practices were so easily disparaged, it is unlikely that they would have survived and proliferated for so long. Our analysis must examine the arguments that the terrorist uses in his own reasoning to justify his actions. For example, some might claim that the inadvertent deaths of innocents is insignificant in light of the larger long-term good that eventually may result as a consequence of policy changes that come about because of the "freedom fighters'" violence. These proponents of terrorist practices believe that while intentionally harming innocent people is *generally wrong,* this principle may be overridden when the beneficial consequences warrant such actions. We will call this the *Consequentialist Argument.*

Those who believe themselves to be carrying out the will of God consider their acts to be morally justified regardless of what they do at "God's command." Similarly, those who are believed to be acting on God's behalf are sometimes regarded by their social peers as heroes and martyrs, irrespective of any incidental suffering their actions might cause others. We will refer to these views respectively as the *Divine Command Argument* and the *Culture Induced Argument.*

Similarly, some terrorists believe that carrying out God's desires will garner them significant rewards in the "afterlife." We will call this the *Self-Interest Argument.*

A thorough examination of each of these viewpoints will aid us in our efforts to articulate *objective and persuasive* moral judgments about which acts of violence constitute terrorism and are, therefore, always morally wrong.

THE DIVINE COMMAND ARGUMENT

The Divine Command Argument is the view that any action becomes morally right when it is commanded by God. This view has its origins in the biblical story of Abraham and Isaac as found in the Book of Genesis 22. According to the Judeo-Christian-Islamic Tradition, God commands Abraham to sacrifice his son as a test of his faith and loyalty.[7] At the last instance, just as Abraham prepares to kill Isaac, God intervenes, the boy is saved, and a ram is offered in sacrifice instead. Following, we get this account.

> By myself I have sworn, says the Lord, because you have done this, and have not withheld your son, I will indeed bless you, and I will multiply your descendants as the stars of heaven and as the sand which is on the seashore. And your descendents shall possess the gate of their enemies, and by your descendents shall all the nations of the earth bless themselves, because you have obeyed my voice. (Genesis 22: 15–18)

Notice that it is not relevant that Abraham does not actually carry out the execution of his son. The point seems to be that the faithful should be willing to perform without question even what is, at least from our temporal perspective, one of the most heinous acts imaginable precisely because God commands it. If so, then even the most abominable act of terrorism would, similarly, be obligatory at God's command.

In the Abraham example, we are told that God was testing the faith of Abraham. One problem with extending this biblical example to other instances of violence is the difficulty of accurately comprehending God's purpose. The terrorist must act under the presumption that the political agenda of her organization is also God's agenda. This is problematic, however, because terrorist acts are seldom successful in achieving a long-term political solution, and if such acts were milestones along the road to fulfilling God's wishes, surely the outcome eventually would be achieved. In retrospect, it seems more likely that those who sponsor terrorism invoke God's will only to lend credibility to their own agenda.[8]

The terrorist might respond, however, that it is not our place to question God's purpose. Consider the plight of Job who endured terrible suffering at the hands of God without even the hint of a reason. When Job questions God's actions, his countryman responds: "The Almighty! we cannot discover him, pre-eminent in power and judgment; his great justice owes no one an accounting" (Job, 37: 23). And God Himself addresses Job out of a swirling maelstrom: "Who is this that obscures divine plans with words of ignorance?" (Job, 38: 2). Thus the terrorist might respond that we must always carry out God's will without demanding any knowledge concerning a rationale for His desires.

Again, however, such an interpretation is troubling because there is a vast difference between suffering harm and perpetrating harm on others. Job endured great calamity, but he did not himself inflict pain and suffering on others. While one might argue that enduring harm at the behest of God without question is the mark of a martyr, inflicting harm on other innocent people requires a higher standard, especially when the command for such action comes through an envoy or other intermediary. Surely those who perpetrate great suffering on innocent people under the umbrella of divine command must recognize the possible corruptibility or self-interest of those who convey such messages to them. In sum, were God to want His faithful to carry out what amounts to the most ignoble actions imaginable under our social order—the intentional harming of innocent people—it seems that He would not make controversial political leaders the conduits of His decrees. Would anyone have expected Abraham to sacrifice his son based on a second- or thirdhand command from heaven relayed to him by a political actor? Of course not. Terrorists, however, who invoke divine command as the basis for their actions are doing just that.

Even in those cases where one believes harming innocent people intentionally is a manifestation of God's will, the standard of certainty for acting on such a belief must be impossibly high. While it may be praiseworthy to endure personal suffering based on a belief regarding the will of God, inflicting harm on others on that basis seems irresponsible. All lucid persons acknowledge the occasional fallibility of our judgments. Given an intellectual awareness of the possibility of false beliefs, of mental lapses and illnesses, of mistaken communications and a myriad of other factors that contribute to the enormous uncertainty of our belief structures, how can anyone ever be certain that intentionally harming innocent people at random is really the will of God? It seems to me that even an omnipotent and omnibeneficent being would find terrorist actions based on sincere but weakly substantiated beliefs concerning His desires to be morally reprehensible.

In sum, we must conclude that while one may reasonably *suffer harm* based on a belief that such suffering is the will of God, one cannot *inflict harm* on innocent people without direct, indubitable, firsthand knowledge that doing so is, indeed, a divine decree.

THE CONSEQUENTIALIST ARGUMENT

Consequentialists believe that the correct moral alternative in any set of circumstances is the one that will produce the best consequences for all involved. Recall that the type of terrorist movement we are examining is limited to those whose members believe they are helping justice to prevail. They believe in justice, but they don't believe that the current state of affairs is just. It is not that they want injustice, but that they want to redefine justice according to their own values. Given this agenda, they conclude that the ends they seek are worthy enough to justify the means they employ. Their argument might be formulated this way: The current state of affairs is unjust, and those actions that help bring an end to the current unjust state of affairs are morally permissible.

While this type of consequentialist reasoning has some intuitive appeal, close analysis exposes several difficulties. The claim that *any* action that helps to bring an end to a perceived unjust state of affairs is permissible seems highly questionable. The terrorist's criticism of the state of affairs that he wishes to change is based on a particular notion of justice, and there is always a limit to the extent of harm (in the form of intentionally killing or injuring innocent people) that one can reasonably carry out *for the sake of justice.* The terrorist violates the very consequentialist principle that he invokes to support his actions when the harm he inflicts outweighs the good that his actions might achieve. The premise that *any* action might be permissible for the sake of bringing about an alternative notion of justice is not tenable from a consequentialist perspective.

Another difficulty for proponents of the Consequentialist Argument derives from a moral judgment concerning the need to change the present conditions. A judgment that ranks one sociopolitical climate as superior to another not only involves a value judgment, but also implies that anyone making the assessment ought to be free to self-determine his or her own social contract and sociopolitical climate. While terrorists might be able to justify the desire for certain changes within their societies (insofar as the things they purport to change actually affect their lives), actions aimed at changing conditions or policies in other societies are not permissible given this line of reasoning. In short, proponents of this view demand a principle of freedom for themselves that they deny to others. A failure to acknowledge reciprocity in what should be valued cannot reasonably justify actions aimed at imposing one's own values on others. In other words, if we claim to value freedom for ourselves, we can't justify violating another society's freedom to choose.[9]

Finally, even if the above difficulties could be overcome, the Consequentialist Argument would only make sense if the "desired" consequences could be assured. In those cases where terrorist actions result in widespread suffering with little or no likelihood of achieving the terrorist's goals, any claimed justification for terror evaporates.

THE SELF-INTEREST ARGUMENT

Sometimes referred to as *egoism,* this is the view that people always act to maximize their own long-term well-being. Terrorist documents and diaries discovered in the aftermath of the 2001 World Trade Center attack referred to the promise of a plethora of rewards as a result of martyrdom, including a variety of material comforts and the "possession" of numerous female virgins in the afterlife. These documents and diary entries became a source of considerable ridicule as they revealed motivations for the suicidal attacks. Nevertheless, for devout believers, the promise of eternal reward can be persuasive.

In the Judeo-Christian-Islamic Tradition, the faithful are rewarded by God for their good deeds, either in this life with wives, children, and material possessions (as is done in the Old Testament), or in the "afterlife," as promised by the New Testament and the Koran. The Koran specifically teaches that those who die in battle will be rewarded by Allah.

> And those who are slain in the way of Allah, He rendereth not their actions in vain, He will guide them and improve their state, and bring them in unto the Garden which He hath made known to them. . . . [In the Garden] there are rivers of water unpolluted, and rivers of milk whereof the flavor changeth not, and rivers of wine delicious to the drinkers, and rivers of clear-run honey: therein for them is every kind of fruit with pardon from their Lord. (Sûrah XLVII 3–6 & 15)

Fundamental teaching in the Judeo-Christian-Islamic Tradition, however, does not support this as a justification for behavior independent of an agent's motives. Good deeds done for self*less* reasons, that is, done from love of others or of God, merit great rewards. Good deeds done for the purpose of garnering a personal reward are selfish acts, not deserving of commendation. Indeed, selfish actions always are considered sinful, rather than praiseworthy. Thus, those who attempt to gain for themselves personal rewards by attacking innocent people in an effort to earn favors from God are behaving selfishly, and have negated any claims for compensation. There is no divine reward for selfish acts, no matter how objectively good they might be. In the Judeo-Christian-Islamic Tradition, an agent's intentions are as much or more important in evaluating his or her actions as are the consequences of the actions. God is not one with whom to bargain for favors.

In short, actions done for the purpose of claiming a divine reward are motivated by self-love (*cupiditas*), not the love of God, and selfishness is never morally praiseworthy. This also applies to those who are motivated by a desire for status within their community or social group either for themselves or for their families.

We must conclude that no sacrifice—no matter how great—that is motivated by a selfish expectation of reward, for self or for family either in this life or the next, can ever be considered praiseworthy. Those who commit such acts are merely using others—taking their lives—for selfish reasons and are deserving of condemnation. Even worse, they sin hiding behind the cloak of God to sanctify despicable selfish deeds.

CULTURAL INDUCED ACTIONS

While moral judgments vary widely among cultures, most ethicists agree that ethical principles are universal. Even though most ethical principles are universally recognized as *prima facie* good, there is often disagreement as how to adjudicate between various of these principles when they come in conflict, as they invariably do in our complex social world. A well-known story recounted by Herodotus in his *History*, illustrates this well.

According to Herodotus, the King of Persia (Darius), brought the representatives of two cultures before him and had each explain how they treated the bodies of their deceased fathers. The Callatians noted that it was customary to eat their bodies, while the Greeks spoke of cremation. Each was horrified at the other's account. Herodotus concludes that judgments about what is right and wrong are relative to a given society, even though both groups ascribed to the principle that children should honor their deceased fathers.

For those who adhere to a virtue-based model of ethics, differences can seem even more disparate. We know from experience that what counts as a virtue can differ widely from culture to culture. Cultures reinforce and prioritize their own particular virtues by giving special status to those who manifest them. A terrorist group's ability to recruit adherents to its cause, especially when the cause involves great sacrifice or even death, is strong evidence that group members receive special status as heroes among their peers. As long as the perception of terrorists as heroes perpetuates in a given society—as long as it is considered virtuous to carry out terrorist acts—there will not be a shortage of new willing recruits. Our goal in this section is to understand why those who commit terrorist acts are revered by their peers and whether such reverence is ever warranted.

We will begin with a discussion of the classical view that the aim of a moral education is to develop virtues, and we will examine how such thinking can contribute erroneously to celebrating terrorists as heroes. It will be helpful to start with a common understanding of what counts as a virtue and why this might vary from culture to culture.

Plato defines a virtue as a quality *in virtue of which* a function is performed well. Consider, for example, a knife used to prune grapevines. Sharpness is a virtue in a pruning knife because sharpness is a quality *in virtue of which* a pruning knife performs its function well. We call this a technical or functional virtue. Nevertheless, we recognize that even the "most virtuous" (i.e., sharpest) pruning knife must be wielded correctly to prune vines for optimum production.

Human virtues are of two kinds: technical and moral. Technical virtues have to do with performance of functions; moral virtues have to do with one's character. For example, physical strength and agility are virtues in a wrestler; objectivity and fairness are virtues in a judge. Physical strength is a technical virtue; fairness is a moral virtue. Moral virtues relate to how a person treats others.

We find that not only are virtues particular to various social roles, but because the status of social roles—judge, warrior, statesman, professor, seamstress, artist, hockey player, priest—differs in different cultures, these cultures are likely to celebrate different behaviors as virtuous. How, then, are we to make any sense of virtue as a means of making ethical judgments? The problem is that moral virtues, just as technical virtues, are not in themselves praiseworthy but take their moral qualities from the ends at which they aim. Perhaps another example will be helpful.

Sharpness is a virtue in an ax; sharpness is a vice in a splitting maul. Both tools are similar in shape and composition and function, but the particular use to which they are put—cutting logs rather than splitting them—causes the desired characteristics to be dissimilar. Analogously, moral qualities in human virtues can only be assessed in terms of the ends they serve. Let us take a quality that is unanimously regarded as a virtue—courage—and use this as a means of illustration.

A person can be said to behave courageously when he or she attempts to achieve a particular goal which entails the threat of a countergoal that he or she wishes to avoid. When the agent endeavors to bring about the desired goal despite the risk of the dreaded countergoal, he or she has acted courageously.

Notice that our conceptual theory for courage makes no claim about the moral quality of the goal or the countergoal. This is because courageous actions are not themselves praiseworthy independent of the purposes toward which the courage aims.

A teenager might take foolish risks in order to impress his peers with his courage, but his actions would have no moral significance. Likewise, a burglar might risk her life to steal something of value, but it would be a misnomer to consider her act an exemplar of moral virtue. Indeed, any daring act done from selfish motives (as we noted in a previous discussion) is not considered praiseworthy according to most religious traditions and should not be considered virtuous.

Thus it is an aberration to praise a terrorist for his courage independent of the purpose for which he manifests this courage. As Emmanuel Kant tells us in his *Groundwork of the Metaphysics of Morals:*

> Intelligence, wit, judgment, and the other talents of the mind, however they may be named, or courage, resoluteness, and perseverance as qualities of the temperament, are doubtless in many respects good and desirable. But they can become extremely bad and harmful if the will, which is to make use of these gifts and which in its special constitution is called character, is not good.[10]

Societies or cultures that celebrate acts of courage independent of the purpose for these acts have badly misunderstood moral virtues and how they relate to character.

A second important distinction for us is the difference between a courageous act and a courageous person. Anyone might perform a single courageous (or otherwise praiseworthy) act under certain circumstances or for a particular motive. A courageous person, however, is one who is willing to behave courageously under the right circumstances for the right reasons. Even a pusillanimous person might give the appearance of having courage by a single daring act; a truly courageous person is the one who can be counted on to act courageously under any circumstance. Given these two accounts, we must find it is unlikely that many terrorists can be said to have the virtue of courage as a component of their character. Furthermore, even if one is successful in behaving courageously in a particular instance, the moral quality of that action is assessed by its consequences, not by the risk or the pain endured by the agent.

SEPTEMBER 11, 2001

Because this single event has had such enormous impact on this nation and around the world, I want to briefly review what happened on September 11, 2001, and how the United States responded to it. This catastrophic event will provide a platform for our discussion of terrorism and Just War Theory.

We noted that terrorism differs from various other types of nefarious, criminal violence because it is done for the purpose of achieving certain political objectives. In response to the September 11 attacks against the Pentagon and the World Trade Center, many reasonably asked, "Why?—why would this group of people from the other side of the world want to murder thousands of innocent people in America?"

The objective of the attack was not to destroy the innocent people who worked in these buildings, but rather to make a political statement against the principles that define America. The terrorists did not care about the thousands of innocent people who died, or about the even greater number of relatives who mourned their losses whom they did not even know. The lives and tranquility of these men and women were simply sacrificed as a means of symbolically attacking America's core values—because we proudly admit to be the ultimate masters of our government and its policies.

The September 11 attack and the U.S. response to it is best understood as the culmination of twenty-five years of terrorist attacks against the United States and its citizens that began with the seizure of the U.S. Embassy in Tehran in November 1979. When neither the United States nor the United Nations chose to mount an effective response to this blatant, outrageous act of war, it encouraged a series of other terrorist actions that ended with the September 11 disaster. Let's review.

In 1983, sixty-three people were murdered when a terrorist attacked the U.S. Embassy in Beirut, an event followed by attacks against a Marine Headquarters in the same city and the U.S. Embassy in Kuwait, resulting in more than 200 additional American deaths. The following year (1984) a second attack was made against the U.S. Embassy in Beirut, followed by attacks against U.S. soldiers in Madrid and Germany a year later. Also in 1985, an American citizen in a wheelchair was murdered by terrorists who seized control of a cruise ship. In 1986, four innocents were killed when a TWA flight was destroyed by terrorists; and in 1988, Pan American Flight 103 was bombed, killing over 200 people.

In 1993, federal employees were shot and killed by terrorists as they entered their workplace in Langley, Virginia. In February of the same year, 6 people were killed and over 1,000 injured when terrorists attempted to blow up the World Trade Center with a rented truck loaded with explosives. Over the next three years, military personnel were attacked twice in Saudi Arabia, resulting in the deaths of twenty-six men and women and injures to hundreds, and the U.S. embassies in both Kenya and Tanzania were also attacked, killing 224 people.

On October 12, 2000, the U.S.S. Cole was attacked while at port in Yemen, resulting in the death of seventeen U.S. sailors, and less than a year later we had September 11.[11]

The most important decision that a democratic country ever makes is whether to go to war. A decision to resort to force proceeds in two parts. First, is the use of force permissible according to international law and the Just War Tradition? Even if it is permissible (i.e., justified), there is the further question of whether it is prudent. Following the attack on the World Trade Center, the United States went to war against those who planned or participated in this attack. As citizens, each of us must make a moral judgment about whether the use of armed force to achieve political objectives is both permissible and prudent. We are, after all, especially in a democracy, at some level responsible for the actions or inactions of our government.

We recognize that whenever a nation resorts to the use of military force to achieve political objectives, it is highly likely that innocent people will be killed. If so, then how is what the United States and its allies did in Afghanistan in response to September 11 different from what the terrorists did—namely, engaging in actions that they knew would result in the deaths of innocent people? Understanding the answer to this question is of great importance to citizens in a democratic nation.

Let us begin by examining freedom and justice as the two fundamental American values and see how these apply in international society. Understanding the values that govern political discourse among civilized nations in the international society of states may help us to understand the world's outrage and response to these terrorist acts.

As we noted in several previous discussions, the two values that form the foundation of the United Nations Charter are territorial integrity and political sovereignty. Territorial integrity means that nations should always be free from the threat of attack. In domestic society, any individual who is attacked has the right to defend himself or herself and, analogously, nations have the same right. Just as the security and safety of my person is sacrosanct to me, so is the security and safety of a state sacrosanct to its citizens. We might think of this international value as corresponding to our nation's core value of justice for all, only the *all* in this case is the international society of states.

The second value, political sovereignty, means that each nation's people are free to choose for themselves how they are to be governed. In domestic society people are free to do as they choose as long as their actions do not interfere with the freedom or well-being of others. Political sovereignty means that people can choose democracy, socialism, monarchy, communism, oligarchy, or whatever they want, as long as their mode of government does not interfere with the freedom or security of other nations. How a populace collectively chooses to be governed is no one's business outside of those who are members of that populace, because they are the only ones who are the subjects of that government.

When the September 11 terrorists attacked America's core individual values of justice and freedom, they also attacked the fundamental international values of political sovereignty and territorial integrity.

Members of those terrorist organizations that were behind the attacks in New York and Washington, D.C. believed that governments that permit freedom beyond the parameters that the terrorists prescribe are decadent and should be overthrown, and that attacks against the people or property of such governments are justified. They attacked the United States and the values it embodies, and they attacked the safety and tranquility of the homes and firesides of America's citizens.

In domestic societies, when a person's freedom or safety is attacked, the police and magistrates intervene on behalf of the state to see that justice is done. In the international society of states, there is no analogous common authority to enforce justice as there is in domestic society. The United Nations has no armed forces at its disposal and little or no influence on the actions of sovereign states. Each state or alliance of states must itself fill the role of police officer, bailiff, and judge when it has been wronged. Just as the use of force is sometimes necessary in dealing with criminals in domestic society, so it is sometimes the only way to bring about justice in international society as well.

TERRORISM AND THE TRADITION OF JUST WAR

War differs from terrorism in that it is a legal remedy for a wrong received. Since antiquity, civilized peoples the world over have recognized the necessity of using force in the name of justice and have delineated concise rules and limits on how and when force may legitimately be used.

As we discussed in chapter 1, every civilized society for which we have written records, whether from Europe, Asia, Africa, the Middle East, or North and South America, has recognized some restrictions on when to use force and how it should be used. Collectively, the principles that underline these restrictions are called the Just War Tradition.

Concerning when it is lawful to go to war, the Just War Tradition says that war can only be declared by a lawful government; that it must be declared publicly to give the other side a chance to meet demands in order to avoid violence; that there must be a just cause for going to war that cannot be resolved any other way—in other words, war is always a last resort. Regarding how a war should be fought, the Just War Tradition states that only military targets can intentionally be attacked.

Terrorism rejects the entire legal framework of war. Terrorists don't conform to Just War Tradition, nor do they narrowly aim at military targets. In fact, terrorist organizations hide behind the Just War Tradition for their own safety. They purposely plan and launch attacks at innocent people and then depend on the moral acumen of their victims to keep themselves and their organizations safe.

In other words, terrorist leaders and supporters intentionally advocate and command others to harm innocent people, then locate themselves in places where it is almost impossible to attack them without endangering innocent people. Terrorist leaders know that those who would attack them must violate the same moral principles that are the cause for being angry at the terrorists in the first place.

To counter a terrorist attack is to face a seemingly impossible dilemma: If the society does not attack back, the terrorist organizations will continue to murder innocent citizens; if it does respond, their retaliatory actions will inadvertently cause innocent people to suffer. Either way, innocent people are harmed, although they may be innocent citizens of different states.

Did innocent Afghanistan civilians die as result of U.S. military actions? Certainly. But any civilian casualties were an unintended side effect of actions aimed at legitimate military targets, the number always to be kept to a minimum by carefully attacking only military targets.

Given the two choices, not strike back against terrorism or strike back while adhering to the tenets of the Just War Tradition, the United States chose the course of action which, in the long term, will result in less harm to all innocent people.

CONCLUSION

Although terrorists may attempt to justify their deeds either through a variety of arguments or an appeal to the Just War Tradition, neither is sufficient to excuse them from the harm that they cause. Even those who sincerely believe in their cause are misguided agents of evil. Those who celebrate terrorists acts against individuals or groups for causes with which they agree are guilty of fostering the spread of evil.

Topics for Further Discussion

1. Following the terrorist attacks of September 11, 2001, the United States declared a "war on terrorism," and the U.S. armed forces received the mission of attacking terrorist strongholds in Afghanistan. Some objected to calling the U.S.'s actions a "war" because that terminology implies that terrorists would be treated as combatants, rather than as international criminals. What are the advantages and disadvantages of referring to U.S. actions in Afghanistan as a war?

2. Members of terrorist organizations who were captured during the U.S. war on terrorism were imprisoned at the Marine base on the island of Cuba, rather than in the United States, primarily so they would not have the protection of U.S. laws during interrogation. Do you believe that the rights of these prisoners were violated"?

Notes

1. I recognize that some who spread terror are simply moral imbeciles motivated by a variety of psychological infirmities. Rather than concern ourselves with these individuals, our discussion will focus on political movements that employ terrorist tactics. Examples extend from the PLO and al Qaeda in the international arena, to certain pro-life and environmental groups in domestic society, many of which have numerous affluent financial supporters who themselves seem oblivious to their role in underwriting terrorism.

2. Changing belief systems is a slow process, often taking place over generations. Emphasis on the importance of this long-term strategy should in no way minimize the importance of a short-term objective of seeking out, punishing, and deterring those who plan, support, or carry out terrorists acts.

3. One problem with this working definition is that by including illegality as a necessary condition for an act to be considered terrorist, we exclude government-sanctioned violence; for example, the government-sanctioned genocide carried out by leaders such as Pol Pot, Stalin, and Hitler. A second problem is the stipulation that victims be "innocent." Some terrorists argue that those they attack are not innocent simply because they represent or support social values that differ from those of the terrorist.

4. Nick Fotion, "The Burdens of Terrorism," in *Value in Conflict*, edited by B. Leiser (New York: MacMillan, 1981), pp. 563–72.

5. Martin Oppenheimer, "Defining Terrorism," in *The Nonviolent Activist* (May–June 1985), reprinted in *Terrorism: Opposing Viewpoints*, edited by David L. Bender (St. Paul, Minn.: Greenhaven Press, 1986), p. 87.

6. The botched raid by the Federal Bureau of Investigation against David Koresh and his community in Waco, Texas is one example where numerous innocent people were killed "legally" for a questionable objective.

7. The Judeo-Christian account is that God commands Abraham to sacrifice Isaac. The Islamic account is that Allah commands Abraham to sacrifice Ishmael. Isaac is the offspring of Abraham and Sara; Ishmael is the offspring of Abraham and Hagar. Sara tricks

Abraham into naming Isaac as his heir, and Hagar and Ishmael are banished, later becoming the wellspring for the Arab nation.

8. All societies steeped in a single religious tradition have invoked their deity on behalf of their political agendas vis-à-vis their neighbors, and approximately 50% of the time their predication has been validated.

9. Plato (Socrates) makes an analogous argument in The *Republic*. In addressing the parable of the Ring of Gyges, Socrates notes that it is inconsistent to will that all members of a social order conform to a particular standard of behavior and at the same time to make oneself an exception to that universal standard. As Immanuel Kant puts it in his own grounding for morality, "we must act always so that we could will the maxim of our action to be a universal law."

10. Immanuel Kant, *Foundations of the Metaphysics of Morals*, translated by Lewis White Beck (Indianapolis, IN: The Bobbs-Merrill Company, 1981), p. 9.

11. The only effective response that the United States made to terrorism was done in April 1986 when President Reagan ordered an air strike against the terrorist regime in Tripoli. The Libyan Head of State, Muammar Qaddafi, had ordered and carried out terrorist attacks against U.S. servicemen and women in Germany. The evidence was irrefutable. Successful air attacks against military targets in and around Tripoli effectively silenced Colonel Qaddafi as a critic of America and proponent of terrorism.

Chapter
12

THE JUST WAR AND WEAPONS OF MASS DESTRUCTION

Despite the differences among nuclear, bacteriological, and chemical (NBC) munitions, all three types are generally treated as "unconventional weapons" in contemporary Just War literature and referred to as "weapons of mass destruction" by the press. One common aspect of the debate on their use is whether they *differ in kind* from conventional ordnance, or whether they merely *differ in degree*. If the latter case is true (i.e., NBC weapons differ from conventional weapons only in terms of their intensity), then their use is likely subject to the same *jus in bello* criteria as conventional weapons. Those who defend this view might argue that as long as these weapons do not inflict *unnecessary* suffering and can be employed in ways that *discriminate* between combatants and noncombatants, then their use is permissible. If, however, NBC weapons are not merely different in degree from conventional weapons but also different in kind, then these weapons would resist analysis under the existing *jus in bello* criteria, and we would either have to develop a new rubric governing their use or reject them altogether.

Notice that this latter alternative is a two-edged sword. One might argue, for example, that because the existing Just War criteria do not apply to nuclear weapons—weapons that are a sign of status among the more powerful nations of the world—that there are no existing principles restricting how they might be employed. Does this mean that they should not be employed at all, or does it mean that their use is limited only by the judgment of political and military leaders possessing such weapons?

The Second Gulf War initiated by the U.S. and Great Britain-led coalition was justified largely by an allegation that Iraq possessed weapons of mass destruction which, if true, placed them in violation of the agreement that terminated hostilities during the First Gulf War ten years prior. Several UN Security Council resolutions during the period between these two wars reiterated the mandate that Iraq destroy all weapons of mass destruction and refrain from acquiring any new weapons. Note, however, that it was not the weapons per se that were the grounds for hostilities, but Iraq's noncompliance with U.N. mandates. After all, it is well known that numerous other nations possess similar and even greater weapons.

In this chapter we will examine nuclear and chemical weapons in some detail to determine whether analysis under the Just War Tradition is reasonable and, if not, what other considerations should govern their use. We will discuss biological weapons only briefly as they are less controversial, and prohibitions against their use are almost universally accepted by the nations of the world. In each case we will focus our discussion of NBC weapons on their implications for human beings and will discuss only briefly the implications of their effects on plants, animals, and the environment.[1]

Our discussion of NBC weapons begins with a detailed historical summary of their use. The horror with which U.S. military forces regard these weapons seems out of proportion to their effectiveness. Familiarity with the past uses of NBC weapons, some instances dating back to antiquity, may alleviate some of this trepidation.

Although Germany's use of chlorine gas against French forces at Ypres in April 1915 is generally considered the first successful use of chemicals in warfare, the history of chemical and biological weapons dates back to antiquity. In 600 B.C., for example, according to the historian Pausanias, when the Kirrhaeans misappropriated land belonging to Apollo's temple, the Athenian leader Solon stopped the flow of a small stream that provided Kirrha with water and contaminated the dammed water with helleborous roots. When he later allowed the flow of water to resume, the thirsty Kirrhaeans satiated themselves, became ill, and the Athenians captured the city.[2]

Thucydides recounts two instances (one successful, one not) where fire, laden with pitch and sulphur, was used against enemy forces during the fifth century B.C., although it is difficult to tell from his accounts whether the resulting noxious fumes were part of the desired effect or simply incidental to the fire.[3] In any event, it is reasonable to regard both fire and smoke as precursors of modern chemical weapons.

Justinius relates that Hannibal achieved victory over King Eumenes of Pergamum by hurling clay pots containing poisonous snakes into enemy ships, which so terrorized the sailors that they yielded.[4] And in another account, he tells us that a Carthaginian general defeated Marharbal in 200 B.C. by appearing to retreat and leaving behind great quantities of wine poisoned with mandragora, a toxic root. After the enemy occupied the camp and became drugged by the poisoned wine, the Carthaginians were able to reenter the camp unopposed and kill their foes in their sleep.[5] Another historian, Dionysius of

Halicarnassus, tells us in *Roman Antiquities* that the Greeks of Megara covered large hogs with tar, ignited them, and loosed these flaming, incendiary pigs against the Macedonians to disrupt their elephant formations.

Plutarch recounts that Quintus Sertorius defeated the Charakitanes in Spain by using the wind to carry a toxic substance that caused coughing and blindness. And Polybius records that the people of Ambrajia used smoke produced by burning feathers in barrels to drive off the Roman sappers who were attempting to tunnel into their city.[6]

The Byzantine Greeks first used "Greek Fire," invented by the Syrian Callinicus, at the siege of Constantinople, and it continued in use in various forms for centuries. Although many knew of its effectiveness in terms of both its incendiary and antirespiratory qualities, its formula was a closely guarded secret.

One of the first modern designs for chemical ordnance was done by John Doughty in 1862. In a letter to Edwin Stanton, the U.S. secretary of war, Doughty enclosed diagrams and a plan for constructing projectiles containing liquid chlorine that would "effectively disqualify every man for service that was within the circle of its influence; rendering the disarming and capturing of them as certain as though both their legs were broken."[7] Doughty closes his letter with the comment that he has contemplated the morality of such a weapon and has concluded that its use would "lessen the sanguinary character of the battlefield," an argument that will be repeated often after similar weapons had become a reality.

Attempts also have been made to employ biological weapons against enemy forces. Gabriel de Mussis, an eyewitness to the Mongol siege of the coastal city of Caffa in 1346, records that the attacking army used a trebuchet to sail plague-infected corpses over the city walls in order to infect the residents. He adds that when he, along with the citizens of the city, fled in ships, they carried the plague to Sicily, Sardinia, Corsica, and Genoa, and from there it spread throughout Europe.[8] And in 1422, according to historian Varillas, after an unsuccessful siege of Carolstein, Corbut had the bodies of his dead soldiers along with 2,000 cartloads of excrement hurled into the city. In his own words, "A great number of the defenders fell victim to the fever which resulted from the stench, and the remainder were only saved from death by the skill of a rich apothecary who circulated remedies against the poison which infected the town."[9]

In 1763, the commander in chief of the British forces in America, Sir Jeffrey Amherst, sent a letter to one of his subordinate commanders, Colonel Bouquet, proposing that a plan be devised whereby the Native Americans with whom they were at war could be infected with smallpox. Colonel Bouquet wrote back, "I will try to inoculate the ____ with some blankets that may fall into their hands, and take care not to get the disease myself." Amherst responded, "You will do well to try to inoculate the Indians by means of the blankets, as well as to try every other method that can serve to extirpate this execrable race." Captain Ecuyer of the Royal Americans, after a meeting with two Indian chiefs, made the following journal entry on June 24, 1763: "Out of regard for them we gave them two blankets and a handkerchief out of the smallpox hospital. I hope it will have the desired effect."

The following year multiple sources (including Captain Ecuyer) reported that a smallpox epidemic was raging among the Native Americans and that numbers of Mingoes, Delawares, and Shawanoes had died from it, indicating that the plan was probably successful.[10]

General W. T. Sherman, describing events following the Battle of Vicksburg in the American Civil War, writes that on July 8, 1863, after a hot march through a region where water was extremely scarce, his troops reached the town of Clinton, only to discover that "General Johnson had marched rapidly, and in retreating had caused cattle, hogs, and sheep to be driven into the ponds of water and there shot down; so we had to haul their dead and stinking carcasses out to use the water."[11] Evidently the practice of contaminating water supplies with bacteria from decaying carcasses was common enough in the history of warfare that this action by General Johnson did not elicit official protests or condemnation.

There have been few recent attempts at using biological weapons, although research to develop such weapons has been extensive. During World War II, American soldiers sometimes scored the ends of their bullets and rubbed human waste on them in order to cause infections (a clear violation of the *jus in bello* prohibition against unnecessary suffering, because it was done solely for the purpose of causing harm after a victim's status as combatant had been terminated).

Also during World War II, Japan used biological agents such as typhoid (plague) and anthrax against at least eleven Chinese cities with some success. After the war, the Soviet Union brought to trial twelve Japanese prisoners for preparing and employing biological agents. The Japanese facility responsible for the research and development of biological weapons was commanded by Lieutenant General Shiro Ishii. Known as Unit 731, it hosted experiments on at least 3,000 American, Chinese, Korean, Soviet, British, and Australian POWs, killing at least 1,000, and perhaps many more. After the war, the United States granted General Ishii and his associates immunity from prosecution in exchange for exclusive possession of the results of their experiments. Publicly, American officials denied that any nation had used biological agents during the war.[12]

Attempts to restrict the use of both chemical and biological weapons also have a long history. When an Italian chemist offered Louis XIV of France a type of biological weapon, the king, instead of using the weapon, is reported to have given the inventor a pension with the stipulation that he never reveal his discovery.[13] And the historical custom against using poison was so strong that Lieber's Code (General Orders 100, dated April 24, 1863) singles it out, along with torture, as two prohibitions that may not be overridden based on military necessity. Lieber writes, "The use of poison in any manner, be it to poison wells, or food, or arms, is wholly excluded from modern warfare. He who uses it puts himself out of the pale of the law and usages of war."[14] It is reasonable to interpret this to include a prohibition against poisoning the air we breathe, although this interpretation was debated following World War I.

The 1899 Hague Convention, ratified by all of the major countries of Europe and Asia, banned the use of "projectiles the sole object of which is the diffusion of asphyxiating or deleterious gases." All the delegates voted in favor of the ban on gases except the U.S. representative Captain Alfred T. Mahan, who had been told by the secretary of state to oppose the measure with the hope that "the dissent of a single powerful nation might render it altogether nugatory." Following the vote approving the resolution concerning gases, Mahan made the following declaration:

> [It is] illogical, and not demonstrably humane, to be tender about asphyxiat-
> ing men with gas, when all were prepared to admit that it was allowable to
> blow the bottom out of an ironclad at midnight, throwing four of five hun-
> dred men into the sea, to be choked by water, with scarcely the remotest
> chance of escape. If, and when, a shell emitting asphyxiating gases alone has
> been successfully produced, then, and not before, men will be able to vote
> intelligently on the subject.

Similar arguments concerning the humane quality of chemical weapons are still being debated a century later.[15]

Prior to Germany's successful use of chemical weapons during World War I, most nations considered their use to be prohibited by either the 1899 Convention, quoted earlier, or the 1907 Hague Convention IV (Article 23), which states that "it is especially forbidden to employ poison or poison weapons." The French were the first to try chemical weapons on the battlefield in World War I, employing 26mm gas grenades in April 1914, but they proved ineffective.[16]

The Germans were careful to design chemical weapons in ways that skirted the 1899 prohibition against weapons "the *sole object* of which is the diffusion of asphyxiating or deleterious gases" by replacing *only part* of the shrapnel and explosives in 105mm artillery rounds with chemicals designed to irritate the mucous membrane. Three thousand of these shells were used against British troops in October 1914, but the soldiers never even realized there had been a chemical attack. A second attempt was made with a modified 15cm howitzer round in January 1915. The Germans fired 18,000 of these rounds (called T-shells), each containing seven pounds of xylyl bromide, as well as a shrapnel charge, against Russian positions at Bolimov, with little or no effect.[17]

Chemical weapons recorded their first success not with German artillery but with the simple release of more than 5,000 canisters containing 168 tons of chlorine that were opened upwind of the front lines. Although the use of gas at this encounter caused panic among the defenders, the Germans were not prepared to capitalize on it and the defensive lines were soon restored. Rather than protesting Germany's use of these chemicals at Ypres in 1915 as a violation of the laws of land warfare (which would have been questionable, given the letter of the 1899 Convention and the means used in delivery), the Allies responded by developing similar weapons for their own use, and on September 24, 1915, the British launched the first Allied gas attack.[18]

Following World War I, the more powerful nations of the civilized world, except the United States and Japan, ratified the Geneva Protocol of 1925, which declared,

> Whereas the use in war of asphyxiating, poisonous or other gases, and of all analogous liquids, materials, or devices, has been justly condemned by the general opinion of the civilised world . . . this prohibition shall be universally accepted as a part of International Law, binding alike the conscience and the practice of nations . . . [and the prohibition extended] to the use of bacteriological methods of warfare.[19]

Some signatories to the 1925 Geneva Protocol stipulated that they reserved the right to use chemical weapons in retaliation, but this at least constituted a prohibition against first use, and with more than 120 nations as signatories, it amounted to the same as a prohibition.

Significantly, neither Germany nor the Allies used chemical weapons during World War II, although it is unclear whether their motivation was a fear of retaliation or simply the realization that chemical weapons had never proved to have any significant effect on overall outcomes.

The United States finally ratified the 1925 Geneva Protocol in 1975, but stipulated that it did not consider the treaty's restrictions to extend to tear gas and other riot control agents, or to chemical herbicides, although the current U.S. policy is that herbicides and riot agents will not be used without presidential approval, except in certain cases that parallel their use in domestic society. From 1956 until 1975, U.S. policy did not rule out first use of either chemical or biological (or nuclear) weapons.

Since World War I there have only been six confirmed instances of first use of chemical weapons internationally: Spain against Morocco in 1925; the Soviet Union against China in 1934; Italy in Ethiopia in 1935; Japan against China from 1937 to 1945; Egypt against Yemen from 1963 to 1967; and Iran against Iraq from 1984 to 1988.[20] This is significant, because given the many dozens of armed conflicts since the end of World War I, it would appear that the prohibition against the first use of chemicals has assumed the status of customary as well as positive international law.

The morally questionable use of nuclear weapons by the United States against Hiroshima and Nagasaki in Japan in August 1945 remains the only case of any nation detonating nuclear weapons in war. Unlike chemical weapons that have never been and probably are not capable of being decisive on the conventional battlefield, nuclear weapons have decisive force.[21] But, unlike chemical and biological weapons, which have a long tradition of being regulated under international law, there are no international treaties restricting the use of nuclear weapons in wartime. The current U.S. policy statement on the use of nuclear weapons is found in Field Manual 27–10, *The Law of Land Warfare*.

> The use of explosive "atomic weapons," whether by air, sea, or land forces, cannot as such be regarded as violative of international law in the absence of any customary rule of international law or international convention restricting their employment.[22]

The United States has always held that nuclear weapons are not subject to existing prohibitions against chemical weapons or poison, and current policy continues to leave open the option of "first use."

Let us now examine the various types of NBC weapons in terms of the Just War Tradition.

CHEMICAL AND BIOLOGICAL WEAPONS

In a report to the United Nations on chemical and bacteriological weapons, prepared in accordance with General Assembly Resolution 2454A (XXIII), we find the following definitions:

> Chemical agents of warfare are taken to be chemical substances, whether gaseous, liquid, or solid, which might be employed because of their direct toxic effects on man, animals, and plants. Bacteriological (biological) agents of warfare are living organisms, whatever their nature, or infective material derived from them, which are intended to cause disease or death in man, animals, or plants, and which depend for their effects on their ability to multiply in the person, animal, or plant attacked.[23]

The use of biological weapons is prohibited by the 1972 Biological Weapons Convention, a treaty that is signed by 103 nations (including the five permanent members of the UN Security Council), which has been in force since March 1975. Parties to this treaty declare that they will

> never in any circumstances develop, produce, stockpile or otherwise acquire or retain (a) microbial or other biological agents or toxins whatever their origin or method of production, of types and in quantities that have no justification

for prophylactic, protective or other peaceful purposes; (b) weapons, equipment or means of delivery designed to use such agents or toxins for hostile purposes or in armed conflict.[24]

Unlike the reservation attached to the U.S. ratification of the 1925 Geneva Protocol on chemical weapons, the official policy regarding biological weapons is that "the U.S. does not reserve the right to retaliate with bacteriological methods of warfare [even] if another state or any of its allies fails to respect the prohibitions of the Protocol."[25]

A second treaty that has recently become relevant to biological type weapons is the 1948 Genocide Convention. With the U.S. ratification in 1986, it has now been ratified by all five permanent members of the UN Security Council, as well as ninety-one additional nations. This treaty declares that genocide, conspiracy to commit genocide, direct and public incitement to commit genocide, attempt to commit genocide, and complicity in genocide are crimes under international law, and expressly includes in its definition of genocide

any of the following acts committed with intent to destroy, in whole or in part, a national, ethnical, racial, or religious group, as such: (a) killing members of the group; (b) causing serious bodily or mental harm to members of the group; (c) deliberately inflicting on the group conditions of life calculated to bring about its physical destruction in whole or in part; (d) imposing measures intended to prevent births within the group.[26]

The significance of this to biological weapons is that ethnic weapons designed to attack only certain national groups—weapons that might be possible through genetic engineering—are forbidden by the Genocide Convention.

Nations all seem to recognize that the use of biological weapons must be prohibited because they cannot discriminate between combatants and noncombatants. The reason that these weapons have been considered inappropriate has nothing to do with their effect on soldiers—that is, they do not cause "unnecessary suffering"—but because of their potential effect on innocents and friendly combatants.

This points out an important difference between biological and chemical weapons. While the nations of the world were able to agree to a prohibition of biological weapons in a relatively short time, the debate regarding the morality of chemical weapons continues to be a topic of controversy. The classic argument for the use of chemical weapons is found in J. B. S. Haldane's *Callinicus*. Haldane argues that chemical weapons should not be outlawed because they are the most humane weapons ever invented and have the capacity to reduce suffering on the battlefield significantly. As he puts it, "The use of mustard gas would render it [war] less expensive of life and property, shorter, and more dependent on brains rather than numbers."[27]

Those who oppose chemical weapons on moral grounds offer a variety of arguments. Frances Harbour states that chemical weapons are immoral because: (a) they are a form of torture, (b) they inflict unnecessary mental and physical suffering, (c) they are dehumanizing, (d) they can result in a dishonorable death, and (e) they are likely to be employed in ways that do not discriminate between combatants and noncombatants.[28] Unfortunately, Harbour does not establish how chemical weapons differ from conventional weapons such as bombs or artillery or mines in terms of their effect on combatants, except for the remarkable claim that wearing chemical protective clothing is immoral because it makes humans look like "insects or space monsters." In chemical protective clothing, she argues, "the soldier is isolated and subject to an undignified and dehumanizing experience." And when weighing the physical suffering caused by chemical weapons against that of conventional weapons, she concedes that they are "at least comparable."

Nevertheless, it is certain that chemical weapons presently cause special psychological effects that conventional weapons do not. Prior to their deployment to Saudi Arabia (in response to Iraq's invasion of Kuwait), U.S. soldiers seemed obsessed with the possibility of facing chemical weapons. Prior to the Second Gulf War, nothing had changed. Not only the armed forces, but the news media seemed obsessed with the possibility that chemical weapons might be employed. Every day during the entire course of the war, national news commentators discussed the possibility of chemical attacks against U.S. or British forces or into a neighboring country. During the First Gulf War, the Israeli government went so far as to issue protective masks to every Israeli citizen.

Haldane attempts to explain this exaggerated dread of chemical weapons as a predisposition of people to fear the unknown. In any event, I report it as an interesting observable phenomena and leave the reader to draw his or her own conclusions regarding its origins and significance.

Despite arguments such as Harbour's, I can find no reason to prohibit chemical weapons on moral grounds. If Harbour's arguments are that chemical weapons should be outlawed because they are dehumanizing, she will have to provide an argument to persuade us that the Just War Tradition should be expanded to include a principle prohibiting weapons that "dehumanize" that is similar to the existing principles that prohibit weapons that cannot discriminate or that cause unnecessary suffering. This would require a new paradigm in the *jus in bello* tradition, as the present restrictions focus entirely on the protection of innocents. Harbour's proposed revision would require a *jus in bello* restriction based on protecting the dignity of combatants. This seems highly unlikely given that, literally speaking, the most extreme form of "dehumanization" is death, an effect that most military weapons are designed to have. If she is referring only to the psychological effects of chemical clothing, I do not understand how it is substantially different from the specialized clothing that many others—surgeons, firefighters, welders, clowns, divers, astronauts, football players—wear in their respective professions.

This does not mean, however, that there are not still sound and prudential reasons for chemical weapons to be outlawed, even if there are no fundamental ethical ones. Indeed, this seems to be the basis for the difference in the way that prohibitions against chemical and biological weapons have been treated under international law. Recall that while the United States signed without any reservations the 1972 Biological Weapons Convention prohibiting the development or production of such weapons, its ratification of the 1925 Geneva Protocol stipulates that it will "cease to be binding . . . in regard to an enemy State if such State or any of its allies fails to respect the prohibitions laid down in the protocol." And although none of the signatories to the convention on biological warfare have stipulated a reciprocity reservation, one-third of those that have ratified the 1925 Protocol on Chemical Weapons (including the United States, France, China, the former Soviet Union, Great Britain, and most other nations with chemical weapons capability) have made similar "first use" stipulations. If the use of chemical weapons was regarded as immoral, as is the use of biological weapons, then nations would not be justified in reserving the right to use them in retaliation. Obviously this is not the case.[29]

Opposition to the use of chemical weapons is prudent for a number of reasons, and the U.S. ratification of the Chemical Weapons Convention in April 1997 seems to reflect this line of thinking. First, there is, as Harbour rightly points out, a historical precedent against the use of chemical weapons that places the burden for justifying their use on those who advocate change. And while chemical weapons as a whole might be no worse than conventional weapons in terms of violating the *jus in bello* principles prohibiting unnecessary suffering and mandating discrimination between combatants and non-combatants, they are certainly no better. The very existence of customary law against using these weapons constitutes a strong argument against their use, and in the absence of a convincing argument to the contrary, the prohibition should stand. (An example of a convincing argument to the contrary might be another party's use of them first.) This is especially persuasive, considering the fact that chemical weapons have historically had no significant impact on the outcome of conflicts.

Second, even though the weapons themselves are not substantially different from conventional weapons in the suffering they cause, increased diversity in weapons technology is likely to adversely affect military units in terms of defensive readiness posture and medical treatment capabilities, and this would probably produce an aggregate increase in human suffering. In other words, not only would an attack that mixed high explosive and chemical ordnance produce more casualties than would an attack using either type of weapon by itself, but troops training to defend against both types of attacks would be less prepared than if they had to train for only one type, including medical treatment units. Thus, chemical weapons themselves need not cause more suffering than conventional weapons; they need only be capable of increasing suffering when used in consonance with other weapon types; and it is prudent for nations to mutually agree to measures that will reduce suffering without having any significant impact on the outcome of the conflict.

Third, it seems prudent to restrict chemical weapons because of the possibility that they could be used by terrorist or other criminal groups operating outside of the law. We know that weapons designed and built for use in war find their way into the arsenals of terrorists, gangsters, drug lords, and others of their ilk. A growing proliferation of chemical weapons increases the likelihood of their use in domestic society enormously, and chemical weapons used by terrorists against unprepared civilians in crowded facilities could be devastating.

Finally, both the storage and destruction of chemical weapons that are obsolete or have outlived their shelf life pose enormous problems for the nations producing them, as the United States and various independent Soviet Republics found out following the Cold War.

These arguments support not only a prohibition against first use of chemical weapons but also a prohibition against the development, production, stockpiling, or acquiring of lethal chemical weapons that parallels existing international restrictions on biological weapons. The Chemical Weapons Convention represents a major breakthrough in the evolution of *bellum justum* and international law, because it not only bans the use of most types of chemical weapons in war, but bans the development, production, and stockpiling of them and mandates the destruction of existing stockpiles. The treaty also requires nations to declare the existence of any surviving inventories and provides for on-site inspections to ensure compliance with treaty provisions.

NUCLEAR WEAPONS

Some have argued that the existence and proliferation of nuclear weapons makes it impossible to ever justify resorting to war, regardless of the provocation. Proponents of this view maintain that given the proliferation of nuclear weapons it is inevitable that *eventually* modern war will escalate to nuclear war, and the consequences of nuclear war are too catastrophic to ever be justifiable, regardless of the circumstances. The only reasonable alternative, they argue, is rejection of war altogether. As Pope John XXIII writes in *Pacem in Terris*, "In this age which boasts of its atomic power it no longer makes sense to maintain that war is a fit instrument with which to repair the violation of justice."[30] Those who defend this view argue that the use of nuclear weapons will make a mockery of both *jus ad bellum* and *jus in bello:* of the former because the long-term dangers of radioactive fallout and environmental contamination—potentially against one's own population or allies—make the utilitarian objection to war insurmountable; and of the latter because nuclear weapons are far too indiscriminate in whom they kill—in both the long term and the short term—for them to ever be employed justly. Renowned psychologist Eric Fromm expresses these sentiments in the following way:

> Whatever the rationale of previous wars may have been—defense against attack, economic gain, liberation, glory, the preservation of a way of life—such rationale does not hold true for nuclear war. There is no defense, no gain, no liberation, no glory, when at the very "best" half the population of one's country has been incinerated within hours, all cultural centers have been destroyed, and a barbaric, brutalized life remains in which those still alive will envy the dead.[31]

One response to this line of reasoning is to question the contention that in modern war the use of nuclear weapons is inevitable. Scores of wars have been fought since 1945 where at least one belligerent possessed nuclear capability, and there has not been a single case where a nuclear weapon, even a tactical one, has been used.[32]

A second objection to the nuclear pacifist's position is that this view seems to assume that nuclear weapons will always be employed—*à outrance*. Certainly we can imagine nuclear weapons being employed tactically in ways that fall short of all-out strategic bombardment or the use of megaton-size weapons.

Even if we reject the final conclusion of the pacifist's argument (that war is never justified), however, we are still faced with the implicit claim that the use of nuclear weapons is never justified. Those defending this view might hold that the use of nuclear weapons in combat will always be morally wrong because (1) their use will result in widespread noncombatant deaths and (2) the destructive effects of such weapons will necessarily be out of proportion to any political or military objectives achieved.

One possible response to this criticism of nuclear weapons might be that it is not an argument against nuclear weapons per se, but against a particular effect that is possible when one uses nuclear weapons. Perhaps it is true that the use of nuclear weapons against another people can never be justified. If so, then it is because of the effects of such weapons—that is, they violate our notions of *bellum justum*—not because they are nuclear weapons. Moreover, with the rejection of the doctrine of mutually assured destruction (MAD) in favor of the doctrine of flexible response, the United States and other nuclear powers have changed their strategic war planning from countervalue targeting (cities) to counterforce targeting (military targets). This shift in planning seems to imply that our political leaders accept nuclear weapons as an alternative under the Just War Tradition (whereas the MAD doctrine implied a rejection of nuclear weapons in the context of Just War).

Others take the position that it is not necessary for the effects of nuclear weapons to pass the *jus in bello* criteria in order for the United States to be justified in constructing and stockpiling them. This can easily be seen if one imagines a case where the detonation of a nuclear weapon might be an acceptable alternative in lieu of war. Suppose, for example, that one could deter a large-scale conflict by demonstrating the power of a nuclear explosion on a lifeless volcanic island (or underground); or imagine deterring an alien attack by detonating a nuclear weapon on the moon (or in space). Indeed, most experts and laypersons alike agree that the use of nuclear weapons in a *deterrence* role did result in a half century of peace between NATO and the Warsaw Pact and did prevent the Cold War from escalating into a conventional war that would have itself constituted a catastrophe of global proportions.

A second reason why strategic nuclear weapons have not been eliminated is the belief that they have contributed to peace. Certainly nuclear weapons served as a deterrent to war between the nations that belonged to NATO and the Warsaw Pact during the Cold War period following World War II.[33] Perhaps it is this deterrent effect that motivated Russia to change its long-standing policy against the first use of nuclear weapons to match the U.S.'s long-standing policy that first use is a viable alternative to conventional aggression.

Even in a deterrence role, however, nuclear weapons are highly controversial. The possibility of accidental launch, launch by a world leader gone mad, launch by terrorist groups, too rapid an escalation in the event of minor hostilities, accidents in storage areas, or launch on the mistaken belief that the other side has initiated an attack should cause concern in all sane peoples. Some argue that issues such as these pose a danger as great or even greater than that posed by war.

Additionally, some claim that war can be deterred equally as well with large numbers of conventional weapons that do not pose the long-term, indiscriminate danger of nuclear weapons. In other words, the gains of nuclear deterrence are not proportional to the costs (in terms of risk, not dollars) of stockpiling nuclear weapons; using conventional weapons, some argue, would accomplish the same objective at a reduced risk.

Examples such as these seem to indicate there are at least some cases where the detonation of nuclear weapons might be a reasonable alternative. And indeed, at the request of the United Nations, the International Court of Justice took up the issue of the legality of the use or threat of nuclear weapons in 1996 and determined (by a split 7-7 vote) that "the Court cannot conclude definitively whether the threat or use of nuclear weapons would be lawful or unlawful in an extreme circumstance or self-defense, in which the very survival of a State would be at stake."

Contrary to the conclusion of the U.N. court, Michael Walzer believes that "nuclear weapons explode the theory of just war."[34] There is certainly at least one aspect of nuclear weapons that offers strong evidence for considering them *different in kind* from conventional weapons, namely the long-term effects of radiation and nuclear fallout. No other weapons system has such far-reaching and long-lasting destructive capability. This seems to make their use in war at least questionable, because by their very nature they tend to be indiscriminate in whom they harm *in the long term.* Even if they can be employed as tactical weapons in ways that minimize innocent deaths at the time of detonation—this itself no mean task—the long-term effects of fallout and the radiological contamination at the detonation site are still extremely difficult to accurately predict.

Considerations such as these provide persuasive reasons for regarding nuclear weapons—at least the type of strategic weapons that characterize the world's arsenals—as different in kind from other types of ordnance, because they cannot be employed in ways that satisfy the *jus in bello* condition of discrimination in the long term.

Given the enormity of the possible consequences associated with nuclear war, one might wonder, Why do the United States, Russia, China, France, Great Britain, Pakistan, and India (along with other nations) continue to build or maintain such weapons? Why haven't the nations of the world been able to reach a comprehensive agreement restricting the deployment and use of nuclear weapons, given such strong objections to their viability as a means of waging war? Let us begin our attempt to answer this question with a very brief summary of the progress achieved by the the world community in regulating nuclear weapons in recent years.

The first series of Strategic Arms Limitation Talks (SALT I) began in 1969 and concluded in 1972 when U.S. President Nixon and Soviet General Secretary Brezhnev signed the Anti-Ballistic Missile Treaty and an interim agreement to limit strategic offensive weapons. The purpose of the SALT II negotiations was to replace the interim SALT I agreement with a long-term treaty that would limit nuclear delivery systems (while maintaining parity). Although this treaty was signed by U.S. President Carter and Secretary Brezhnev in 1979, it was never ratified in the U.S. Senate, primarily as retaliation by the U.S. for the Soviet Union's invasion of Afghanistan. U.S. ratification became moot, however, as the United States quickly violated the spirit of the SALT agreements by developing multiple warheads for existing delivery systems.

In July 1991, after ten years of negotiations, the United States and the Soviet Union agreed to the Strategic Arms Reduction Treaty (START I), the first treaty ever aimed at reducing nuclear arsenals. (With the breakup of the Soviet Union in 1992, the independent republics of Ukraine, Belarus, Kazakhstan, and Russia all signed the START I treaty several months later.) This treaty, which reduced the number of intercontinental nuclear weapons by thirty percent, went into effect in December 1994.

START II (signed by President Bush and President Yeltsin and ratified by the U.S. Senate and Russian Duma) eliminates all "heavy" intercontinental ballistic missiles as well as those with multiple warheads and limits the numbers of strategic (intercontinental) warheads to a number two-thirds below pre-START I levels (about 3,000 each).

In March 1997, Russian President Yeltsin and U.S. President Clinton agreed to begin negotiations for a START III agreement which, unlike its predecessors, would require reductions in the inventories of nuclear warheads (i.e., those not deployed on delivery systems), to include the irrevocable disposition of the plutonium in the warheads. This treaty would also further reduce the number of intercontinental weapons to between 1,500–2,500 each. On May 24, 2002, U.S. President Bush and Russian President Putin signed the Moscow Treaty on Strategic Offensive Reductions, requiring a reduction in strategic nuclear warheads in each country to 1,700–2,200 by the end of 2012.

Two related international agreements on nuclear weapons deserve mention. The Nuclear Non-Proliferation Treaty, approved by the United Nations in 1968, is the most widely accepted arms agreement, with over 185 signatories. The only nations that that are not party to the nonproliferation agreement are Cuba, Israel, India, Pakistan, and North Korea (which withdrew in 2003). A second international document relating to nuclear weapons is the Comprehensive Test Ban Treaty, approved by the United Nations General Assembly in 1996. This treaty, which would ban nuclear test explosions for any reason whatsoever, has been signed by over 150 nations. Given the world's present unsatisfactory but somewhat promising state of affairs, let us attempt to understand how we got into this nuclear predicament, and then speculate on what we might imagine the future to look like in terms of nuclear weapons, especially among nations that are not presently part of the nuclear club.

First, imagine that we are official government policy makers for a powerful nation; call it the Federation of States. Our charge from our constituents is to ensure our nation's independence and security, especially vis-à-vis our political adversaries, whom we will call the Romulan Republic. We have the ability to produce nuclear weapons, and we are trying to decide whether we should do so. We reason that if we have a strong nuclear arsenal and the Romulans do not, our independence and security will be assured. (We have no intention of using said weapons, we only see them as a means of ensuring our security.) Naturally, if the Romulans ever develop a strong nuclear arsenal, then there is even more reason for us to have one in order to protect ourselves.

In fact, it seems that it does not matter whether the Romulans have nuclear weapons or not; our own security vis-à-vis the Romulans is enhanced if we arm ourselves with nuclear weapons. Thus, as political leaders charged with providing security for the nation, it seems that our best course of action toward this end is to build nuclear weapons. The Romulans, of course (and the responsible leaders of all sovereign nations) reason precisely the same way, and both sides begin building such weapons. Nuclear proliferation seems inevitable.

The paradox is that at some point the nuclear arsenals themselves seem to jeopardize security by their very presence. In other words, the security of the citizens of the respective nations is threatened because the nuclear arsenals themselves pose more of a threat than the conflict they were designed to deter; this is because there is not a linear relationship between the security achieved by building one nuclear weapon and the security achieved by building a number of nuclear weapons. In this case, the collective utility of an aggregate of identical actions is less than the sum of the utilities of each action taken individually.[35] While each individual act of building a single nuclear weapon increases security, the aggregate of acts of building all of them reduces security (hence, SALT and START treaties to reverse the trend). This seems true whether we consider just two nations with large arsenals, or many scores of nations with small ones.

Nevertheless, nuclear deterrence seems to be an inevitable policy consequence if we have security as our paramount political objective. Suppose, however, that rather than providing security, our constituents charge us with the mission of preventing war? Perhaps this would help us avoid the difficulties caused by pursuing increased security through nuclear deterrence.

What if we were to accept the claim that the best way to prevent war is to maintain parity in strength? It is reasonable to assume that nations that are political, economic, or geographic rivals are more likely to remain at peace and solve their differences without violence if they each believe themselves to be equal in strength to their potential adversaries. Certainly nations are less likely to start wars when it is not in their interests to do so, and it is never in a nation's interest to start a war it does not believe (or at least is uncertain) it can win. When one nation believes itself militarily superior to a rival nation, and there is a conflict of interests, the likelihood of that nation initiating hostilities increases.

Given the assumption that parity increases our chances for peace, and assuming that peace is truly our objective, let us see how this affects our thinking about nuclear weapons.

Again, take two nations, the Federation of States and the Romulan Republic, with widely divergent political views. Because the people of each nation do not trust their counterparts in the rival nation, and because they are in competition for limited resources and status among the other nations of the world, the likelihood of armed conflict remains consistently high. Both have the capacity to build nuclear weapons, although neither side has done so.

If the Federation builds nuclear weapons and the Romulans do not, the temptation to use coercive force will be increased, and the likelihood of war increases. The same is true if the Romulans build nuclear weapons and the Federation does not, because the likelihood of war increases as the disparity in strength does—regardless of which side is stronger. If both sides either build nuclear weapons or do not build nuclear weapons, then parity is maintained and the likelihood of war is reduced. Consider the following four alternatives:

1. Romulans build nuclear weapons—Federation does not;
2. Federation builds nuclear weapons—Romulans do not;
3. both sides build nuclear weapons;
4. neither side builds nuclear weapons.

The best choice would be number 4—neither side builds nuclear weapons. The second-best alternative would be number 3—both sides build them—because this would be another way to maintain parity.

Now suppose that you are a member of the Romulan Republic and you believe that the Federation of States intends (or has started) to build nuclear weapons. Of the two choices available to you—number 3, follow suit and build your own nuclear weapons, or number 2, not build them—which one is most likely to prevent war? Does it matter that the Federation tells you that its weapons are for defensive purposes only? Does it matter that the Federation claims that its weapons will only be used to maintain peace, that is, to prevent war? No. The Romulans must build nuclear weapons to maintain parity. *National security policy is always based on enemy capabilities, not intentions.* After all, not only is deceit possible, but intentions might change overnight.

Given that one side is going to arm, the other side has no choice but to arm too—not only for self-defense, but also as a deterrent to war. From this simplistic example, we see one of the paradoxes of nuclear deterrence: In some circumstances, the only way to reduce the chance of war is to build weapons for war. This same reasoning also can be applied to disarmament. If one side disarms, the likelihood of war increases; if neither side does, we have nuclear deterrence; if both do, we have disarmament. Of course, as we can see from ongoing arms negotiations during the past twenty-five years, the process of reducing strength while maintaining parity as well as enough arsenal for deterrence is painfully slow.

This leads us to our second difficult discussion issue concerning nuclear deterrence: *Is it ever morally permissible to intend to do something that it would be morally wrong to actually do?* Notice that we will continue to work under the assumption that a strategic nuclear exchange would be morally reprehensible because of the effects discussed previously. The problem now, however, does not concern the actual detonation of nuclear weapons, but simply the conditional intention to detonate them under certain circumstances.

The debate on this topic is highly complex, with some scholars investigating relevant topics such as what it means to form an intention, second-order versus first-order intentions, distinctions between intentions, threats, and bluffs, and so on. Our approach will be more fundamental. For purposes of our discussion, we will assume that for the threat to use nuclear weapons to be credible, there must be a sincere intention to carry it out. This assumption is reasonable, given the open and democratic nature of our government. We do not expect our political leaders to declare publicly one policy while privately planning to carry out another; rather, to some extent at least, we expect national policy to reflect the will of the people. This means that if the official policy of the United States is to use strategic nuclear weapons under certain conditions, it is reasonable to expect government leaders to carry out this policy when those conditions obtain. When government leaders threaten to use nuclear weapons in the event of an attack, they are not bluffing. Our two premises, then, are

> It is wrong to use strategic nuclear weapons.
>
> The United States intends to use strategic nuclear weapons under certain conditions.

Naturally, those who advocate deterrence argue that by forming a conditional intention (i.e., if they attack, we will retaliate) one can prevent the antecedent of the conditional from occurring. And it does seem plausible that by threatening to use nuclear weapons a nation can decrease the likelihood that it will have to use them. In other words, the best way to prevent *either side* from using nuclear weapons is for the other side to threaten (intend) retaliation.[36] But herein lies the source of the dilemma: If it is wrong to perform some act, is it not also wrong to intend to perform it? By not intending to perform the immoral act, however, the likelihood of nuclear war actually occurring increases.

One might respond to the dilemma by concluding that because the use of nuclear weapons is wrong, the intent to use them also is wrong. (This is referred to as the wrongful intention principle.)[37] Therefore, we simply should not use or even threaten to use them. Those who take this view often advocate unilateral disarmament.

One might also argue that the issue of intent is logically independent from the issue of use, and even though the use of nuclear weapons is morally wrong, intending or threatening to use them is permissible. Finally, one may take the position that if an intent (or threat) to do something is permissible because it is likely to bring about desirable consequences (in this case because it reduces the likelihood of war), then acting on that conditional intent (or threat) in the appropriate circumstances does not require a separate justification.[38]

I doubt that there is any consensus on this issue forthcoming. Perhaps we could change tactics and ask ourselves, What would happen if the U.S. government renounced its intention to use strategic nuclear weapons? In other words, what if the United States kept certain weapons in accordance with treaty limitations but renounced its intention ever to use them? Would the mere presence of the weapons be as good of a deterrent as would their presence coupled with a statement of intent to use them if provoked?

In 1982, the Soviet Union officially adopted a policy of no first use of nuclear weapons. (Russia has since retracted that policy.) The United States's response to the Soviet position was to belittle and label it as "a clever ploy" aimed at the United Nations.[39] A more recent commentator on the Soviet position writes

> The point is not hypocrisy . . . but the vacuity of verbal pledges, no matter how solemnly uttered. Nations plan for war not by listening to their rivals' commitments but by looking at their capabilities. As long as NATO has nuclear weapons in the field, they might be used. . . . Thus an NFU [no first use] declaration on the part of NATO could not change the basic objective of Soviet planners.[40]

The point here is not the Soviet's renunciation of the first use of nuclear weapons but the United States's response to it. As we observed previously, national security policies are based on capabilities, not intentions. If this is true, then the deterrent effect of nuclear weapons would be based on their existence rather than on a political leader's intentions concerning their use. Thus, nuclear weapons would have the same deterrence capacity whether policy called for first use, no first use, or no use, as long as the weapons are on hand and functional.[41]

This approach to the deterrence dilemma is not without its own problems. Probably the most troubling one concerns the need to articulate national policy in order to subject it to public debate. The United States could not, for example, renounce the policy of first use without replacing it with a new policy, and this might cause considerable consternation among members of the European Community. Still, with the dissolution of the Warsaw Pact and the restructuring of the Soviet Union, the argument that nuclear weapons are a legitimate means of deterring conventional war seems less plausible—even though as of this writing most of the independent republics that once formed the USSR have decided to destroy their nuclear arsenals. Certainly if nuclear weapons are not needed to deter conventional war, then there is no need to reserve the right of first use. Thus a renunciation of the first use of nuclear weapons seems to be the minimum acceptable position to take in the immediate future.

What would be the repercussions of adopting a policy of "no use" of *strategic* nuclear weapons?[42] I doubt that such a policy would have any effect whatsoever on the deterrence capacity of the strategic arsenal. Predictably, the Russian reaction would be similar to the U.S. response to the 1982 Soviet declaration of no first use—it did not change American policy one bit. Nor would such a policy necessarily entail that the weapons be dismantled. The United States could justify keeping an arsenal of strategic nuclear weapons to deter attack or to deter other nonnuclear nations from building nuclear weapons. The weapons also could be used as bargaining chips during disarmament negotiations. Finally, one could keep them based on the possibility that the world political climate could change in ways that might justify renouncing the no-use policy, although the numbers of weapons would probably be reduced drastically.

In sum, the following principles seem to represent a reasonable direction for U.S. nuclear policy to take in the next decade. The United States should:

1. declare its intent to refrain from using strategic nuclear weapons under any foreseeable circumstances;
2. renounce first use of all nuclear weapons;
3. continue to negotiate reductions in nuclear weapons with Russia and other nations with nuclear capabilities.

In 1992, Boris Yeltsin, president of the Russian Republic, announced that the Russian nuclear arsenal would no longer be targeted at American cities. As the great intercontinental nuclear arsenals of the superpowers are slowly dismantled, the peoples of the world must resolve not to be subjected to the threat of strategic nuclear war as a means of ensuring peace. But this is not enough. It is imperative that the nations of the world act now to codify rules restricting nuclear weapons in terms of development, size, storage, target planning, and both tactical and strategic use. We must not wait to see the destructive capabilities firsthand—as we have done historically with conventional weapon systems—before we develop laws and doctrines that extend the tenets of the Just War Tradition to nuclear technology. The proposed START IV treaty would involve all declared nuclear nations, but there is not yet an agreement on the time frame of negotiations.

Topics for Further Discussion

1. International law expressly prohibits the use of both chemical and biological weapons. The United States has agreed to a policy of "no first use" of chemical weapons, and a policy of "no use"—even in retaliation—regarding biological weapons. Suppose, however, that the United States could develop a biological weapon that would make soldiers sick for three to five days without any long-term effects. What would be the legal and moral considerations governing the use of such a weapon?
2. The 1995 Protocol IV on Blinding Laser Weapons stipulates that laser weapons may not be specifically designed for the sole purpose of causing

permanent blindness (less than 20/200 vision). Do you believe that a laser or microwave weapon that could destroy the retinas of eyes without doing any other damage to the body would be a violation of the principles of Just War? Or is this simply another case of prudential restraint?

3. The United States attacked two Japanese cities, Hiroshima and Nagasaki, with atomic bombs during World War II. Supporters of these attacks point out that fewer lives were lost by bombing these cities than would have been lost had the United States invaded the Japanese mainland. Critics of the attacks claim that Japan was already willing to accept reasonable conditions for surrender and that the real motive for the bombing was to force Japan's unconditional surrender before Stalin and the Soviet Union entered the war. What alternative measures might have brought an end to the war short of bombing these two cities? *Note:* (a) The United States had only enough uranium for two bombs; (b) The United States had conducted only one test in the desert and did not know for certain the extent of damage the bombs would cause; (c) Hiroshima was bombed on August 6, the U.S.S.R. declared war on Japan on August 8, Nagasaki was bombed on August 9, Japan agreed to surrender unconditionally on August 10; (d) Approximately 120,000 people were killed and 100,000 were injured in the two bombings—not counting the long-term effects of radiation and fallout.

4. If it is morally wrong to use nuclear weapons because of their long-term, indiscriminate effects, is it also morally wrong to threaten to use them? Why or why not?

5. Based on the evidence gathered in the aftermath of Hiroshima and Nagasaki, we know that one of the long-term effects of nuclear radiation is an increase in deformed babies. Do you believe it is possible to have moral obligations to other humans who have not yet been conceived? If you believe we have moral obligations to future generations, how might this influence decisions about whether to use nuclear weapons? If you believe we have no obligations to unborn generations, develop an argument to support your position.

6. Modern antitank missiles often are constructed from depleted uranium because of its high density. Some argue that such weapons violate the Just War Tradition since they can cause radioactive contamination on the battlefield. Evaluate these projectiles using the *jus in bello* criteria discussed in previous chapters.

7. Some argue that there is a nonlinear relationship between the utility of individual acts and the aggregate utility of a number of the same acts. One simplistic example that they claim illustrates this is overindulging at meals. One might, for example, eat (or drink) a large portion of a particular dish and derive tremendous pleasure (and no harm) from it. If, however, one were to repeat this same behavior over a period of weeks

(or years), the individual instances of pleasure might be overwhelmingly outweighed by certain negative consequences, such as disease, obesity, addiction, failed relationships, and so on. Similar examples include taking a shortcut across the grass, skipping brushing one's teeth after meals, cutting class, and so on. How might one apply this theory of nonlinear utility—that is, there may be a nonlinear relationship between the deterrent quality of a single nuclear weapon and the enormous danger of a nuclear arsenal—to argue against our present nuclear strategy?

8. Developing national policy on nuclear weapons might be likened to driving a large truck full of explosives down a steep, winding, mountain dirt road that you've never driven before, at night, in a torrential rainstorm, and with no brakes—but there is no need to worry because the rearview mirror works just fine. Recall that in June 1981, Israel attacked a nuclear reactor under construction in Iraq by French scientists. The president of Iraq at the time, Saddam Hussein, publicly stated that the reactor would be used to supply weapons-grade plutonium for nuclear weapons and that he expected to have a nuclear arsenal by 1991. When the French government refused to cease construction of the reactor, Israeli aircraft destroyed it. At the time the attack was widely condemned by the U.S. press (the *Los Angeles Times* called it "state sponsored terrorism" and the *New York Times* called it "an act of inexcusable short-sighted aggression"), but after Desert Storm in 1991, Secretary of Defense Dick Cheney sent General David Ivry, Israel's mission commander for the attack, a note thanking him for the successful raid ten years earlier and stating that his actions "made our job much easier in Desert Storm." Given the level of danger and the number of long-standing animosities in various regions, what should U.S. policy be toward nations such as North Korea and Iran that are working to develop nuclear weapons? Is the use of force justified in order to prevent their development?

9. Although land mines are not considered unconventional weapons in the same way NBC weapons are, they still are highly controversial. U.N. Protocol II on Prohibitions or Restrictions on the Use of Mines, Booby-Traps and Other Devices (1980) (along with the 1996 Amendments to this protocol, ratified by the United States) stipulates the following restrictions (among others): (1) Remotely delivered mines must be antipersonnel type only and must be equipped with a self-destruction device, and (2) All feasible precautions shall be taken to protect civilians, both in the short and long term, from the effects of mines and booby traps.

    a. Proponents of a total ban on the production, stockpiling, and use of land mines, especially antipersonnel land mines, argue that the mines cannot be used in ways that discriminate between combatants and noncombatants. Opponents of a ban respond that a ban would amount to *noblesse oblige*

arms control, as long as China, Iraq, Iran, and North Korea continue to produce and supply mines on the world market. Write an argument either in
support of or against an international ban on antipersonnel land mines. If
you argue in support of such a ban, what do you believe the U.S. policy on
these mines should be in the absence of a ban?

b. The 1997 Ottawa Convention on the Prohibition of the Use, Stockpiling,
Production and Transfer of Anti-Personnel Mines and on their Destruction
(accepted by a large number of nations) was not signed by the United States,
China, India, Pakistan, or Russia because these nations believed that there
are good reasons to have antipersonnel mines in particular circumstances.
Investigate and evaluate the United States's arguments for its position vis-à-
vis this convention.

c. Mines at sea are regulated primarily by the 1907 Hague Convention (VIII).
Two recent violations of this convention include Iran's use of antiship mines
in the Persian Gulf during its war with Iraq, and the United States's use of
mines against Nicaragua in international waters in 1984. What specific prohibitions of the 1907 Hague Convention were violated in each case?

Notes

1. I believe that the relationship between warfare and the environment will become increas-
    ingly important. The 1977 U.N. Convention on the Prohibition of Military or Any Other
    Hostile Use of Environmental Modification Techniques was passed largely as a response
    to the U.S.'s use of defoliates (Agent Orange) during the Vietnam War. The Convention
    limits restrictions to damage that is "widespread and long-lasting," a phrase vague enough
    to make enforcement extremely difficult. Saddam Hussein's malicious burning of the
    Kuwaiti oil wells in the First Gulf War, and his attempts to ignite his own nation's wells
    in the Second, were wanton, vicious attacks against the environment. Neither he nor his
    subordinates were ever called to account for these crimes before the world community.
    For an insightful introduction to the topic of military operations and the environment, see
    Merritt Drucker, "The Military Commander's Responsibility for the Environment,"
    Environmental Ethics (Summer 1989).
2. Curt Watchel, *Chemical Warfare* (New York: Chemical Publishing Company, 1941), p. 17.
3. Thucydides, *History of the Peloponnesian War,* translated by Rex Warner (New York:
    Penguin Books, 1971), Book II, "The Siege of Plataea," p. 171, and Book IV, "Athenian
    Defeat at Delium," p. 325.
4. J. H. Rothschild, *Tomorrow's Weapons: Chemical and Biological* (New York: McGraw-
    Hill, 1964), pp. 12–13.
5. Watchel, *Chemical Warfare*, pp. 14–15.
6. Ibid., p. 20.
7. Colonel Alden Waitt, *Gas Warfare: The Chemical Weapon, Its Use, and Protection Against
    It* (New York: Duell, Sloan, and Pearce, 1942), pp. 9–11.
8. Vincent J. Derbes, "De Mussis and the Great Plague of 1348," *Journal of the American
    Medical Association* 196; no. 1 (April 4, 1966): 179.
9. Ibid., p. 179. As the source for this passage, Derbes cites Varillas, *Histoire de l'Heresie
    de Viclef, Jean Hus, et de Jerome de Prague* (Lyon, France: Chez Iean Certe, 1682),
    vol. 2, p. 117.

10. Francis Parkman, *The Conspiracy of Pontiac* (New York: The Library of America, 1991), p. 648.

11. W. T. Sherman, *Memoirs,* vol. I (New York: The Library of America, 1990), p. 346.

12. *Biological and Toxin Weapons Today,* edited by Erhard Geissler (Oxford, England: Oxford University Press, 1986), pp. 10–11.

13. Ibid., p. 8.

14. Richard Shelly Hartigan, *Lieber's Code and the Law of War* (Chicago: Precedent Publishing, 1983), pp. 48, 58.

15. Waitt, *Gas Warfare,* pp. 12–13.

16. Major Charles E. Heller, *Chemical Warfare in World War I: The American Experience, 1917–1918,* Leavenworth Paper No. 10, (Fort Leavenworth, Kans.: Combat Studies Institute, U.S. Command and General Staff College, 1984), p. 6.

17. Ibid.

18. Ibid., p. 11.

19. *Documents on the Laws of War,* edited by Adam Roberts and Richard Guelff (New York: Oxford University Press, 1982), pp. 137–45.

20. I omit—with considerable reservation—from this list the use by the United States of defoliants in Vietnam and Iraq's use of chemicals against its own citizens (the Kurds). Included is Egypt's use of chemicals against Yemen, even though Egypt still denies the allegation. There have been other allegations that are unsubstantiated (although perhaps true).

21. Edward M. Spiers, *Chemical Warfare* (Chicago: University of Chicago Press, 1986), p. 31.

22. Department of the Army, *Law of Land Warfare,* Field Manual 27–10 (Washington, D.C.: U.S. Government Printing Office, 1956), chap. 2, para. 35, p. 18.

23. Willlam Epstein and others, *Chemical and Bacteriological (Biological) Weapons and the Effects of Their Possible Use* (New York: United Nations, 1969), p. 5.

24. Geissler, *Biological and Toxin Weapons Today,* p. 135.

25. *Law of Land Warfare,* Field Manual 27–10, Change 1, dated July 15, 1976, para. 38c, p. 2.

26. Geissler, *Biological and Toxin Weapons Today,* p. 132.

27. J. B. S. Haldane, *Callinicus: A Defense of Chemical Warfare* (New York: Garland Publishing, 1971), p. 51.

28. Frances V. Harbour, "Chemical Weapons and Soldiers' Rights," paper presented at the Joint Services Conference on Professional Ethics (JSCOPE), National Defense University, Washington, D.C., January 12, 1990.

29. In *A Moral Military* (Philadelphia: Temple University Press, 1989), Sidney Axinn confuses the relationship between the Just War Tradition and the international laws of war concerning chemical and biological weapons. He writes, "Why we reserve the right to retaliate against chemical but not biological weapons is unclear," p. 75.

30. *Pacem in Terris,* 1st ed., S.264 (London: Catholic Truth Society, 1967), para. 127. Quoted in Bruce Kent, "A Christian Unilateralism," in *Ethics and Nuclear Deterrence,* edited by Geoffrey Goodwin (New York: St. Martin's Press, 1982), p. 56.

31. Eric Fromm, *The Heart of Man,* vol. 12 in the Religious Perspectives Series, edited by Ruth Nanda Anshem (New York: Harper & Row, 1964), p. 56. Reprinted in "The Impossibility of Civilized Warfare," in *The Morality of Peace and War,* edited by Martin T. Woods and Robert Buckenmeyer (Santa Barbara, Calif.: Intelman Books, 1974), p. 229.

32. Examples include the Korean War, Vietnam War, Falklands War, Afghanistan War, and United Nations–Iraq War. Nations known or believed to have the ability to produce nuclear weapons include the United States, Russia, the United Kingdom, France, India, South Africa, Canada, China, Israel, and Pakistan.

33. Robert Paul Holmes disagrees. He argues that "there is little reason to believe that deterrence has worked in the past, or that it will continue to work in the future." And, of

course, the statement that "without nuclear weapons there would have been war in Europe" during the Cold War period cannot be proven. However, when one considers that Europe, with its historical nationalism and residual unresolved conflicts from World War II, remained an island of peace for almost fifty years while there were more than 150 wars worldwide, and that such inflammatory incidents between the United States and the former Soviet Union as the Berlin and Cuban missile crises were handled without escalating into violence, Holmes's argument seems terribly unpersuasive. Additionally, the brutal religious- and nationalistic-inspired violence that erupted following the breakup of the Soviet Union implies that it was nuclear deterrence that kept the dogs of war tethered for so many years. See *On War and Morality* (Princeton, N.J.: Princeton University Press, 1989), p. 236.

34. Michael Walzer, *Just and Unjust Wars: A Moral Argument with Historical Illustrations* (New York: Basic Books, 1977), p. 282.

35. For more on the nature of the relationship between the utilities of individual acts and an aggregate of the same acts, see Harry S. Silverstein, "Utilitarianism and Group Coordination," *Nous* 13 (1979): 336.

36. The official U.S. position is that nuclear weapons may be used in response to even a conventional attack. Thus, they are used as a deterrent not just to nuclear war but also to conventional war.

37. See Gregory S. Kavka, "Some Paradoxes of Deterrence," in *Ethics and the Military Profession*, 2d ed., edited by Malham M. Wakin (Boulder, Colo.: Westview Press, 1986), pp. 444–62.

38. Ronald Dworkin briefly summarizes these alternatives and cites examples of those who have defended each position in "Nuclear Intentions," *Ethics* 95 3 (April 1985): 445 60. The article appears in a special issue of *Ethics*, focusing solely on nuclear deterrence.

39. See Josef Joffe, "Nuclear Weapons, No First Use and European Order," *Ethics*, 95 3 (April 1985): 608; and Richard H. Ullman, "Denuclearizing International Politics," ibid., p. 578.

40. Joffe, "Nuclear Weapons, No First Use," p. 609.

41. Regarding nuclear deterrence, Bernard Brodie has argued that "we do not need . . . to threaten that we will use [nuclear weapons] in case of attack . . . their being there is quite enough." Quoted in Walzer, *Just and Unjust Wars*, p. 281. Walzer cites George Quester, *Deterrence Before Hiroshima* (New York: Wiley, 1966), p. 67, as the source for this quotation.

42. I am considering as strategic all nuclear warheads, delivered either by long-range bombers, from submarines, or by long-range land-based missiles. Those that are portable or fired from artillery guns I am considering tactical. The official policy is more complex.

SECTION

IV

PROFESSIONAL AND HUMANITARIAN OBLIGATIONS

Professions differ from other forms of employment in that membership therein implies a commitment to certain abstract ideals that are shared by others in the same profession worldwide. Those who choose to become members of a profession often cite a sense of "calling" to serve their society or even humankind as their motivation. The question of whether military officers are members of a profession in the classical sense is an important one because it would mean that the Just War Tradition is the common ethical template that officers would share, regardless of their nationality. In this section we will examine certain ethical issues specific to military officers and consider the tensions inherent in regarding them as members of a bonafide profession.

Chapter

13

THE ENEMY: COLD-BLOODED KILLERS OR COMRADES IN ARMS?

Up to this point our discussion of international law has not distinguished between the rules governing *jus in bello* and *jus ad bellum,* although what we have been saying seems to be more relevant to political (i.e., *jus ad bellum*) decisions. In this chapter we will attempt to see how Hart's concept of rules, which derive their normative force from an internal point of view, can help us understand soldiers and their relationship to *jus in bello.*

When we focus on the conduct of war from a historical perspective, as we did in chapter 1, we find that there is a tendency among military personnel of all cultures to take an internal point of view toward *certain* rules that are spelled out in international law. Together these rules comprise what might be called the "Professional Military Ethic," or the "warrior ethos." The origin of this tradition among military people stems from their sharing certain values common to the profession of arms, such as courage, honor, loyalty, and obedience. This notion of a warrior ethos harkens us back to a passage cited earlier (chapter 2) by Saint Ambrose, where King David of Israel praises his enemy (Abner) for his valor, honors him with a banquet after his defeat, weeps for him when he is killed, and requires that the same justice be shown to Abner's soldiers as to his own men.

Sailors of all nations recognize certain customs of the high seas, and the code of chivalry that pilots on both sides observed during World War I is well known.[1] Michael Walzer discusses instances of the warrior code's significance during World War II, when it was customary for the victorious commander to receive the commanding general of the vanquished out of respect for his profession. Walzer writes, "Historically, such visits were not merely matters of courtesy; they were occasions for the reaffirmation of the military code."[2]

J. Glenn Gray, in his classic *The Warriors: Reflections on Men in Battle*, chides General Dwight Eisenhower for ignoring his staff's recommendations that he allow the captured German General Jurgen von Armin to call on him. Gray observes, "One of the most time-honored and persistent images of the enemy, today very suspect in democratic lands, is the one held by the professional soldier, who regards all military men as comrades in arms."[3]

General Linderman, writing about the American Civil War, relates that "when General John Bell Hood realized that the enemy troops he was about to attack were unaware of the Southerners' presence, he ordered, 'Major, send a shell first over their heads and let them get in their holes before you open with all your guns.'"[4] Linderman argues that the source of this tradition of camaraderie between enemy soldiers lies in the shared reverence for that virtue that is intrinsic to success as a fighting person—courage. Linderman cites the following personal account by a Union soldier as an example of how soldiers could experience such a bond:

> I saw an officer on a milk-white horse ride forth from the woods in the rear of the Confederate work. Confident that he would be torn to bits by shells, I dropped my pipe, and glued my glass on him and waited for the tragedy. He trotted briskly over the plain where shells were thickly bursting, and into the fort. I saw him hand a paper to the officer in command of the work. He sat calmly on his horse, and talked and gesticulated as quietly as though he were on dress parade. My heart went out to that man. I hoped he would not be killed. I wished I had the aiming of the guns. He lifted his hand in salute to the visor of his cap. He turned his white horse and rode slowly across the open ground where shot and shell were thickly coursing. Dust rose above him. Tiny clouds of smoke almost hid him from view. Shot struck the ground and skipped past him, but he did not urge his horse out of a walk. He rode as though lost in meditation and deaf to the uproar that raged around him. He rode into the woods, disappeared in the timber and was safe. With a "Thank God that brave man was not killed," I rejoined my gun.[5]

It is easy to see how a common bond based on shared values could develop among members of the profession of arms. While traditional moral reasoning provides the rational basis for the *jus in bello* dimension of the Just War Tradition, it is an internal point of view toward the rules of war or the warrior ethos that is at its heart.

During both World Wars, especially in the European Theater, there was much mutual admiration between soldiers on opposite sides. One soldier, describing a German detachment in October 1918, wrote,

> I grew proud of the enemy who had killed my brothers. They were two thousand miles from home, without hope and without guides, in conditions bad

enough to break the bravest nerves. Yet their sections held together, sheering through the wrack of Turk and Arab like armoured ships, high-faced and silent. When attacked they halted, took position, fired to order. There was no haste, no crying, no hesitation. They were glorious.[6]

For another veteran, John Roberts, the same war held.

No personal hostility whatever. Indeed, when an enemy position had been taken, one tended to take the same attitude of care and welfare to the dead and wounded as if they belonged to our own side. There was an abhorrence of any maltreatment of prisoners . . . especially when they had put up a good fight.[7]

An American infantryman in Vietnam describes a similar experience.

One day during a fire fight, for the first time in my life, I heard the cries of the Vietnamese wounded, and I understood them. When somebody gets wounded, they call out for their mothers, their wives, their girlfriends. There I was listening to the VC cry for the same things.[8]

Another veteran of Vietnam made the following observation during the war:

It occurred to me that we were becoming more and more like our enemy. We ate what they ate. . . . We endured common miseries. In fact, we had more in common with the Viet Cong than we did with that army of clerks and staff officers in the rear.[9]

American officers writing about their experiences in the Middle East during the recent United Nations war with Iraq record similar experiences. One captain, in describing his experience with an elderly, captured Iraqi soldier who had been wounded, writes,

Here was a man who could have been my grandfather with a hole in his chest, with no shoes on his blackened feet, and apparently starving from lack of food. My memory drifted back to thoughts of hot summers like the one I just experienced, sitting on my grandfather's knee listening to him tell stories. . . . In this sudden moment, this Iraqi, although not near the man in size that my grandfather is, resembled him by his strong quiet presence. I wondered if he had grandchildren.[10]

Another captain, recounting his unit's capture of an Iraqi force during the same war, describes his enemy counterpart thus,

I am not sure what I really expected him to look like. As I watched the haggard band of tired Iraqis move in our direction, I knew he was in charge. He moved with that quiet dignity that is reserved for the conqueror. Even in defeat, he was firmly in command. He exhibited a kindness and compassion that I had believed his people incapable of showing. We spoke for quite some time. . . . I finally saw the face of my enemy. . . . He was not so different from me.[11]

After this encounter was over, the same officer writes, "His compassion and sophistication had dashed my conception of the evil, illiterate bedouin."

The current U.S. Army publication on the conduct of war, *The Law of Land Warfare*, requires that belligerents "conduct hostilities with regard for the principles of humanity and chivalry."[12] The Air Force publication on the same topic is even more specific.

> *Chivalry.* Although difficult to define, chivalry refers to the conduct of armed conflict in accord with well-recognized formalities and courtesies. During the Middle Ages, chivalry embraced the notion that combatants belonged to a caste, that their combat in arms was ceremonial, that the opponent was entitled to respect and honor, and that the enemy was a brother in the fraternity of knights in arms. Modern technological and industrialized conflict has made war less a gentlemanly contest. Nevertheless, the principles of chivalry remain in specific prohibitions such as those against poison, dishonorable or treacherous misconduct, misuse of enemy flags, uniforms, and flags of truce. The principle of chivalry makes armed conflict less savage and more civilized for the individual combatant.[13]

The empirical evidence, however, indicates that soldiers have frequently refused to regard their opponents as moral equals. In other words, soldiers have recognized the *jus in bello* rules, taken an "internal point of view" toward them, and still not always extended them to certain enemy soldiers because they regarded these soldiers as being outside the bounds of moral judgment. This is Dwight Eisenhower's explanation for refusing to acknowledge German General Jurgen von Armin as a moral equal, an action that became the topic of national debate and criticism. In his memoirs, General Eisenhower explains,

> Daily as it [the war] progressed there grew within me the conviction that as never before in a war between many nations the forces that stood for human good and men's rights were this time confronted by a completely evil conspiracy with which no compromise could be tolerated. . . . The war became for me a crusade in the traditional sense of that often misused word.[14]

Nazi Germany presents us with a difficult case because the Third Reich was one of the most objectively evil political regimes the world has known. General Eisenhower's assessment is representative of the reasoning that allows soldiers on the one hand to take an internal point of view toward certain rules applicable to their profession, while on the other hand to fail to acknowledge the applicability of these rules toward a particular class of persons. Military and political leaders often are guilty of characterizing the enemy as being less than human in order to lend righteousness to the cause for which the war is fought. As J. Glenn Gray puts it,

> Equally ancient, and apparently as persistent, is the image of the enemy as a creature who is not human at all. Especially common to simple uneducated soldiery when fighting a foe of another color or race, it is by no means unknown to educated unimaginative men. They regard the enemy as subhuman, a peculiar species of animal with indeterminable qualities and habits, all evil.[15]

An example of this can be seen in the contrast between the rules that were generally observed in World War II among European military forces who recognized a common culture and heritage with their belligerents, and those that prevailed in the Asian Theater, where a common heritage was lacking. Reports of battles with Japanese soldiers often contain metaphors connoting animals or insects, such as "they came in hordes," or "they appeared as swarms of yellow," or "they burrowed into the mountains." Gray cites the following passage from Herman Wouk's *The Caine Mutiny* as being indicative:

> Like most of the naval executioners at Kwajalein, he seemed to regard the enemy as a species of animal pest. From the firm and desperate taciturnity with which the Japanese died, they seem on their side to believe they were contending with an invasion of large armed ants.[16]

One explanation, then, for the historical fact that soldiers have sometimes failed to observe rules of humane treatment, even though they recognized certain moral obligations that should govern behavior between human beings, is that they compartmentalized their beliefs in ways that allowed them to view the enemy as being less than human. A second explanation for such behavior is to collectively view the enemy as being guilty and deserving of punishment. Unfortunately, it is not difficult to imagine either of these views being held by citizens of even the most civilized nations today. One need only recall the brutal injustices of My Lai or the manner in which Muslims and Christians treated one another in the Bosnian–Serbian conflict.

Nevertheless, it is, as Grotius put it, a fiction to conceive of the enemy as forming a single body. "Generals," he writes, "are responsible for the things which have been done while they were in command; and all the soldiers that have participated in some common act, as the burning of a city, are responsible for the total damage."[17] Elsewhere, Grotius notes that "guilt is personal. . . . Let those responsible for crimes be held for them; and let not the fear of punishment extend beyond those in whom an offense may be found."[18]

And concerning the guilt that a community might bear for crimes initiated by the majority,

> When the community is at fault through the crime of the majority, . . . and when, for this cause, it loses things [such as] political liberty, fortifications, and other profitable things, the loss is felt also by the individuals who are innocent, but only in respect to such things as belonged to them not directly but through the community.[19]

We can understand that this is so when we consider the possibility of holding a military leader such as General Robert E. Lee personally responsible for the American Civil War,[20] or even for the crimes committed at Andersonville Prison, where 45,000 Union soldiers died.[21]

Perhaps improvements in communications media, increased travel, access to satellite television, proliferation of English as an international language, and international financial interdependence have all contributed to an increased awareness of the common emotions that are shared by all of the diverse peoples of the world, as well as the common problems (such as pollution, ozone depletion, and the nuclear threat) with which they must contend. If so, then it is reasonable to believe that this trend will continue. Certainly people are less likely to cling to a false belief in the innate inferiority of a particular group when there is increased interaction. In any event, professional soldiers of all nations must continue to regard the rules of war as their rules if the humanitarian principles of *jus in bello* are to be effective in reducing the brutality of war. In Hart's terms, they must take an "internal point of view" toward the *jus in bello* rules and contribute to their refinement, promulgation, and enforcement. One goal of the military establishment should be to reconcile revolutionary technological innovations with traditional principles before battlefield scenarios prove the last war's rules to be obsolete. This should be a military responsibility, because these are soldiers' rules, not rules imposed on them by a political system.

Samuel Huntington, in his discussion of military officers and the Professional Military Ethic, writes,

> An officer corps is professional only to the extent to which its loyalty is to the military ideal. What appeals politically one day will be forgotten the next. What appeals politically to one man will inspire the hatred of another. Within the military forces only military loyalty to the ideal of professional competence is constant and unifying: loyalty of the individual to the ideal of the Good Soldier, loyalty of the unit to the traditions and the spirit of the Best Regiment. The most effective forces and the most competent officer corps are those which are motivated by these ideals rather than by political or ideological aims. Only if they are motivated by military ideals will the armed forces be the obedient servants of the state.[22]

Moreover, there must be an increased effort to promulgate the laws of war and the ethos of the warrior in peacetime. International conferences and treaties should include stipulations that soldiers of all services and nations receive periodic instruction in the Just War Tradition, the laws of war reflecting this tradition, and the ethos of the soldier. International agreements to this effect should receive the same or greater priority—to include emphasis on verification—as arms control efforts. Without changes in this aspect of *jus in bello,* many will continue to treat the laws of war as theoretic ideals rather than legal and moral mandates.[23]

Topics for Further Discussion

1. Is it reasonable to expect soldiers to have respect for the enemy combatants they are engaged in attempting to destroy? What does the "moral equality of soldiers" have to do with the warrior ethos?
2. Vitoria argues that, while soldiers are responsible for *jus in bello,* they are always imbued with "invincible ignorance" as far as *jus ad bellum* is concerned. Was General Eisenhower rejecting the *jus in bello–jus ad bellum* distinction when he refused to permit a visit from General von Armin in accordance with military tradition?
3. One way people "justify" unequal treatment of others is by characterizing them as being inferior or different in some way. When this is done to a group it is called prejudice and often results in discrimination. Provide both military and domestic examples where groups have done this.
4. Religious wars—Protestant against Catholic, Buddhist against Hindu, Christian or Jew against Muslim—have often been exceptionally ruthless because the objective of such wars is frequently the virtual annihilation of the other side. Some argue that patriotism is really a disguised form of religion and that blind loyalty to one's country or nationality can generate similar ruthlessness. With this in mind, consider the following questions:

    a. How are political and religious affiliations similar? How do they differ? Consider similarities and differences between documents containing political or religious theory (constitution or bible), icons (founders, heroes, martyrs), symbols (flags, statues, ornaments), financial support (donations, taxes, fees), conditions for membership (sacrifices, oaths, exams), and various forms of sanctions for misbehavior.
    b. What might be done to prevent intense patriotic loyalty, either to a nation or to a political ideology, from motivating genocide? Could this be why Samuel Huntington (see quotation, page 229) argues that the loyalty of the professional

military person must be to the professional military ethic, rather than to a polit-ical ideal?

c. Does the Just War Tradition permit intervention in the internal affairs of another nation in order to prevent genocide? Develop a set of criteria for when a nation would be justified in intervening in the internal affairs of another nation for humanitarian reasons. Apply these criteria to two recent internal conflicts that involved widespread humanitarian abuse. Some examples might include the following: Iraq (under Saddam Hussein), Serbia–Bosnia–Croatia (former Yugoslavia), Somalia, Cambodia, Sudan, Uganda (under Idi Amin), or the Soviet Union (under Stalin).

5. Because of its importance to success on the battlefield, courage might rightly be labeled as "the soldier's virtue," and it is important that mili-tary officers be able to distinguish courage as a virtuous act from daring and other types of foolish risk-taking. Courageous actions all have the same syntax—that is, there is a goal that the agent wants to bring about, and a countergoal that he or she wants to avoid, and when an agent pur-sues a goal despite the danger of a dreaded countergoal, then he or she has acted courageously. The worthiness of the desired goal and the mag-nitude of negative consequences associated with the countergoal are what distinguish courage from ersatz courage, daring, or bravado. Below are five examples of courageous actions, three involving soldiers and two from peacetime. In each case, identify the desired goal that the agent attempts to bring about and the undesirable countergoal (or risk) that causes the act to be considered courageous, and assess the merits of each.

a. On the night of March 30, 1976, in the Quang Tri Province, Republic of Vietnam, the headquarters of Company I, 3d Battalion, 9th Marine Regi-ment, 3d Marine Division was attacked with heavy machine-gun and mortar fire by a superior force of well-trained North Vietnamese regulars. Second Lieutenant John P. Bobo from Buffalo, New York, organized his headquar-ters group into a hasty defense and began moving from position to position providing encouragement to his soldiers and directing the battle. For his heroic actions that night he was awarded the Medal of Honor (posthu-mously). The following description of the battle is taken from the award citation: "When an exploding enemy mortar round severed Second Lieu-tenant Bobo's right leg below the knee, he refused to be evacuated and insisted upon being placed in a firing position to cover the movement of his soldiers to a better defensive location. With a web belt around his leg serv-ing as a tourniquet and with his leg jammed into the dirt to curtail the bleed-ing, he remained in this position and delivered devastating fire into the ranks of the enemy attempting to overrun the marine position. He was mortally wounded while firing his weapon into the main point of the enemy attack, but his valiant spirit inspired his men to heroic efforts, and his tenacious stand enabled the command group to gain a protective position where it repulsed the enemy onslaught."

b. Our second example concerns the actions of a medical specialist rather than a combat soldier. Donald Ballard was a naval hospital corpsman from Kansas City, Missouri, serving with the 3d battalion, 4th Marine Regiment, 3d Marine Division in the Quang Tri Province, Republic of Vietnam on May 16, 1968. His citation reads, in part: "Hospital Corpsman Ballard was returning to his platoon from an evacuation-landing zone when his unit was ambushed by a North Vietnamese Army unit employing automatic weapons and mortars, and sustained numerous casualties. Observing a wounded marine, HC Ballard unhesitatingly moved across the fireswept terrain to the injured man and rendered medical assistance to his comrade. As he and four additional marines prepared to carry a wounded marine to safety, an enemy soldier suddenly left his concealed position and, after hurling a hand grenade near the casualty, commenced firing upon the small group of men. Instantly shouting a warning to the marines, HC Ballard fearlessly threw himself upon the lethal explosive device to protect his comrades from the deadly blast. When the grenade failed to detonate, he calmly arose from his dangerous position and resolutely continued his determined efforts in treating other marine casualties. HC Ballard's heroic actions and selfless concern for the welfare of his companions served to inspire all who observed him and prevented possible injury or death to his fellow marines. His courage, daring initiative, and unwavering devotion to duty in the face of extreme personal danger sustain and enhance the finest traditions of the US Navy."

c. During the presidential elections of 1872, Susan B. Anthony and fourteen supporters walked into a voting booth and cast their ballots for president of the United States. A few days later she was arrested, brought before a judge, and charged with having illegally entered a voting booth. When the judge asked her how she pleaded, she replied:

"Guilty! Guilty of trying to uproot the slavery in which you men have placed us women. Guilty of trying to make you see that we mothers are as important to this country as are the men. Guilty of trying to lift the national standard of womanhood, so that men may look with pride upon their wives' awareness of public affairs. But Your Honor, not guilty of acting against the Constitution of the United States, which says that no person is to be deprived of equal rights under the law. How can it be said that we women have equal rights, when it is you and you alone who take upon yourselves the right to make the laws, the right to choose your representatives, the right to send only sons to higher education. You have become the slaveholders of your mothers and wives."

"I am forced to fine you one hundred dollars," the judge said.

"I will not pay it," she replied and walked from the courthouse.

Ten years after her death, states ratified the Nineteenth Amendment to the Constitution guaranteeing equal rights for women, and there is no doubt that

Susan Anthony's opposition to the injustices of the ruling government was a catalyst that influenced the change.

d. On January 13, 1982, Air Florida Flight 90 crashed into the Potomac River shortly after take-off in a blizzard from Washington's National Airport, killing more than seventy passengers. It was rush hour and the banks of the Potomac were quickly crowded with people watching while helicopters attempted to pull survivors from the floating ice and water. When it became obvious to the spectators that one survivor, Priscilla Tirado, was too weak to hold onto the rescue rings that were lowered to her from the helicopter, one of the witnesses decided to do something. Lenny Skutnik was a twenty-eight-year-old mail clerk who lived in a $325 monthly apartment and was paid $14,000 a year. He later told reporters that he enjoyed an occasional night out by taking his wife and two kids to Brother's Pizza. As he put it, "Every once in a while I just close my eyes and blow a couple of bucks." After diving into the frigid water and pulling Miss Tirado to safety, he gave his coat to Joseph Stiley, a survivor who had broken both legs in the crash and was shivering, then he refused to get into an ambulance to be taken to the hospital until he received assurances that it wasn't going to cost him anything.

e. The following account is taken from Martin Middlebrook, *The First Day on the Somme* (Allen Lane, 1971), reprinted in *The Oxford Book of Military Antecdotes*, edited by Max Hastings (Oxford University Press, 1985). "Neville was a young officer who liked to stand on the fire-step each evening and shout insults at the Germans. His men were to be in the first wave of the assault near Montauban and he was concerned as to how they would behave, for they had never taken part in an attack before. While he was on leave Neville bought four footballs [soccerballs], one for each of his platoons. Back in the trenches, he offered a prize to the first platoon to kick its football up to the German trenches on the day of the attack. . . . Neville himself kicked off. 'As the gunfire died away [wrote one survivor], I saw an infantryman climb onto the parapet and into No Man's Land, beckoning others to follow. As he did so, he kicked off a football; a good kick, the ball rose and traveled towards the German line. That seemed to be the signal to advance.' The winning footballers of the 8th East Surreys were unable to collect the prize from their commander. Captain Neville was dead."

6. Historically, societies have distinguished between "professions" and "vocations." Members of the former are expected to have a sense of "calling," to be educated and certified by other members of the profession, and to commit to a set of abstract ideals. Once one joins the medical or legal profession, for example, it is a lifetime certification that can only be taken away or forfeited for cause as determined by one's peers. Most military officers regard themselves as members of a profession and, indeed, our society expects them to adhere strictly to a set of abstract ideals such as loyalty, selflessness, and obedience to civilian authority. The officer corps is managed, however, according to a business or corporate model, where officers work in a highly vertical organizational structure, are evaluated regularly by superiors in this hierarchical structure (rather than their peers), are selected for promotions and financial rewards based on these evaluations, work in an environment where those not selected for promotion are forced to retire, and are subjected to lay-offs (euphemistically referred to as "selective early retirement boards" or "drawdowns") based on political or budgetary decisions. In short, although we expect our officers to conform to a professional model, we manage them according to a corporate or managerial model.

a. Is membership in the officer corps best understood as constituting membership in a profession, or should officers be considered "managers of violence" or some other type of executive expert according to their military specialty? What are the pros and cons of each alternative?

b. Would it be more effective to reduce the warrior ethos to a set of positive laws governing how military officers should act, rather than expect officers to "voluntarily" adhere to a set of professional abstract ideals?

Notes

1. One pilot provides the following account of having successfully attacked a German plane: "I was almost equally gratified the next second to see the German pilot level off his blazing machine and with a sudden leap overboard into space [with a parachute] let the Fokker slide safely away without him. . . . I truly wished him all the luck in the world." Edward Rickenbacker, *The Fighting Circus* (Garden City, N.Y.: Doubleday, 1965), pp. 251–52.

2. Michael Walzer, *Just and Unjust Wars: A Moral Argument with Historical Illustrations* (New York: Basic Books, 1977), p. 37.

3. J. Glenn Gray, *The Warriors: Reflections on Men in Battle* (New York: Harper & Row, 1970), pp. 142, 146–147.

4. Gerald F. Linderman, *Embattled Courage: The Experience of Combat in the American Civil War* (New York: The Free Press, 1987), p. 68.

5. Ibid., p. 69. Linderman cites Frank Wilkeson, *Recollections of a Private Soldier in the Army of the Potomac* (New York and London: G. P. Putnam's Sons, 1886), pp. 113–14, as the source for this passage.

6. T. E. Lawrence, quoted by Richard Holmes in *Acts of War: The Behavior of Men in Battle* (New York: The Free Press, 1986), p. 373.

7. Ibid., pp. 373–74.

8. Ibid., p. 372.

9. Philip Caputo, *A Rumor of War* (New York: Ballantine Books, 1977), p. 262.

10. Captain Darryl Williams, United States Military Academy, untitled, unpublished work prepared for the Eisenhower Graduate Program in Leader Development.

11. Captain James Stevens, United States Military Academy, untitled, unpublished work prepared for the Eisenhower Graduate Program in Leader Development.

12. U.S. Department of the Army, *Law of Land Warfare*, Field Manual 27–10 (Washington, D.C.: U.S. Government Printing Office, 1956), para. 3, p. 3.

13. U.S. Department of the Air Force, *International Law—The Conduct of Armed Conflict and Air Operations*, Air Force Pamphlet 110–31 (Washington, D.C.: U.S. Government Printing Office, 1976), chap. 1, p. 6 (1–6).

14. Dwight Eisenhower, *Crusade in Europe* (New York: Doubleday, 1948), pp. 156–57, quoted by Gray, *The Warriors*, p. 147. Walzer cites this example and provides a provocative assessment of the distinction between the crime *of* war for which political leaders are responsible and crimes *in* war that are a military responsibility. He cites Erwin Rommel as an example of a German general who is widely admired because of his adherence to the laws of war in the face of Hitler's orders to the contrary, but Walzer "sympathizes" with Eisenhower's decision. Walzer, *Just and Unjust Wars*, pp. 37–38.

15. Gray, *The Warriors*, p. 148.

16. Ibid., p. 149.

17. Grotius, *The Law of War and Peace*, Bk. III, chap. 10, IV, p. 719.

18. Ibid., Bk. II, chap. 21, XIII, pp. 539–40.

19. Ibid., Bk. IX, pp. 537–38.

20. General Lee's orders to his forces prior to moving into Maryland and Pennsylvania are an excellent articulation of elements of the Professional Military Ethic put into practice and, as such, are worth noting: "The duties exacted of us by civilization and Christianity are not less obligatory in the country of the enemy than in our own. The commanding general considers that no greater disgrace could befall the army, and through it our whole people, than the perpetration of the barbarous outrages upon the innocent and defenseless and the wanton destruction of private property that have marked the course of the enemy in our country. . . . The commanding general, therefore, earnestly exhorts the troops to abstain with most scrupulous care from unnecessary or wanton injury to private property, and he enjoins upon all officers to arrest and bring to summary punishment all who shall in any way offend against the orders on this subject." Quoted in Peter Karsten, *Law, Soldiers, and Combat* (Westport, Conn.: Greenwood Press, 1978), p. 103. Lee was charged with treason, but never tried. He spent the last years of his life as president of Washington College in Virginia.

A speech by Lieutenant Colonel Tim Collins, Commander of the Royal Irish battle group, to his soldiers in Kuwait in March 2003, has a similar ring to it: "We go to liberate, not to conquer. We will not fly our flags in their country. We are entering Iraq to free a people, and the only flag that will be flown in that ancient land is their own. Don't treat them as refugees, for they are in their own country. I know men who have taken life needlessly in other conflicts. They live with the mark of Cain upon them. If someone surrenders to you, then remember they have that right under international law, and ensure that one day they go home to their family. The ones who wish to fight, well, we aim to please. If there are casualties of war, then remember that when they woke up and got dressed in the morning they did not plan to die this day. Allow them dignity in death. Bury them properly, and mark their graves. You will be shunned unless your conduct is of the highest, for your deeds will follow you down in history. Iraq is steeped in history. It is the site of the Garden of Eden, of the Great Flood, and the birth of Abraham. Tread lightly there. You will have to go a long way to find a more decent, generous and upright people than the Iraqis. You will be embarrassed by their hospitality, even though they have nothing. . . . There may be people among us who will not see the end of this campaign. We will put them in their sleeping bags and send them back. There will be no time for sorrow. Let's leave Iraq a better place for our having been there. Our business is north." Quoted by Ben Macintyre in a press release.

21.   The commandant of Andersonville Prison, Captain Henry Wirtz, was tried and found guilty of violating Lieber's Code and was hanged on November 11, 1865. For a summary of the case, see Friedman, *The Law of War: A Documentary History*, vol. I, pp. 783–98.

22.   Samuel P. Huntington, *The Soldier and the State* (Cambridge, Mass.: The Belknap Press of Harvard University, 1957), reprinted in *War, Morality, and the Military Profession*, 2d ed., edited by Malham M. Wakin (Boulder, Colo.: Westview Press, 1986), p. 48.

23.   How should soldiers who are actively engaged in an attempt to destroy one another behave when the fighting temporarily ceases, due to surrender, injury, capture, or truce? When Immanuel Kant declares that we should treat others as ends in themselves and never merely as means to our own ends, he means that they should be treated according to the roles that they have freely chosen for themselves. When one treats a waiter as a means to getting dinner, it is acceptable because we are treating him appropriately given the end that he has freely chosen for himself; that is, we are treating him as an end in himself. When Kant claims that we should act so that we could will the maxim of our action to be a universal law, he means that we should act the way that we would want others to act given the particular role we (and they) have freely chosen. To do otherwise, he argues, is irrational because it is advocating a particular set of rules for a particular role, and then personally behaving in a way that violates these rules. Put either way, it means that people should not give preference to themselves at the expense of others, except as is reasonable, given their respective roles. Thus, soldiers deserve the respect appropriate to that profession; criminals and those that abuse others should be treated accordingly. In wartime, soldiers may be killed because that is treating them appropriately as soldiers. Soldiers who terminate their status as combatants are no longer proper objects of attack. Thus, the *jus in bello* laws of war do not violate Kant's categorical imperative.

Chapter

14

UNJUST WARS
AND PROFESSIONAL
OBLIGATIONS*

In 1995, during a number of interviews corresponding with the release of his book on the Vietnam War, Robert McNamara, who was the secretary of defense during the early years of Vietnam (1961–1968), stated that he was convinced— fully seven years before the war ended—that it was both unwinnable and that the United States should withdraw. Our discussion in chapter 6 noted that in order for a war to be just, there must be a reasonable chance of success. The fact that the secretary of defense believed that the United States was fighting an unjust war in Vietnam is shocking. Had the U.S. government acted on McNamara's assessment at that time (which he kept from the public), close to 50,000 U.S. soldiers and many, many more Vietnamese soldiers and civilians who died in the war might still be alive today.

What does this mean for the U.S. military profession? Are professional soldiers culpable in some way for fighting in a war that the secretary of defense believed was unjust? Should those of us who were military leaders at the time have resigned our commissions—assuming that we, like the secretary of defense, believed the war to be an unjust one? Should we have undertaken some form of civil disobedience? What should we do in the future if similar instances arise?

Until recently, the answers to these questions seemed too obvious to warrant detailed discussion. Our long-standing tradition of civilian control of the military meant that soldiers go where and when they are told to go, provided that the telling is done by legally elected officials imbued with the power to make such decisions. This is the view to which military professionals have

*An earlier version of this chapter was first published in *Parameters* XXV, no. 3 (Autumn 1995): 4–8, and is included here with permission of the publisher.

traditionally given their adherence and their lives. Following the publication of the first edition of this text, where in chapter 6 I mention this view only in passing, a number of my colleagues have taken issue with this position. They suggest that although this position may be true from a legal perspective, it is not the case from a moral one. Some have argued that no person can ever abrogate his or her moral agency, and that just as military officers should refuse to obey immoral orders from their superiors when they are fighting *in war*, so they must do so when they are ordered *to war*.

Such arguments require us to rethink the notion of whether soldiers are morally obligated to fight in wars they believe are unjust. Having rethought the proposition thoroughly, I believe that our long-held position on this topic is dead right. The purpose of this chapter is to explain why this is so.

POLITICAL AND MILITARY RESPONSIBILITIES

In Shakespeare's dramatic account of the Battle of Agincourt, Henry V, on the evening before the battle, in an effort to assess the morale of his forces, disguises himself as a common soldier and visits some of his troops in the British encampment. When he encounters three infantrymen who wish that they were safely back in England (rather than France, where the battle occurs), the king, still in disguise, responds, "Methinks I could not die anywhere so contented as in the king's company, his cause being just and his quarrel honorable."

"That's more than we know," one of the infantryman replies. And a second soldier adds, "Ay, or more than we should seek after, for we know enough if we know we are the king's subjects. If his cause be wrong, our obedience to the king wipes the crime of it out of us."

Thus, does Shakespeare teach his seventeenth-century British audience about the Just War distinction between political and military responsibility regarding warfare.

The notion that soldiers are only praised or blamed for how they fight in a war—for military virtues such as courage, honor, and loyalty—rather than the justness of the war itself is not an idea that begins with Shakespeare. As we saw in chapter 1, civilized nations since antiquity have recognized a logical separation between *jus ad bellum* (the justice of wars) and *jus in bello* (justice in wars). According to the Just War Tradition, decisions regarding whether force should be used to achieve political objectives are always political decisions, while decisions concerning *how* that force is employed—the actual conduct of war—are the responsibility of the professional soldier. It is the former concept, that of *jus ad bellum,* or decisions concerning going to war, that are of primary concern to the question at hand, and although this will be our focus, we will mention a few things about both aspects to review why these concepts are distinct from one another.

CIVILIAN CONTROL OF THE MILITARY

Fundamental to the U.S. political system is the concept of civilian control of the military. Army Field Manual 100–5 identifies "Proper subordination to political authority" as one of the core values that makes up our army's identity. What does this mean? Does it mean that civilians such as the secretary of defense or the chairman of the Senate Armed Services Committee can tell the military how to train, how to fight, how to interrogate prisoners, how to treat civilian refugees in a war zone, or how much ammunition to carry? No! These are issues that only members of the military profession are competent to decide.

The reason we maintain an armed forces led by a highly trained, technically proficient, and well-compensated group of professionals is because as a nation we recognize that war fighting is an incredibly difficult, challenging skill that requires considerable specialized expertise. It would be ludicrous to permit persons from outside of the profession to make technical decisions regarding how force should be managed in training or on the battlefield. Deciding about the conduct of war falls under *jus in bello,* justice in war, and such decisions are the responsibility of military professionals.

Subordination of the military to political authority means that the responsibility and authority for going to war rests with the political leadership. Notice that this limits the military in a number of ways. On the one hand, the guardians of the state (the soldiers) cannot make decisions regarding either going to war or negotiating for peace without the authority of their political constituency. Such actions would be morally and legally wrong. Thus, Plato, for example, writing 2,500 years ago, notes that generals who either go to war or negotiate peace without the approval of the political establishment should be executed.

On the other hand, subordination to properly constituted civil authority means that military professionals cannot refuse to go when the political establishments order them to do so. Again, such actions are morally and legally wrong.

In many countries, the separation between political and military decision making is considered so important that soldiers are not even allowed to vote. In this country, military persons on active duty can vote because they are considered *citizen* soldiers—but they are prohibited by law from being politically active.

Recall from our discussion in chapter 6 that the restriction on political decision making concerning war provided the basis for President Harry Truman's relief of General Douglas MacArthur during the Korean War. General MacArthur had made public pronouncements concerning the war's political objectives. This same conceptual dichotomy concerning war caused difficulties for General Norman Schwartzkopf when he made ill-advised comments to the news media lamenting the U.S./U.N. decision not to invade Iraq. He later publicly retracted his statements.

During the same war, Air Force General Mike Dugan was not so lucky. When he made public statements about U.S. political objectives that he had established for his forces, he was relieved as the Air Force Chief of Staff and had to retire from military service.

To take this principle one step further, suppose that the president and Congress have decided that force is not called for, but many military leaders believe that it is warranted; surely we would not want military leaders to embark on offensive operations without political approval, even if such operations only included "minor actions" like mining foreign harbors.

Military leaders may privately make recommendations to the national leadership when they are asked for them, but they are prohibited from establishing or publicly influencing political objectives. Even the notion of resignation seems circumscribed where decisions on the use of force are at issue. A military officer's resignation when called to arms, especially that of a senior officer, would constitute a public statement about that officer's assessment of the political objectives. Just as officers should not fight when the president decides against the use of force, they should not refuse to fight when the president orders them to do so.

FORMALLY JUST WARS

A second consideration for understanding this issue is the legal stipulation that soldiers (qua soldiers) be immune from the crime of war. Soldiers are, as legal philosopher Vitoria tells us, considered imbued with invincible ignorance as far as the justice of a war is concerned. Thus soldiers who fight in an unjust war are protected from prosecution when the war is over. So when the International Tribunal at Nuremberg charged German leaders with crimes against peace, only a few very senior military leaders who were actively involved in political decision making regarding acts of aggression were prosecuted for this crime.

The fact is that we often never know objectively and with any degree of certainty which side in a war is just, even in retrospect. Just as in domestic society we agree to abide by a system of formal justice, recognizing that ideal or objective justice often is impossible to achieve, and so it should be regarding political decisions in international society. This system of accepting formal justice is well established and accepted in democratic countries, and the concept should apply similarly to professional soldiers and their approach to *jus ad bellum* issues. Perhaps an example will be helpful here.

Consider a highly publicized murder trial, for example. After the evidence is presented by both sides in accordance with accepted rules, a judge or jury will deliberate and reach a verdict of guilty or innocent. In many cases, we will never know for certain whether the accused committed the crime, but our society accepts the verdict of the jury as long as the proper formal procedures were followed because we believe that this method is the one most likely to give justice. We regard adherence to the formal process of justice to be so sacrosanct that when proper formal procedures are not followed, even in obvious cases of guilt, charges are dismissed and convictions are overturned.

Analogously, when the American people enter a national debate regarding the use of force, and Congress, following proper constitutional procedures, decides either to use force to achieve some political objective, or to refrain from doing so, that decision is formally just. It is as close to objective justice as we know how to get. Our elected leaders in this case are the judge and jury, and we in the armed forces agree to abide by the decision of the court.

Moreover, it is profoundly arrogant for officers to take the view, as some military officers do, that after the national debate takes place, and the president and Congress decide to act, then the officers should have the latitude to follow their own conscience, either assenting or declining to follow the order of the president. And, of course, if such an individual assessment were to be morally permissible for officers, then it must be morally permissible for soldiers of all ranks. Accepting this position inevitably leads to one of two unsatisfactory conclusions. One is that we permit soldiers to leave military service whenever they do not agree with a political decision. The other option is to acknowledge that requiring them to fight a war against their will is immoral, but to make such a political decision legally binding on them anyway. The first alternative would make a mockery of the very notion of having a standing army, and the second one would make a mockery of our legal system.

When the American people hire, train, equip, and support a professional officer corps, they expect them to be responsive to an elected authority regarding *when they should do the job for which they have been hired, trained, and equipped.*

MILITARY OFFICERSHIP: PROFESSION OR VOCATION?

Part of what it means to be a member of a profession is having a deep commitment to a set of abstract values and principles that define the profession. This means that members of a profession accept certain values that are specific to their profession as being more fundamental than other values. For example, the Hippocratic oath, written around the fifth century B.C., states, in part,

> I will apply medicinal measures for the benefit of the sick according to my ability and judgment: I will keep them from harm and injustice. I will not give a deadly drug to anybody if asked for it, nor will I make a suggestion to this effect.

Military officership also entails commitment to a set of principles. When one takes the oath of office in the profession of arms, he or she swears to *support and defend the Constitution of the United States against all enemies, foreign and domestic.* This constitutes an agreement to abide by political authority for all *jus ad bellum* decisions: that is, an agreement to fight in wars that are formally just, and also to fight them according to the Just War Tradition and warrior ethos that defines the professional military ethic. A refusal to go when called upon constitutes an abandonment of the oath of office, the profession of arms, and the soldiers who depend on their officers for competent leadership—it is a betrayal of the national trust.

Topics for Further Discussion

1. Under the leadership of Adolf Hitler, Germany's armed forces engaged in acts of aggression against neighboring states. Should German military officers have refused to participate in these actions? Were those who did participate guilty of a crime?

2. There is a long tradition in the United States that grants the status of **conscientious objector** to those who refuse military service based on a spiritual- or religious-based objection to violence. What would you tell a professional soldier who invoked conscientious objector status as a rationale for refusing to participate in a war that he or she believed unjust?

3. What would you say to a soldier who refused to deploy with his or her unit as part of a U.N. or NATO mission on the grounds that he or she had volunteered to fight on behalf of his or her own political community, but not on behalf of another political body? (Hint: See Article VI (2) of the U.S. Constitution.)

Chapter

15

THE ROLE OF THE UNITED NATIONS*

Using armed forces for peacekeeping and humanitarian missions presents new challenges for traditional Just War arguments. Neither peacekeeping nor humanitarian missions satisfies our previous definition of just cause—namely, in order for the just cause criterion to be met, there must be an injury received. In peacekeeping and humanitarian interventions, force is employed not by those injured, but by a third party on behalf of others who have received injury or are undergoing extreme hardship.

In this chapter we examine the legal and moral implications of humanitarian intervention. The question we explore is, When (if ever) should the United States—acting either unilaterally or in conjunction with the United Nations—forcibly intervene in the internal affairs of another sovereign nation–state for humanitarian reasons?

Our analysis proceeds in three parts. First we discuss the relationship between the moral and legal aspects of humanitarian intervention. We want to distinguish humanitarian intervention from other types of international "interference," such as peacekeeping. Historical and legal references will provide the background for the definition we develop in this initial section.

Next we examine the relevant moral principles that underlie customary practices and the formal legal framework, and we develop arguments for how conflicts in these principles might be resolved. We conclude with a discussion of a set of criteria that might assist political decision makers considering using military forces for humanitarian missions. Taking the tenets of Just War Tradition (*jus ad bellum*) as our model, we sketch a framework that nations may use for assessing scenarios where they are contemplating the use of force for humanitarian reasons.

*An earlier version of this chapter was first published in *Philosophy and Public Affairs* 10, no. 2 (April 1996): 103–19, and is included here with the permission of the publisher.

THE LEGALITY OF HUMANITARIAN INTERVENTION

There is a strong, long-standing presumption in the international community against states interfering in each other's internal affairs. Article 2(7) of the United Nations Charter specifically prohibits U.N. intervention in the domestic affairs of any state and guarantees that states will not be subjected to U.N. "settlements" concerning domestic issues. Article 2(4) requires that all members refrain from "the threat or use of force against the territorial integrity or political independence of any state."[1] And although Chapter VII (Art. 42) of the Charter does permit the Security Council to "take such action by air, sea, or land forces as may be necessary to maintain or restore international peace and security," members have normally considered domestic issues to fall outside of this provision. The only apparent just cause for the unilateral use of armed force is found in Article 51 of Chapter VII. "Nothing in the present Charter shall impair the inherent right of individual or collective self-defense if an armed attack occurs." Protection of nationals abroad (and sometimes protection of property interests) is generally considered to fall under this self-defense provision. Notice that such wording clearly prohibits the type of multilateral action against Iraq planned and conducted by the United States and Great Britain without security council approval in 2003, Iraq's refusal to fully comply with previous security council resolutions not withstanding.

As articulated in the U.N. Charter, then, the absolute nature of the prohibition against humanitarian intervention seems patent. Nations should never forcibly intervene in the internal domestic affairs of other nations in the international community. But there is more to the story than this.

International law is composed of both positive law, as codified in the U.N. Charter and various international treaties, as well as customary law based on historical precedents and accepted practices, as we have noted in earlier discussions. The author of the first modern text on international law, Hugo Grotius, in his classic, *The Law of Peace and War*, specifically lists humanitarian intervention as one of the just causes of war. He writes,

> The fact must also be recognized that kings, and those who possess rights equal to those of kings, have the right of demanding punishments not only on account of injuries committed against themselves or their subjects, but also on account of injuries which do not directly affect them but excessively violate the law of nature or of nations in regard to any persons whatsoever.[2]

And elsewhere,

> This is a matter of controversy, whether there may be a just cause for undertaking war on behalf of the subjects of another ruler, in order to protect them from wrong at his hands. ... If the wrong is obvious, in case some [cruel

leader] should inflict upon his subjects such treatment as no one is warranted in inflicting, the exercise of the right vested in human society is not precluded.[3]

Grotius mentions cannibalism, piracy, abuse of the elderly, rape, and castration of male subjects as examples of just causes for humanitarian intervention.[4] He concludes his discussion with "this word of warning, that wars that are undertaken to inflict punishment are under suspicion of being unjust, unless the crimes are very atrocious and very evident."

John Stuart Mill, in his classic defense of nonintervention, allows for limited exceptions to his exhortation that "one country is not justified in helping the people of another in a struggle against their own government for free institutions." He continues,

> When the contest is only with native rulers, the answer I should give to the question of the legitimacy of intervention is, as a general rule, No. . . . If a people does not value [freedom] sufficiently to fight for it, and maintain it against any force which can be mustered *within* the country, it is only a question in how few years or months that people will be enslaved. . . . When a people has had the misfortune to be ruled by a government under which the feelings and the virtues needful for maintaining freedom could not develop themselves, it is during an arduous struggle to become free by their own efforts that those feelings and virtues have the best chance of springing up. . . . It can seldom, therefore—I will not go so far as to say never—be either judicious or right, in a country which has a free government, to assist, otherwise than by the moral support of its opinions, the endeavors of another to exhort the same blessing from its native rulers.[5]

Oppenheim's classic, *International Law*, sums up the historical precedents in the following way:

> There is general agreement that, by virtue of its personal and territorial supremacy, a state can treat its own nationals according to discretion. But there is a substantial body of opinion and of practice in support of the view that there are limits to that discretion and that when a State renders itself guilty of cruelties and persecution of its nationals in such a way as to deny their fundamental human rights and to shock the conscience of mankind, intervention in the interest of humanity is legally permissible. Great Britain, France, and Russia intervened in 1827 in the struggle between revolutionary Greece and Turkey when public opinion reacted with horror to the cruelties committed during the struggle. . . . Undoubtedly the practice of intervention had not been as frequent as occasion seems to have demanded.[6]

Later, in the same work, the author attempts to reconcile the historical precedents with the more recent U.N. Charter by forbidding unilateral action but permitting intervention undertaken by the United Nations.[7]

The Just War Tradition also recognizes humanitarian intervention as a just cause for the use of force. In his highly influential *Just and Unjust Wars,* Michael Walzer argues that humanitarian intervention justifies the use of force when "the violation of human rights within a set of boundaries is so terrible that it makes talk of community or self-determination or 'arduous struggle' seem cynical and irrelevant."[8]

While both the historical legal documents and the Just War Tradition each provide a strong argument that the U.N. Charter's prohibition against intervention is not the last word on this topic, recent practices provide an even stronger one. Since the founding of the United Nations following World War II, there have been numerous cases of nations (acting unilaterally or regionally) deploying military units to foreign soil for "humanitarian" reasons. India's excursion into Pakistan, Zimbabwe's action in Uganda, Vietnam's involvement in Cambodia, and U.S. interventions in the Dominican Republic, Grenada, and Panama have all been justified, at least in part, under the rubric of humanitarian intervention. U.N. intervention in Somalia in 1993, sanctioned in part by the Security Council under Chapter VII (Art. 42) of the Charter, has been touted as an example of humanitarian intervention. Nations have cited the protection of refugees, the prevention of genocide, the protection of nationals abroad, the safeguarding of democracy, the stabilization of civil unrest, or other variations of human rights violations as their provocation for these humanitarian interventions.

We must take care to distinguish humanitarian intervention as it is traditionally understood in international law from other types of external intervention, such as peacekeeping, which falls under Chapter VI of the Charter.[9] Following recent precedents, our discussion of humanitarian intervention shall include only those cases when a nation or group of nations uses armed force to intervene in the internal affairs of another nation for humanitarian reasons. These reasons might include disaster relief, protection of refugees, prevention of genocide, curtailment of human rights violations, or other forms of human suffering, whether inflicted intentionally or by natural causes. The common factor in all cases of humanitarian intervention is that the intervening nation(s) *uses its armed forces in a coercive role* to cause some effect in the internal affairs of another nation and, after this humanitarian objective is achieved, the intervening force withdraws. It does not matter whether the intervening nation(s) actually engages in hostilities; simply that it uses armed force in a coercive role is sufficient. Humanitarian *aid,* supplied either by private or governmental organizations or peacekeeping forces sent at the request of the legitimate government do not qualify as humanitarian intervention because of the absence of coercive force. Neither does the protection of nationals abroad, which, as we noted previously, is more properly classified as an issue of self-defense.[10]

Finally, unlike humanitarian intervention, peacekeeping is not expressly forbidden under the U.N. Charter and rightfully should be considered in a separate category from humanitarian intervention, because it does not conflict with the principle of national sovereignty. A recent intervention that illustrates the important but fine distinction between peacekeeping and humanitarian intervention is the U.S. military incursion into Haiti in September 1994. Recall that following UN Security Council Resolution 940, which authorized the formation of a 6,000-person multinational force and the "use of all necessary means" to facilitate the departure of the military regime in Haiti, President Clinton ordered elements of the 82nd Airborne Division to prepare for an "assault" into the island. While U.S. troops were poised armed and ready for deployment on the airfield at Fort Bragg, North Carolina, awaiting President Clinton's order to depart, a delegation, which included former President Jimmy Carter, Senator Sam Nunn, and General Colin Powell, was in Haiti attempting to persuade Haitian leaders to sign an agreement "inviting" U.S. forces into their nation. This was crucial because such an agreement would ensure that any military action by the United States would fall under the rubric of peacekeeping rather than humanitarian intervention. Furthermore, given this background, it becomes obvious why numerous undocumented reports of atrocities, including the kidnapping and murdering of orphans, were widely circulated by U.S. propaganda elements. If no agreement was reached between U.S. and Haitian leaders inviting in U.S. forces, reports of extensive heinous humanitarian abuses would be used to constitute sufficient cause for humanitarian intervention.

Because there is no clearly stated policy or rule that addresses when, if ever, humanitarian intervention is permissible (or perhaps even morally obligatory), national debate in this country regarding the possible intervention in Haiti, as well as Somalia and the former Yugoslavia, focused primarily on self-interest and cost to the United States, with limited consideration given to questions of morality or justice. Not only is international law practically useless for the adjudication of such questions, the relevant moral principles and precedents are equally unclear. Even though there are numerous historical precedents where nations have justly and successfully intervened on foreign soil for humanitarian reasons, there are no clearly articulated guidelines for when it is appropriate to do so. And while President Clinton promised U.S. allies a Presidential Decision Directive specifying conditions for U.S. involvement in U.N. peacekeeping missions,[11] and the U.S. Army has recently written Field Manual 100–23, *Peace Operations*,[12] there are no plans for developing a similar set of guidelines for humanitarian interventions.

How are we to reconcile the gap between accepted practices and positive law as found in the U.N. Charter? One way might be to argue that humanitarian intervention is *always legally prohibited* but *sometimes morally permissible*. In discussing India's 1971 intervention into Pakistan to stop the brutal massacre of the Bengali people, Ellen Frey-Wouters argues,

> While the political and moral justification for the Indian intervention may have been compelling, in my opinion the intervention must be considered a

violation of existing international law dealing with the use of force. I admit that forceful unilateral intervention may have to be practiced in certain unique and extreme genocidal situations, but international law need not authorize or encourage it.[13]

But surely in those cases where we find our legal and moral rules at odds, we should endeavor to reconcile these differences, especially when we are able to identify potential conflicts in advance. According to Frey-Wouters' argument, we should accept the facade that humanitarian intervention is illegal—that is, absolutely forbidden by the U.N. Charter—but nevertheless we should condone it in cases where it is morally appropriate. Clearly the law in this case is not responsive to policy or in agreement with our moral sensibilities. If one accepts that the prohibition against intervention is *prima facie* rather than absolute, inherent in this recognition is an obligation at least to attempt to articulate the grounds for when the prohibition may justifiably be overridden. Ideally, of course, one would like the legal code to include any overriding criteria.

Perhaps we will not be able to agree on a set of conditions that trump the *prima facie* obligation not to intervene; but we can only know this after we have attempted to develop them. Frey-Wouters seems satisfied with acknowledging the incongruity between the moral and legal dimensions and simply throwing up her hands about it without any attempt at resolution. If we are ever going to have an effective system of obligations and constraints in the international community, there must be some congruence between formal laws and our accepted practices and moral intuitions.

Another way to reconcile the differences between the U.N. Charter and customary practices might be to define "crimes against humanity" as outside domestic jurisdiction.[14] The very expression "crimes against humanity" seems to suggest acts the condemnation of which transcends any national legal code. Under this interpretation, intervention could be justified under Chapter VII (Articles 39–41) of the U.N. Charter, which authorizes the Security Council to use a variety of measures—including armed force—to "maintain or restore international peace and security." Those who defend this view might argue that because one of the express purposes of the U.N. Charter is to "promote and encourage respect for human rights and for fundamental freedoms for all" (Art. 1,[3]), it would be hypocritical to permit member nations to invoke the Charter (Art. 2,[7]) as a basis for protecting themselves from outside interference while they violate the very rights the Charter is designed to protect.

Even if we accept either of these "explanations," a number of difficulties still remain. For example, if we accept both that a) humanitarian intervention is legally permissible, and b) nations sometimes have a moral obligation to intervene, then why hasn't the United Nations done so in past cases of genocide and widespread humanitarian abuse—such as the Khmer Rouge's brutal actions in Cambodia, to name just one? Moreover, if humanitarian intervention is sometimes justified, can it legitimately be done as a unilateral or regional undertaking, as has most often happened in practice, or must it always be part of a U.N.-sanctioned activity? And finally, how might the formal legal rules be modified to better reflect customary practice and our moral intuitions regarding humanitarian intervention?

Some might object that the flux and turmoil of international law (especially in the post–Cold War world) are such that any attempt to codify moral principles now might limit flexibility and obstruct the evolution of criteria for highly diverse scenarios. This appeal to future scenarios is not persuasive when one considers that there are always national or religious groups embroiled in crucial life-and-death scenarios in various locations around the globe. We must sort out the relevant moral principles now and develop policies based on these principles rather than continue to "fly by the seat of our pants" in such high stakes circumstances as those that we presently face.

Relevant Moral Principles

Before we can assess the merits of the arguments for and against humanitarian intervention, we must examine the moral reasoning behind certain key concepts. It is sophistry to invoke sovereignty as a rationale for prohibiting humanitarian intervention without examining the foundations of this key international "value." Nor is it persuasive to herald intervention for humanity's sake without critically examining the source of this alleged obligation to do good. Having examined these foundational issues, we will then be ready to discuss intelligently whether there are certain conditions that make humanitarian intervention permissible and, if so, what they might be.

The purpose that the principle of nonintervention is designed to accomplish in international society is to guarantee that political communities are free to determine their own internal affairs. We find the foundation for this principle in a domestic analogy. In civil society individuals (and families) are free to live as they choose, as long as they do not harm or otherwise interfere with the lives of others. When translated into the language of rights, these individual freedoms manifest themselves as the rights of life and liberty. In the society of nations, the individual rights of life and liberty are rendered as "territorial integrity and political independence," and this is the way they are expressed in the U.N. Charter.

For every right one enjoys, one also incurs a reciprocal duty. In the case of domestic society, citizens have the right to life and liberty and the duty not to interfere with the life and liberty of others. In international society, nations have the right to political independence and territorial integrity and the duty not to interfere with the territorial integrity or political independence of others, hence the principle that nations should not interfere in the internal affairs of other nations.

It is easy to reason in these terms because talk of rights is at the very core of our political system, and it is also central to the U.N. Charter. On reflection, however, we realize that the purpose of granting or acknowledging rights for political entities such as states is not for the "benefit" of the states themselves, but to protect the fundamental freedoms of the constituents of those states. Abstract entities like nations cannot be happy or sad, guilty or praiseworthy, evil or good. States cannot "enjoy" liberty. Emotions and dispositions are attributes of moral agents—of human beings. We recognize state's rights, not so that states may be protected from harm but to guarantee that the citizens of those states are left free to determine the political processes by which they will be governed. Protecting the liberty of constituents is what motivates the principle of nonintervention. Because the *raison d'être* for a nation's "absolute" sovereignty is to protect political independence and self-determination, the right of "absolute" sovereignty is conditional based on its fulfillment of this purpose.[15] When states adopt policies of genocide, slavery, or other heinous injustices, talk of self-determination or political sovereignty is ludicrous.

While this argument persuades us that humanitarian intervention is at least sometimes permissible, we have said nothing to establish whether it is obligatory. Let us return to the domestic analogy and see if this helps us.

Under civil government, it is not permissible for private citizens to punish criminals regardless of the nature of the crimes they commit; those who do so are themselves guilty of a crime. While it is clearly the right of each individual to protect herself and punish criminals in the absence of a government structure, in civil society this individual right has been "collected" from the citizens at large and consolidated in the office of the magistrate.[16] Where law enforcement or the punishment of transgressors is *permissible* by all in the absence of a common authority, it becomes *obligatory* once a common authority is established, which reserves the responsibility for law enforcement for itself.

The state, by taking away from individuals the right to punish lawbreakers, has assumed a duty to punish those who transgress. What had been permissible for individuals to do in the absence of a civil government, now becomes obligatory for the government to do. The situation is similar in international society. By "collecting up" the right to intervene for humanitarian reasons from its member nations, the United Nations has assumed an obligation to do so itself. When the United Nations fails to fulfill its duty in obvious cases— such as Pakistan, Cambodia, Uganda, and Bosnia–Serbia–Croatia—unilateral action becomes justified. When the formal system of law breaks down, the "old natural liberties" revert back to individuals.

Because there are persuasive moral grounds for humanitarian intervention, the United Nations cannot reasonably or effectively reserve the right to intervene for itself and then repeatedly fail to exercise it when the situation calls for it. Obvious failure to carry out one's duties to others negates any claim one might have had to a franchise on those duties. In cases where the result of U.N. inaction is obvious—genocide, for example—the right to intervene reverts to those who are willing to act on it.

One might question why, in the absence of common authority, humanitarian intervention is permissible rather than obligatory. This is because while there is a universal, enforceable, *prima facie* obligation not to do harm, there is no similar universal obligation to do good. (In chapter 10 we referred to the obligations as "Moral Truths," MT_1 and MT_2.) Individuals and governments may reasonably use force to ensure that members do not harm one another, but it is unreasonable to attempt to force one's fellows to do good.[17] Obligations to do good arise from special relationships, such as a parent to a child, a soldier to his nation, a ship captain to her passengers. In the absence of a formal agreement, no such enforceable obligations obtain between citizens of different nations.

Thus we must reject Oppenheim's contention (cited previously) that humanitarian intervention is permissible only as a collective action under the auspices of the United Nations. *Either it must be obligatory as a collective action or permissible as a unilateral (or regional) one.* By reserving for itself the franchise on humanitarian intervention, the United Nations has entered a special relationship with its member nations that obligates humanitarian intervention as a moral and legal duty.

Now we must determine what the conditions are that warrant overriding the principle of nonintervention for humanitarian reasons.

OBJECTIVE CRITERIA

Humanitarian intervention constitutes the use of armed force to achieve a political objective—namely, the cessation of gross moral injustices. Because the Just War Tradition provides a set of objective criteria for decision makers contemplating the use of force against another sovereign nation, it seems to be a good place to begin our search for some criteria to govern humanitarian intervention. We must keep in mind, however, that while we may crave objectivity, even the most objective criteria must be subjectively applied. Hence any decision in such matters will always be a matter of prudent judgment. One always endeavors to make decisions that are objectively just, but loyalties, emotions, and the exigencies of various situations often can be barriers to objectivity, even for a "neutral" party like the UN Security Council. Often the best one can do is to adhere to an accepted decision-making process, thereby ensuring that decisions are formally just. Let us examine certain key tenets of *jus ad bellum* and attempt to modify them as necessary to suit our topic.

There Must Be a Just Cause.   Grotius believes that humanitarian intervention is justified when a leader inflicts "upon his subjects such treatment as no one is warranted in inflicting." Oppenheim contends that a state forfeits its claim to nonintervention when it is "guilty of cruelties and persecution of its nationals in such a way as to deny their fundamental human rights and to shock the conscience of mankind." And as we noted previously, Michael Walzer argues that intervention is justified "when the violation of human rights within a set of boundaries is so terrible that it makes talk of community or self-determination or 'arduous struggle' seem cynical and irrelevant, that is, in cases of enslavement or massacre."

Let us agree that a state forfeits its right to nonintervention when its *leaders intentionally engage in practices that result in widespread, catastrophic human suffering.* These practices may be either overt actions aimed directly at causing the suffering, or simply a refusal to initiate action to curtail accidental or chance suffering when the means are available. Thus the requirement of intentionality can be met in principle by inaction as well as purposeful acts. Moreover, when a particular segment of the population or members of an identifiable social group are the primary victims of such suffering, one may assume that it is intentional.

To clarify what the term *just cause* encompasses, it is perhaps just as useful to identify certain cases that do not constitute just causes. As Grotius himself observes, one must take care that differences in political or religious values or customs are not interpreted as a cause for intervention, and that such pretexts often "serve to conceal greed for what is another's."[18] "Defense of democracy," for example, is not a just cause for humanitarian intervention. A democratically elected government can sanction slavery or perpetuate genocide just as efficiently as any other. Intervention to impose a political system on another people violates the principle of self-determination and is a form of subjugation. It is no different than intervention "for a people's own good" in order to ensure Buddhism, Paganism, Islam, or Christianity.

Nor does the maintenance or restoration of peace in a civil war constitute a just cause. Violence is one method of self-determination and, in many cases, it may be the only method available. The primary difference between an internal struggle (civil war) and genocide directed against one segment of the population is the purpose of the fighting, respective casualty rates notwithstanding.

The Political Objective Be Publicly Declared by Lawful Authority in Advance. The legitimate use of force must always be a public, political act. Covert and clandestine operations, when not part of a larger publicly declared policy, are always morally reprehensible. (They may also be morally reprehensible when they are part of a larger political goal, but are not necessarily so.) A public declaration of intent to intervene to end humanitarian abuses at once opens the issue to internal debate within one's own political community and sends notice to the government responsible for the abuses that it must cease immediately or be the object of forceful intervention. Furthermore, a public declaration entails a formal statement of the political objectives of the contemplated intervention. This is crucial because any military actions conducted in excess of the publicly stated objectives requires additional justification, as we noted in chapter 6.

For actions undertaken by the United Nations, the Security Council is the only recognized decision-making authority.[19] The question of who in the United States has the lawful authority to wage war remains unsettled.[20] The War Powers Act gives the president the authority to commit forces for up to sixty days to protect our national interests. This justification does not persuade when applied to humanitarian interventions, however. The president is charged with protecting the citizens of the nation he represents; he has no similar obligation to citizens of other nations. Humanitarian interventions should reflect the will of the populace and should only be undertaken by congressional mandate.

Humanitarian Intervention Must Be a Last Resort.   This condition is more difficult to apply than it initially seems. There are, after all, always additional measures one may undertake short of armed force. There are always more threats to make, more talks to hold, and more sanctions to apply (and for a longer time). Additionally, it often may be the case that imposition of measures short of force would only exacerbate difficulties for the abused population and increase their suffering. Embargoes and economic sanctions most certainly affect those at the bottom of the economic hierarchy first and worst. The condition of last resort serves to emphasize the gravity of the resort to force. There can be no set number of alternatives one must undertake in order for this condition to be met. The condition is met when reasonable nonviolent efforts have been unsuccessful and there is no indication that future attempts will fare any better. When the United Nations fails to act to curb the systematic murder of innocent people by the government of a member nation, the condition of last resort is met simultaneously with a public declaration by a member nation or regional organization of its intent to intervene.

The Costs Must Be Proportional to the Expected Objectives.   What might be an acceptable proportional relationship between the humanitarian goal one endeavors to achieve by intervening and the costs associated with achieving this goal? Keep in mind that it is the costs to innocents that are of concern here, not the costs to those who are guilty of perpetrating the injustices. Recall from our previous discussions that there are no limits to how many would-be murderers one may reasonably kill in self-defense, or in defense of an innocent. The issue of proportionality is really an issue of how many innocents one may put at risk in order to achieve a worthy political objective—in this case, ending humanitarian abuse. Therefore, the question is best understood from a self-interest perspective rather than an ethical one. Decision makers in nations considering intervention must ask themselves how many of their own citizens (i.e., soldiers) they are willing to put at risk in order to protect the citizens of another nation. Barring some special relationship—such as that of an army to its nation's citizens—there is no moral duty for one to risk his or her life to save another; such actions are normally regarded as supererogatory.[21] There will be cases where nations are not willing to risk the lives of their own citizens in order to end certain humanitarian abuses, *even though humanitarian intervention is justified*. Likewise, there will continue to be cases where nations are only willing to intervene because of certain political benefits that they might expect. Such prudential considerations do not in any way affect the moral permissibility of intervention. Perhaps an example will be helpful here.

In 1971, the prime minister of India, Indira Gandhi, ordered her nation's forces into East Pakistan to protect the Bengali people, who were being systematically slaughtered by the Pakistan military. There is no doubt that India, as well as Mrs. Gandhi, personally, reaped considerable benefits from this action. Pakistan's support of guerrilla activity ceased, enormous refugee problems ended, the growing popularity of the Communist Party in India was curbed, and Mrs. Gandhi was hailed as a hero worldwide. While any or all of these consequences may have influenced Mrs. Gandhi's decision to intervene, they have no bearing whatsoever on the issue of whether the intervention was morally permissible. Actions that are objectively just do not become unjust based on the motive of the agent who performs them. Motives have to do with the moral character of agents, not the normative status of particular acts. While political considerations may play a crucial role in national policy decisions, they are only incidental to the moral issue at stake. India's speedy withdrawal after her humanitarian objectives were achieved is *prima facie* evidence that the humanitarian objectives were not a ruse for the subjugation of Pakistan.

From the perspective of the United Nations, however, its failure to take any action whatsoever in response to Pakistani atrocities underscores its impotence as an international arbiter of justice.

These criteria—just cause, proportionality, last resort, and public declaration by lawful authority—seem to me to constitute a set of necessary conditions which, taken together, are jointly sufficient for determining the permissibility of humanitarian intervention. Thus, while the expression "just cause" seems to imply a sufficient justification, it is simply a necessary one.

CONCLUSION

Although the paralysis that inflicted the United Nations for the past four decades is cured, it seems to have been replaced by neurosis. It is likely that there will continue to be numerous opportunities in the immediate future for the United Nations to fill the role for which it was designed: promoting human rights and fostering world peace. The issue of humanitarian intervention is a new one for the United Nations, but it is in keeping with the fundamental purpose for which the organization was formed. Without clear guidelines for harmonizing this policy with the long-standing principle of nonintervention in domestic affairs, however, it is likely the United Nations and the United States will continue to struggle with balancing the moral, legal, and prudential elements of political decisions. In our chaotic world community, it is crucial that we debate, refine, and publish formal criteria that will provide the margins for acceptable behaviors in international society, and then act on them. As a minimum, we should identify those moral principles operative in the society of nations and subject their relationship to one another to national public debate in advance of new conflicts. Only in this way will we, as a nation, be prepared to make informed moral choices concerning our role in the world community.

Topics for Further Discussion

1. Following the collapse of the Soviet Union, national and religious animosities that had been held in check by a strong central communist government in Yugoslavia erupted into violence. Beginning in May 1992, following Bosnian independence, Bosnian Serbs (Christians) initiated policies aimed at ridding certain regions of their Muslim population. Political actions included sieges of cities; blockade of food, fuel, and medical supplies; destruction of water supplies; systematic rape of Muslim women; and random artillery, armor, and sniper attacks against innocent civilians. In response to Serbian violence, the UN Security Council discussed sending 10,000 peacekeeping troops. None were sent, but the Security Council passed a resolution imposing a no-fly zone over Bosnia, and the United States and NATO repeatedly threatened to conduct air attacks against Serbian artillery positions if the shelling of cities continued. Nevertheless, the situation worsened, and even humanitarian relief efforts were routinely blocked in order to inflict further suffering on isolated Muslim populations and to speed the dirty business of ethnic cleansing.

   a. Would the use of military forces in this case be permissible or obligatory, either as a peacekeeping or humanitarian intervention mission?
   b. Why should the United States, United Nations, or NATO have done more (or less) in response to the violence in the former Yugoslavia?
   c. Some of the leaders who ordered criminal acts against innocents were charged by a World Court convened specifically to address this case, but capturing them proved difficult. Would the use of military force in order to capture these suspected criminals be justified? If so, how could such force be justified under the Just War Tradition?

2. In April 1992, in response to catastrophic suffering in Somalia—more than 300,000 people dead from starvation, including nearly 100 percent of those under ten years of age—UN Security Council Resolution 751 committed fifty observers to monitor relief efforts there. Four months later, UN Security Council Resolution 775 authorized 3,500 soldiers to assist in the relief effort. Both of these peacekeeping missions were conducted under Chapter VI of the U.N. Charter. Several months later, the UN Security Council approved Resolution 794, which changed the Somali mission from one of peacekeeping under Chapter VI to peace*making* under Chapter VII, and authorized U.N. forces to use all necessary force to accomplish their mission. Soldiers were needed because warring factions and the lack of an effective central government were thwarting international relief efforts. The United States subsequently increased its presence in Somalia to approximately 25,000 soldiers in a U.S.-led relief effort aimed at feeding millions of starving Somalis temporarily until the United Nations could rally support from other nations and assume command and control responsibility itself. Other nations quickly began contributing forces to the U.N. mission, and by June 1993, U.S. soldiers had been augmented with a multinational force representing thirty-two nations under U.N. control.

    Sometime during this buildup period, U.S. military forces adopted a policy of searching and disarming Somali citizens in the capital city of Mogadishu in order to achieve "long-term stability." Enforcement of this policy led to a rapid deterioration of the relationship between U.N. soldiers and Somali citizens, and on June 5, members of a Somali political faction headed by Mohammed Aidid attacked and killed twenty-four Pakistani soldiers who were part of the U.N. force. In response to a U.N. resolution calling for the arrest of those responsible, the United States sent 400 highly trained Rangers to Somalia to search for and capture Mr. Aidid. On October 3, while conducting offensive operations aimed at capturing Mr. Aidid, the Ranger unit fought a battle that resulted in 18 U.S. soldiers killed, 77 wounded, and more than 1,000 Somali casualties, many of them innocents. Initially, the United States responded by sending 100 armored vehicles, four attack helicopters, and 1,700 more troops to Somalia. Shortly afterwards, however, the United States distanced itself from the U.N. operation and began advocating a political settlement.

    a. Was there a just cause for humanitarian intervention in Somalia prior to the U.S. deployment?
    b. Did the United States meet the requirement that its military intervention be "publicly declared"? Do UN Security Council Resolutions authorizing intervention affect this Just War requirement?

c. Should the Somalis who attacked the Pakistani forces on June 5 be considered terrorists or soldiers, assuming they carried their arms openly and wore distinctive insignia? How about the Somalis who successfully defended Mr. Aidid against capture by the U.S. Rangers on October 3?

d. Assuming that humanitarian intervention was justified, did U.S./U.N. forces exceed the margins of their mission when they began disarming Somali citizens, or was this a reasonable step in the relief effort?

e. In terms of the legitimate use of military force (i.e., minimum rules of engagement), what are the differences between peacekeeping, peacemaking, and humanitarian interventions?

3. Following the 1991 Gulf War between the United Nations and Iraq, the Iraqi government refused to allow U.N. inspectors into various facilities suspected of containing chemical or biological weapons and long-range delivery systems capable of employing such weapons. After several years of unsuccessfully attempting to conduct the U.N.-mandated inspections, the United States declared that if the U.N. teams were not allowed to complete their inspections, that the U.S. would use military force to coerce Iraq into compliance.

a. Was military force in this case justified under the Just War Tradition?

b. Was the unilateral use of force by the U.S. justified?

c. If other nations in the region were permitted to stock weapons of mass destruction, why should the Iraqi people not be afforded the same means of self-defense? Would your answer be different if the government that initiated the Gulf War (i.e., Saddam Hussein) were overthrown?

d. In early March 2003, President Bush stated publicly that he would force members of the UN Security Council to "show their cards" by forcing a vote on whether to use military force to disarm Iraq and force compliance with earlier U.N. resolutions. A vote against the use of force would, as senior U.S. officials put it, "make the UN irrelevant." Later (March 14), the U.S. administration changed its position and the secretary of state (Colin Powell) stated publicly that the United States would not require a vote, and that a vote was not needed to justify the use of force. Why was it politically important not to have a vote, given that it would almost certainly oppose U.S. military action?

4. Grotius states that justifications for humanitarian intervention into a sovereign state by another include abuse of the elderly, rape, and castration of males. As I write this, the "castration" of females, female genital mutilation (FGM) has been carried out on approximately 135 million women worldwide and is widely practiced in dozens of countries. World health organizations estimate that about two million women a year are at risk for this extremely painful, harmful, and unnecessary procedure. Why (or why not) would the use of military force to stop the physical mutilation of women (FGM) in a neighboring country be justified?

Notes

1. There also are two General Assembly Resolutions that reinforce the prohibition against interference: The 1960 Declaration on the Granting of Independence to Colonial Countries and Peoples and the 1965 Declaration on the Inadmissibility of Intervention (GAR 2131).

2. Hugo Grotius, *The Law of War and Peace*, translated by Francis W. Kelsey (Indianapolis, IN, and New York: Bobbs-Merrill Company, Inc., 1962), Bk. II, Chap. XX, Sect. XL, Para. 1, p. 504.

3. Ibid., Bk. II, Chap. XXV, Sect. VIII, Para. 2, p. 584.

4. Ibid. The discussion of rape as a cause for intervention is found in Bk. III, Chap. IV, Sect. XIX, Para. 1, pp. 656–57; the other causes mentioned are found in Bk. II, Chap. XX, Sect. XL, Para. 3, pp. 505–06.

5. John Stuart Mill, "A Few Words on Non-Intervention," in *Dissertations and Discussions: Political, Philosophical, and Historical*, vol. III (New York: Henry Holt and Company, 1873), pp. 259–60.

6. Lassa F. Oppenheim, *International Law: A Treatise*, 8th ed., edited by H. Lauterpacht (New York: David McKay Co., Inc., 1955), pp. 312–13.

7. Oppenheim writes, "The Charter of the United Nations, in recognizing the promotion of respect for fundamental human rights and freedoms as one of the principal objects of the Organization, marks a further step in the direction of elevating the principle of humanitarian intervention to a basic rule of organized international society. . . . As a matter both of history and of principle the prohibition of intervention must be regarded primarily as a restriction which International Law imposes upon States for the protection of the independence of other members of the international community. For this reason the notion and the prohibition of intervention cannot accurately extend to collective action undertaken in the general interest of States or for the collective enforcement of International Law." Ibid. pp. 313, 319. Interestingly, Oppenheim's later discussion of the humanitarian intervention runs contrary to the very historical precedents he cites. He attempts to circumvent the difficulty by permitting some "non-dictatorial" forms of collective "intervention" by the United Nations. Thus he seems to rule out both unilateral action and the use of force as a means of intervention. See ibid., p. 320.

8. Michael Walzer, *Just and Unjust Wars: A Moral Argument with Historical Illustrations*, 2d ed. (New York: Basic Books, 1992), p. 90. Walzer's views are derived from John Stuart Mill, "A Few Words on Non-Intervention," in *Dissertations and Discussions*, vol. III (New York: Henry Holt and Company, 1873) pp. 238–63.

9. Since 1956, when the General Assembly passed a resolution authorizing the secretary general to send forces to keep the peace between Israel and Egypt under Chapter VI of the U.N. Charter, peacekeeping missions have been accepted as an exception to the prohibition against interference. As I write this, "blue hats" are stationed in more than ten nations around the globe as a means of preserving peace, and it appears likely that the number of nations requesting U.N. assistance will continue to increase. Thus both peacekeeping and humanitarian missions aim at securing the well-being of a third party. But while recent (since the founding of the United Nations) humanitarian interventions seem to have evolved from peacekeeping missions ("mission creep," as some commentators put it), they differ in significant ways. Peacekeeping, for example, is always conducted with the consent of the major legitimate political factions involved and is authorized by the UN Security Council; humanitarian interventions are most often conducted unilaterally and, except in the case of the relief effort in Somalia, are not sanctioned by the United Nations. And while peacekeeping missions do not conflict with the U.N. Charter

or other international treaties, moral and legal questions concerning humanitarian interventions are less clear.

10. The United States incorrectly invoked humanitarian intervention for the purpose of protecting nationals abroad when it sent forces to the Dominican Republic in 1965 and Grenada in 1983. U.S. law (War Powers Act or Javits–Stennis Bill) authorizes the president to intervene in order to protect the lives of U.S. citizens, but these are more properly considered cases of self-defense.

11. Paul Lewis, "U.S. Plans Policy on Peacekeeping," *New York Times*, November 18, 1993, p. A7.

12. Sean D. Naylor, "No Peace in Peacekeeping," *Army Times*, October 11, 1993, pp. 14–15.

13. *Humanitarian Intervention and the United Nations*, edited by Richard B. Lillich (Charlottesville, VA: University Press of Virginia, 1973), p. 107. Thomas M. Franck and Nigel S. Rodley defend a similar view in "After Bangladesh: The Law of Humanitarian Intervention by Military Force," *American Journal of International Law* 304 (1973).

14. Concerning India's actions in Bangladesh and in response to Ellen Frey-Wouters comments earlier, Frank Newman argues, "I don't think it is an Article 2(7) situation; it seems to me that we have plenty of precedents to establish that crimes against humanity are not essentially within the domestic jurisdiction." Ibid., p. 111.

15. It is not that unusual for instrumental policies aimed at some primary objective to assume a value of their own, even to the extent that they can actually impede the attainment of the objective they were designed to achieve. In international society, the principle of non-intervention has become sacrosanct, even to the point of disregarding the reasons that underlie its formulation in the first place. Another example that comes to mind is the practice of assigning grades in academia. While this practice undoubtedly began as an expedient for measuring and motivating the quest for knowledge, many students now view the education process as a quest for the grades themselves, even to the extent that they cheat in order to "do well." Thus the practice of awarding grades can have the opposite effect of the very purpose it was instituted to achieve. Another example might be the relationship between winning and "playing well" in sports.

16. Grotius writes, "As soon as numerous families were united at a common point judges were appointed, and to them alone was given the power to avenge the injured, while others are deprived of the freedom of action wherewith nature endowed them." *The Law of War and Peace*, Bk. II, Chap. 20, VII, p. 473. John Locke makes the same point a century later. "The inconveniences [caused] by the irregular and uncertain exercise of the power every man has of punishing the transgressions of others make them . . . willing to give up everyone his single power of punishing, to be exercised by such alone as shall be appointed to it amongst them. . . . And in this we have the original weight of both the legislative and executive power, as well as of the governments and societies themselves." *Two Treatises of Government* (New York: New American Library, 1963), Bk. II, Sect. 127, p. 397. See the discussion of this topic in chapter 5.

17. In Kantian terms, all have a perfect duty not to do harm and an imperfect duty to do good. Perfect duties do not depend on one's inclinations, while imperfect duties do. Mill's "harm principle" results in a consequentially equivalent prescription. "The only purpose for which power can be rightfully exercised over any member of a civilized community, against his will, is to prevent harm to others." See Immanuel Kant, *Groundwork of the Metaphysic of Morals*, translated by H. J. Patton (New York: Harper Torchbooks, 1964), p. 89 (53, n. 53); John Stuart Mill, *On Liberty* (Indianapolis, IN: Bobbs-Merrill Company, 1956), p. 13.

18. Ibid., Bk. II, Chap. XX, Sect. XLI and Sect. XLIII, Para. 3, pp. 507–08.

19. The U.N. organization is outdated and desperately in need of reform. The permanent members of the Security Council (United States, Russia, China, France, and England) are

a vestige of World War II, with the result that France and England have authority that far exceeds their economic and military influence. Reform is blocked, however, because all decisions can be vetoed by any member of the Security Council, and France and England would not approve of any reforms that reduced their political influence.

20.   Certainly the War Powers Act authorizes the president to use military force for a period of up to sixty days in order to give Congress time to debate the issue. And as we noted in an earlier discussion in chapter 6, while President Bush claimed that he did not need congressional approval to commit forces to the U.N.–Iraq War in 1991, many did not agree. Although the Senate voted 51 to 48 to support the president's policy, suppose the vote had been slightly different—suppose the Senate had voted *against* U.S. support for Kuwait? When President Clinton faced a similar situation regarding the deployment of U.S. forces to Haiti, he insisted that the mission begin on a Friday because Congress was scheduled to debate it on Monday of the following week, and he wanted to avoid confronting this issue head on.

21.   Soldiers, of course, are under the special obligation to put their lives at risk to protect innocents whenever the political community they represent directs them to do it.

GLOSSARY

a priori   A proposition that is known or justified by reason alone, independent of (or prior to) sensory experience.

act utilitarianism   A theory that claims that the moral worth of an action is determined by the good and bad consequences (i.e., utility) it produces. Under this account, an act is morally right if and only if it produces more utility than any alternative act the agent could have done instead.

bellum justum   This expression, "Just War," encompasses both *jus ad bellum* and *jus in bello*.

benevolent severity   Punishing someone or inflicting pain upon people for their own good and out of love for them.

caritas   The love of God, or selfless love.

civitas Dei   The City of God. According to Augustine, the City of God is composed of God, the Angels, and those individuals who have been granted efficacious grace.

civitas terrena   The City of Earth. All of mankind except those few who have been granted efficacious grace—a society of the reprobate.

concupiscence   Desires of the flesh.

conscientious objector   A legal category for those who are excluded from military service because they object to the use of violence based on either religious or spiritual reasons. Those who object to violence for political reasons are not considered conscientious objectors. (Some conscientious objectors elect to perform military service in noncombatant roles.)

cupiditas   Love of self. Even those benevolent actions that are motivated by expectation of reward, either earthly reward or reward in the hereafter, are a form of *cupiditas*.

de facto **laws**   Those rules operative among members of a group that are independent of formal declarations or juridical sanctions.

de jure **laws**   Rules that are declared by a lawfully constituted authority and backed up by sanctions.

deontological   From *deon*, meaning moral duty, and *logos*, meaning account or explanation of. Any one of a number of theories that claim that the moral

261

worth of actions is determined by rules or principles rather than the consequences of the actions.

double effect   The Christian doctrine (first formulated by Thomas Aquinas as a justification for self-defense) that states it is permissible to perform an act that has both good and bad consequences, provided that the bad consequences are unintended, unavoidable, and proportional to the good consequences.

efficacious grace   Sufficient grace for salvation. If all human beings bear the blight of Original Sin, as Augustine argues, then only those who are granted efficacious grace by God are saved.

eschatological promise   The promise by Christ that he would return to earth on the Day of Judgment and lead the forces of good against the forces of evil in the Battle of Armageddon.

external point of view   This is the expression that H. L. A. Hart uses to describe the perspective of those who are motivated to obey their society's laws or rules because of a fear of sanctions.

first fratricide   Cain's murder of his brother Abel. This symbolizes the disposition human beings have to act violently toward their fellows.

formally just   Formal procedures are often adopted as a means of improving objectivity in decision processes. Wars are *formally* just when they conform to a set of established criteria, the *jus ad bellum* conditions, for example. Some might argue that an act could be "formally just" but still morally wrong (i.e., unjust) because of other relevant factors not included as criteria in the formal determination.

Four Cardinal Virtues   In the Ancient Greek and Roman traditions, the supreme virtues are knowledge, justice, temperance, and courage. In the Christian canon, knowledge is often referred to as prudence and courage as fortitude.

internal point of view   The perception that certain rules or laws should be obeyed for no other reason except that "they are *my* laws." H. L. A. Hart contrasts this with the "external point of view" taken by those who obey laws only because of the fear of sanctions.

invincible ignorance   This describes a condition when it is not possible to ascertain the truth or falsity of one's beliefs. Francisco de Vitoria argues that soldiers are always possessed of "invincible ignorance" concerning whether the cause they are fighting for is just. Hence, soldiers are not responsible for the justice of the war (*jus ad bellum*) in which they fight.

jihad   A holy war undertaken as a sacred duty, especially in the Islamic tradition.

jus ad bellum   The justice of war. This is the traditional phrase used to refer to the justifications for resorting to force as a means of achieving political objectives. The classical *jus ad bellum* criteria are: (a) there must be a just cause; (b) war must be a last resort; (c) the political objectives must be proportional to the costs of fighting; (d) war must be declared by a lawful authority; (e) war must be publicly declared; (f) there must be a reasonable chance of success; (g) the war must be prosecuted for rightful intentions; and (h) the war must be fought justly. In chapter 6, I argue (agreeing with Grotius) that the last of these two are not necessary.

jus in bello Justice in war. This is the traditional expression for considerations on how a war is prosecuted. The two classical *jus in bello* concerns are: Who can lawfully be attacked, and what means can be used to do it? These are usually understood as prohibitions against employing weapons or methods that inflict unnecessary suffering, or intentionally attacking noncombatants or prisoners. I argue that *jus in bello* is primarily a military responsibility.

military necessity Under international law, "military necessity" constitutes a sufficient reason for performing actions "indispensable" to subduing the enemy as quickly as possible, but which would otherwise be prohibited. This effectively prohibits violence not done for military purposes, but permits almost anything done for military objectives. The expression is necessarily vague.

military realism The view that moral factors are not relevant to the conduct of war. Those who defend this position argue that the resort to force constitutes a rejection of the rule of law, and that therefore it is ridiculous to attempt to pass laws to govern an activity that represents lawlessness. If military realism is true, then following *jus in bello* rules is foolery.

natural law Those obligations or principles binding on all persons that are accessible through reasoned examination of human nature and relationships.

necessary and sufficient conditions The conditions where the only way to bring about R is for C and D to occur, and that if C and D both occur, R will inevitably follow. For example, the necessary and sufficient conditions for combustion are fuel, kindling temperature, and oxygen. Each is necessary, because without any one of them there cannot be combustion; they are jointly sufficient because when they are all present combustion is inevitable.

normative This implies an obligation; it refers to that which "should" be done, or "ought" to be done.

objectively just Justice as determined by an "ideal observer," or someone who has no personal stake in the matter.

ontological status From the Greek *onta*, "the really existing things," and *logos*, "the study of." The expression is used to describe those things that exist as categories.

Original Sin The sins of Adam and Eve in the Garden of Eden. St. Augustine argues that all human suffering is divine retribution for Original Sin.

pacifism Opposition to war or violence as a legitimate means of settling disputes. Pacifism as a moral doctrine should not be confused with instances of individual opposition to violence in particular cases or under certain conditions. In the context of the discussions in this text, pacifism is the view that the use of violence is never justified as a means of obtaining political objectives.

political realism This is the view that moral considerations are not relevant to sovereign states acting in the international society of nations. Thomas Hobbes defends this view in the *Leviathan* when he argues that states are always in a "state of nature" because there is no social contract or common authority to enforce standards of right and wrong and punish transgressors. If political realism is true, then *jus ad bellum* is a chimera.

positivism   Logical positivism is the view that statements only have meaning if they are empirically verifiable. Legal positivism is the view that laws should serve as functions that link specific types of behaviors to punishments.

prima facie **duty**   "Prima facie" means, literally, "at first look." A prima facie duty is one that obligates, unless there are other duties or factors that override or invalidate it.

promulgate   To make known by decree or to announce formally.

reductio ad absurdum   A form of argument where one proves that a claim is false by showing that if it were true it would lead to an absurdity.

reprisal   An act of violence that normally would be illegal, but that is permitted under international law when it is carried out against a target group in response to illegal acts committed by members of that target group. I distinguish between reprisals conducted in wartime as a response to *jus in bello* violations, and reprisals conducted in lieu of war. In either case, reprisals are supposed to be used as a means of forcing the other side back into compliance with the law, rather than as a means of revenge.

rule utilitarianism   The theory that acts are right if and only if they are in accordance with rules that, if followed universally, would produce better consequences (i.e., utility) than any alternative rules.

sufficient justification   A condition that permits certain actions but does not require them. For example, even if one has sufficient justification for the resort to force, it is not necessary that one act on it. See also *necessary and sufficient conditions*.

supererogatory   Morally praiseworthy acts that are considered by some to be "over and above the call of duty." Some consider jumping on a hand grenade to protect one's comrades from the shrapnel an example of a supererogatory act. According to utilitarianism, such acts are simply obligatory.

teleological   From the Greek *telos*, meaning "end," and *logos*, meaning "account or explanation of." Any moral theory that claims that the moral worth of actions is determined by their consequences.

volitional laws   Rules, norms, and/or conventions particular to social roles or individual groups. Grotius identifies three types of volitional laws: domestic (concerning family relationships), municipal (concerning relationships in civil society), and international (concerning conduct in the international society of nations).

SELECTED BIBLIOGRAPHY

ALRUTZ, KENNETH E., ET AL., EDS. *War and Peace.* Lynchburg College Symposium Readings, Series One, Vol. V. Washington, D.C.: University Press of America, 1982.

AMBROSE, SAINT. *Nicene and Post-Nicene Fathers*, Vol. X. Edited by Philip Schaff. Grand Rapids, Mich.: Eerdmans Publishing Co., 1969.

AQUINAS, ST. THOMAS. *The Political Ideas of St. Thomas Aquinas.* Edited by Dino Bigongiari. New York: Hafner Publishing Co., 1957.

———. *Selected Political Writings.* Edited by A. P. D'Entreves. Oxford, England: Basil Blackwell, 1959.

———. *Summa Theologica.* Translated by Fathers of the English Dominican Province. London: R. & T. Washbourne, 1917.

ARISTOTLE. *The Complete Works of Aristotle*, Vol. 2. Edited by Jonathan Barnes. Princeton, N.J.: Princeton University Press, 1984.

AUGUSTINE, SAINT. *A Select Library of the Nicene and Post–Nicene Fathers*, Vols. I–VIII. Edited by Philip Schaff. Grand Rapids, Mich.: Eerdmans Publishing Co., 1969.

———. *The Problem of Free Choice.* Translated by Dom Mark Pontifex. Westminster, Md.: The Newman Press, 1955.

———. *The Political Writings of St. Augustine.* Edited and with an introduction by Henry Paolucci. Chicago: Regnery Gateway, 1962.

AXINN, SIDNEY. *A Moral Military.* Philadelphia: Temple University Press, 1989.

BAIRD, ROBERT M., AND STUART E. ROSENBAUM, EDS. *Morality and the Law.* New York: Prometheus Books, 1988.

BALLIS, WILLIAM. *The Legal Position of War: Changes in Its Practice and Theory from Plato to Vattel.* New York: Garland Publishing, 1973.

BARNES, JOHN. *Morale: A Study of Men and Courage.* Garden City, N.Y.: Avery Publishing Group, 1988.

BEST, GEOFFREY. *Humanity in Warfare.* New York: Columbia University Press, 1980.

CADY, DUANE L. *From Warism to Pacifism: A Moral Continuum.* Philadelphia: Temple University Press, 1989.

CICERO, MARCUS TULLIUS. *De Officiis*. With an English translation by Walter Miller. Cambridge, Mass.: Harvard University Press, 1961.

———. *De Re Publica and De Legibus*. With an English translation by Clinton Walker Keyes. New York: G. P. Putnam's Sons, 1928.

———. *Cicero: Letters to Atticus*, Vol. II. Translated by E. O. Winstedt. New York: Macmillan, 1912.

CLAUSEWITZ, CARL VON. *On War*. Edited and translated by Michael Howard and Peter Paret. Princeton, N.J.: Princeton University Press, 1976.

COHEN, MARSHALL, THOMAS NAGEL, AND THOMAS SCANLON, EDS. *War and Moral Responsibility*. Princeton, N.J.: Princeton University Press, 1974.

COHEN, SHELDON M. *Arms and Judgment: Law, Morality, and the Conduct of War in the Twentieth Century*. Boulder, Colo.: Westview Press, 1989.

DEANE, HERBERT A. *The Political and Social Ideas of St. Augustine*. New York: Columbia University Press, 1963.

DWORKIN, RONALD. *Law's Empire*. Cambridge, Mass.: Harvard University Press, 1986.

DYER, GWYNNE. *War*. New York: Crown Publishers, 1985.

EPPSTEIN, JOHN. *The Catholic Tradition of the Law of Nations*. Washington, D.C.: Catholic Association for International Peace, 1935.

FALK, RICHARD A. *Law, Morality and War in the Contemporary World*. New York: Praeger, 1963.

———, GABRIEL KOLKO, AND ROBERT JAY LIFTON, EDS. *Crimes of War*. New York: Vintage Books, 1971.

———, FRIEDRICH KRATOCHWIL, AND SAUL H. MENDLOVITZ, EDS. *International Law: A Contemporary Perspective*. Boulder, Colo.: Westview Press, 1985.

FOSTER, MARY LECRON, AND ROBERT A. RUBINSTEIN, EDS. *Peace and War*. New Brunswick, N.J.: Transaction, 1986.

FOTION, NICHOLAS, AND GERALD ELFSTROM. *Military Ethics: Guidelines for Peace and War*. Boston: Routledge & Kegan Paul, 1986.

FRIEDMAN, LEON, ED. *The Law of War: A Documentary History*, Vols. I & II. New York: Random House, 1972.

GOLDSTEIN, JOSEPH, BURKE MARSHALL, AND JACK SCHWARTZ, EDS. *The My Lai Massacre and Its Cover-Up*. New York: The Free Press, 1976.

GOODRICH, LELAND M., AND EDWARD HAMBRO. *Charter of the United Nations: Commentary and Documents*. Boston: World Peace Foundation, 1949.

GOODWIN, GEOFFREY, ED. *Ethics and Nuclear Deterrence*. New York: St. Martin's Press, 1982.

GRAY, J. GLENN. *The Warriors: Reflections on Men in Battle*. New York: Harper & Row, 1970.

GREEN, L. C., ED. *Essays on the Modern Laws of War*. New York: Transnational Publishers, 1985.

GROTIUS, HUGO. *The Law of War and Peace*. Translated by Francis W. Kelsey. Indianapolis and New York: Bobbs-Merrill, 1962.

HACKETT, GENERAL SIR JOHN. *The Profession of Arms*. New York: Macmillan, 1983.

HARE, J. E., AND CAREY B. JOYNT. *Ethics and International Affairs*. New York: St. Martin's Press, 1982.

HART, H. L. A. *The Concept of Law*. Oxford, England: Clarendon Press, 1961.

————. *Law, Liberty, and Morality.* Stanford, Calif.: Stanford University Press, 1963.

HARTIGAN, RICHARD SHELLY. *The Forgotten Victim: A History of the Civilian.* Chicago: Precedent Publishing, 1982.

————. *Lieber's Code and the Law of War.* Chicago: Precedent Publishing, 1983.

HARTLE, ANTHONY E. *Moral Issues in Military Decision Making.* Lawrence, Kans.: University of Kansas Press, 1989.

HOLMES, RICHARD. *Acts of War: The Behavior of Men in Battle.* New York: The Free Press, 1986.

HOLMES, ROBERT PAUL. *On War and Morality.* Princeton, N.J.: Princeton University Press, 1989.

HUNTINGTON, SAMUEL P. *The Soldier and the State.* Cambridge, Mass.: The Belknap Press of Harvard University, 1957.

JOHNSON, JAMES TURNER. *Ideology, Reason, and the Limitations of War: Religious and Secular Concepts, 1200–1740.* Princeton, N.J.: Princeton University Press, 1981.

————. *Just War Tradition and the Restraint of War.* Princeton, N.J.: Princeton University Press, 1981.

————. *The Quest for Peace.* Princeton, N.J.: Princeton University Press, 1987.

KALSHOVEN, FRITS. *Belligerent Reprisals.* Dordrecht, The Netherlands: Martinus Nijhoff Publishers, 1971.

————. *Constraints on the Waging of War.* Dordrecht, The Netherlands: Martinus Nijhoff Publishers, 1987.

KARSTEN, PETER. *Law, Soldiers, and Combat.* Westport, Conn.: Greenwood Press, 1978.

KEEGAN, JOHN. *The Face of Battle.* New York: Viking Press, 1976.

KIPNIS, KENNETH, AND DIANA T. MEYERS, EDS. *Political Realism and International Morality.* Boulder, Colo.: Westview Press, 1987.

KNOLL, ERWIN, AND JUDITH NIES MCFADDEN, EDS. *War Crimes and the American Conscience.* New York: Holt, Rinehart, 1970.

LEWY, GUENTER. *America in Vietnam.* New York: Oxford University Press, 1978.

LINDERMAN, GERALD. *Embattled Courage: The Experience of Combat in the American Civil War.* New York: The Free Press, 1987.

LUPIS, INGRID DETTER. *The Law of War.* New York and Cambridge, England: Cambridge University Press, 1987.

MATTHEWS, LLOYD J., AND DALE E. BROWN, EDS. *The Parameters of Military Ethics.* Published under the auspices of the U.S. Army War College Foundation, Inc., by Pergamon–Brassey's International Defense Publishers Inc., 1989.

MELZER, YEHUDA. *Concepts of Just War.* Leyden, The Netherlands: A. W. Sijthoff, 1975.

MONTROSS, LYNN. *War Through the Ages.* New York: Harper & Bros., 1960.

MORAN, LORD. *The Anatomy of Courage.* Garden City, N.Y.: Avery Publishing Group Inc., 1987.

MURPHIE, JEFFRIE G., AND JULES L. COLEMAN. *The Philosophy of Law.* Totowa, N.J.: Rowman & Allanheld, 1984.

NAGEL, WILLIAM J., ED. *Morality and Modern Warfare.* Baltimore: Helicon Press, 1960.

NIEBUHR, REINHOLD. *Moral Man and Immoral Society: A Study in Ethics and Politics.* New York: Charles Scribner's Sons, 1932.

NUSSBAUM, ARTHUR. *A Concise History of the Law of Nations.* New York: Macmillan, 1954.

O'CONNELL, ROBERT L. *Of Arms and Men: A History of War, Weapons, and Aggression.* New York and Oxford, England: Oxford University Press, 1989.

OPPENHEIM, LASSA F. *International Law,* Vol. II. Edited by H. Lauterpacht. New York: David McKay Co., 7th ed., 1952. (Original work published in 1906.)

PASKINS, BARRIE. *The Ethics of War.* Minneapolis, Minn.: Minnesota University Press, 1979.

PHILLIPS, ROBERT L. *War and Justice.* Norman, Okla.: University of Oklahoma Press, 1984.

PLATO. *The Collected Dialogues of Plato.* Edited by Edith Hamilton and Huntington Cairns. Princeton, N.J.: Princeton University Press, 1961.

POTTER, RALPH B. *War and Moral Discourse.* Richmond, Va.: John Knox Press, 1973.

RAMSEY, PAUL. *The Just War: Force and Personal Responsibility.* New York: Charles Scribner's Sons, 1968.

―――. *War and the Christian Conscience.* Durham, N.C.: Duke University Press, 1961.

ROBERTS, ADAM, AND RICHARD GUELFF, EDS. *Documents on the Laws of War.* New York: Oxford University Press, 1982.

ROSENBLAD, ESBJORN. *International Humanitarian Law of Armed Conflict.* Geneva, Switzerland: Henry Dunant Institute, 1979.

RUSSELL, FREDERICK H. *The Just War in the Middle Ages.* London: Cambridge University Press, 1975.

RYAN, JOHN K. *Modern War and Basic Ethics.* Milwaukee, Wis.: Bruce Publishing Co., 1940.

SHANNON, THOMAS A. *What Are They Saying About Peace and War?* New York: Paulist Press, 1983.

STERBA, JAMES P., ED. *The Ethics of War and Nuclear Deterrence.* Belmont, Calif.: Wadsworth Publishing, 1985.

SUAREZ, FRANCISCO. *Selections from Three Works of Francisco Saurez.* Edited by G. L. Williams, A. Brown, and J. Waldron in *Classics of International Law,* Vol. 2. James Brown Scott, ed. Oxford, England: Clarendon Press, 1944.

TAYLOR, TELFORD. *Nuremberg and Vietnam: An American Tragedy.* Chicago: Quadrangle Books, 1970.

TEICHMAN, JENNY. *Pacifism and the Just War.* New York: Basil Blackwell, 1986.

TONER, JAMES H. *The American Military Ethic.* New York: Praeger, 1992.

―――. *The Sword and the Cross.* New York: Praeger, 1992.

TOOKE, JOAN D. *The Just War in Aquinas and Grotius.* London: S.P.C.K., 1965.

TUCKER, ROBERT W. *The Just War: A Study in Contemporary American Doctrine.* Baltimore: Johns Hopkins University Press, 1960.

VATTEL, EMMERICH VON. *The Law of Nations.* Washington, D.C.: Carnegie Institution, 1916.

VITORIA, FRANCISCUS DE. *De Indis et De Ivre Belli Reflectiones.* Edited by Ernest Nys, in *Classics of International Law,* Vol. 7, James Brown Scott, ed. Washington, D.C.: Carnegie Institution of Washington, 1917, reprinted 1944.

WAKIN, MALHAM M., ED. *War, Morality, and the Military Profession.* Boulder, Colo.: Westview Press, 1979.

WALZER, MICHAEL. *Just and Unjust Wars: A Moral Argument with Historical Illustrations.* New York: Basic Books, 1977.

WASSERSTROM, RICHARD A., ED. *War and Morality.* Belmont, Calif.: Wadsworth Publishing, 1970.

WELLS, DONALD A. *War Crimes and the Laws of War.* Lanham, Md.: University Press of America, 1984.

WHITE, ANDREW DICKSON. *Seven Great Statesmen.* New York: The Century Co., 1912.

WOODS, MARTIN T., AND ROBERT BUCKENMEYER, EDS. *The Morality of Peace and War.* Santa Barbara, Calif.: Intelman Books, 1974.

WRIGHT, QUINCY. *The Role of International Law in the Elimination of War.* New York: Oceana Publications, 1961.

———. *A Study of War.* Vols. 1–2. 1942. (Reprint). Chicago: University of Chicago Press, 1965.

YODER, JOHN H. *When War Is Unjust: Being Honest in Just-War Thinking.* Minneapolis, Minn.: Augsburg, 1984.

UNITED STATES GOVERNMENT PUBLICATIONS

Extract of Interim Historical Report. Korea War Crimes Division. Cumulative to 30 June 1953. U.S. Army Korea Communications Zone. On file at the National War College, Carlisle Barracks, Pa.

Nazi Conspiracy and Aggression. Office of the United States Chief Counsel for Prosecution of Axis Criminality. Washington, D.C.: U.S. Government Printing Office, 1946.

Trial of the Major War Criminals Before the International Military Tribunal. Nuremberg, Germany, 1947.

U.S. Army War College. *Law for the Joint Warfighter,* Vol. 1. Carlisle Barracks, Pa., 1988.

U.S. Department of the Air Force. *International Law—The Conduct of Armed Conflict and Air Operations,* Air Force Pamphlet (AFP) 110–31. Judge Advocate General Activities, 19 November 1976.

U.S. Department of the Army. *The Army,* Field Manual 100–1. Washington, D.C.: U.S. Government Printing Office,1986.

———. *Law of Land Warfare,* Field Manual 27–10. Washington, D.C.: U.S. Government Printing Office, 1956.

———. *Leadership and Command at Senior Levels,* Field Manual 22–103. Washington, D.C.: U.S. Government Printing Office, 1980.

———. *The Peers Commission Report.* Edited version of the many-volume behemoth found in *The My Lai Massacre and Its Cover-up.* Edited by Joseph Goldstein, Burke Marshall, and Jack Schwartz. New York: The Free Press, 1976.

———. *Protocols to the Geneva Conventions of 12 August 1949,* Department of the Army Pamphlet 22–1–1. Washington, D.C.: U.S. Government Printing Office, 1979.

———. *Rules of Land Warfare.* Washington, D.C.: U.S. War Department, Office of the Chief of Staff, 1914.

ARTICLES IN JOURNALS AND OTHER PERIODICALS

BARRY, ROBERT. "Just War Theory and the Logic of Reconciliation." *New Scholastic* 54 (Spring 1980): 129–52.

BRAND, G. "The Development of the International Law of War." *Tulane Law Review* 25 (February 1951): 186–204.

CHRISTOPHER, P. "Unjust War and Moral Obligation: What Should Officers Do?" *Parameters* XXV, no. 3 (Autumn 1995): 4–8.

———. "Humanitarian Interventions and the Limits of Sovereignty." *Public Affairs Quarterly* 10, no. 2 (April 1996): 103–19.

COHEN, MARSHALL. "Moral Skepticism and International Relations." *Philosophy and Public Affairs* 13 (Fall 1984): 299–346.

EZORSKY, GERTRUDE. "War and Innocence." *Public Affairs Quarterly* 1, no. 2 (April 1987): 111–16.

GENOVESI, VINCENT. "Just War Doctrine: A Warrant for Resistance." *Thomist* 45 (October 1981): 503–40.

HART, H. L. A. "Are There Any Natural Rights?" *The Philosophical Review* 64, no. 2 (April 1955): 175–90.

HARTIGAN, RICHARD SHELLY. "Saint Augustine on War and Killing: The Problem of the Innocent." *Journal of the History of Ideas* 27 (1966): 195–204.

HARTLE, COLONEL ANTHONY E. "Humanitarianism and the Laws of War." *Philosophy* 61 (1986): 109–15.

HAUERWAS, STANLEY. "Pacifism: Some Philosophical Considerations." *Faith and Philosophy* 2 (April 1985): 99–102.

JOHNSON, JAMES TURNER. "Toward Reconstructing the *Jus ad Bellum*." *Monist* 57 (October 1973): 461–88.

———. "Natural Law as a Language for the Ethics of War." *Journal of Religious Ethics* 3 (Fall 1975): 217–42.

———. "Just War and Human Rights." *Philosophy and Public Affairs* 9 (Winter 1980): 160–81.

WOODRUFF, PAUL. "Justification or Excuse: Saving Soldiers at the Expense of Civilians." *Canadian Journal of Philosophy.* Supplemental Vol. VIII (1982): 159–76.

INDEX